HEALTHY
GOURMET
COOKBOOK

HEALTHY GOURMET COOKBOOK

RECIPES
PAMELA SHELDON JOHNS

TEXT AUTHOR AND NUTRITION CONSULTANT
MARY ABBOTT HESS
ASSISTED BY JANE GRANT TOUGAS

FOOD PHOTOGRAPHY
PHILIP SALAVERRY

FOOD STYLIST
SUE WHITE

CollinsPublishersSanFrancisco
A Division of HarperCollinsPublishers

First published in USA 1994
by Collins Publishers San Francisco

Produced by Weldon Owen Inc.
814 Montgomery Street
San Francisco, CA 94133 USA
Phone (415) 291-0100   Fax (415) 291-8841

Weldon Owen Inc.:
Chairman: Kevin Weldon
President: John Owen
General Manager: Stuart Laurence
Co-Editions Director: Derek Barton
Publisher: Jane Fraser
Managing Editor: Anne Dickerson
Editorial Assistant: Jan Hughes
Copy Editor: Zipporah Collins
Proofreaders: Sharilyn Hovind, Toni Murray, Alice Klein
Captions: Jane Horn
Production: Stephanie Sherman, Mick Bagnato
Design: Tom Morgan, Blue Design
Design Assistant: Jennifer Petersen
Illustrations: Diana Reiss-Koncar
Index: Ken Dellapenta
Assistant Food Stylist: Bruce Yim
Prop Stylist: Amy Glenn
Assistant to Food Photographer: David Williams

Library of Congress Cataloging-in-Publication Data:

Johns, Pamela Sheldons, 1953-
    Healthy gourmet cookbook / recipes, Pamela Sheldon Johns ; text
    author and nutrition consultant, Mary Abbott Hess ; assisted by Jane
    Grant Tougas ; food photography, Philip Salaverry ; food stylist,
    Sue White.
    p.   cm. — (Healthy gourmet series)
    Includes index.
    ISBN 0-00-255373-2
    1. Cookery. 2. Low-fat diet —Recipes. 3. Salt-free diet —Recipes.
    4. Sugar-free diet —Recipes. I. Hess, Mary Abbott. II. Tougas, Jane
    Grant. III. Salaverry, Philip. IV. Title. V. Series.
    TX714.J595 1994
    641.5'637 —dc20
                                                    94-6392
                                                    CIP

Manufactured by Mandarin Offset, Hong Kong
Printed in China

A Weldon Owen  Production

Endpapers: Apples glow in the autumn morning mist.

Pages 2–3: Wheat is the world's most popular cereal grain. Harvest begins in a golden field in New South Wales, Australia.

Page 4, top to bottom: Pasta with Clams, Spinach and Tomatoes; Grilled Pizza Carciofi (recipes on page 129)

Right: A fruit vendor in Sri Lanka stands proudly before his carefully arranged display. The natural appeal of fresh ingredients at their seasonal peak inspires cooks the world over.

Page 8, clockwise from top: Strawberry-Champagne Sorbet; Caramelized Bread Pudding; Ken Hom's Northern Chinese Steamed Pears (recipes on page 181)

Pages 10–11: A venerable grove of silver-leafed olive trees creates welcome shade.

Pages 62–63: Apple trees bloom at the base of Mt. Hood in the Pacific Northwest.

Pages 98–99: A feild of radiant sunflowers brightens the countryside.

Pages 144–145: Autumn foliage creates a canopy of color in an orchard.

Pages 182–183: The purple hues of winter envelope the farmlands of Oregon.

CONTENTS

HEALTHY GOURMET

Healthy Gourmet

WITH EVERY SEASON COMES A NEW OPPORTUNITY
TO TASTE THE RICHNESS OF THE HARVEST, TO
RECONNECT WITH CULTURAL TRADITIONS AND TO
EXPLORE THE MANY FLAVORS OF HEALTHFUL EATING.

For more than a decade, an abundance of health and nutrition information has filled our airwaves, newsstands and bookstores. Certainly, if health recommendations and nutrition advice were enough to change the way we eat, we would have changed long ago. So often, it seems, one critical ingredient has been overlooked: taste. When food doesn't taste good, we don't want to eat it—no matter how healthful it may be.

Top: Bumpy-skinned crookneck squash blaze with sunny color in a backyard garden. Left: From one season to the next, nature tempts us with a changing harvest. Bins of just-picked Canadian apples wait to be shipped.

Year after year, Food Marketing Institute surveys show that U.S. consumers rank taste as their number one consideration in food selection, followed closely by nutrition. A reflection of this abiding interest is the campaign by the American Institute of Wine and Food urging culinary leaders and health experts to treat taste and nutrition as inseparable parts, the yin and yang of a whole food experience.

Healthy Gourmet does just that. It is about cooking and eating delicious foods—rich in flavor, freshness, color, texture *and* healthful nutrients. Our ingredients are a back-to-basics harvest of fruits, vegetables, grains, cheese, poultry and seafood, seasoned with an international flair. We have accented ethnic diversity in the recipes, because food has always been an eloquent expression of cultural heritage. Within the context of taste and health, "eating well" means exploring and celebrating our many food traditions.

Before technology and transportation dissolved the barriers to global communication and commerce, humans ate what they found each season in their immediate environs. In the earliest times, a diet of grains and legumes flavored with fruits, vegetables and, later, meats was typical. Getting food was an important social activity for early civilizations, a task that inspired cooperation and group solidarity. Sharing meals and celebrating rituals integrated food deeply into the culture. We can easily see the threads of these primitive practices running through our daily lives when we participate in a family dinner, enjoy a meal with others, observe a religious tradition or celebrate a holiday.

The industrial revolution made reliance on fresh, locally available foods a thing of the past. A diet rich in the complex carbohydrates and fiber of grains, fruits and vegetables was modified with refined sugars, salt, saturated fats and increasingly processed foods. Today science and medicine are telling us that a return to our more "primitive" food style may be critical to our health and well-being. We are being called to the kitchen to regain control over the foods we choose, prepare and eat.

Unlike our early ancestors, however, we aren't constrained by season and geography. Our fresh food choices abound. We can rediscover the flavors of our own ethnic heritage and experience the culinary traditions of others as well. It's not surprising to discover that the cuisines of so many cultures, while flavored differently, have at their heart a reliance on the grains, legumes, fruits and vegetables that were basic to our earliest common experience.

Notes food journalist Robert Barnett, "If we based our meals more on whole grains, legumes, vegetables, and fruits, . . . with a little fat for flavoring and technique and even a truly high-fat indulgence thrown in from time to time, . . . we might learn that our sense of taste, given a bounty that's closer to our evolutionary roots, actually wakes up. We might learn that healthful food actually tastes good."[1]

As you read and cook with *Healthy Gourmet*, we think you will agree. With every season comes a new opportunity to taste the richness of the harvest, to reconnect with cultural traditions and to explore the many flavors of healthful eating. *Healthy Gourmet* provides guidance that can help you rethink and improve your daily food choices without compromising good taste for good health.

Opposite: Two women pause for trade and talk at a floating market in Thailand. Below: Markets are traditional gathering spots. It's likely that this Russian woman dispenses the news of the day to her customers along with fresh produce.

Nutrition Basics

Remember the 4 food groups? Prior to 1980, we were encouraged to eat 2 servings each day from both the milk group and the meat group plus 4 servings from the fruit and vegetable group and 4 servings from the grain group. When more and more research began to show that food choices can have a significant impact on disease prevention, the U.S. government issued its first set of Dietary Guidelines for Americans, recommending that people reduce their consumption of fat, cholesterol and sodium and increase their intake of complex carbohydrates and fiber. A 1990 revision of the guidelines puts an even greater emphasis on health promotion.

To help people use the guidelines in their everyday lives, in 1991 the federal government introduced the Food Guide Pyramid (see page 25). The pyramid illustrates how 6 food groups—grains, fruits, vegetables, meat, dairy and fats/oils/sweets—contribute proportionately to a diet that promotes good health. To understand the philosophy behind the Food Guide Pyramid, let's take a closer look at the Dietary Guidelines:

1. EAT A VARIETY OF FOODS

Humans need more than 40 nutrients, including various vitamins and minerals. Even though many foods are good sources of several nutrients, no single food provides all the nutrients we need. That's one reason why variety is so important. It is better to rely primarily on different foods for necessary nutrients than on vitamin pills or other supplements and fortification (the addition of vitamins and minerals to some foods). Here's why: nutrients in naturally occurring combinations often complement each other in healthful ways. For example, milk provides calcium, phosphorus and vitamin D, which are absorbed together to build strong bones. A calcium pill may not provide the phosphorus and vitamin D the

Above: An assortment of glistening fresh vegetables are displayed in an outdoor market in Hong Kong. Opposite: Heart-healthy unsaturated fats, like the oil pressed from corn and other plants, stay liquid at room temperature. Animal-based saturated fats like butter remain solid; use them sparingly.

body needs to use calcium fully. In addition, nutrition science is still discovering the role and importance of many trace elements in foods that aren't supplied by supplements or fortification. And, of course, eating a lot of different foods is just plain fun.

But eating a lot of different foods does not necessarily mean eating a lot. If you are inactive or want to lose weight, try to choose foods that are low in calories but rich in nutrients and flavor.

2. MAINTAIN HEALTHY WEIGHT

The concept of healthy weight is easily misunderstood, especially in a culture that places such great value on being thin—often too thin.

A healthy weight depends not so much on your appearance but rather on how much of your weight comes from fat, where in your body the fat is located (excess weight in the stomach area is a bigger health risk than weight in other areas) and whether you have weight-related health problems—high blood pressure, for example. People tend to become a little heavier as they grow older; generally, this weight gain does not produce a health risk.

To figure out your healthy weight, consult a registered dietitian or your physician. If you feel you must diet continuously, even when you are not creating any health advantage for yourself, it's probably time to take a long hard look at your motivation. Remember, foods are not

DIETARY GUIDELINES FOR AMERICANS

- Eat a variety of foods.
- Maintain healthy weight.
- Choose a diet low in fat, saturated fat and cholesterol.
- Choose a diet with plenty of vegetables, fruits and grain products.
- Use sugars only in moderation.
- Use salt and sodium only in moderation.
- If you drink alcoholic beverages, do so in moderation.

FAT: THE HIGHS AND LOWS

Quick chemistry lesson: Fats are made up of several fatty acids (usually 3). There are 24 kinds of fatty acids commonly found in foods. Fatty acids can be grouped according to length of molecule chain or according to degree of saturation—saturated, monounsaturated or polyunsaturated. We call these the types of fat.

All fat found in food is a combination of saturates, monounsaturates and polyunsaturates. When one type of fat is dominant in a food, we tend to identify that particular food as such. For example, we talk about the saturated fat in red meat or the monounsaturated fat in olive oil. (See the chart under "Fat" in the glossary.) Each type of fat affects the human body in specific ways. Consequently, it's smart to know not only *how much* fat your diet contains, but also *what types* of fat it includes.

In terms of dietary choices, unsaturated fats are considered more heart-healthy than saturated, and monounsaturated fats may be preferable to polyunsaturated ones. Most saturated fats come from animal sources. Plants and fish are sources of unsaturated fat, which is usually liquid at room temperature. Monounsaturates include olive, canola and peanut oils. Polyunsaturates include corn, safflower and soybean oils. Sesame oil has almost equal amounts of poly and monounsaturated fat. Exceptions to the rules: Coconut oil, used mainly to keep foods such as crackers crisp, is far more saturated than beef fat or butter. Conversely, chicken fat, although of animal origin, is primarily monounsaturated.

Olive oil and other highly monounsaturated oils are thought to help lower overall blood cholesterol, lower damaging low-density lipoprotein (LDL) cholesterol and maintain healthy high-density lipoprotein (HDL) cholesterol. That Mediterranean populations have relatively low blood cholesterol levels is attributed at least in part to their use of olive oil.

Some foods that are high in poly- and monounsaturates can be processed in a way that creates *trans fatty acids*, fatty acids that remain poly- or monounsaturated but act like saturates, tending to raise LDL and blood cholesterol levels. When hydrogenation is used to harden liquid oil into margarine and shortening, structural changes occur in the fat molecules, producing trans fatty acids. Mainstream dietary advice is to choose tub or soft margarines rather than stick margarines because softer margarines have less trans fatty acids. Sometimes a bit of butter makes food taste better. Try to reserve the use of butter only to enhance flavor, and use liquid oils the rest of the time. Neither butter nor oils contain trans fatty acids.

Regardless of the benefits associated with particular fats, try to limit your fat consumption. National health advice is to keep total fat to about 30 percent of your calories over a several-day period and to restrict saturated fat to 10 percent of calories. The 30 percent guide should not be applied to single foods or recipes. These goals don't mean that eating should be a series of mathematical calculations. Check the Fat Formula chart below for your fat target in calories and grams. If you are unsure how to do this, have a registered dietitian help you analyze your current diet, set fat goals and discuss other changes if they are needed.

Using your recommended daily fat intake as a guide, you can pursue a low-fat diet without following a strict regimen. Virtually all foods can fit into a healthy diet. It's a matter of choice—of selecting fairly low-fat choices most of the time. That way you'll have room for some high-fat foods that are special to you. If you want these special foods fairly often, limit your portions to small amounts—just enough to enjoy and savor. Remember that following a healthful diet is a *process* occurring over a lifetime, not in isolated 24-hour periods.

We have calculated total fat as well as saturated, monounsaturated and polyunsaturated fat grams for each recipe in *Healthy Gourmet*. The new food label (see page 32) will tell you how many calories and how much fat are in packaged foods.

THE FAT FORMULA

Using the 30 percent formula, your goals for daily calories from fat, grams of fat and grams of saturated fat will vary depending on total calories.

Calories/Day	Calories from Fat (30%)	Grams of Fat in 30% of Calories	Grams of Saturated Fat in 10% of Calories
1200	360	40	13
1500	450	50	17
2000	600	67	22
2500	750	83	28
3000	900	100	33
3500	1050	117	39

"good" or "bad" by nature. If you steadfastly deny yourself your favorite foods, you'll want more of them and want them more often. Have that slice of apple pie, but make it half your usual portion. And open your mind to new foods prepared in healthy, flavorful ways. Using *Healthy Gourmet* is a great way to start.

3. CHOOSE A DIET LOW IN FAT, SATURATED FAT AND CHOLESTEROL

In countries with diets high in fat, obesity and certain forms of cancer are more prevalent than in countries with lower-fat diets. Higher levels of saturated fat are linked with heart disease. Fat contains more than twice the calories of carbohydrates or protein. Thus, when you eat a diet low in fat, it's much easier to enjoy a variety of foods without consuming excessive calories.

Cholesterol is present in all of the body's tissues and is a substance essential to life. High blood cholesterol, however, is a well-documented risk factor for heart disease. Many people confuse cholesterol levels in food (dietary cholesterol) with the cholesterol level in their own bodies. Most of the cholesterol in your body—your serum or blood cholesterol—is made by you, at the rate of about 1000 mg a day. Your blood cholesterol is likely to increase when you eat foods high in total fat and particularly saturated fat. But some components of saturated fat, such as the stearic acid found in red meat and chocolate, don't seem to raise blood cholesterol. In addition, the omega-3 fatty acids found in some fish help reduce the risk of heart disease by shifting blood fats from low-density lipoproteins (LDLs) to the healthier high-density lipoproteins (HDLs) and reducing the tendency of the blood to clot (strokes are the result of blood clots in the brain). Eating fish about 3 times a week provides ample amounts of these protective fatty acids.

According to a November 1990 statement by the National Institutes of Health, the average American man consumes about 435 mg of *dietary* cholesterol every day, while the average woman consumes 304 mg daily. For health promotion, it is wise to limit dietary cholesterol to about 300 mg daily. Animal products are the source of all dietary cholesterol; egg yolks and liver, for example, are high in dietary cholesterol. Plant foods do not contain cholesterol, but high-fat vegetable-based foods can prompt the body to make more cholesterol. Current thinking is that it is more important to reduce total fat and saturated fat than to stringently

For the most complete nutrition, eat a balanced diet that features a variety of foods.

Above: Red chili peppers dry in the hot, arid sunshine of Mallorca, Spain. Left: Not only do fruits, vegetables and grains provide important nutrients and dietary fiber, their texture, flavor and color make eating more pleasurable.

reduce foods that contain cholesterol. Most cholesterol-rich foods also have lots of essential vitamins and minerals. Cutting down on foods of animal origin can reduce your intake of iron, calcium, zinc and vitamins needed for good health.

Foods rich in soluble fiber—dried peas and beans, fruits, vegetables, barley and oats—can help lower serum cholesterol. Studies have shown that polyunsaturated and monounsaturated fats lower LDLs, or "bad" blood cholesterol. But fats are still fats. If you're concerned about controlling your weight or lowering your blood cholesterol, boost your intake of vegetables, fruits and grains, particularly whole grains and legumes.

4. CHOOSE A DIET WITH PLENTY OF VEGETABLES, FRUITS AND GRAIN PRODUCTS

If there is one guideline at the heart of *Healthy Gourmet,* this is it. Vegetables, fruits and grains are not only a vital part of the varied diet recommended in guideline 1 but also the foundation of the Food Guide Pyramid. In addition to nutrient value, they add texture, flavor and color, generally enhancing meals.

Whole fruits, vegetables and grains are preferable to juices and refined grains because they contain a wider range of nutrients plus dietary fiber. Fiber-rich foods—whole grains, legumes, vegetables and fruits—play a positive role in preventing both heart disease and cancer. They also aid elimination and reduce the risk of diseases of the intestinal tract. Some of these benefits come from the foods themselves—their unique combinations of food components and nutrients—not simply from fiber. That is why it is important to choose fiber-rich foods over fiber supplements. Fiber values are given for every *Healthy Gourmet* recipe.

5. USE SUGARS ONLY IN MODERATION

If you have a sweet tooth (who doesn't?), don't despair. "In moderation" doesn't mean "never." Moderation means smaller portions or less frequency. Moderation does not mean consuming almost 25 percent of total calories from sugar, which is the average for Americans. Many foods that contain a lot of added sugar are both high in calories and low in nutrients. Unneeded calories yield unwanted pounds, which can produce health risks.

As the tip of the Food Guide Pyramid suggests, make sugary foods more the exception than the rule. For a healthy sweet, choose fruit—a

Opposite: The cuisines of many cultures, although flavored differently, have at their heart a common reliance on grains, legumes, fruits and vegetables. A busy Peruvian market bustles with energy. Below: Recent studies suggest that a glass or two of red wine a day may offer some healthy benefits. Clusters of dusky zinfandel grapes ripen on a vine in California's Napa Valley.

food with naturally occurring sugars combined with fiber, vitamins and minerals. It is prudent for all of us to limit candy, sugar syrups, sugared soft drinks and very sweet desserts. But don't be sugar phobic. Enjoy some sugar to enhance the flavor of fruits, beverages, baked goods and cereals.

Parents are often concerned about the sugar in presweetened cereal. The added sugar is about equal to the sugar many people spoon on plain cereal. For children, some dietitians and pediatricians recommend mixing equal parts of sweetened and unsweetened cereal, making a healthy, nutrient-dense snack that kids enjoy.

The only specific health risk associated with eating sugar in moderation is tooth decay. Brush your teeth after eating sugary foods or rinse your mouth with an unsweetened liquid.

6. USE SALT AND SODIUM ONLY IN MODERATION

In countries with diets low in salt, high blood pressure is less common than in countries such as the United States, where people typically eat far more salt and sodium than they need. One in three U.S. adults has high blood pressure (hypertension). Reducing salt intake may help alleviate the condition. Some people with hypertension are not salt-sensitive; they may need to take medications to reduce their blood pressure.

There is no way to predict whether you might develop high blood pressure and might benefit from sharply reducing sodium intake. If you have good kidney function and do not have high blood pressure, you simply excrete the sodium you eat. Chances are, though, you are eating much more sodium than you need. Breaking the salt habit now could be a lot easier than wrestling with it later.

Nutrition experts recommend that adults limit their sodium intake to about 2400 mg a day. One teaspoon of table salt contains about 2300 mg. Other foods high in sodium include condiments such as soy sauce and Worcestershire sauce; hard cheeses such as Parmesan and cheddar; dill pickles; canned soups; smoked fish; and sausages. Many packaged foods are also high in sodium. The product's nutrition panel lists the sodium level. Sodium values are given for every recipe in *Healthy Gourmet*.

7. IF YOU DRINK ALCOHOLIC BEVERAGES, DO SO IN MODERATION

Alcoholic beverages supply calories but few or no nutrients. Some recent evidence suggests that alcohol in moderation, particularly red wine, may offer some health benefits, but the situation is still controversial (see page 48). For women, 1 drink a day is considered "moderate"; for men, 2 drinks. A drink is defined as 12 fl oz (375 ml) of regular beer, 5 fl oz (160 ml) of wine or 1½ fl oz (45 ml) of distilled spirits (80 proof).

Wine and other alcohol-containing beverages may be used to add flavor in cooking. As these liquids simmer, most of the alcohol evaporates, but their flavors remain. If you are sensitive to alcohol or choose not to use it, omit the alcohol-containing ingredients in *Healthy Gourmet* recipes and substitute equal amounts of alcohol-free wine or fruit juice.

WHAT IS A SERVING?

A "serving" in the Food Guide Pyramid is a standardized portion of food—but not necessarily the amount of food you put on your plate. Most people agree that 1 cup or 8 fl oz (250 ml) is a "glass" of milk, and that happens to be the portion used in the Pyramid. Many people, however, eat more than 3 oz (90 g) of cooked meat, poultry or fish and more than ½ cup (2½ oz/75 g) of cooked rice or pasta as a portion. (The Pyramid's relatively small ½-cup serving of grains makes it easier to reach the recommended 6–11 daily servings, however.)

Unfortunately, the standardized serving sizes on new food labels do not necessarily correspond to Pyramid servings. Food label servings are more in line with the portions people really eat. For example, on a food label, 2 slices of bread is considered a serving, while in the Pyramid, 1 slice is a serving.

To complicate matters further, the "food exchange" system used by individuals with diabetes mellitus (up to 10 percent of the United States population) and in various weight-loss programs is based on yet another measurement for servings—at least for some foods. For example, using the Food Guide Pyramid, ¾ cup (6 fl oz/180 ml) is 1 serving of fruit juice. Under the food exchange system, 1 serving of fruit juice varies from ½ cup (4 fl oz/125 ml) of apple or orange juice to ⅓ cup (3 fl oz/80 ml) of grape or prune juice. In exchange systems, the portion of each fruit is adjusted so that each has a similar amount of carbohydrate.

As the new food label regulations were being developed in Washington, D.C., many health and nutrition groups argued for conformity—at least between the food label and the Pyramid serving sizes—but to no avail. If you are using the Food Guide Pyramid to help manage your diet, it will just take a little practice to translate food label servings into Pyramid servings when there are discrepancies.

The Food Guide Pyramid

Since the late 1980s, United States national health policy has focused on the Dietary Guidelines for Americans (see sidebar on page 17). Meanwhile, various health-related groups have been very vocal about their own dietary guidelines. For example, the American Heart Association recommends a low-fat, low-cholesterol diet, while the American Cancer Society stresses eating a lot of vegetables (particularly cruciferous ones—see "cruciferous" in the glossary), fruits and whole grains. Other countries, such as Canada and Japan, have health recommendations similar to the Dietary Guidelines for Americans.

Today's approach to the Dietary Guidelines for Americans is definitely action-oriented. In a subtle yet powerful shift in perspective, we are now advised to eat to *promote health*, not just to prevent disease. And rather than considering each Dietary Guideline and food group in isolation, we are encouraged to take control of the big picture. The Food Guide Pyramid helps us see that big picture. It turns food guidelines into *food choices*.

The United States Department of Agriculture and the United States Department of Health and Human Services developed the Food Guide Pyramid after extensive consultation with health and nutrition experts, consumer advocates and food industry representatives around the country. The Pyramid was introduced to the public in 1991. It is a graphic representation—a blueprint—of the "total diet," depicting recommended food groups and numbers of daily servings from each group. Companion information identifies foods in each group and defines Pyramid serving sizes.

The Food Guide Pyramid depicts 5 nutrient-rich food groups: (1) grains (bread, cereal, rice and pasta); (2) vegetables; (3) fruits; (4) milk, yogurt and cheese; and (5) meat, poultry, fish, dry beans, eggs and nuts. Recommended daily servings are expressed as a range. Your optimal servings are based on your calorie needs. For example, 6 daily servings from the grain group may be ideal for a sedentary woman or older adult who takes in about 1600 calories per day. An athletic teenage boy or very active adult who eats 2800 daily calories, however, will need the maximum 11 recommended servings of bread, cereal, rice or pasta. For each recipe in *Healthy Gourmet* we tell you the number of servings of each Pyramid food group that is supplied.

A sixth food group—fats, oils and sweets—is at the tip of the Pyramid. It is recommended that we eat moderately from this group—only enough to make food enjoyable. For example, salad dressing containing oil is a part of this group. The idea is to aim for plenty of salad but use only a small amount of dressing.

Within each food group, there are *preferred* choices. Among breads and cereals, for example, whole grains are preferred. Similarly, deep green and orange vegetables pack a bigger nutrition punch than their paler cousins.

WORKING FROM THE BOTTOM UP

Basic to the concept of the Food Guide Pyramid is the notion of proportion. Although the Pyramid depicts 6 food groups, it clearly illustrates that, for optimal health, some foods should play a larger role than others in the daily diet. These foods are at or near the base of the Pyramid.

GRAINS: 6–11 SERVINGS. At the foundation of the Pyramid are foods from grains that provide complex carbohydrates, minerals and fiber: bread, cereal, rice and pasta. Contrary to popular beliefs, bread and other grain-based foods are not "fattening." It's the butter, cream cheese, oil or rich sauces added to them that make their fat and calorie levels soar. Because you need a lot of the nutrients from grain-based foods over the course of a day, try to include at least 2 servings with every meal. Favor items that are made with whole grains or enriched flour and are not laden with fat and sugar.

One serving equals 1 slice of bread, 1 oz (30 g) of ready-to-eat cereal, ½ cup of cooked cereal, rice or pasta, 3–4 small crackers, 1 small slice of cake, 1 pancake. Often you will want 2 servings for an adequate portion. One cup of rice or pasta or a whole sandwich bun counts as 2 servings and will help you reach the goal of 6 to 11 daily servings more quickly.

VEGETABLES: 3–5 SERVINGS. Vegetables share the second tier of the Food Pyramid with fruits. Try to include 2 servings of vegetables with every meal except breakfast. If necessary, meet the goal with snacks such as crisp raw carrot sticks. Naturally low in fat, vegetables provide

THE FOOD GUIDE PYRAMID

A Guide to Daily Food Choices

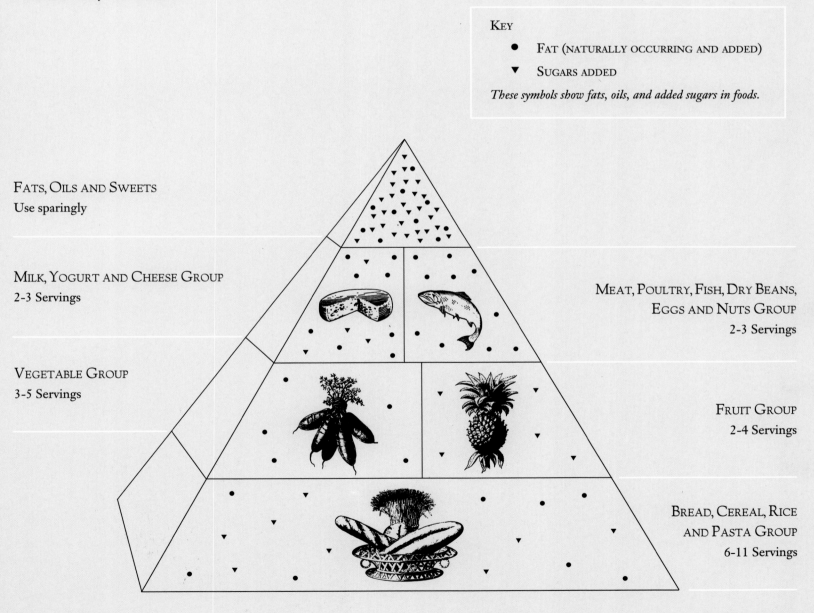

KEY

• FAT (NATURALLY OCCURRING AND ADDED)

▼ SUGARS ADDED

These symbols show fats, oils, and added sugars in foods.

FATS, OILS AND SWEETS
Use sparingly

MILK, YOGURT AND CHEESE GROUP
2-3 Servings

VEGETABLE GROUP
3-5 Servings

MEAT, POULTRY, FISH, DRY BEANS,
EGGS AND NUTS GROUP
2-3 Servings

FRUIT GROUP
2-4 Servings

BREAD, CEREAL, RICE
AND PASTA GROUP
6-11 Servings

vitamins such as A, C, folic acid and biotin as well as minerals such as iron (see the vitamin and mineral tables after the index). Vegetables are also a good source of fiber. Most of us consume only about 12 g of fiber daily and need 20–35 g!

Make variety as characteristic of your vegetables as it is of your overall diet. Take a quick look at the vegetable chart on pages 58–60 if you're worried that there aren't enough choices! Different types of vegetables provide different nutrients. Quickly cook or steam fresh vegetables to preserve nutrients, color and texture. Limit fried vegetables, especially the one that Americans consume most, the French fry! And go easy on the sauces and salad dressings. Better yet, opt for low-fat toppings whenever possible.

One serving equals 1 cup of raw leafy vegetables, ½ cup of other vegetables (cooked or chopped raw), ½ cup of dense salads such as potato salad or coleslaw, and 6 fl oz/180 ml of vegetable juice. *Healthy Gourmet* recipes containing vegetables may count as 2 servings depending on their size. (Occasionally, we have used some fat in the preparation of *Healthy Gourmet* vegetable recipes—but only enough to enhance taste. This accords with the Pyramid recommendation to use the fats/oils/ sweets group sparingly. You should watch the contents and amounts of other sauces, toppings and dressings containing fat that you use.)

FRUITS: 2–4 SERVINGS. Fruits and 100-percent fruit juices provide vitamins A and C as well as folic acid and potassium. Citrus fruits, berries and melons are particularly high in vitamin C. Whole fruits are higher in fiber than fruit juices. If you are using canned or frozen fruits, avoid those packed in heavy syrup. When fruit recipes used for desserts require sugar syrup, eat just a little of the syrup. See the chart on pages 57–58 for a harvest of fresh fruit ideas.

One serving equals a medium apple, banana or orange; ½ cup of chopped, cooked or canned fruit; 6 fl oz/180 ml of fruit juice; or ¼ cup of dried fruit.

MILK, YOGURT AND CHEESE: 2–3 SERVINGS. From this group 2 servings are adequate for most people. Pregnant or breast-feeding women, teenagers and young adults under 25 should aim for 3 daily servings. Milk products provide protein, vitamins and minerals. Milk,

Left: Working close to the earth is a soothing antidote to the stresses of daily life. A Tuscan farmer heads off to this vineyards on a misty autumn morning. Below: A Mexican bicyclist deftly balances a delivery of fresh bread as he navigates narrow streets.

WHAT'S THE BEEF?

Recipes in *Healthy Gourmet* celebrate the year-round harvest of fresh fruits and vegetables. They also use seafood, poultry, legumes and some dairy foods. Although this particular cookbook does not include beef, lamb, pork, veal or game meat recipes, lean meat has a place in a healthful, flavorful diet. Lean meat is an excellent source of protein, iron, zinc, phosphorus, vitamin B_{12} and niacin. A lean 3-oz (90-g) portion of meat provides 20–100 percent of the daily need for each of these nutrients in 8 percent or less of a day's calories. A look at the vitamin and mineral tables after the index reveals the many nutrients meats supply.

If you eat meats, choose lean cuts and eat a moderate 3- or 4-oz (90- or 120-g) cooked portion. Extend meats by combining them with vegetables, as in shish kebabs or chili, or with grains, as in spaghetti with meat sauce, or fajitas or beef barley soup. Most lean beef cuts have the word *loin* or *round* in their names. Lean pork cuts often contain the word *loin* or *leg*.

Trim any separable fat from meat before cooking. If you leave some fat on during cooking, trim it off before serving. Separate and discard fat from drippings, too, when you make gravies and sauces. Grill, bake or roast meats on a rack to raise them above their fat drippings. When you stir-fry or sauté, use a nonstick pan and a minimum amount of oil.

No matter how lean, all meats—in fact all animal products, even chicken and fish—contain about 20–30 mg of cholesterol per oz. If you eat a small portion (3 oz/90 g), however, you'll take in only 60–90 mg of cholesterol—less than a third of the recommended daily maximum of 300 mg. That leaves room for some dietary cholesterol from milk, other dairy foods, eggs and butter.

LEAN CUTS

Here are some lean cuts of meat that are especially good choices:

Per 3-oz (85-g) Cooked and Trimmed Serving

Cut	Calories	Fat (g)	Sat Fat (g)	Chol (mg)
BEEF				
Brisket, flat half	189	8.2	2.7	81
Chuck arm pot roast	183	7.1	2.6	86
Eye round roast	143	4.2	1.5	59
Flank steak	176	8.6	3.7	57
Sirloin steak	165	6.1	2.4	76
Tenderloin steak	179	8.5	3.2	71
Top loin steak	176	8.0	3.1	65
Top round steak	153	4.2	1.4	71
PORK				
Center loin roast	165	6.1	2.2	66
Ham, whole roasted	187	9.4	3.2	80
Loin chop, broiled	165	6.9	2.5	70
Tenderloin, roasted	133	4.1	1.6	67
LAMB				
Cubes, broiled or grilled	158	6.2	2.2	77
Foreshank	159	5.1	1.8	89
Leg, shank portion, roasted	153	5.7	2.0	74
Loin, broiled	183	8.3	3.0	80
VEAL				
Arm steak	171	4.5	1.3	132
Cubes, braised	160	3.7	1.1	124
Cutlet, breaded, pan-fried	175	5.3	1.4	96
Rib roast	151	6.3	1.8	97
PROCESSED MEAT				
Canadian bacon, grilled	156	7.2	2.4	48
Ham, extra lean	123	4.7	1.5	45
Roast beef, lean	150	3.3	1.4	36

Source: The Meat Board, Lessons on Meat (National Live Stock and Meat Board, Chicago, Il.: 1991).

yogurt and cheese are the very best sources of calcium. However, many dairy products, such as ice cream, are high in fat. You can get all the nutrients without the fat in nonfat (skim) milk, low-fat (1-percent) milk and nonfat yogurt. In fact, nonfat milk gives twice the amount of calcium as plain ice cream by volume with only a third of the calories. Choose "part skim" or low-fat cheeses. When you eat a high-fat cheese, choose one with a bold flavor, and let a little go a long way. If you love ice cream, try substituting ice milk or low-fat frozen yogurt . . . most of the time.

One serving equals 8 fl oz/250 ml of milk or yogurt; 1½ oz (45 g) of natural cheese; 2 cups of cottage cheese; 2 oz (60 g) of processed cheese. Equivalents for these groups are based on calcium content, realistically you will probably choose ½ serving (1 cup) of cottage cheese.

MEAT, POULTRY, FISH, DRY BEANS, EGGS AND NUTS: 2–3 SERVINGS. Meat, poultry and fish are excellent sources of protein, B vitamins, iron and zinc. Dry beans, eggs and nuts are similar to meat in the nutrients they provide, but they contain iron in a form that is not as well utilized by the body. The best sources of iron—a nutrient particularly needed by

PROTEIN ALTERNATIVES TO MEAT

Each of these choices provides 7 g of protein, the amount of protein in 1 oz of lean meat, fish or poultry (55 calories).

1 cup (2 oz/60 g) cooked broccoli or brussels sprouts (50 calories)

¼ cup (1⅓ oz/40 g) cottage cheese (55 calories)

⅓ cup (3 oz/90 g) tofu (75 calories)

1 large egg (80 calories)

1 cup (250 ml) soy milk (80 calories)

½ cup (3½ oz/105 g) cooked legumes (80 calories)

1 oz (30 g) Cheddar cheese (115 calories)

7 fl oz (210 ml) low-fat (1-percent) milk (90 calories)

7 fl oz (210 ml) whole milk (130 calories)

1 cup (5½ oz/165 g) cooked egg noodles (210 calories)

1 cup (8 oz/240 g) oatmeal (145 calories)

1 small slice (2½ oz/225 g) cheese pizza (170 calories)

1–2 oz (30–60 g) nuts or seeds (150–200 calories)

1¾ tablespoons peanut butter (160 calories)

2½ tablespoons tahini (sesame butter) (220 calories)

2 pieces (5 oz/150 g) corn bread (350 calories)

The day's catch dries in the sun in Hong Kong, where fish is a favorite ingredient as it is throughout Asia. Eating 3 servings per week can help reduce the risk of heart disease.

women, teenagers and children—are liver; lean pork, beef and lamb; the dark meat of poultry; fish and shellfish. Sources of iron other than meat include legumes, enriched grains, dried fruit and some leafy green vegetables. From the meat group, lean meat (see sidebar on page 28), poultry without skin, shellfish, fish and dried beans and peas are the choices lowest in fat. Sausages and cold cuts are generally high in fat, except those clearly marked "fat reduced." Lean ham, roast beef and turkey breast are among the leanest deli choices.

Eggs are very rich in nutrients, but egg yolks are high in cholesterol. Enjoy no more than 4 whole eggs or egg yolks per week. If you must limit your dietary cholesterol, use double portions of egg whites or egg substitutes. Go easy on the nuts, too. They are good protein sources but high in fat.

One serving equals 2–3 oz (60–90 g) of cooked lean meat, poultry or fish; ½ cup cooked dried beans; 1 egg; ⅓ cup nuts (or 2 tablespoons of peanut butter are equivalent to 1 oz of cooked meat, or about ⅓ serving).

VEGETARIAN CHOICES

Gone are the days when the word *vegetarian* conjured up images of flower children and alternative lifestyles. Vegetarianism has gone mainstream. It is estimated that 5–10 percent of Americans consider themselves vegetarians—from vegans (those who avoid all foods of animal origin) to semivegetarians (those who eat dairy products and eggs, maybe a little fish and chicken, but no red meat). Even people who eat red meat only occasionally may consider themselves vegetarians of sorts. Some people set aside "vegetarian days" for themselves. True vegans account for only .1 percent of the total U.S. population.

One of the biggest advantages of a vegetarian diet is a lower-than-average intake of fat, saturated fat and cholesterol. As a result, vegetarians often have lower-than-average blood cholesterol levels and lower blood pressure than meat eaters. They also tend to have a healthy weight. These factors may help protect vegetarians from heart disease.

Vegetarians have fewer digestive system disorders and a reduced risk for adult-onset diabetes. The high-fiber vegetarian diet (or any high-fiber diet, for that matter) improves control of blood sugar, which is

a plus for people with diabetes. There is also some evidence that vegetarians have a lower risk of colon and lung cancer. Of course, all of these advantages also may have something to do with other lifestyle tendencies among vegetarians (less smoking and alcohol consumption, more exercise, etc.), who are likely to be more health-conscious than nonvegetarians.

Vegans who carefully plan what they eat to ensure they receive all the nutrients they need are at no greater risk for nutrient deficiencies than are meat eaters. And vegetarians who eat some dairy products, and some chicken or fish are generally at little risk for nutrient deficiencies.

Getting enough vitamin B_{12} which is found only in animal products can be a problem if you avoid all dairy products, meat and eggs. True vegans should seek nutritional yeasts or foods fortified with vitamin B_{12} (some commercial cereals and soy beverages are).

Calcium, zinc and iron deficiencies can be of particular concern to vegetarian women. Broccoli, kale, collard and mustard greens, chick-peas and legumes have calcium. So does tofu processed with calcium. Calcium fortified bread has recently been introduced and calcium fortified juices have been available for several years. Zinc is found in

peas, lentils, wheat germ and wheat bran. Fortified cereals, legumes, potatoes, dried fruits, enriched breads and prune juice provide iron. It is important for vegetarians to eat fruits or vegetables that contain vitamin C at each meal, to enhance their absorption of iron from plant foods.

Many grains, legumes and seeds are good sources of protein. In combination with each other or with vegetables—red beans and rice, corn and beans, split pea soup and rye bread, or peanut butter and bread, for example—the resulting protein is adequate to promote health. In early civilizations and in areas where meat is scarce and expensive, these combinations are a diet mainstay.

If you are following a vegetarian regimen of any kind, the most important factor to remember is variety. If your choice has been made purely for health reasons, keep in mind that small servings of lean meat, poultry or fish will not undermine your efforts. If your vegetarian decision is based on religious or environmental principles, give your health priority too by planning meals to ensure you get all the nutrients you need. And no matter what your motivation, vegetarian or not, explore the wide variety of fruits, vegetables, grains and legumes that makes any diet flavorful and healthful.

FATS, OILS AND SWEETS: Use Sparingly. Small circles and triangles throughout the Food Guide Pyramid indicate the presence of naturally occurring or added fat and sugars. As you look from the base of the Pyramid to the tip, you see that fats and sugars become more concentrated. At the very top of the Pyramid are foods that provide calories but few vitamins and minerals. Fruits, vegetables and grains are naturally low in fat; we alter that profile when we use cooking oils, butter, salad dressings and high-fat sauces and gravies. Sugar is part of the nutrient package found naturally in fruit and milk; *added* sugar provides extra calories but few vitamins and minerals.

Much of the added sugar in our diet comes from food in the Pyramid tip, such as candy, soft drinks, jellies and table sugar. Try to substitute foods lower in the Pyramid for high-sugar or high-fat snacks. For example, choose fresh or dried fruit instead of candy. Try popcorn or pretzels instead of corn chips or potato chips. For beverages, enjoy fruit or vegetable juice, milk, yogurt drinks or water instead of sugared soft drinks.

For a healthy sweet, instead of candy choose fruit—a food with naturally occurring sugars combined with fiber, vitamins and minerals. Apricots dry on trays on a warm California day.

THE NEW LABEL FORMAT

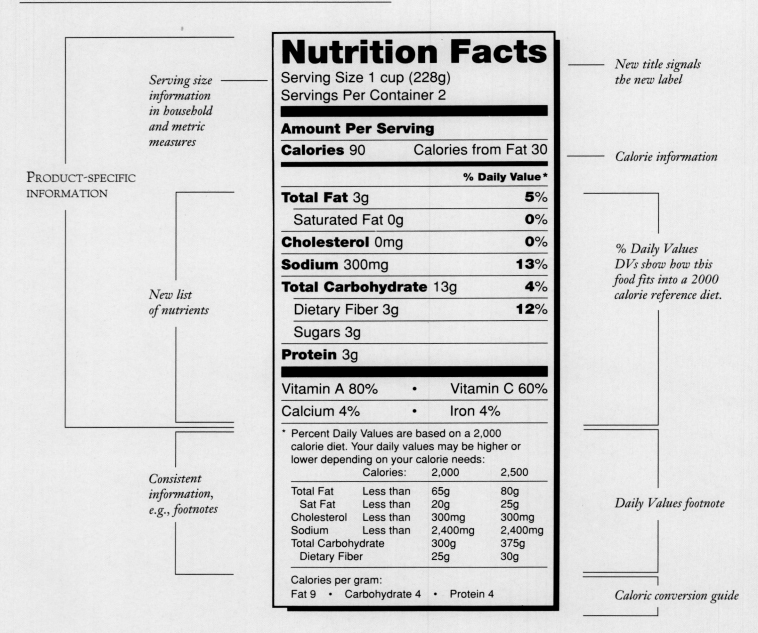

Serving size information in household and metric measures

PRODUCT-SPECIFIC INFORMATION

New list of nutrients

Consistent information, e.g., footnotes

New title signals the new label

Calorie information

% Daily Values DVs show how this food fits into a 2000 calorie reference diet.

Daily Values footnote

Caloric conversion guide

Nutrition Facts

Serving Size 1 cup (228g)
Servings Per Container 2

Amount Per Serving

Calories 90   Calories from Fat 30

                                    % Daily Value*

Total Fat 3g   **5%**

  Saturated Fat 0g   **0%**

Cholesterol 0mg   **0%**

Sodium 300mg   **13%**

Total Carbohydrate 13g   **4%**

  Dietary Fiber 3g   **12%**

  Sugars 3g

Protein 3g

Vitamin A 80%   •   Vitamin C 60%

Calcium 4%   •   Iron 4%

* Percent Daily Values are based on a 2,000 calorie diet. Your daily values may be higher or lower depending on your calorie needs:

		Calories:	2,000	2,500
Total Fat	Less than		65g	80g
Sat Fat	Less than		20g	25g
Cholesterol	Less than		300mg	300mg
Sodium	Less than		2,400mg	2,400mg
Total Carbohydrate			300g	375g
Dietary Fiber			25g	30g

Calories per gram:
Fat 9 • Carbohydrate 4 • Protein 4

HOW TO READ FOOD LABELS

Read any good labels lately? Until recently, inconsistencies in terms, serving sizes and health and content claims made food labels confusing at best. In 1990, the United States Congress leveled the field with passage of the Nutrition Labeling and Education Act. The Food and Drug Administration (FDA), which oversees all packaged foods, and the United States Department of Agriculture (USDA), which is responsible for labeling meat and poultry, cooperated in drafting a standard nutrition label mandated to appear on almost all processed foods.

No more unsatisfied curiosity. No more guessing. Now a complete list of ingredients, standard serving sizes, reliable health and content claims, and a reader-friendly format make the label a useful tool for making informed food choices.

JUST THE FACTS

Items that must be listed on the new nutrition label include total calories, calories from fat, total fat, saturated fat, cholesterol, sodium, total carbohydrate, dietary fiber, sugars, protein, vitamins A and C, calcium and iron. From these 14 nutrients, it's clear that the redesigned nutrition label is intended to help you manage what you eat to avoid recognized health risks. More information, such as amounts of monounsaturated and polyunsaturated fat or levels of other vitamins and minerals, is optional. But when a food is fortified or enriched or when a health claim related to an optional nutrient is made, those values must appear on the label.

In addition to nutrient-per-serving information, the new label displays Daily Values. With the exception of vitamins and minerals,

Daily Values are expressed in grams or milligrams and as a percentage. Each percentage, based on a 2000-calorie-per-day "reference" diet, tells you how much of your daily "allowance" for the particular nutrient is met by 1 serving of that food. For example, if the label says that 1 serving of a food contains 13 g of fat or "20% Daily Value," you know that 1 serving of the food gives you 20 percent of the 65-g fat allowance recommended for a 2000-calorie daily diet.

If you are using nutrition labels to help manage what you eat, remember that the label information is based on a 2000-calorie daily diet and on the specific serving size indicated. If you eat less than 2000 calories a day, your total percentage Daily Values for fat, saturated fat, carbohydrate and protein should equal less than 100 percent. Conversely, if you eat more than 2000 calories a day, your percentages for these will probably total more than 100 percent of the Daily Values on the label. Needs for other nutrients, including fiber, sodium, choles-

As Time Goes By ...

Your nutrient and calorie needs aren't the same as they were 10 years ago. And as time goes by, they will continue to change. As a general guideline, adults should consume *at least* the lower number of servings from each food group in the Food Guide Pyramid (see page 25). With modest amounts of added fat and sugar, this plan provides about 1600 calories—enough for a sedentary woman, young children and some older adults. Depending on body size and physical activity, many adults need more than 1600 daily calories. Most men and very active women, for example, can consume in the middle to upper middle of the Pyramid's serving ranges. The lower to middle numbers are good for most women. Athletes and active teens, especially boys, may go for the top of the range.

WOMEN'S SPECIAL NEEDS

More and more research is showing the link between nutrition and disease prevention among women. Both the National Institutes of Health's Women's Health Initiative and the American Dietetic Association's Nutrition and Health Campaign for Women focus on the unique health needs of women and how food choices can contribute to health.

Current concerns include increasing calcium throughout a woman's life to build and maintain bone mass, which prevents osteoporosis. In addition, many women do not get enough iron, which can lead to anemia. (Low iron intake can also result in anemia in teenagers and very young children.) Heart disease and breast cancer are both statistically associated with diets high in fat, although it is important to note that heredity is a major risk factor for both conditions.

Women who may become pregnant are now encouraged to get plenty of folic acid from vegetables or supplements, as folic acid has been found to reduce the incidence of birth defects. It is a generally accepted fact that pregnant and breast-feeding women need additional calcium, iron and folic acid. At least 3 daily servings from the dairy group, plus extra grains, fruits and vegetables help to meet these higher vitamin and mineral needs. Most pregnant women are advised to take supplemental iron pills or a prenatal multivitamin-mineral.

A MATURE OUTLOOK

Americans over age 65 made up 11 percent of the population in 1984. By 2030, the number will rise to 17 percent—50 million people. Interest in healthy, flavorful eating will grow right along with this population. Some older people can continue to eat the way younger adults do, but others need fewer calories as hormone levels change and metabolism slows. As people age, their taste buds become less sensitive, and intense flavors may be more enjoyable.

Lean body mass decreases with age, so that the body loses muscle and adds fat. If you eat fewer calories to help maintain a healthy weight, make sure the calories you do consume are rich in valuable nutrients.

Elderly people can experience less efficient nutrient absorption, loss of appetite and nutrient deficiencies resulting from medications. They may need more vitamin A, C and E, found in fruits, vegetables and whole grains, to help strengthen their immune systems and fight cataracts, cancer and heart disease. Calcium and vitamin D are important to reduce the risk of osteoporosis, and iron-rich foods help to prevent anemia.

Although it is best to rely on foods for nutrients, people who are unable to eat well due to illness or age, may need to take vitamin-mineral supplements. Unfortunately, many people who take supplements without the advice of an expert (preferably someone who is *not* selling a product) select the wrong nutrients, take an inappropriate dose or form, or use products with no documented positive effect on human nutrition. If you think you or a loved one might need nutrition screening and counseling, consult a registered dietitian.

terol, vitamins A and C, iron and calcium, are not related to calorie intake; you should simply aim for 100 percent of the stated Daily Value. For optimal nutrition and health, you may want to exceed Daily Values for vitamins A and C, calcium and fiber. To determine your specific nutrient goals, see a registered dietitian for evaluation and counseling.

Some labels also have a footnote listing Daily Values for 6 basic nutrients in both 2000-calorie and 2500-calorie daily diets. These values are based on widely accepted public health recommendations. Basically, the numbers indicate that if you need (or eat) more calories, you can have a bit more total fat, saturated fat, carbohydrate and fiber. Regardless of calorie intake, public health experts advise trying to limit cholesterol to a maximum of 300 mg and sodium to about 2400 mg a day. In fact, if your kidneys work well and you have no personal or family history of high blood pressure, you may not need to restrict sodium. You will simply excrete about as much as you eat.

Rice originated in Asia and is its major food. Some of the grain harvested from this Japanese paddy will be ground into flour for noodles.

HIGHS AND LOWS

Nutrient content claims on foods have caused significant confusion in the past. For example, some unscrupulous manufacturers labeled their products "cholesterol free," suggesting a unique advantage over their competition, when in fact the food by its very nature never contained any cholesterol in the first place. Today, staking a health claim isn't quite so easy. Absolute claims, such as "low sodium" and "fat free," are strictly regulated. All food labeled "low-fat" has 3 grams or less of fat per serving. And products making implied claims that subtly suggest a food might be healthful in some way—for example, "high in oat bran"—now must meet the criteria required for making the corresponding absolute claim—in this case, "high fiber." For further details see "Nutrient content claims" in the glossary.

Healthy Eating

It's on the nightly news and in the morning paper. It's fodder for magazine articles, books, seminars and lectures. Everywhere you turn, you'll find more and more information about diet and health. Often it is difficult to separate fact from fiction. Here is a fact: Diet cannot cure chronic disease. But a well-balanced diet low in fat and high in complex carbohydrates, vitamins and minerals can reduce the risk of disease and complement medical treatment of disease if it occurs.

HERBAL MEDICINE

Common plants, especially herbs, have been used through the ages to ward off illness, to relieve symptoms and, some maintain, to cure disease. For example, capsaicin, the alkaloid oil that makes chilies and red peppers hot, is thought to relieve bronchial congestion, reduce blood clotting that can lead to strokes, increase the metabolic rate and improve mood by causing the brain to produce natural opiates called endorphins.

Garlic, a member of the lily family, may have antibiotic properties. Research suggests that an ounce of garlic, the equivalent of one head, lowers blood fats, has anticlotting effects and may lower blood pressure. But garlic used in the amounts needed for pharmacologic effect may cause gastrointestinal distress as well as unpleasant body odor. Capsules of odorless garlic have not been tested for effectiveness. Botanically related to garlic, onions may have cholesterol-lowering and anticancer properties.

Research indicates that basil, cumin and turmeric may possess cancer-preventing properties. Basil, coriander, dill, fennel leaves, mint, parsley and rosemary are sources of beta-carotene. A number of other herbs and spices—including allspice, celery seed, clove, ginger, lemongrass, marjoram, pepper, rosemary and sage—have antioxidant properties. Caraway, dill, peppermint, marjoram and anise can act as digestives (aids to the digestion of food). (European *digestif* liqueurs are based on ancient herbal recipes.) Both cinnamon and ginger have been used to relieve upset stomach.

There are no scientifically based "recommendations" for amounts of herbs and spices, and more is not necessarily better. Plants and their

derivatives are full of surprises. Regulations on herbal remedies and supplements are quite loose, and some potentially toxic substances are sold without warning labels. Herbal essential oils, for example, are highly concentrated and can be toxic.

Although many prescription drugs are based on chemicals found in plants, more research is needed on the medicinal qualities of plants before we try to self-medicate. For now, use plenty of herbs and spices to enhance the flavor and aroma of foods. They are important as *ingredients* in a well-balanced, healthful, good-tasting diet.

Heart disease accounts for more United States deaths annually than any other disease. It is, in fact, the number one killer of both men and women. According to the American Heart Association, high blood

Fresh herbs pack a powerhouse of flavor, yet need very little room to grow. Dried spices also add an exotic taste sensation to simple recipes. As a seasoning, both are a healthy alternative to salt, butter and heavy sauces.

GRAB THE FLAVOR, CUT THE SALT

When broiling or sautéing fish or poultry, rub seasonings on fillets or poultry pieces. Mix chopped fresh herbs with bread crumbs and perhaps a few ground nuts to coat fish or skinned poultry. For vegetables and grains, add herbs and spices to the cooking liquid or mix them with the cooked food. Fresh herbs are generally more flavorful and fragrant, but dried ones can be used if fresh aren't available. Use whole spices for poaching fruit; sprinkle ground spices over raw or baked fruit.

HERB/SPICE COMBINATIONS FOR FOODS

VEGETABLES

Beans, green	Chives and fresh lemon zest
	Marjoram, basil and/or rosemary
	Caraway seeds and mustard
Broccoli	Gingerroot and garlic
	Sesame seeds
Carrots	Cinnamon and nutmeg
	Gingerroot and basil
Peas	Mint, onion and parsley
	Rosemary and marjoram
Potatoes	Dill, onion and parsley
	Cumin or caraway seeds and onion
Spinach	Nutmeg and onion
	Sesame seeds and fresh garlic
Tomatoes	Basil and rosemary
	Cinnamon and onion

FRUITS

Apples	Cinnamon, allspice and nutmeg
	Gingerroot
Bananas	Allspice
	Nutmeg and ground ginger
Oranges	Cinnamon and cloves
	Poppy seeds
Peaches	Nutmeg
	Cinnamon and cloves
Pears	Cardamom
	Freshly ground black pepper
Strawberries	Cinnamon
	Freshly ground black pepper

GRAINS

Pasta	Basil, fresh garlic and parsley
	Fresh garlic, onion and red pepper
Rice	Chili powder, fresh orange peel and cumin
	Curry powder, ginger, turmeric and ground coriander
Poultry	Rosemary and thyme or marjoram
	Tarragon, onion and fresh garlic
	Bay leaf, cumin and turmeric
	Curry powder, cumin, mustard, fresh garlic and paprika
	Gingerroot, cinnamon, allspice, anise seeds and cloves
	Mustard, fresh garlic and honey
Seafood	Thyme, nutmeg and black and red peppers
	Tarragon, thyme, parsley flakes, onion and garlic
	Thyme, fennel seeds, black and red peppers, and saffron
	Sesame seeds, ginger and white pepper

FOR THE LIFE OF SPICE

When stocking your spice rack, buy only as much as you think you'll use in a few months' time. Protect your flavor investment with these simple tips:

- Store spices in a cool, dry place in airtight containers. Excessive heat dissipates essential oils; high humidity tends to cake ground spices. Don't store spices near the stove.
- Date spices and herbs as you buy them, and use older packages first.
- When measuring spices, use dry utensils to prevent caking.
- Close spice bottles and tins soon after measuring what you need. Prolonged exposure to air or light causes loss in flavor and aroma.

cholesterol, high blood pressure and unhealthy weight are among the risk factors for heart disease. Following the Dietary Guidelines and the Food Guide Pyramid will help you control these risks. Be especially careful about fat; if you are eating too much, limit your total fat, saturated fat and dietary cholesterol. Become aware of your personal risks by having your blood cholesterol and blood pressure checked when you go to the doctor. Take specific actions based on your family history, test results and personal habits.

When you cook with fruits, vegetables and herbs rushed to market from a local farm or harvested from your own garden, the result is incomparably fresh and flavorful.

Research shows that 40–60 percent of all cancers are related to food choices. The American Institute for Cancer Research notes that nutrients found in fruits, vegetables and whole grains can help lower risk for many cancers. Eat a diet rich in these foods and lower your fat intake to increase your protection.

Certain substances in fruits and vegetables—including (but not limited to) fiber, vitamin C and beta-carotene—protect against cancer. Diets high in carotenes significantly reduce the risk of lung and skin cancers. Other nutrients, including vitamin E, selenium, vitamin B_6, folic acid (folacin), pantothenic acid and vitamin B_{12} have also been

SERVING THE SEEDS OF FLAVOR

Is there anything quite like the taste of a juicy tomato right off the vine or sweet corn on the cob fresh from the field? Have you ever marveled at the beauty of a delicate squash blossom or a ruffled purple leaf of kale? So great is our reliance on processed foods these days that younger generations and city dwellers may not know how fresh produce really tastes, feels and looks.

One reaction to a stressful, fragmented late-twentieth-century lifestyle has been a return to the garden. Working close to the earth puts us in harmony with nature's rhythm. And home-grown fruits and vegetables not only taste great but are economical too. Certainly the labor involved is more relaxation than work!

If you don't have a patch of land to devote solely to vegetable gardening, intersperse a few vegetable plants and berry bushes with your annuals and perennials. Some vegetables, such as squash, have interesting flowers; and some flowers, such as nasturtiums and pansies, make tasty salad ingredients. Just be sure that they are grown without pesticides or insecticides.

If you have no land to cultivate, try patio tomatoes and peppers, specifically bred to grow in pots. And don't overlook herbs. They take very little space to grow. With bright light and moisture, most will thrive indoors on a windowsill year round. With just a snip or a pinch, you have a powerhouse of flavor to add zest to anything from a simple salad to a robust main course.

Here are some herb growing tips:

• Basil is an annual. Snip the stems, use just leaves. Keep stems pinched back to prevent flowering.

• Chives are perennial. For best yield, keep plants well trimmed.

• Dill is an annual. Sow seeds in succession to ensure an ongoing supply. Harvested seeds are ready to use when they have turned dark.

• Mint is an invasive perennial. Cut it back often, and give it room to spread.

• Oregano, a perennial, likes full sun. Its purplish pink flowers are an attractive addition to the garden. Cut spent stems for maximum yield.

• Parsley, a biennial, is grown as an annual because second-year leaves are not very plentiful. Parsley does best in full sun. For variety, try Italian parsley, an intensely flavored flat-leafed variety.

• Rosemary, an aromatic, shrublike perennial, can grow 3–4 ft (1–1.2 m)

high. Rosemary grows best in full sun. In cold-winter regions, move plants indoors.

• Sage is a perennial. Keep it pinched back after it blooms.

• Thyme is a low-growing, bushy perennial. After it has flowered, trim the plant completely to encourage new growth.

Two more sources for the freshest produce are roadside stands and local farmers' markets. For example, you may not have room to grow brussels sprouts in your own garden, but how can you resist that impressive stalk of sprouts at the Saturday morning market? (You might be surprised to learn how many people—and not just children—have never seen a stalk of brussels sprouts.)

Buying directly from farmers in your area also means you'll be cooking with the freshest food available in your locale. Many growers have "pick your own" arrangements for berries, apples and pumpkins. These outings are a fun way to teach children about food right at the source. (One warning: Avoid buying apple cider from roadside stands and small growers. If it's not processed under strict sanitary conditions, apple cider can be tainted with dangerous *E. coli* bacteria.)

found to have anticancer properties. Some nonvitamin, nonmineral chemicals found in fruits and vegetables activate enzymes and destroy carcinogens. Substances that inhibit the spread of malignant tumors have been found in soybeans, chick-peas, lima beans and potatoes. The bacteria found in yogurt may contribute to preventing colon cancer. (These bacteria are used to ferment the milk and are "healthy"; in fact, they aid digestion.)

Breast cancer strikes 180,000 American women each year. Although the role of diet in preventing this cancer is not yet completely understood, we do know that breast cancer is more common in countries where women's total fat and saturated fat consumption is high. And there is evidence suggesting that a diet rich in fiber as well as vitamins A and C can decrease the risk of breast cancer. (For more information on women's special nutritional needs, see page 33.)

Osteoporosis, a weakening of the bones, leads to more than 1.5 million fractures every year. Of the 25 million Americans afflicted with osteoporosis, most are women. In fact, the disease is a major cause of disability in older women. Although there is no cure for osteoporosis, there are preventive strategies, and now is the time to start.

Calcium is essential to reducing osteoporosis. The Recommended Dietary Allowance (RDA) for calcium is 800 mg per day. Adolescents, young adults and pregnant and lactating women are advised to consume 1200 mg daily. Most women, however, eat only about half the recommended amount. Choosing a calcium source at each meal is a good strategy. Try skim milk, cheese or low-fat yogurt. Some experts recommend that postmenopausal women up their calcium intake to 1500 mg per day.

Try to get most of your calcium from the foods you eat. Naturally occurring calcium interacts with other nutrients, such as vitamin D, for maximum absorption. Dairy products are a good source of calcium, but choose mostly low-fat varieties. One cup (8 fl oz/250 ml) of milk provides 300 mg of calcium; 8 oz (250 g) of yogurt, 300–400 mg. Yogurt, frozen yogurt, sardines and canned salmon (with bones) are great calcium sources. Dark green leafy vegetables are another good

Opposite: Food has always been an eloquent expression of cultural heritage. Within the context of taste and health, "eating well" means exploring and celebrating our many food traditions. Below: Early civilizations in the New World thrived on a diet of corn supplemented with other vegetables, legumes and grains. Eaten in combination, these foods are a good source of protein.

source. Calcium-fortified fruit juices are a good beverage for people who don't like, or cannot drink, milk. Bread fortified with calcium is now available. Check with your physician or a registered dietitian to find out what is best for you.

One bonus of a diet fairly high in calcium is a potential reduction in risk for hypertension (also known as high blood pressure). Traditionally, however, hypertension is associated with sodium. If you have high blood pressure or a family history of the condition, you may be advised to choose a diet low in salt, the most common dietary form of sodium. For many people, a reduction in salt lowers risk for hypertension, stroke and heart attack.

Develop a palate for a wide range of herbs, spices and seasonings to reduce your reliance on saltiness as a primary flavor. This habit will enhance your enjoyment of meals whether or not you are prone to hypertension.

In addition to researching diet and disease prevention, scientists are also exploring the role various nutrients play in brain chemistry and immunity. For example, we know that tryptophan, a common amino acid found in protein foods, causes the brain to produce serotonin, a substance that causes drowsiness and increases tolerance for pain. Carbohydrates also provide tryptophan to the brain. (Don't be tempted to try tryptophan in pill form; there is potential for contamination and toxicity.)

Researchers studying the immune system have learned that starvation as well as obesity adversely affects immunity. A diet high in calories and fat but low in vital nutrients can leave you dangerously vulnerable

to illness. Antioxidants such as vitamins E and C and minerals such as zinc, iron and selenium are critical for the immune system to function properly. Yogurt may boost the immune system as well. Research among elderly people has shown that increasing weakness in the immune system may actually be related more to poor nutrition than to age. (For more information on nutrition and aging, see page 33.) At any age, good nutritional status is associated with increased immunity and resistance to disease.

Based on all this science, is there a magic pill to keep us all young and healthy? No. Individual nutrients work best in their natural context, interacting in ways we do not yet fully comprehend. And a magic pill would take all the fun out of the food experience—taste, texture, aroma and all the customs that define the art, not the science, of cooking and eating.

Keeping Food Safe

Delicious, safe, healthy food is everyone's goal. Keeping good food safe is a challenge that requires both education and vigilance by cooks as well as government agencies. Many people become sick needlessly because they are unaware of the basic precautions necessary to lessen their exposure to dangerous food-borne bacteria, viruses, parasites and chemicals. Simply stated, the major causes of food contamination are improper preparation, storage and handling.

Three basic rules go a long way toward keeping your kitchen safe:

1. KEEP FOOD CLEAN.

Wash your hands with soapy water frequently when handling food, and use clean utensils, dishes, sponges and towels. Wash the tops of cans thoroughly before opening; wash the cutting edge of your can opener with soap and water. Keep all refrigerated foods well wrapped or covered. Wipe up refrigerator spills immediately.

2. KEEP HOT FOODS HOT.

All cooked foods should be cooked to at least 140°F (60°C) and kept hot. Don't allow cooked foods to sit at room temperature for more than 1 hour.

3. KEEP COLD FOODS COLD.

All cooked foods to be served cold or stored should be cooled rapidly to 40°F (4°C) or below in your refrigerator. Freeze foods at 0°F (−18°C). Refrigerate leftovers and fresh perishables promptly. Keep foods out of the 40°–140°F (4°–60°C) danger zone where bacteria

WELL DONE FOR SAFETY

Type of Meat	Cook to an internal temperature of	
	Whole	Ground
Beef	145°F (63°C)	160°F (72°C)
Pork	160°F (72°C)	160°F (72°C)
Lamb	145°F (63°C)	180°F (82°C)
Veal	160°F (72°C)	160°F (72°C)
Poultry	170°F (77°C)	165°F (74°C)
Stuffed Poultry	180°F (82°C)	

Although much of the world's rice crop is grown in wet lowland paddies, another common method is to plant on terraced hillsides like these picturesque Balinese fields.

thrive. Thaw frozen foods in the refrigerator or under cold running water. If you thaw food in your microwave, cook it immediately. Never thaw foods at room temperature.

MICROWAVING AND GRILLING SAFELY

Safe microwaving and grilling require some special precautions. Arrange food in the microwave to promote even heating. Always follow the manufacturer's instructions for microwaving prepared foods, including turning and stirring as well as standing time. When microwaving meats and poultry, remember that they should reach the same internal temperature recommended for conventionally cooked meats and poultry.

When grilling meats, choose lean cuts. Some evidence indicates that fat dripping onto the grill's heat source forms a potential carcinogen that is transferred to the meat via smoke. You can also avoid this risk by putting foil directly under meat before grilling or by precooking meat in the microwave and reducing the grill time. Always remove cooked, grilled foods to a *clean* plate. And never pour marinade with juices from raw meat, poultry or fish over cooked food.

BUYING AND STORING STRATEGIES

When you grocery shop, make sure the frozen foods you select are frozen solid and that refrigerated foods are cold. Select these foods last, especially in warm weather. Don't buy damaged cans or packages, and double-check "sell by" and "use by" dates on perishable packaged foods. Once you are home, store refrigerated and frozen foods promptly. Label and date leftovers and other foods you freeze to avoid aged "mystery packages" whose contents have deteriorated in quality. Be sure to store grain products away from heat sources. Refer to the charts on pages 57–60 for storage tips on fresh fruits and vegetables. Organize your refrigerator, freezer and cupboards so that it's easy to use the oldest foods first.

IRRADIATION AND PESTICIDES: WHAT'S WHAT?

Just the word itself conjures up all sorts of high-tech horrors. In fact, irradiation does have a useful—and safe—role to play in our food supply. Yet, although more than 50 foods in 40 countries are already irradiated, the United States lags in using this technique.

Irradiated food has been exposed to gamma rays to destroy harmful bacteria such as salmonella and to kill insects on produce, thus reducing the need for post-harvest fumigation. Irradiation can also prolong shelf life by delaying ripening and sprouting and by interfer-

In Italy's northeast corner, the snow-covered peaks of the Dolomites provide a dramatic backdrop to the softly rolling farmland that has sustained the residents of this border region for generations.

A farmer's market offers a constantly changing array of the season's best produce. Shoppers in Nuremberg, Germany, inspect the day's offerings.

ing with organisms that promote spoilage. Irradiated food does *not* become radioactive. Irradiation does, however, chemically alter food. Of course, so does cooking.

To irradiate or not to irradiate—the decision remains controversial. Irradiating poultry could have a significant positive impact on public health by destroying salmonella and other bacteria. Pork has also been approved for irradiation so that fewer nitrites are needed for flavoring and preserving cured pork. Irradiating spices to kill insects may be a better alternative to using ethylene oxide, a chemical fumigant with potentially harmful residues. Irradiating strawberries, however, simply to extend their shelf life for a week or so, seems much less noble and clearly more market-driven.

All irradiated foods sold in the United States, except spices and some other dry ingredients, must bear the radura symbol. It looks like this:

Pesticides are commonly used to control crop damage inflicted by insects and disease and to prevent food spoilage. Like pharmaceuticals, pesticides are extensively tested and regulated by a number of federal and state agencies. Farmers are legally obligated to comply with standards for pesticide use. According to the United States Food and Drug Administration (FDA), the majority of foods—whether fresh or processed—have no detectable pesticide residue.

Many grocery stores now carry organic produce, and it can be found at some farmers' markets and health food stores. Organic produce may be more flavorful, and you may find different varieties of fruits and vegetables grown locally on organic farms, but it is almost always more expensive. Organically grown produce is not necessarily safer or more nutritious than produce grown using pesticides. In fact, when nutrient analysis is done from actual samples, scientists cannot differentiate organic from regular produce.

A rose is a rose is a rose? Maybe not. Using biotechnology, scientists can control an organism's reproductive process to favor certain genetic attributes. Enzymes used in food processing may now be produced through genetic engineering. Dairy cows are sometimes treated with a genetically engineered protein hormone that increases milk supply. Even human insulin and growth hormones are produced using genetic engineering techniques.

In genetic engineering, like any emerging technology, safety is a primary concern. Is the process controllable? Predictable? What will be the effect of altered foods on future generations? What impact does biotechnology have on the environment? What is its impact on delicately balanced ecosystems? What are the moral and social implications? These questions and others posed by vigilant watchdog groups continue to challenge the scientific community.

Currently, the FDA does not require any special labeling for genetically engineered foods, unless they contain a potential allergen not previously present. The first genetically altered produce to hit the market was a tomato that is sold red and ripe but has an extended shelf life. Other genetically engineered produce will surely follow.

FOODS VULNERABLE TO HEALTH RISKS

Government inspection and regulation have made our food supply increasingly safe over time, but new pathogens present a continuous challenge. The now infamous *E. coli* (*Escherichia coli*) microbe that wreaked such havoc in the early 1990s was recognized as a threat to humans only in 1982. The experts' best advice is: Don't take chances, especially with vulnerable foods known to harbor dangerous organisms occasionally. Raw and soft-cooked eggs, raw and undercooked meats and poultry and raw fish and shellfish are considered high-risk foods.

Eggs. Raw and undercooked egg yolks can be a source of salmonella bacteria. The smart choice is to avoid soft-cooked eggs and prepared foods that include raw egg yolks as an ingredient—for example, mayonnaise, Caesar salad, soft meringues and eggnog. Use only clean, uncracked eggs. Fresh eggs can be stored in the refrigerator for 3 weeks; hard-boiled (hard-cooked) eggs can be kept in the refrigerator up to 1 week.

Monounsaturated olive oil is a staple of Mediterranean cooking, one explanation, perhaps, for the relatively low blood cholesterol level of the people of that region.

Poultry and meat. Fresh chicken, turkey, duck and small game birds can be stored in the coldest part of your refrigerator for 2 days. Recent research has found that much of the raw chicken sold is contaminated with salmonella bacteria and therefore requires special handling. Rinse raw chicken with cold water, and thoroughly wash with hot soapy water *all* surfaces and utensils that raw chicken touches—including the sink, countertop, cutting board, plates, cutlery and your own hands. Anything you touch before washing your hands—even a cupboard door or water faucet—can become contaminated. Fortunately, thorough cooking inactivates and destroys these bacteria.

Don't let juices from raw poultry drip onto other foods in your refrigerator. This residual juice can contaminate foods that you might not be using right away. Stuff poultry just before you cook it. And remember that a stuffed bird takes longer to cook. Remove stuffing from the cavity before storing leftover poultry, and cover the bird in plastic wrap to preserve moistness.

Other than purchasing irradiated poultry, heating food to a high enough internal temperature is the only way to assure that bacteria are destroyed (see chart on page 42). Cook meat and poultry thoroughly, and use a meat thermometer to check temperatures. Reheat leftovers to an internal temperature of at least 160°F (72°C); reheat gravies and meat sauces to a rolling boil.

Seafood. Seafood is particularly nutritious and heart-healthy, but it requires special care in handling. Always buy your fish and seafood from respectable vendors who know their sources. Fresh fish should not smell "fishy" or like ammonia. Purchase smaller fish; they tend to be younger and therefore less exposed to contaminants. A fresh fish should have firm flesh; bright, clear, bulging eyes; and intact skin covered with a film that looks like a bright varnish. Choose fish steaks and fillets that have a translucent sheen and moist, firm flesh. The shells of clams, mussels and oysters should be closed or should close tightly when tapped. Store mollusks covered with a damp towel in the coldest part of your refrigerator.

Buy fish that is well chilled or on ice. Don't buy fish that is displayed under hot lights or that is piled up haphazardly. Refrigerate fresh fish as soon as possible in the coldest part of your refrigerator. Rinse it under cold water, pat it dry with paper towels and place it in an airtight plastic bag. Use fresh fish within 1 day or freeze it.

Always cook seafood thoroughly. Eating raw or undercooked fish, particularly shellfish, is risky. It can be contaminated with bacteria, viruses, parasitic worms and dangerous chemical residues. PCBs and DDT are still found in some fin fish. Trim fish skin and cut away dark areas where chemicals tend to accumulate. Cooked fin fish should be opaque and flake easily with a fork.

International Fare: Healthy Traditions

In many countries, a traditional healthful diet is simple "peasant-style" fare—locally grown foods prepared using uncomplicated cooking methods. At the core of several perennially popular international cuisines, you'll find not only healthful ingredients but also distinct taste profiles that have evolved over the centuries. Recipes in *Healthy Gourmet* often take their inspiration—for both ingredients and flavor—from traditional ethnic cuisines.

China. The low-fat, high-carbohydrate Chinese diet is exactly what the doctor ordered, according to many Western cancer experts. Rice and wheat are diet staples in China, complemented by more than 2000 vegetables. Authentic Chinese stews and stir-fried dishes use very little oil. Western adaptations of Chinese food, however, emphasize more meat, fried ingredients and sugary or salty sauces. For a more traditional—and more healthful—experience, make rice and steamed or stir-fried vegetables the main course.

France. The French have much lower rates of heart disease than Americans despite the fact that as much as 37 percent of their calories come from fat—15 percent from saturated fat. This so-called French Paradox might be attributed to the fact that the French consume more fresh vegetables and fruits—both sources of antioxidants that may inhibit fatty deposits along artery walls. The French often use olive oil, a monounsaturated fat, as well as butter for cooking. Many French foods, particularly those with rich sauces, are beautifully presented in rather modest portions. The French also have a very different lifestyle pace. They walk more, dine leisurely and seldom snack.

Although wine consumption is decreasing in France, the French still drink about 10 times more wine than Americans do. The red wine they consume with their meals may increase HDL (good) cholesterol and lower LDL (bad) cholesterol. Studies have suggested that *moderate* alcohol consumption—1 or 2 drinks a day, not necessarily limited to red wine—may have some positive health effects. While the French have less heart disease than Americans, their rate of liver disease is much higher than ours, suggesting that excess alcohol is a major health risk. The "red wine connection" and all other aspects of the French Paradox are under study by scientists on both sides of the Atlantic.

Japan. The traditional Japanese diet is low in fat and high in fiber, featuring soy products, fish, vegetables, noodles and rice. The emphasis is on rice or noodles—the base of the Food Guide Pyramid. Meat is used as a garnish rather than a main course. This diet is credited with helping

Buying directly from a farm means that you are cooking with the freshest of ingredients. Many farmers sell their own cheeses and other dairy products, or have "pick your own" arrangements for tree fruit, berries and pumpkins.

to keep heart disease low in Japan. A traditional Japanese meal is far more than food; it is ceremony. In addition to advocating balance and moderation, the Japanese Dietary Guidelines call for making "all activities pertaining to food and eating pleasurable ones." We should take a lesson from the Japanese in this respect!

Mediterranean Region. Studies among Mediterranean populations have revealed a surprisingly low incidence of heart disease. A typical Mediterranean diet—found in southern Italy, for example—consists of pasta, olive oil, fruits, vegetables, bread and sometimes seafood. Mediterranean people in general eat far more bread than Americans, and legumes are a diet staple. Even the simplest Mediterranean meal is an event, an experience to be enjoyed by family and friends.

The role of olive oil in the Mediterranean diet has received much publicity. While it is true that olive oil, a monounsaturated fat, is preferable to saturates and polyunsaturates, the bottom line is that olive oil is still a fat. To emulate the Mediterranean diet, don't add olive oil to your diet; substitute it for other fats you are already using and continue to limit *all* fat.

Mexico. Corn, beans, fish, chicken and vegetables are staples of traditional Mexican cuisine. Mexican food as popularized in the United States, especially fast food, bears little resemblance to the real thing. In traditional Mexican fare, corn and beans are a part of every meal, providing complementary proteins. The chili peppers and tomatoes so characteristic of south-of-the-border cuisine are sources of antioxidant vitamins A and C. Avocados, the heart of guacamole, are high in calories from fat, but most of that fat is monounsaturated, like olive and canola oils, and thus is thought to have some heart-healthy benefits. Much traditional Mexican food, including tortillas, is cooked in lard, which has almost equal amounts of saturated and monounsaturated fat. Substituting a more heart-healthy fat or cooking corn or flour tortillas by methods other than frying boosts the nutrient profile of Mexican foods.

Opposite: Compared to Americans, the French have much lower rates of heart disease, perhaps because they know how to enjoy life at a more leisurely pace. Below: Contrary to popular belief, grain-based foods like pasta are not fattening. In fact, your goal should be six to eleven half-cup servings per day. In China, noodles dangle from wooden dowels as they dry.

Maximizing Flavor

As author Lionel Tiger reminds us in *The Pursuit of Pleasure*,[2] food is not simply a matter of survival. Indeed, University of Chicago professor of psychology Mihaly Csikszentmihalyi has made a study of the inherent joy in some of life's common activities, including cooking. Csikszentmihalyi maintains that many cooks find transforming raw ingredients into meals the kind of "peak experience" that brings order and harmony to everyday life.[3]

Unfortunately, he laments, people who don't pay enough attention to what they eat miss a significant source of pleasure. Taking control of food and cultivating taste are investments well worth the energy they take. In eating and in cooking, exploration and adventure transform the experience.

HOW YOU COOK IT COUNTS

The cooking methods used in *Healthy Gourmet* play a significant role in enhancing fresh foods. These techniques are simple, preserving the healthful qualities of food and creating the foundation for a full range of flavor.

Steaming. Steamed foods are prepared without added fat, and steaming preserves nutrients because no part of the food comes in direct contact with water. Take care to remove food from the steam as soon as it is cooked to maximize flavor. One drawback to steamed foods, however, is their sometimes bland taste. Resist the temptation to serve them with flavorful high-fat sauces. Instead, use herbs and spices on the food itself and in the steaming water. Serve steamed foods with zesty salsas and relishes or low-fat sauces prepared from reductions and purées.

Grilling. Hardwood chips, such as mesquite and apple, and various fresh herbs, such as rosemary and thyme, can be sprinkled over hot coals to impart a distinct taste and aroma to grilled foods. Dried herbs, including herb blends, should be soaked in water for a few minutes before putting them over the hot coals. Go easy with these aromatics; you don't want to overpower the food's natural flavor.

Foods are sometimes marinated before grilling, both to tenderize and to add flavor. We use some oil-based marinades in *Healthy Gourmet*, and you might be concerned about the ¼–½ cup (2–4 fl oz/60–125 ml) of oil called for in these recipes. Rest assured that after the marinade is drained off the food, only a small amount of oil is actually consumed. We have adjusted the nutrition calculations accordingly. Oil-free marinades can also be made: use a base of citrus juice, wine or vinegar. You can brush these marinades over food as it grills without adding fat.

Meats, poultry, seafood, vegetables and fruits—even pizza and tortillas—are great for the grill. Some items may require precooking before being finished over the intense heat. (For some food safety tips on marinating and grilling, see page 45.)

Roasting. Roasting (baking) uses the heat of an enclosed oven to cook food. Roasted foods tend to be dry and unappealing if overdone. It is this dryness that inspires us to use rich sauces and gravies. When food is roasted properly and its moisture is protected, it doesn't need high-fat accompaniments.

Whole birds and fish, large cuts of meat and whole vegetables are generally said to be "roasted," while fish fillets, smaller cuts of meat and poultry pieces are usually "baked"—though the process is essentially the same. If you roast poultry with its skin on to preserve moisture, eat it with the skin removed. You may also want to keep a bit of the exterior fat on meat to add moisture during roasting, but trim it off before serving. Fish fillets and skinless poultry breasts can be dipped in seasoned bread crumbs or crushed whole-grain cereal before baking. The coating creates a surface that helps seal in moisture.

Sautéing. Traditionally, sautéed foods are prepared with oil over high heat. Using a nonstick pan with a very small amount of cooking oil or oil spray helps you reduce the added fat. Chopped onion, garlic and herbs are often sautéed before being added to a dish. Stir-frying sliced vegetables, meats and poultry is really sautéing with extra stirring. In a nonstick pan or wok, try using a small amount of chicken stock, wine or apple juice instead of fat to stir-fry or sauté.

Microwaving. Ideal for retaining food color and nutrients, microwaving is now a standard operating procedure in most American kitchens.

Just-shelled green peas need only the briefest steaming to enhance their sweet flavor. Peas are low in fat and high in nutrients and fiber.

Sweeping farmland near Boyd, Oregon presents a timeless vista. When the nation was young, most Americans produced the food that appeared on their table, but no longer.

Microwaving requires no added fat and dramatically speeds cooking of foods suited to the process.

Some fresh vegetables, such as potatoes and squash, are particularly good candidates for microwave cooking; others, such as green beans and peas don't fare as well. Berries, particularly raspberries and blueberries, make quick and delicious sauces when cooked in the microwave.

Remember that foods often cook unevenly in the microwave, and microwave-safe containers must be used. Use a microwave cookbook for complete directions, and follow instructions carefully about covering, stirring and rotating containers. Microwaved foods may be easy and delicious or complete disasters, depending on differences in technique and time. (For more about food safety and the microwave, see page 45.)

A TASTE FOR ALL SEASONS

Low-fat cooking methods get a flavor boost from the creative use of herbs and spices. Although the words *herb* and *spice* are used interchangeably, spices actually come from bark, buds, roots, seeds and stems, while herbs usually come from leaves.

Each herb and spice has its unique flavor, and certain combinations have come to characterize international cuisines. That doesn't mean you can't be creative. If you are curious about an unfamiliar fresh herb, take a whiff of it. Crush a leaf or two. Taste the herb, then taste and smell what you're cooking. Do the flavors and aromas complement each other? Experiment. After all, who would have thought herbal sorbet would be a hit?

When cooking with dried herbs, use one-third as much as the fresh herb. Packaged fresh herbs keep up to a week in the refrigerator. Bunches of a fresh herb such as parsley keep well in the refrigerator in a plastic bag. Wrap stems first in a moist paper towel, or place stalks upright with stem ends in water, and cover tops with plastic wrap. Don't wash herbs until just before you're ready to use them.

Mild herbs such as basil, parsley and dill are at their peak taste when used raw or cooked just slightly and added just before the food is served. Stronger herbs such as rosemary, bay leaves, sage and thyme, however, are enhanced by cooking.

A FRESH LOOK AT SAUCES

If you think the word *sauce* is just another way of saying *high fat*, think again. Today's sauces have a healthful, high-flavor profile. Reductions, purées, relishes, salsas, flavored oils and flavored vinegars make hollandaise and béarnaise yesterday's news.

Stocks and fruit juices can be slowly reduced over heat to an essence of flavor robust enough to be used sparingly with great results. We've included recipes for making your own chicken, fish and vegetable stocks (see the glossary). Preparing your own stock gives you control over its flavor intensity and sodium level. Add puréed vegetables or legumes to reduced stock for a flavorful sauce. For a "cream" sauce, add evaporated nonfat milk.

Colorful relishes are a tasty way to add more fruits, vegetables and legumes to your daily fare while cutting down on salty, high-fat sauces and condiments. Relishes go by different names in different cultures— salsas in Mexico, chutneys in India, sambals in Indonesia and Malaysia, chowchows in the American South. What these relishes have in common are their intense, full flavor, their ease of preparation and their flexibility. Use them to add zest to rice and pasta, to legumes, to steamed vegetables and to simple meats, fish and poultry.

Summer delights include juicy tomatoes in a sun-drenched palette of reds, oranges and yellows. Their sweetness adds sparkle to low-fat sauces and relishes.

Relishes have been an integral part of the cuisines of many cultures for hundreds of years. They are usually highly spiced, may be hot or cold and vary in consistency from chunky to smooth. From the time of ancient traders to today's immigration and travel, globetrotting relish recipes have showcased locally available ingredients. As a result, the culinary borders are beginning to blur. Salsas no longer rely exclusively on fresh cilantro (fresh coriander), lime juice and jalapeño chili peppers. Chutneys accompany dishes other than curries, and sambals go beyond a paste of chilies and spices. Like the world itself, these international relishes are becoming a global melting pot.

Aromatic flavored oils such as sesame, hazelnut, almond and walnut are much more intense in taste than vegetable, canola or safflower oil.

Consequently, just a little goes a long way. These oils are delicate and must be kept refrigerated. A touch of balsamic vinegar, *mirin* or flavored vinegar over steamed vegetables wakes up quiet tastes. A whipped vinaigrette on vegetables and seafood can take the place of a cream sauce, reducing fat while increasing flavor.

Quick and Easy

Time is of the essence, the old saying goes. With many demands made on our precious time, we occasionally hoard it, reluctantly share it and often feel guilty about wasting it. The driving force behind an explosion in convenience foods over the last two decades has been time savings. While some convenience products have a useful role, many have contributed to producing a generation of Americans sadly unaware of how great cooking from scratch *tastes.*

The fact is that many of us just don't have the time to prepare everyday family dinners, let alone a formal dinner party, a Sunday brunch or a special intimate dinner for two. Yet preparing a flavorful and healthful meal with fresh ingredients is not synonymous with struggling against the clock to complete several time-consuming recipes. For example, invest your time in Tuscan-style rosemary chicken (recipe on page 120) or orange roughy poached in red wine (recipe on page 189) and complement the main course with a simple medley of steamed fresh vegetables enhanced with a squeeze of lemon or a touch of flavored vinegar and a fresh fruit. Add fruit with a small wedge of cheese for dessert.

If you don't have time to do your own baking, buy a fresh loaf of multigrain bread from your favorite bakery—and skip the slathering of

INTERNATIONAL TICKET TO TASTE

Cuisine	Flavorings
Caribbean	Lime, allspice, ginger, chilies, mustard seed, peppers
Chinese	Gingerroot, garlic, star anise, pepper, orange peel, soy sauce, sesame seeds
French	Chives, tarragon, chervil, parsley, rosemary, thyme, fennel, basil, mustard, black pepper, marjoram, mint
Greek	Lemon, garlic, rosemary, cinnamon, bell peppers (capsicums), onion, oregano
Indian	Chilies, turmeric, cumin, fenugreek, tamarind, mustard, gingerroot, coriander, cinnamon, cloves, curry leaves
Indonesian	Peanut, lime, gingerroot, sesame seeds, onion, chili peppers, cayenne, coriander, nutmeg, cinnamon
Italian	Garlic, oregano, basil, rosemary, thyme, olives
Japanese	Gingerroot, garlic, mustard powder, lemon peel, fish stock (dashi), horseradish, soy sauce
Mexican	Cumin, oregano, garlic, chili peppers, fresh cilantro (fresh coriander), tomatillos, onion
Moroccan	Cardamom, mace, allspice, cloves, gingerroot, mint, black pepper, cayenne, coriander, cumin, onion
North African	Mint leaves, garlic, sesame seeds, lemon peel, onion
Thai	Chili peppers, coriander seeds, cloves, gingerroot, lemon grass

butter or margarine. Homemade breads taste great unadorned if you give them a chance; they make good breakfast toast and lunchtime sandwiches, too. (To finish off a loaf that's no longer fresh, make homemade melba toasts: slice the bread very thinly, arrange the slices on a cookie sheet or sheet of aluminum foil and bake them in a 275°F (135°C) oven for about 45 minutes. You'll have a healthy, crunchy snack. Melba toast slices that contain raisins or nuts are as tasty and crunchy as cookies.)

If you prefer to spend your time preparing a grain or vegetable dish rather than a main course, buy a whole rotisseried chicken. Accent the chicken with a relish or salsa for extra flavor. Chicken left over from a dinner can be used in a luncheon salad or hearty soup.

If your household is small, buying whole fruits and vegetables is not always practical, because the produce spoils before you can use it. Instead, head for the best supermarket salad bar in your area. There you will find all sorts of cut vegetables and fruits for steaming, stir frying, snacks, desserts, relishes and garnishes. Some supermarket produce sections also offer fresh cut vegetables, such as broccoli, cauliflower and carrots, as well as cut fruits, such as melons, pineapples and oranges. This 1990s convenience food—called "speed scratch" by trend watchers—may seem to be expensive but no more so than throwing out spoiled produce when you need only small amounts of several ingredients. And "speed scratch" foods are worth every cent when you consider the taste, variety, texture, color and nutrients they add to your meals.

Some ethnic dishes call for special ingredients you may prefer to buy canned or frozen to save time. Frozen phyllo dough, for example, is as easy to use as it is versatile. Prepared wonton wrappers are available in the refrigerator case at some stores. Jarred grape leaves are a smart choice, especially if you don't live near a Middle Eastern food market. Canned legumes, such as chick-peas (garbanzo beans) and kidney beans, are as nutrient-dense as dried, soaked beans, but if you are watching your sodium intake be sure to rinse them before using them in recipes. Canned broths are seldom as flavorful as homemade stocks, but they can save the day if you don't have prepared stock or need just a few ounces. When time isn't of the essence, homemade stock recipes are provided in the glossary.

Some canned fruits and vegetables—pumpkin, peas, corn, kidney beans and beets, to name a few—are surprisingly nutritious, but they may contain a lot of sodium. The label tells you how much. If you drain the liquid from the can's contents, sodium will be drastically reduced.

Don't rule out frozen vegetables. Flash-freezing technology makes some frozen vegetables (snow peas, sugar snap peas and baby lima beans) "fresher" than out-of-season supplies in the produce department. Cruciferous varieties, such as broccoli, brussels sprouts and cauliflower maintain their texture and flavor very well when frozen. In general, select whole frozen vegetables rather than chopped. Frozen broccoli spears and asparagus, for example, are more tender than the chopped versions.

An easy way to impart a healthy boost to some of the foods you routinely prepare is to add some fresh fruits and vegetables. For color and crunch, mix fresh grapes, diced apples, chopped celery or red bell pepper in your chicken or tuna salad. Top your morning cereal with fresh fruit, and mix some more with your low-fat cottage cheese for lunch. Add a couple of spinach leaves to your sandwiches, and load your pasta sauces, soups and chilis with extra vegetables. If you want a simple appetizer, make it sliced fresh fruit. Try shifting your cultural culinary paradigm by putting a generous serving of vegetables or grains in the center of your plate—the spot Western cultures usually reserve for the meat, fish or poultry.

Fruits and vegetables also provide a quick way to dress up a plate—after all, part of eating well is the experience of beautiful food. One of the compliments we bestow is that something "looks good enough to eat." Vegetables and fruits add color, shape and dimension without adding a lot of fat or calories. And their crunch can act as a foil to smoother-textured foods.

What's in Season?

FRUITS

With such an abundance from which to choose, how can we ever get our fill of ripe, juicy, sweet, delicious fruit? Rich in vitamins, minerals and carbohydrates and an important source of dietary fiber, fruit is a top pick among healthful great-tasting foods.

Storage times for fruits vary depending upon temperature, humidity and ripeness. In general, use fruits as soon as possible after they are ripe.

According to produce industry surveys, America's top-selling fruits are apples, bananas, seedless green grapes, strawberries and cantaloupes.

VEGETABLES

A year-round harvest of vegetables enhances the taste, texture and beauty of our everyday meals. Fat-free, high-fiber and rich in important vitamins and minerals, vegetables do double duty as healthful and flavorful food choices.

Storage time for fresh vegetables depends on temperature and humidity. In general, use vegetables as soon as possible after purchase.

According to produce industry surveys, America's five favorite vegetables are head lettuce, carrots, tomatoes, celery and cucumbers. When shopping for vegetables, be selective and flexible. Choose the highest quality and consider the many alternatives. Enjoy a variety of fresh vegetables when they are most abundant and at the peak of flavor and quality.

FRUIT TABLE

TYPE	PEAK AVAILABILITY (NORTH AMERICA)	FRESHNESS/QUALITY INDICATORS	STORAGE CONDITIONS
Apples	October–March August–December from California	Firm, crisp, bright-skinned, unbruised fruit.	Refrigerate or store in cool, ventilated, dark place.
Apricots	May–August	Unbruised, bright orange with apricot scent; flavor best when fruit ripe and soft.	Ripen at room temperature; then refrigerate.
Atemoyas	August–November	Green skin darkens as fruit ripens; ready when fruit separates from stem or yields to gentle pressure.	Ripen at room temperature; then refrigerate.
Avocados	Year-round August–January from Florida	Assorted shapes, sizes, colors and textures; buy firm fruit; ripen at home; ripe fruit yields to gentle pressure.	Ripen in brown paper bag to avoid bruising and promote ripening; test daily; never refrigerate; can purée and then freeze.
Bananas	Year-round	Clear skin, unbruised, light green or light yellow; generally ripen in few days; use overripe bananas with spotted or black skin in baking.	Ripen at room temperature; never refrigerate.
Blackberries	May–September	Jet black color, dry and clean; avoid berries stuck together and packages with seepage.	Refrigerate.
Blood oranges	January–July	Orange or red skin with red pulp; firm; heavy in relation to size.	Refrigerate.
Blueberries	June–August	Large, dry, plump; "bloom" (powdery coating) is clue to freshness; wild blueberries are very dark in color; cultivated berries, medium blue.	Refrigerate.
Cantaloupes	June–September	Firm, unbruised fruit with light, yellowish skin.	Ripen at room temperature; then refrigerate.
Carambolas (star fruits)	August–February	Golden yellow when ripe; may have brown edges; skin is edible.	Store green-tinged fruits at room temperature in paper bag until golden and fragrant; then refrigerate.
Cherimoyas (custard apples)	November–May	Plump, dull khaki-green, slightly soft.	Ripen at room temperature; check daily; refrigerate when ripe.
Cherries	May–July	Large, dark, firm fruit with green stems firmly attached; avoid any that are sticky or wet; bing has best flavor.	Refrigerate.
Cloudberries	Rare; from Scandinavia	Firm, dry, yellow berries.	Refrigerate; use immediately.
Cranberries	October–November	Very firm, dry, dark, shiny berries.	Refrigerate up to 3 weeks or freeze.
Crenshaw melons	August–December	Firm, unbruised fruit with yellow, velvety skin.	Ripen at room temperature; then refrigerate.
Currants	June–August	Firm, translucent red berries.	Refrigerate; use in 2 days or freeze.
Dates	Year-round	Plump, glossy, soft fruit.	Refrigerate up to 2 weeks.
Feijoas	September–June	Full, rich aroma; when ripe, feels like firm plum.	Ripen at room temperature in paper bag; then refrigerate.
Figs	June–October	Light and dark varieties fresh-smelling; unbruised; yields to touch.	Refrigerate; eat within 2 days.
Gooseberries	Variable; most imported	Light green, firm, like tiny veined green grapes; very tart; only eaten sweetened and cooked.	Refrigerate up to 2 weeks.
Grapes	July–October	Firm, plump, dry fruit; freshest ones have "bloom" (powdery coating); seek yellowish color in green grapes, deep colors in red or blue varieties.	Refrigerate.
Grapefruits	December–June	Heavy, thin-skinned fruit; Indian River and Orchid Island Florida and red-fleshed Texas usually best.	Will keep at room temperature up to 2 weeks; can refrigerate.
Guavas	May–February	Yellow, tender fruit with intense aroma.	Ripen at room temperature until fruit yields to pressure; check daily; then refrigerate 1 day.
Honeydews	June–September	Unbruised, fragrant, cream-colored skin, velvety but not soft; freckles signal high sugar content; blossom end yields to gentle pressure when ripe.	Refrigerate.
Kiwis	Year-round	Plump, fairly firm, unbruised fruit.	Ripen at room temperature; then refrigerate.
Kumquats	November–May	Orange, clear skins; heavy, bright, glossy; tart flavor; edible skins and all.	Refrigerate up to several weeks.
Lemons	Year-round	Thin-skinned; firm; heavy for size.	Refrigerate up to 4 weeks.
Limes	June–December	Dark green color; thin skin; heavy for size.	Refrigerate up to 4 weeks.
Litchis (lychees)	June–July	Unshriveled, with stems; shells range from rusty red to pinkish yellow.	Refrigerate up to several weeks.
Mandarin oranges	November–March	Firm, colorful, thin-skinned.	Keep at room temperature or refrigerate.
Mangoes	May–August	Firm, unbruised, yields to touch; color depends on variety; must be fully ripe to eat.	Ripen at room temperature until soft; then refrigerate.
Nectarines	June–September February–March from Chile	Colorful, unbruised, medium-to-large fruit.	Ripen at room temperature; then refrigerate.
Oranges	January–May from California, Arizona; November–May from Florida	Thin skin; heavy in relation to size; firm; may be orange or greenish.	Refrigerate.
Papayas	Year-round	Well-colored fruit; skin at least half yellow when edible.	Ripen at room temperature; then eat.
Passion fruits (granadillas)	Year-round	Purplish brown, gold or reddish color with firm shell; pulp should be soft with tiny seeds.	Ripen at room temperature until skin dimples; then refrigerate.

TYPE	PEAK AVAILABILITY (NORTH AMERICA)	FRESHNESS/QUALITY INDICATORS	STORAGE CONDITIONS
Peaches	May–September from California, Georgia, South Carolina July–September from New Jersey	Firm, colorful, unbruised fruit; yields to touch when ripe.	Ripen at room temperature; then refrigerate.
Pears	September–December July–October from California	Firm, unbruised fruit; shape, flavor, size depend on variety.	Ripen at room temperature; then refrigerate.
Persimmons	October–December	Firm, unbruised fruit; color, size, shape differ with variety.	Ripen at room temperature until very soft to touch; then refrigerate.
Pineapples	March–July Year-round from different tropical countries	Firm, unbruised fruit with trace of orange color; does not ripen after picking; flesh of ripe pineapple appears glossy and wet; Hawaiian generally sweetest.	Store at room temperature; refrigerate if cut; blackens when refrigerated. If cut, refrigerate and use within 2 days.
Plantains	Year-round	When peel is green, flavor is bland and texture starchy; when peel is black, texture is softer and flavor sweeter; never eaten raw.	Ripen at room temperature; do not refrigerate.
Plums	June–September	Good color with bright, unbruised skin; many varieties, colors, flavors, levels of tartness.	Ripen at room temperature; then refrigerate.
Prickly pears (cactus pears)	September–May	Firm but not hard; reddish or greenish fruit; deep color, not faded.	Ripen at room temperature; then refrigerate.
Quinces	August–January	Skin yellow and smooth when ripe; smell is fragrant; never served raw; always cooked and sweetened.	Store in cool, dry area up to several months.
Raspberries	May–September	Firm, dry, colorful fruit; avoid packages with seepage.	Refrigerate; use within 2 days.
Rhubarb	March–June	Firm, erect stalks, either cherry red or blushing pink; has tart flavor; always cooked and sweetened; botanically a vegetable but used as a fruit. Leaves are toxic; discard them.	Refrigerate; frozen rhubarb of particularly good quality.
Sapotes, white	October–January	Firm, unblemished fruit; when ripe, soft as ripe plum.	Ripen at room temperature; then refrigerate and use promptly; can be frozen whole.
Seville (bitter) oranges	February–March	Plump, heavy, firm fruit with orange, yellow or greenish skin.	Refrigerate.
Strawberries	March–July	Firm, dry, uniformly dark red berries with fresh green caps; size does not influence flavor or quality; tiny wild alpine strawberries have strong flavor and fragrance.	Refrigerate.
Tamarillos	June–October	Glossy, egg-shaped fruit.	Ripen at room temperature; then refrigerate.
Tangerines, tangelos	November–March	Firm, colorful, thin-skinned.	Keep at room temperature or refrigerate.
Ugli fruits	January–May	Green, loose-fitting skin has orange tint when ripe; avoid shriveled or brown fruit.	Refrigerate.
Watermelons	May–August	Firm, dark flesh; no clue to ripeness of whole melon, so best to buy cut melon.	Refrigerate cut fruit; store uncut fruit at room temperature.

VEGETABLE TABLE

TYPE	PEAK AVAILABILITY (NORTH AMERICA)	FRESHNESS/QUALITY INDICATORS	STORAGE CONDITIONS
Acorn squashes	October–December	Firm; smooth-ridged skin, green-orange or with orange patches.	Store in cool, dry area up to 3 months.
Artichokes	March–August	Firm, tight, fresh olive green leaves; size not a quality factor; best ones heavy for size.	Refrigerate.
Arugula (rocket, Italian watercress)	July–August	Crisp, fresh, green color.	Wrap and refrigerate.
Asparagus	March–June	Fresh odor; dry, tight, firm, pointy tips; green, uniform-size spears; white part is woody and discarded, except in specially grown white asparagus.	Refrigerate vertically with stem ends in water.
Bean sprouts: mung, soy, alfalfa, radish	Year-round	Fresh, moist tips.	Refrigerate; use within 2 days.
Beet greens	March–July	Young, green, crisp, velvety-feeling leaves.	Wrap and refrigerate.
Beets (beetroots)	March–July	Firm, smooth, dark red globes; freshest have attached greens; small and medium sizes more tender	Refrigerate.
Belgian endive (witloof, chicory)	Year-round	Firm, crisp; unblemished pure white heads with yellow tips.	Wrap and refrigerate.
Bell peppers (capsicums): red, yellow, green, purple, orange, Holland	Year-round October–June from Florida August–November from California January–March from Mexico	Deep, bright color; firm, smooth; firm stem end.	Wrap in a plastic bag and refrigerate.
Bibb (limestone) lettuce	Year-round	Small heads with tender, dark green leaves; soft texture.	Wrap and refrigerate; wash before using, not before storage.
Black-eyed peas (cow peas)	Year-round	Small to medium size; firm, not shriveled.	Wrap and refrigerate.
Boston (butterhead) lettuce	Year-round	Pale green, loose, soft leaves.	Wrap and refrigerate; wash before using, not before storage.

TYPE	PEAK AVAILABILITY (NORTH AMERICA)	FRESHNESS/QUALITY INDICATORS	STORAGE CONDITIONS
Broccoli	Year-round	Firm, bright, compact clusters of dark green buds.	Refrigerate.
Broccoli rabe (rapini)	Year-round	Fresh green, plump, crisp stems and leaves.	Refrigerate.
Brussels sprouts	October–April	Small, firm, green, hard, compact sprouts.	Refrigerate.
Butternut squashes	October–December	Firm; unblemished, buff-colored skin.	Store in cool, dry area up to 3 months.
Cabbage: red, green, Napa, Chinese	Year-round January–May from Florida, Texas August–December from New York June–July from North Carolina	Solid, heavy, firm, tightly packed heads.	Refrigerate up to 2 weeks.
Calabaza squash	October–December	Very firm, unblemished; small size more tender.	Store in cool, dry area.
Callaloo (leaves of malanga root)	Year-round	Crisp, dark green leaves.	Wrap and refrigerate.
Cardoon	October–March	Firm, erect stalks; outer stalks usually discarded.	Refrigerate.
Carrots	Year-round September–January from Canada	Small or medium, colorful, smooth, very firm, with pointy tips; freshest have greens attached; greens are inedible.	Remove greens; wrap and refrigerate.
Cassavas (yuccas)	Year-round	Completely bark-covered tubers that smell clean and fresh; no cracks or darkening near stem.	Use immediately or peel and store, covered with water, up to 1 day; can peel and freeze chunks.
Cauliflower	Year-round	Heavy, compact head; no brown spots; green leaves.	Refrigerate.
Celery	Year-round December–June from Florida July–October from Michigan	Crisp, unscarred bunches.	Refrigerate up to 2 weeks.
Celeriac (celery root)	October–April	Small, smooth roots; greens inedible except as soup greens.	Refrigerate up to 1 month.
Chayote squash	October–December	Very firm, unblemished; small size more tender.	Refrigerate.
Chicory (curly endive)	Year-round	Deep green outer leaves with crisp yellow heart.	Wrap and refrigerate.
Chili peppers: Anaheim (mild green), banana, jalapeño (hot green), habañero, poblano (ancho), serrano	Year-round	Plump, crisp, glossy, unblemished.	Refrigerate in paper bag up to 2 weeks; can be frozen.
Collard greens	November–March	Young, green, crisp, velvety-feeling leaves.	Wrap and refrigerate.
Corn	May–August August–October from New York, Midwest	Freshly picked ears (cobs) with plump, cool-to-touch kernels; avoid hard or shriveled kernels.	Refrigerate; eat soon after picking; loses sweetness during storage.
Cucumbers	Year-round	Clear-skinned, dark green; fairly thin diameter.	Refrigerate.
Eggplants (aubergines), Japanese eggplants	Year-round	Firm, unscarred, glossy black with green cap; medium size often best; eat cooked only; Japanese variety is small, thin.	Refrigerate.
Escarole	Year-round	Bitter, dark green leaves; usually used cooked or in soups.	Wrap and refrigerate.
Fava beans	April–June	Pale green, velvety pods; beans edible only when young/immature; some people allergic to favas.	Refrigerate; use within 2 days.
Fennel (finocchio, anise)	September–April	Medium to large; fresh green foliage and unbruised white bulb.	Refrigerate.
Fiddlehead ferns	April–June	Fresh, small shoots with tightly furled heads.	Refrigerate unwashed; use within 1 day.
Garlic	Year-round	Firm, dry, sprout-free heads.	Store in cool, dry area.
Gingerroot	Year-round	Fresh-looking, firm root; small sprouts have more delicate flavor than large bulbs.	Refrigerate up to 2 weeks.
Green (spring) onions	Year-round	Dark green leaves; clear white root end.	Wrap and refrigerate.
Horseradish	March–May	One slender, round end and one fatter, gnarled end; firm with no soft spots or sprouts.	Refrigerate.
Hubbard squashes	October–December	Large with green or orange skin; firm, orange flesh; often sold in wedges.	Store in cool, dry area up to 3 months.
Iceberg lettuce	Year-round, December–May from Florida, Arizona	Solid, crisp, tightly packed heads.	Wrap and refrigerate; wash before using, not before storage.
Jerusalem artichokes (sunchokes)	October–April	Firm, light-colored tubers; no peeling required; discolors when cut; keep white with lemon water.	Refrigerate.
Jícama (yam bean)	Year-round	Tuberous root with unblemished thin skin.	Refrigerate, unwrapped, 1 or more weeks; wrap if cut.
Kale	November–March	Crisp, colorful, deep green leaves.	Wrap and refrigerate; wash before using, not before storage.
Kohlrabi	May–June	Purple or green small-to-medium bulbs.	Refrigerate bulbs up to 1 week, leaves up to 3 days.
Leaf lettuce: green, red	Year-round	Soft leaves, mild flavor, fairly crisp texture.	Wrap and refrigerate; wash before using, not before storage.
Leeks	Year-round	Fresh looking, flexible stalks; firm bulbs.	Wrap and refrigerate.
Lima beans	Year-round	Flat, kidney-shaped; full, green, velvety pods; green inner beans have better flavor, texture than yellow or white.	Refrigerate.
Morel mushrooms	Supplies erratic	Dark brown, cone-shaped, hollow caps; fresh-looking, dry.	Refrigerate; use within 1 day.

TYPE	PEAK AVAILABILITY (NORTH AMERICA)	FRESHNESS/QUALITY INDICATORS	STORAGE CONDITIONS
Mushrooms: white (button), brown	Year-round	Beige or "natural" white, plump, round, firm mushrooms with closed caps and short stems; unless package says "natural," many prepackaged white mushrooms may be chemically treated with sulfite; loose mushrooms should feel dry to touch.	Wrap loosely and refrigerate.
Mushrooms, wild and domesticated "wild": boletus (cèpes, porcini), chanterelle, Cremini, *enoki*, Italian brown, *matsutake*, oyster, Portobello (Roma), shiitake, straw, tree ear (wood ear)	Year-round but supplies erratic	Dry, firm, fresh-looking specimens; wetness indicates rot.	Wrap loosely and refrigerate; use within 2 days.
Mustard greens	November–March	Young, green, crisp, velvety-feeling leaves.	Wrap and refrigerate.
Nopales (cactus pads)	Year-round	Small, firm pads; remove thorn eyes, rims and fibrous areas.	Wrap and refrigerate up to 2 or more weeks.
Okra	June–September	Small pods; velvety to touch.	Refrigerate.
Onions	Year-round	Firm, dry, well-shaped; free of sprouts or dark spots.	Store in cool, dry area.
Parsnips	January–March	Firm, crisp, free of cracks, cream-colored; medium size best.	Remove and discard greens; then refrigerate.
Pattypan squashes	March–October	Green color; unblemished, firm; smaller size with small seeds more tender, flavorful.	Refrigerate.
Peas	Year-round	Glossy, bright green, smooth-skinned pod; blossom end fresh and green.	Refrigerate up to 2 days.
Potatoes: white, red, yellow	Year-round	Firm, unbruised, dry, free of cuts; avoid ones with greenish cast or gray spots.	Refrigerate new potatoes; store mature potatoes in cool, dry area.
Pumpkins	October–November	Squat, light brown variety called "cheese" pumpkin and small orange-skinned sugar pumpkin have best flavor; large bright ones best for decorative purposes.	Store in cool, dry area.
Radicchio	Year-round	Fresh-looking, red-purple leaves; smooth texture.	Wrap and refrigerate.
Radishes: red, daikon	November–May Daikon, year-round	Firm, crisp, unblemished; freshest ones have attached greens; daikons are large, white, carrot-shaped.	Remove and discard greens; then refrigerate.
Romaine (cos) lettuce	Year-round	Long, narrow crisp leaves with white or golden hearts.	Wrap and refrigerate; wash before using, not before storage.
Rutabagas (yellow turnips, Swedes)	October–January	Heavy, roundish, very hard.	Store in cool, dry area; remove leaves (if any) before storage.
Salsify (oyster plant)	October–January	Medium-size root.	Wrap and refrigerate up to 2 weeks.
Shallots	Year-round	Dull, parchment skin; firm, dry; free of sprouts.	Store in cool, dry area.
Snow peas (mangetouts)	Year-round	Bright, fresh crisp pods; free of mold at stem end.	Refrigerate; use within 2 days.
Sorrel	Year-round	5 in (13 cm) or less in length; bright, crisp, green leaves.	Wrap and refrigerate.
Spaghetti squash	October–December	Very firm, unblemished; small size more tender.	Store in cool, dry area.
Spinach	Year-round	Crisp, dark green.	Wrap and refrigerate.
String beans: green snap, *haricot vert*, Chinese long, wax, pole	May–August	Pliable but crisp, velvety pods, unbruised; should snap when fresh.	Refrigerate.
Sweet potatoes	August–October	Firm, medium size; unmarked skin; some are kiln-dried ("cured") to remove moisture and extend shelf life.	Store in dry area up to 4 weeks; do not refrigerate; will turn black.
Swiss chard	Year-round	Crisp green leaves.	Wrap and refrigerate; use within 2 days.
Tomatillos	Year-round	Very firm; dry; clear color with husks free of blackness and mold.	Refrigerate up to 1 month.
Tomatoes: red, yellow, Roma (plum/egg), cherry	Year-round; varies by location; peak July–August	Smooth, bright colored, clear skin. Vine-ripened tomatoes best flavor; "forced" tomatoes ripened with harmless ethylene gas; genetically engineered tomatoes have extended shelf life while ripe.	Never refrigerate; store at room temperature. Eat when firm but yields to pressure.
Turnips, white	Year-round	Smooth, round globes with purple crowns; firm flesh; heavy in relation to size; small size more flavorful.	Store in cool, dry area.
Water chestnuts	Year-round	Rock hard, unshriveled; check for soft spots.	Store in paper bag in coolest part of refrigerator.
Watercress	Year-round	Very green, fresh-looking leaves; firm stems.	Wrap and refrigerate.
Yellow squashes (vegetable marrow): crookneck, straightneck	March–October	Deep yellow color; unblemished, firm; smaller size with small seeds more tender, flavorful.	Refrigerate.
Zucchinis (courgettes)	March–October	Green color; unblemished, firm; smaller size with small seeds more tender, flavorful; zucchini blossom is edible delicacy.	Refrigerate; use blossoms immediately.

The Nutritional Analysis of *Healthy Gourmet* Recipes

Each recipe in *Healthy Gourmet* includes a calculation of its nutrient content: calories, protein, carbohydrate, fiber, total fat, types of fat (saturated, polyunsaturated and monounsaturated), cholesterol and sodium. These values not only tell you what nutrients are in the food but also allow you to compare the recipes to the nutrition labels of similar foods. In addition, we indicate foods that are excellent sources (20 percent or more of Daily Value) of iron, calcium, vitamin A and vitamin C. We express vitamin and mineral amounts in percentages of your daily need for that nutrient, as commercial nutrition labels do. Numbers are generally rounded according to rules stated in the *Federal Register*. For example, calories over 50 are rounded to the nearest 10-calorie increment.

Sometimes total fat is expressed as less grams than the *combined* sum of saturated, polyunsaturated and monounsaturated fats. This apparent discrepancy occurs because we round grams of fat to the nearest whole number (or nearest .5 gram if under 5 grams). In addition, for analytic purposes, some molecular configurations of fat (numbers of carbon atoms in the chemical chain) are *not* included in the saturated–unsaturated values but are included in the *grand* total.

What is important is that you limit *total* fat on a daily basis and understand that saturated fats are the least heart-healthy. No more than 30 percent of total fats (or 10 percent of total calories) should be from saturated fats. The fat breakdown accompanying each recipe shows you the proportion of each type of fat.

The Food Pyramid information for each recipe (represented by a pyramid icon under the nutrition information for each recipe) shows how that recipe contributes to meeting the recommended daily servings. Sometimes a recipe contributes servings from more than one food group. Sometimes the specified portion provides 2 servings from one food group. For example, 1 cup of grain provides 2 servings of the 6–11 recommended per day, because a standard serving of cooked grain in the Food Pyramid is ½ cup. A larger portion will help you meet daily totals, and, in the case of some grains, 1 cup is a more realistic adult portion.

In many recipes, there is a small amount, but not a full serving, of a fruit, vegetable, milk, oil or other food. In these cases, we have *not* suggested counting the food toward daily food group totals. Of course, nutrients from these foods are included in the accompanying nutrition information. When recipes list an ingredient as optional, that ingredient is *not* included in the nutrient calculation.

Whenever recipes say "salt and pepper to taste," we have not included any salt or pepper in the calculated values. If you add salt, you are adding 2300 mg of sodium for each teaspoon of regular salt and 1800 mg per teaspoon of coarse-ground kosher or sea salt. The addition of pepper does not alter nutrient values.

The number of servings is based on a serving size suggested by the recipe developer. The nutrient calculations are based on that portion, but you may in fact eat more or less. When you plan your meals, allow 1½ or 2 servings for hearty eaters. Also remember that larger servings exceed the stated nutrient values.

Some recipes use chicken, fish or vegetable stock. Look for these recipes in the glossary.

Every season offers a new taste experience; fresh blueberries are a favorite example of summer's bountiful harvest.

Spring

Spring is the season of fresh asparagus, juicy strawberries and the first harvest of crisp garden lettuce. Celebrate nature's reawakening with *les fleurs farcies*—zucchini blossoms stuffed with ratatouille. Baby vegetables stuffed with peas and mushrooms showcase miniature potatoes, turnips and pattypan squash. Fresh spring peas add the definitive touch.

Fresh young asparagus spears are a spring delicacy. Serve them sautéed in lemon butter with crabcakes or use asparagus in a delicious onion and mushroom frittata, too. Enjoy the luxury of fresh raspberry vinegar in a salad of salmon, lentils and tender garden greens.

Multigrain currant scones with rose-petal cream go well with spring's first raspberries or strawberries. Delicate rose petals make the ultimate seasonal garnish. Make a fresh strawberry sauce to complement ginger roulade. The fresh berries and tropical fruits of spring make wonderful smoothies. Try a creamy, refreshing mango lassi or a strawberry-rhubarb-orange smoothie.

Phyllo Pouches with Scallops and Spinach

Phyllo Pouches with Scallops and Spinach

The fruity apricot flavor of chanterelles is enhanced by a little apricot liqueur.

12 oz (375 g) fresh spinach
3 tablespoons olive oil
2 shallots (white onions), finely minced
2 cloves garlic, finely minced

4 oz (125 g) chanterelle mushrooms, julienned
2 tablespoons apricot liqueur
½ cup (4 fl oz/125 ml) chicken stock (see glossary)
1 lb (500 g) fresh sea scallops
salt and freshly ground pepper to taste
2 tablespoons safflower oil
1 lb (500 g) phyllo dough

1. Preheat an oven to 400°F (200°C). Line a sheet pan with parchment paper.
2. Blanch the spinach leaves in boiling water for 15 seconds. Refresh immediately in ice water to stop cooking. Drain well, squeezing as much water as possible from the spinach, and chop coarsely.

3. Heat the olive oil in a large sauté pan. Add the shallots and garlic, and cook until soft but not browned. Add the chanterelles, and cook for 2 minutes.

4. Deglaze the pan with the apricot liqueur, and reduce the liquid to a glaze. Add the chicken stock, and reduce to half the volume.

5. Add the spinach and scallops, and cook until the scallops are firm, about 5 minutes. Season to taste with the salt and pepper. Set aside to cool.

6. Cut the phyllo dough into 72 rounds 6 in (15 cm) in diameter. Brush 3 pieces lightly with safflower oil, and stack them. Place 2 tablespoons of filling in the center of each stack, and gather the edges up, pinching to close the phyllo into a little pouch.

7. Place the pouches on the baking sheet, brush the tops with a little safflower oil, and bake for 15 minutes, until golden brown.

8. Transfer to a heated platter, and serve immediately.
Makes 24

---

2 pouches per serving: Calories 210, Protein 10 g, Carbohydrates 24 g, Fiber 1 g, Total fat 8 g (Saturated 1 g, Monounsaturated 3.5 g, Polyunsaturated 3.5 g), Cholesterol 10 mg, Sodium 260 mg, Vitamin A 25%.
▲ *1 Bread, ½ Meat*

SOUPS / ITALY

Sopa di Piccioncino

SQUAB AND SWISS CHARD SOUP

This is a hearty version of pasta e fagioli *with the addition of squab and Swiss chard. Serve it with a fresh salad and garlic crostini (recipe follows). If you substitute Cornish game hens or other poultry, allow additional cooking time.*

½ cup (3½ oz/105 g) dry borlotti beans or cannellini beans
2 squabs, cleaned and skinned
2 tablespoons olive oil
½ cup (2½ oz/75 g) diced onion
3 cloves garlic, minced
½ cup (4 fl oz/125 ml) red wine
5 cups (40 fl oz/1.25 l) chicken stock (see glossary)
½ lb (250 g) Swiss chard (silverbeet) or beet (beetroot) greens, coarsely chopped
1 teaspoon fresh rosemary, finely minced
4 oz (125 g) penne pasta
salt and freshly ground pepper to taste
2 tablespoons freshly grated *parmigiano reggiano* (Italian Parmesan cheese) (optional)

1. Soak the beans overnight in water to cover. Place them in fresh water, and cook over medium heat for 1½ hours, until tender. Drain.

2. Cut the squabs lengthwise with kitchen shears or a sharp knife. Remove any visible fat. Rinse, and pat dry.

3. Heat the olive oil in a stockpot. Add the onion and garlic, and sauté until soft. Add the squabs, and lightly brown them on all sides. Add the wine and 1 cup (8 fl oz/250 ml) of the chicken stock; continue cooking, turning the squabs frequently until the meat is

very tender, about 15 minutes. Remove the squabs from the pot to cool.

4. Add the remaining chicken stock to the stockpot and bring to a boil. Reduce to a simmer, and add the chard, rosemary, beans and pasta. Cook for 10 minutes.

5. Remove the bones from the squabs, and add the meat to the soup. Heat through, and season with the salt and pepper.

6. Ladle into warm bowls, sprinkle with cheese, if desired, and serve immediately.
Serves 8

---

1 cup per serving: Calories 190, Protein 12 g, Carbohydrates 21 g, Fiber 2 g, Total fat 6 g (Saturated 1 g, Monounsaturated 3 g, Polyunsaturated 1 g), Cholesterol 25 mg, Sodium 70 mg.
▲ *½ Bread, ½ Meat*

GARLIC CROSTINI

3 tablespoons olive oil
2 cloves garlic, finely minced
16 slices Italian bread

1. Preheat an oven to 375°F (190°C).

2. In a small saucepan, heat the olive oil and garlic. Lightly brush one side of each slice of bread with garlic oil, and place the slices oiled side down on a sheet pan.

3. Bake 15 minutes, turning once, until golden brown. Serve immediately.
Makes 16 slices

---

2 pouches per serving: Calories 210, Protein 10 g, Carbohydrates 24 g, Fiber 1 g, Total fat 8 g (Saturated 1 g, Monounsaturated 3.5 g, Polyunsaturated 3.5 g), Cholesterol 10 mg, Sodium 260 mg, Vitamin A 25%.
▲ *1 Bread, ½ Meat*

Left to right: Squab and Swiss Chard Soup, Garlic Crostini

Salade Niçoise Nouvelle

Freshen up a classic. Instead of canned tuna, which is high in sodium, use grilled fresh tuna. Quail eggs are so small that the amount of dietary cholesterol is much less than in hen's eggs. And in keeping with the miniature look, use small or baby vegetables.

1½ lb (750 g) tuna fillets

2 tablespoons lemon juice

2 tablespoons red wine vinegar

1 clove garlic, finely minced

1½ teaspoons Dijon mustard

½ cup (4 fl oz/125 ml) extra virgin olive oil

1 teaspoon minced fresh tarragon

¼ teaspoon salt

freshly ground pepper to taste

1 lb (500 g) small new potatoes, boiled 10–15 minutes until fork tender

6 baby artichokes, blanched 3–4 minutes and halved length-wise (see glossary)

Ingredients for Onion, Mushroom and Asparagus Frittata

½ lb (250 g) *haricots verts*, blanched 30 seconds, or green beans blanched 1 minute (see glossary)

1 head Boston or Bibb (butterhead) lettuce

6 hard-boiled (hard-cooked) quail eggs, quartered lengthwise

12 small white onions or green (spring) onions, cut into thin rings

1 green bell pepper (capsicum), seeded and julienned

2 cups (12 oz/375 g) cherry tomatoes, halved

12 *Niçoise* olives

1 tablespoon capers

1. Preheat a grill or broiler.
2. Cut the tuna into 6 portions. Grill it over hot coals or in a broiler for 2 minutes on each side, so that it is still rare inside. Remove from the heat.
3. To make the dressing, in a medium mixing bowl, combine the lemon juice, vinegar, garlic and mustard. Slowly drizzle in the olive oil, whisking constantly. Add the tarragon, salt and pepper.
4. Toss the dressing with the potatoes, artichokes and *haricots verts*. Let stand 30 minutes. Drain the vegetables, and reserve the dressing for another use.
5. Line each plate with lettuce leaves. Spoon the dressed vegetables on the lettuce. Place a piece of grilled tuna on top, and arrange the remaining ingredients around it. Chill briefly, and serve.

Serves 6

1 serving: Calories 370, Protein 33 g, Carbohydrates 33 g, Fiber 5 g, Total fat 13 g (Saturated 2 g, Monounsaturated 8 g, Polyunsaturated 1.5 g), Cholesterol 125 mg, Sodium 450 mg, Iron 25%, Vitamin A 35%, Vitamin C 90%.

▲ *2 Vegetable, 1 Meat*

Onion, Mushroom and Asparagus Frittata

This frittata is perfect for brunches and entertaining. Much of the preparation can be done ahead, and the frittata can even be baked before guests arrive and served at room temperature. The American Heart Association says that most people can eat up to 4 egg yolks per week with no problem, but if cholesterol is a concern, substitute 4 whole eggs plus 8 egg whites in this recipe.

2 tablespoons olive oil

1 red (Spanish) onion, sliced ¼ in (6 mm) thick

1 cup (3 oz/90 g) sliced mushrooms

½ lb (250 g) asparagus, blanched (see glossary)

8 eggs, lightly beaten

¼ teaspoon salt

freshly ground pepper to taste

¼ cup (1 oz/30 g) grated Parmesan cheese

1. Preheat an oven to 425°F (220°C).
2. Heat the olive oil in a large, ovenproof frying pan. Sauté the onion until lightly browned. Add the mushrooms, and cook until they are soft and the liquid has evaporated. Remove from the heat.

Salade Niçoise Nouvelle

3. Arrange the asparagus in the pan on top of the onions and mushrooms. Pour the eggs over the vegetables. Season with the salt and pepper, sprinkle the Parmesan on top and bake for 15–20 minutes, until a knife inserted in the center comes out clean. Serve hot immediately or at room temperature later.
Serves 4

1 serving: Calories 270, Protein 17 g, Carbohydrates 8 g, Fiber 2 g, Total fat 19 g (Saturated 5 g, Monounsaturated 10 g, Polyunsaturated 2 g), Cholesterol 450 mg, Sodium 380 mg, Vitamin A 20%.
▲ *1 Vegetable, 1 Meat*

Left to right: Rushta, Turnip Pickles

Rushta

Dolly Granatelli of Santa Barbara, California, recalls her mother making this Lebanese stewlike dish, an excellent source of many vitamins and minerals. The flavor secret is to get the onions as dark brown as possible but not black. Rushta is traditionally served with turnip pickles (recipe on following page).

4 large onions, sliced ¼ in (6 mm) thick

½ cup (4 fl oz/120 ml) olive oil

1 lb (500 g) lentils, rinsed

1 bunch (12 oz/375 g) Swiss chard (silverbeet) or 2 bunches (16 oz/500 g) fresh spinach leaves, julienned

½ lb (250 g) fresh egg noodles, cut into 2-in (5-cm) squares, or dry noodles and increase water by 1 cup (8 fl oz/250 ml)

salt and freshly squeezed lemon juice to taste

1. In a large saucepan, sauté the onions in the olive oil over medium heat, stirring occasionally, for 10 minutes. Continue to cook over medium heat, stirring more frequently to brown the onions evenly, for 30–40 minutes, until the onions are as dark as possible but not black.
2. Add 8 cups (64 fl oz/2 l) of boiling water (be careful of splattering), and bring to a boil. Add the lentils, reduce to a simmer and cook for 20 minutes. Add the Swiss chard, and simmer for another 10 minutes.
3. Bring the soup to a rapid boil, add the noodles and cook until they are done, about 3 minutes for fresh noodles, 8 minutes for dry.
4. Season with salt and lemon juice, and serve.

Serves 12

1 cup per serving: Calories 300, Protein 15 g, Carbohydrates 39 g, Fiber 7 g, Total fat 10 g (Saturated 1.5 g, Monounsaturated 7 g, Polyunsaturated 1 g), Cholesterol 15 mg, Sodium 40 mg, Iron 30%, Vitamin A 50%, Vitamin C 30%.

▲ *1 Bread, 1 Vegetable, 1 Meat*

Turnip Pickles

The beet gives these pickles their eye-catching color. Salt is used to soften the vegetables so they will absorb the pickling juices better. Most of the salt is rinsed off before the pickles are packed in the seasoned vinegar. You can refrigerate them for up to a month.

2 lb (1 kg) turnips, peeled and sliced

1 beet (beetroot), peeled and sliced

2 tablespoons sea salt

1½ cups (12 fl oz/375 ml) vinegar

1 teaspoon sugar

3 cloves garlic

1 chili pepper, slit lengthwise (optional)

1. Place the turnip and beet slices in a bowl. Sprinkle with the salt, toss and set aside for 1 hour.

2. In a medium saucepan, heat the vinegar and sugar with 1½ cups (12 fl oz/375 ml) of water. Bring to a boil, and simmer until the sugar is dissolved, about 3 minutes. Remove from the heat.

3. Rinse and drain the turnip and beet slices. Place them in a nonreactive container with the garlic and chili pepper. Pour the vinegar mixture over, and refrigerate, covered, for 1 week before using.

Makes 1 quart (1 l)

½ cup per serving: Calories 35, Protein 1 g, Carbohydrates 9 g, Fiber 2 g, Total fat 0 g (Saturated 0 g, Monounsaturated 0 g, Polyunsaturated 0 g), Cholesterol 0 mg, Sodium 520 mg, Vitamin C 40%.

▲ *1 Vegetable*

Sopa de Lima

SOUP WITH LIME AND SQUASH BLOSSOMS

To reduce saturated fat, choose flour tortillas made without lard, and bake them, instead of buying deep-fried chips. Adjust the amount of jalapeño in the soup to your taste.

4 flour tortillas

1 lime, cut in half

¼ teaspoon salt

4 cups (32 fl oz/1 l) chicken stock (see glossary)

½ cup (2 oz/60 g) chopped red (Spanish) onion

½ cup (½ oz/15 g) fresh cilantro (fresh coriander)

1 red bell pepper (capsicum), chopped coarsely or cut into strips

1 zucchini (courgette), sliced crosswise ¼ in (6 mm) thick

1 tablespoon minced fresh oregano

1 teaspoon minced fresh thyme

3 cups (1¼ lb/625 g) shredded cooked chicken

2 Anaheim (mild green) chilies, roasted, peeled and cut into strips (see glossary)

2 jalapeño chili peppers, seeded and thinly sliced crosswise

juice of 3 limes

salt and freshly ground pepper to taste

8 zucchini (courgette) flowers, blanched (see glossary)

2 limes cut into wedges for garnish

1. Preheat an oven to 350°F (180°C).

2. Brush across the tortillas with the cut side of the lime halves, and sprinkle them lightly with the salt. Cut them into 1-in (2.5-cm) strips, and spread them on a baking sheet. Bake for 10 minutes, until golden brown. Set aside.

3. In a large stockpot, heat the chicken stock to a boil. Reduce to a simmer, and add the onion, cilantro, bell pepper, zucchini, oregano and thyme. Simmer for 10 minutes, until the vegetables are tender. Add the chicken, Anaheim chilies, jalapeños and lime juice. Heat through. Season with the salt and pepper.

4. Just before serving, add the zucchini flowers. Serve with the tortilla chips and lime wedges.

Serves 8

---

1 cup per serving: Calories 190, Protein 18 g, Carbohydrates 16 g, Fiber 1 g, Total fat 6 g (Saturated 1.5 g, Monounsaturated 2 g, Polyunsaturated 1.5 g), Cholesterol 45 mg, Sodium 210 mg, Vitamin C 100%.

▲ *½ Bread, 1 Meat*

Soup with Lime and Squash Blossoms

Temaki-Zushi

HAND-WRAPPED SUSHI

Sushi is the perfect vehicle for enjoying tidbits of ingredients that you should use in moderation. While caviar (tobiko) contains a high level of dietary cholesterol and sodium, it has a moderate fat content; it supplies a high level of vitamin B_{12} and some omega-3 fatty acids. Avocados are very high in fat (Florida avocados are actually lower in fat and calories than the California ones), mostly monounsaturated, and should be used sparingly to keep an eye on total daily fat intake.

Hand rolling sushi is easy to do and great fun for a party. Arrange some or all of the ingredients listed below and let guests choose their favorites. It is a good idea to make a few sushi in advance and arrange them on a platter.

¼ cup (2 fl oz/60 ml) plus 2 tablespoons unseasoned rice vinegar

2 cups (14 oz/440 g) short-grain rice

3 tablespoons sugar

½ teaspoon salt

1 tablespoon black or toasted white sesame seeds

20 sheets of *nori* (dried seaweed)

1 English (hothouse) cucumber, julienned

3 in (7.5 cm) daikon radish, julienned

1 red bell pepper (capsicum), seeded and julienned

2 carrots, peeled and julienned

½ lb (250 g) pencil-thin asparagus, blanched and cut into 2-in (5-cm) lengths (see glossary)

¼ lb (125 g) snow peas (mangetouts), blanched (see glossary)

½ avocado, thinly sliced

10 green *shiso* leaves or watercress sprigs

2 oz (60 g) radish sprouts

3 oz (90 g) *enoki* mushrooms

½ lb (250 g) steamed crabmeat

½ lb (250 g) shrimp (prawns), shelled, deveined, skewered lengthwise to prevent curling and parboiled 2–3 minutes

2 oz (60 g) *tobiko* (flying fish roe)

¼ cup (2 fl oz/60 ml) *shoyu* (low-sodium soy sauce)

1 tablespoon *wasabi* (Japanese horseradish) mixed with water to make a paste

6 oz (185 g) pickled ginger

1. Prepare the *tezu* (hand vinegar) by mixing 2 tablespoons of the rice vinegar with 1 cup (8 fl oz/250 ml) water in a finger bowl. Set aside.

2. To prepare the *shari* (seasoned sushi rice), rinse the rice several times, until the water runs clear. Let the rice drain for 1 hour. Place it in a medium saucepan with 2¼ cups (18 fl oz/560 ml) water, and cover tightly. Bring to a boil, then reduce the heat to low. Cook 15 minutes without opening the lid. Remove from the heat, uncover, quickly spread a towel over the rice and replace the cover; let stand, covered, for 15 minutes.

3. In another saucepan, heat the remaining rice vinegar, sugar and salt, stirring until the sugar is dissolved. Set aside to cool.

4. Moisten the inside of a large glass or wooden bowl with 2 teaspoons of the *tezu*. Place the rice in the bowl, fluffing it with a wooden spatula or rice paddle. Add the vinegar-sugar mixture,

and fold it into the rice while fanning constantly to cool the mixture. Continue fanning and folding, taking care not to smash the rice kernels, until all the liquid has been absorbed and the mixture is cool, about 10 minutes.

5. Dip your fingers in the *tezu*, and form the rice into 1-in (2.5-cm) balls. Squeeze gently to elongate the balls and place them on a serving platter. Do not stack them. Sprinkle them with the sesame seeds, and cover with a clean towel. Keep at room temperature until ready to use (not more than 1 hour).

6. Using scissors, cut the sheets of *nori* into quarters, and toast them by passing one side over a gas flame 2 or 3 times, until they are crisp. Stack them on a serving dish.

7. Arrange a platter with the other ingredients needed to make the sushi rolls: cucumber, daikon, red pepper, carrots, asparagus, snow peas, avocado, *shiso* leaves or watercress sprigs, radish sprouts, *enoki* mushrooms, crab, shrimp and *tobiko* (in a small dish).

8. Place about 2 teaspoons of *shoyu* in a small bowl for each person. Pass dishes of *wasabi* and pickled ginger for guests to add to their own taste.

9. To hand roll the *sushi*, hold 1 piece of *nori* in your hand, shiny side down. Place a rice ball and choice of fillings inside, shape the *nori* into a cone, and squeeze slightly. Eat immediately.

Serves 16 (about 48 rolls)

---

3 rolls per serving: Calories 190, Protein 11 g, Carbohydrates 30 g, Fiber 2 g, Total fat 2.5 g (Saturated .5 g, Monounsaturated 1 g, Polyunsaturated .5 g), Cholesterol 50 mg, Sodium 410 mg, Iron 30%, Vitamin A 60%, Vitamin C 30%.
▲ *½ Bread, 1 Vegetable, ½ Meat*

Cold Soba Noodles with Scallion-Soy Dipping Sauce

Dashi, a fish and seaweed stock, is an essential ingredient in most Japanese recipes. It is available in instant form in Asian stores, or you can make your own by heating 4 cups (32 fl oz/1 l) of water with 1 oz (30 g) of konbu (dried kelp). Just before it boils, remove the konbu, and add 1 oz (30 g) of bonito flakes. Bring the mixture to a boil, and immediately remove from the heat. Strain before using. If you must limit sodium in your diet, this recipe isn't suitable.

1½ lb (750 g/2 packages) dried *cha-soba* (Japanese buckwheat noodles made with green tea)

1 cup (8 fl oz/250 ml) dashi (see note above)

2 tablespoons soy sauce

2 teaspoons *mirin* (sweet cooking sake) or 1 teaspoon sugar

1 tablespoon sugar

3 green (spring) onions, white parts and some green thinly sliced

1 sheet *nori* (dried seaweed)

2 teaspoons *wasabi* (Japanese horseradish) paste

Top to bottom: Temaki-Zushi, Cold Soba Noodles with Scallion-Soy Dipping Sauce

1. Cook the *cha-soba* in boiling water 3–5 minutes, until tender. Drain, and rinse in cold water. Chill until ready to use.

2. To prepare the dipping sauce: combine the dashi, soy sauce, *mirin* and sugar in a saucepan, and heat just until the sugar dissolves. Chill. Stir in the scallions, and place in 8 individual serving bowls.

3. Place the *cha-soba* on 8 bamboo trays or small plates. Toast the *nori* by passing it over an open flame 2 or 3 times. Cut it into thin strips or crumble it, and sprinkle it over the noodles. Place the dipping sauce in individual serving bowls, and add one to each tray.

4. Serve at once, with the *wasabi* on the side. Add *wasabi* to the dipping sauce to taste and dip the noodles in the sauce.

Serves 8

1 serving: Calories 310, Protein 13 g, Carbohydrates 67 g, Fiber 0 g, Total fat 1 g (Saturated 0 g, Monounsaturated 0 g, Polyunsaturated 0 g), Cholesterol 0 mg, Sodium 1000 mg.

▲ *3 Bread*

Top to bottom: Mango Lassi, Aromatic Rice Pudding, Curried Chicken and Mango Chutney Salad

Mango Lassi

This creamy refreshing drink has almost no fat and provides 16 percent of your daily calcium requirement as well as generous amounts of vitamins.

24 oz (750 g) plain low-fat yogurt
2 ripe mangoes, peeled, seeded and cubed
1 ripe banana
¼ cup (2 oz/60 g) sugar
20 ice cubes

1. Place the yogurt, mango, banana and sugar in a blender, and blend until well mixed.
2. Add the ice cubes, and continue to blend until the ice is almost completely pulverized and the mixture is frothy.
3. Pour into chilled glasses, and serve at once.
   Serves 8

---

1 glass per serving: Calories 130, Protein 5 g, Carbohydrates 24 g, Fiber 1 g, Total fat 2 g (Saturated 1 g, Monounsaturated .5 g, Polyunsaturated 0 g), Cholesterol 5 mg, Sodium 60 mg, Vitamin A 40%, Vitamin C 25%.
▲ *½ Fruit, ½ Milk*

SALADS / BRITAIN

Curried Chicken and Mango Chutney Salad

Britain's years in India bred a love for the spices and chutneys available there. This is not a traditional dish but rather a modern adaptation using traditional ingredients.

¼ cup (2 fl oz/60 ml) dry white wine
2 whole chicken breasts, skinned and boned
1 clove garlic
1 serrano (hot) chili, seeded
2 tablespoons half-and-half (half cream and half milk)
1 tablespoon curry powder
¼ cup (2 fl oz/60 ml) safflower oil
freshly ground pepper to taste
½ cup (4 fl oz/125 ml) mango chutney (recipe follows)
6 ribs celery, sliced crosswise
Boston or Bibb (butterhead) lettuce leaves for garnish
¼ cup (1¼ oz/35 g) cashew halves for garnish (optional)

1. Preheat an oven to 450°F (230°C).
2. Sprinkle the wine over the chicken breasts, and bake them, uncovered, for 15 minutes. Remove from the oven, and cool them. Slice them across the grain, place the slices in a large mixing bowl and set aside.
3. In a food processor with the motor running, drop in the garlic and chili. Add the half-and-half and curry powder. Mix well, scraping the sides at least once to blend all the ingredients. With the machine running, very slowly drizzle in the safflower oil. Season with freshly ground pepper.
4. Add the dressing, chutney and celery to the chicken, and mix well. Line a serving plate with the lettuce leaves, place the chicken on top and garnish with the cashews.
   Serves 6

---

1 serving: Calories 220, Protein 19 g, Carbohydrates 9 g, Fiber 1 g, Total fat 12 g (Saturated 2 g, Monounsaturated 2 g, Polyunsaturated 7 g), Cholesterol 50 mg, Sodium 85 mg, Vitamin C 20%.
▲ *½ Fruit, 1 Meat*

MANGO CHUTNEY

2 mangoes, peeled and coarsely chopped
½ cup (2½ oz/75 g) diced onion
½ cup (3½ oz/105 g) firmly packed brown sugar
½ cup (4fl oz/125 ml) white wine vinegar
4 cloves garlic, minced
1 jalapeño (hot green) chili, seeded and minced
1 tablespoon minced fresh gingerroot
¼ teaspoon ground cloves
salt and freshly ground pepper to taste

1. In a nonaluminum saucepan, simmer all the ingredients for 20 minutes. Cool and refrigerate.
   Makes 2 cups (16 fl oz/500 ml)

¼ cup per serving: Calories 75, Protein 1 g, Carbohydrates 20 g, Fiber 1 g, Total fat 0 g (Saturated 0 g, Monounsaturated 0 g, Polyunsaturated 0 g), Cholesterol 0 mg, Sodium 5 mg, Vitamin A 40%, Vitamin C 30%.
▲ *1 Fruit*

BREAKFAST / INDIA

Aromatic Rice Pudding

This creamy, eggless rice pudding is a nice choice for dessert as well as breakfast. It requires whole milk for its creamy texture. All milk, whether low-fat or whole, provides lots of calcium for bone and tooth strength throughout life. Serve the pudding with a bowl of kumquats, figs, and dried apricots in honeyed rose water (recipe on page 216).

4½ cups (36 fl oz/1.1 l) whole milk
½ cup (4 oz/125 g) sugar
½ cup (3½ oz/105 g) *basmati* rice, rinsed well
¼ cup (1½ oz/45 g) raisins
3 tablespoons coarsely chopped blanched almonds (optional; see glossary)
¼ teaspoon ground cardamom
¼ teaspoon saffron threads
1 tablespoon coarsely chopped pistachios (optional)
3 oz (90 g) kumquats, sliced (optional)

1. In a large saucepan, heat the milk and sugar, stirring until the sugar is dissolved. Add the rice, and simmer for 1¼ hours, stirring frequently and mixing any skin that forms back into the pudding. The rice will be very tender, and the milk will thicken.
2. Add the raisins, almonds, cardamom and saffron, and simmer for 10 minutes. Remove from the heat.
3. Serve at room temperature or chilled, sprinkled with the pistachios or sliced kumquats.
   Serves 6

¾ cup per serving: Calories 250, Protein 7 g, Carbohydrates 42 g, Fiber 1 g, Total fat 6 g (Saturated 4 g, Monounsaturated 2 g, Polyunsaturated 0 g), Cholesterol 25 mg, Sodium 90 mg, Calcium 20%.
▲ *½ Bread, 1 Milk*

Aromatic Smoked Tilapia

A visitor to China may get a taste of river life by spending a day on the Li River. Special boats take visitors on leisurely rides that include lunch. The galley is a small platform off the back of the boat, and the meal-to-be is often submerged in a bamboo cage behind the boat and pulled along. This smoked fish is reminiscent of just such a trip. It is delicious with Chinese long beans and mushrooms in black bean sauce (recipe on page 174).

¼ cup (1¾ oz/50 g) rice
¼ cup (1¾ oz/50 g) firmly packed brown sugar
2 tablespoons orange or tangerine peel
4 tablespoons black tea leaves
1 tablespoon star anise
6 tilapia fillets, 2 lb (1 kg), or other fresh fish of choice
2 tablespoons soy sauce
2 tablespoons rice vinegar
1 teaspoon minced garlic
¼ teaspoon sesame oil
1 tablespoon orange zest

1. Improvise a smoker by lining a wok or stockpot with foil, leaving enough excess to close over the top like a tent. In the bottom, place the rice, brown sugar, orange peel, tea and star anise. Place a small rack over these in the bottom of the wok.
2. Arrange the fish on the rack, and crimp the foil closed over it. Smoke over medium heat for 10 minutes. Remove from the heat, and let stand 10 minutes before opening. Transfer the fish to a serving platter and discard the other ingredients in the wok.
3. In a small bowl, combine the soy sauce, rice vinegar, garlic and sesame oil. Brush over the fish, sprinkle with the orange zest and serve at once.
Serves 6

1 fillet per serving: Calories 200, Protein 32 g, Carbohydrates 8 g, Fiber 0 g, Total fat 4 g (Saturated .5 g, Monounsaturated 1 g, Polyunsaturated 1.5 g), Cholesterol 70 mg, Sodium 360 mg.
▲ *1 Meat*

Chinese Egg Noodles with Baby Bok Choy

This one-dish meal is quick to prepare and full of fresh flavor.

1 lb (500 g) fresh Chinese noodles or fresh thin egg noodles
1 lb (500 g) baby bok choy
¼ cup (2 fl oz/60 ml) *hoisin* sauce
2 tablespoons soy sauce
2 tablespoons Chinese rice wine or dry sherry
2 teaspoons sesame oil

2 tablespoons peanut (groundnut) oil
3 cloves garlic, sliced
3 green (spring) onions, sliced crosswise
1 tablespoon minced fresh gingerroot
¼ cup (2 fl oz/60 ml) chicken stock (see glossary)
1 teaspoon sesame seeds

1. Cook the noodles in boiling water for 3–4 minutes, until al dente. Drain.
2. Remove the tough base of the bok choy. Cut one whole head in quarters lengthwise, and blanch for 1 minute; immerse immediately in ice water, drain and set aside. Slice the remaining bok choy crosswise, separating the stems and leafy greens. Set aside.
3. In a small bowl, mix together the *hoisin* sauce, soy sauce, rice wine or sherry and sesame oil.
4. In a wok, heat the peanut oil until very hot but not smoking. Add the garlic, green onions and ginger; stir-fry for 1 minute. Add the quartered and sliced bok choy, and stir-fry for another minute.
5. Add the *hoisin* mixture and chicken stock to the wok, and stir until slightly thickened. Add the noodles, tossing to incorporate the sauce and bok choy. Heat through, transfer to a warm platter and sprinkle with the sesame seeds. Serve immediately.
Serves 6

1 serving: Calories 320, Protein 11 g, Carbohydrates 52 g, Fiber 1 g, Total fat 8 g (Saturated 1.5 g, Monounsaturated 0 g, Polyunsaturated 0 g), Cholesterol 55 mg, Sodium 560 mg, Iron 20%, Vitamin A 50%, Vitamin C 70%.
▲ *2 Bread, 1 Vegetable*

Four Seasons Dumplings with Dipping Sauce

Siu Mai dumplings come in many forms, sold by street vendors and in teahouses for dim sum. The four seasons are symbolized in this dumpling, which is steamed and served with a delicious simple sauce.

DIPPING SAUCE
3 tablespoons peanut (groundnut) oil
¼ cup (¾ oz/20 g), finely minced green (spring) onions
¼ cup (2 fl oz/60 ml) soy sauce
4 teaspoons sugar
1 green (spring) onion, thinly sliced
DUMPLINGS
6 dried Chinese black mushrooms
1 teaspoon sugar
1½ lb (750 g) shrimp (prawns), shelled, deveined, and coarsely chopped
1 egg white
½ cup (3 oz/90 g) peeled and minced fresh water chestnuts, or minced canned water chestnuts
1 teaspoon grated fresh gingerroot

Clockwise from top right: Four Seasons Dumplings with Dipping Sauce; Aromatic Smoked Tilapia; Chinese Egg Noodles with Baby Bok Choy

2 green (spring) onions, minced, plus 3 green (spring) onions, green parts only, very finely minced

1 teaspoon finely minced tangerine or orange peel

1 tablespoon minced fresh cilantro (fresh coriander)

½ teaspoon salt

1 teaspoon cornstarch (cornflour)

1 tablespoon Chinese rice wine or dry sherry

2 teaspoons Chinese sesame oil

1½ teaspoons peanut (groundnut) oil

30 round wonton skins or square ones with the corners trimmed off

1 carrot, peeled and finely grated

1 red bell pepper (capsicum), finely minced

3 fresh white mushrooms, stemmed and finely minced

1. To make the dipping sauce, heat the peanut oil until it is very hot, almost smoking. Add the minced green onions and remove immediately from the heat. Let stand 10 minutes. Strain, pressing the onions in a sieve to get as much flavor in the oil as possible. Discard the onions.

2. In a small bowl, combine the green-onion oil with the soy sauce and sugar. Stir in the sliced green onion, and set aside until ready to serve.

3. To make the dumplings, fill a wok or large stockpot with water to a level near the bottom edge of a Chinese bamboo steamer placed inside. Remove the steamer, and bring the water to a boil.

4. Soak the Chinese black mushrooms in ½ cup (4 fl oz/125 ml) hot water with the sugar for 20 minutes, until the mushrooms are soft. Drain; remove and discard the stems; cut the mushrooms into ¼-in (6-mm) dice, and set aside.

5. In a large mixing bowl, combine the shrimp, egg white, water chestnuts, ginger, 2 minced green onions, tangerine peel, cilantro and salt. Add the cornstarch, rice wine, sesame oil and peanut oil. Mix until smooth.

6. To form the dumplings, place a heaping teaspoon of the filling in the center of each wonton skin. Bring opposite edges together and pinch, forming 4 cloverleaf loops. Fill 1 loop with green onion (spring), 1 with grated carrot (summer), 1 with red pepper (autumn), and 1 with mushrooms (winter).

7. Lightly oil each tier of the steamer, and put the dumplings in, one layer in a tier. Place the tiers over boiling water in the wok, reduce the temperature slightly and steam 2–3 minutes, covered tightly. Switch the positions of the tiers, and steam another 2–3 minutes.

Makes 30 dumplings

---

3 dumplings per serving: Calories 230, Protein 17 g, Carbohydrates 21 g, Fiber 1 g, Total fat 7 g (Saturated 1.5 g, Monounsaturated 3 g, Polyunsaturated 2.5 g), Cholesterol 105 mg, Sodium 700 mg, Vitamin A 50%, Vitamin C 30%.

▲ *1 Bread, 1 Meat*

Syrian Whole-Wheat Pita Bread

Fresh pita (pocket bread) is great stuffed with your favorite sandwich fillings or as a simple accompaniment to vegetables, hummus (recipe on page 102) and baba ghanouj *(recipe on page 103).*

1 package (¼ oz/7 g) active dry yeast
4 teaspoons sugar
¼ teaspoon salt
4 teaspoons vegetable oil
3½ cups (17½ oz/575 g) all-purpose (plain) flour
2 cups (10 oz/315 g) whole-wheat (wholemeal) flour
½ cup (2½ oz/75 g) yellow cornmeal (yellow maize flour)
   mixed with ½ cup (2½ oz/75 g) all-purpose (plain) flour

1. Line a baking sheet with parchment, and dust it lightly with flour.
2. Dissolve the yeast with the sugar in 2 cups (16 fl oz/500 ml) of warm water (105°–115°F/41°–46°C). Add the salt and oil.
3. In a large mixing bowl, combine the yeast mixture with the 3½ cups (17½ oz/575 g) of all-purpose flour, and mix until the dough is not lumpy. Gradually add the whole-wheat flour until the dough is too stiff to stir.
4. Turn the dough onto a lightly floured work surface, and knead until smooth and elastic, about 10 minutes.
5. Place the dough in a lightly oiled bowl, cover and let rise until doubled, about 45 minutes.
6. Punch down, form into a ball and let rest, covered, for 30 minutes.
7. Divide into 12 equal balls.
8. On a work surface dusted with the cornmeal and flour mixture, roll each ball to approximately 6 in (15 cm) in diameter. Turn as you roll to ensure an even thickness.
9. Brush off any excess flour, and place the rounds on the baking sheet. Cover, and let rise until slightly puffy, about 20 minutes.
10. While the rounds are rising, preheat an oven to 450°F (230°C). Carefully turn the rounds over, and bake for 5–7 minutes.

Makes 12 pitas

---

1 pita per serving: Calories 260, Protein 8 g, Carbohydrates 52 g, Fiber 4 g, Total fat 2 g (Saturated .5 g, Monounsaturated .5 g, Polyunsaturated 1 g), Cholesterol 0 mg, Sodium 50 mg.
▲ *2 Bread*

Falafel

Instead of deep-frying falafel (chick-pea patties), this version uses a small amount of oil and a nonstick pan. Chick-peas are an excellent source of many vitamins and minerals, a particularly good substitute for high-fat red meats, with a fiber bonus.

½ lb (250 g) chick-peas (garbanzo beans), soaked overnight,
   or 24 oz (750 g) canned
½ cup (2 oz/60 g) coarsely chopped onion

8 cloves garlic
3 tablespoons lemon juice
¼ cup (¼ oz/8 g) minced fresh parsley
2 tablespoons minced fresh cilantro (fresh coriander)
2 teaspoons ground cumin
2 teaspoons ground coriander
¼ teaspoon turmeric
¼ teaspoon salt
freshly ground black pepper to taste
2 tablespoons all-purpose (plain) flour
1 teaspoon baking powder
2 tablespoons olive oil
3 rounds of pita bread (preceding recipe), halved
1 tomato, chopped coarsely
1 English (hothouse) cucumber, peeled and diced
¼ cup (2 fl oz/60 ml) hummus (recipe on page 102)
½ cup (4 oz/125 g) dill-scented yogurt (recipe on page 110)

1. Drain the soaked chick-peas, place them in a saucepan with fresh water to cover and bring to a boil. Reduce to a simmer, and cook for 1 hour. Drain and cool. (Canned chick-peas do not need to be cooked, only drained.)
2. Place the chick-peas in a food processor with the onion, garlic, lemon juice, parsley and cilantro. Pulse until evenly ground. Add the cumin, coriander and turmeric, and blend well. Season with the salt and pepper. Stir in the flour and baking powder.
3. Form the mixture into 12 rounded 2-in (5-cm) patties with your hands.
4. Heat a little of the olive oil in a nonstick skillet. Brown a batch of the patties lightly, about 5 minutes on each side. Keep them warm as you cook the next batch.
5. Serve the falafel hot in the pita halves with the tomato, cucumber and hummus. Top with the dilled yogurt sauce.

Serves 6

---

1 serving: Calories 370, Protein 14 g, Carbohydrates 61 g, Fiber 6 g, Total fat 10 g (Saturated 1.5 g, Monounsaturated 4.5 g, Polyunsaturated 2.5 g), Cholesterol 0 mg, Sodium 170 mg, Iron 30%, Vitamin C 35%.
▲ *1 Meat, 1 Bread*

Tageen of Cornish Hens in Honey Sauce with Apricots

Tageens are a specialty in Moroccan homes. The word tageen *refers to the savory stew as well as the earthenware platter with a conical lid in which it is served. Moroccan-born Kitty Morse, author of* Come with Me to the Kasbah: A Cook's Tour of Morocco, *offers this recipe using Cornish hens in place of the traditional pigeons. For variations, she suggests trying other seasonal fruits, such as figs, instead of the apricots. Because each serving is a whole bird, the calorie and nutrient levels of this recipe are very high, but most people will not eat the wings, skin and some meat, so actual intake will be lower. Since the* tageen *is rich and the portions generous, serve it with simple cooked rice or couscous.*

3 tablespoons olive oil

⅛ teaspoon Spanish saffron, crushed

1 teaspoon turmeric

4 small Cornish game hens, 12–16 oz (375–500 g) each

3 onions, thinly sliced

1 cup (1 oz/30 g) parsley, chopped

¾ cup (6 fl oz/180 ml) chicken stock (see glossary)

1 lb (500 g) ripe apricots, halved and pitted, or ½ lb (250 g) dried apricots, soaked in water for 20 minutes

½ cup (6 fl oz/185 ml) honey

salt and freshly ground black pepper to taste

¼ cup (1¼ oz/35 g) whole blanched almonds, toasted (see glossary)

1. In a small bowl, mix the oil with the saffron and turmeric. Pat this mixture onto the hens, and place them in a small Dutch oven or large pot with a cover.

2. Add half of the onions, half of the parsley and the stock. Cover, and cook over low heat on a stove until the hens are tender, about 1 hour. Transfer the hens to a platter, and keep warm, reserving the sauce.

3. Set aside 8–10 apricot halves for garnish. Bring the sauce to a boil. Add the remaining apricots, onions and parsley and the honey. Cook over medium heat until the sauce is reduced by a third, about 10 minutes. Season with the salt and pepper.

4. To serve, pour the sauce over the hens, and garnish with the reserved apricots and the toasted almonds.

Serves 4

1 hen per serving: Calories 790, Protein 53 g, Carbohydrates 60 g, Fiber 6 g, Total fat 40 g (Saturated 9 g, Monounsaturated 20 g, Polyunsaturated 7 g), Cholesterol 155 mg, Sodium 160 mg, Iron 25%, Vitamin A 80%, Vitamin C 45%.

▲ *2 Fruit, 2 Meat*

Top to bottom: Syrian Whole-Wheat Pita Bread, Falafel, Tageen of Cornish Hens in Honey Sauce with Apricots

Crabcakes and Asparagus Sautéed in Lemon Butter

Crabmeat is particularly rich in minerals, including zinc, which helps to boost immune function. Ostrich fern shoots are a delicacy in the spring in Maine. They are a wonderful substitute for the asparagus in this recipe, if available. If you must limit sodium in your diet, this recipe isn't suitable.

1 lb (500 g) asparagus or ostrich fern shoots, dry brown
    leaves and coating removed
salt to taste
1 tablespoon olive oil
1 shallot (white onion), minced
3 tablespoons plus 1 teaspoon freshly squeezed
    lemon juice
1 teaspoon finely grated lemon zest
¼ cup (2 fl oz/60 ml) plain low-fat yogurt
1 egg
½ teaspoon dry mustard
1 lb (500 g) fresh crabmeat
1 cup (4 oz/125 g) dry bread crumbs
freshly ground pepper to taste
2 tablespoons unsalted butter
2 teaspoons lemon zest

1. Preheat an oven to 400°F (200°C), and lightly oil a nonstick muffin pan.
2. Rinse the asparagus or ferns and blanch them in boiling salted water for 3 minutes. Immerse them immediately in ice water, and drain. Set aside.
3. Heat the olive oil in a nonreactive medium saucepan. Add the shallot, and sauté until soft but not browned. Add 1 teaspoon of the lemon juice and the finely grated lemon zest, and remove from the heat to cool.
4. When the mixture has cooled, add the yogurt, egg and mustard. Carefully fold in the crabmeat and bread crumbs. Season with salt and pepper.
5. Place the muffin pan in the oven for 5 minutes. Remove, and quickly spoon heaping spoonfuls of the crab batter into the cups. Bake for 3–4 minutes, remove the pan, turn the crabcakes and return the pan to the oven for an additional 3–4 minutes, until the crabcakes are golden brown.
6. Heat the butter in a sauté pan. Add the asparagus and toss lightly. Heat through. Add the remaining lemon juice and lemon zest, tossing to mix. With tongs, remove the asparagus to a serving platter.
7. Arrange the crabcakes on top of the asparagus, drizzle any remaining lemon butter over and serve immediately.
Serves 4

1 serving: Calories 330, Protein 29 g, Carbohydrates 25 g, Fiber 2 g, Total fat 13 g (Saturated 5 g, Monounsaturated 5 g, Polyunsaturated 1 g), Cholesterol 120 mg, Sodium 1170 mg, Vitamin C 30%.

▲ *1 Vegetable, 1 Meat*

Baby Vegetables Stuffed with Peas and Mushrooms

What could be more indicative of spring than fresh peas and baby vegetables? Include these savory mouthfuls as part of a crudité tray or as a first course with red pepper sauce (recipe on page 90).

½ lb (250 g) peewee potatoes (1–1½ in/2.5–4 cm
    in diameter)
½ lb (250 g) baby turnips
½ lb (250 g) baby pattypan squash
½ lb (250 g) fresh peas, shelled
2 tablespoons freshly squeezed lemon juice
2 teaspoons minced fresh parsley
½ teaspoon minced fresh tarragon
salt and freshly ground pepper to taste
2 tablespoons olive oil
2 shallots (white onions), minced
1 clove garlic, minced
1 lb (500 g) white mushrooms, minced
½ teaspoon minced fresh thyme
3 tablespoons thinly sliced chives

1. Blanch the potatoes, turnips and pattypans about 2 minutes, until just tender. Refresh immediately in ice water. Drain. Slice off the vegetable tops, and slice a small amount from the bottoms so the vegetables will sit level. Scoop out a small hole in each vegetable with a melon baller. Save the scoopings for stock or soup.
2. To make the pea purée, blanch the peas for 1½ minutes. Refresh immediately in ice water. Drain. Place in a food processor or blender, and purée until smooth. Add the lemon juice, 1 teaspoon of the parsley and the tarragon. Season with the salt and pepper. Set aside.
3. To make the mushroom stuffing, heat the oil in a medium skillet, sauté the shallots and garlic until soft but not browned. Add the mushrooms and cook until all liquid has evaporated, about 5 minutes. Add the remaining parsley, thyme, salt and pepper. Remove from the pan to cool.
4. Place the pea purée in a pastry bag and fill the scooped-out turnips.
5. Place the mushroom mixture in a pastry bag, and fill the hollowed-out potatoes and squash.
6. Sprinkle the chives on top of the stuffed vegetables, and arrange them on a platter. Serve at once.
Serves 8

1 serving: Calories 100, Protein 4 g, Carbohydrates 14 g, Fiber 3 g, Total fat 4 g (Saturated .5 g, Monounsaturated 2.5 g, Polyunsaturated .5 g), Cholesterol 0 mg, Sodium 50 mg, Vitamin A 40%, Vitamin C 50%.

▲ *2 Vegetable*

Top to bottom: Baby Vegetables Stuffed with Peas and Mushrooms, Crabcakes and Asparagus Sautéed in Lemon Butter

Limpa

SWEDISH RYE BREAD

This bread is good anytime, but it is especially tasty with seafood. Since rye flour is low in the proteins needed for a good elastic dough, this recipe also uses a high-protein all-purpose or bread flour. The result is a fairly dense and flavorful loaf.

    1 package (¼ oz/7 g) active dry yeast
    2 tablespoons brown sugar
    1½ cups (7½ oz/235 g) rye flour
    ¼ cup (2 fl oz/60 ml) molasses
    1 teaspoon fennel seeds
    2 teaspoons orange zest
    2 tablespoons safflower oil
    1½ teaspoons salt
    5–5½ cups (25–27½ oz/780–795 g) all-purpose (plain) flour

1. Line a baking sheet with parchment paper.
2. Dissolve the yeast and brown sugar in 2 cups (16 fl oz/500 ml) of warm water (105°–115°F/41°–46°C). Add the rye flour, molasses, fennel seeds and orange zest. Stir until smooth to create a sponge for the bread. Cover and let rise until doubled, about 1 hour.
3. Stir in the safflower oil, salt and 1 cup (5 oz/155 g) of the all-purpose flour. Beat until smooth. Continue to add the flour, ½ cup (2½ oz/75 g) at a time, until the dough is soft and not lumpy.
4. Turn the dough onto a lightly floured work surface, and knead until smooth and not sticky, about 10 minutes.
5. Lightly oil a large bowl. Place the dough in the bowl, covered, to rise until doubled in bulk, about 1 hour.
6. Punch down the dough, and form 2 round loaves. Place them on the prepared baking sheet, and slash an *X* with a razor on top. Cover the loaves, and let them rise until doubled in bulk, about 1 hour.
7. While the loaves are rising, preheat an oven to 350°F (180°C).
8. Bake 45–55 minutes, until browned and hollow sounding when tapped. Cool on a rack before slicing.

Makes 2 loaves (24 slices)

---

1 slice per serving: Calories 140, Protein 3 g, Carbohydrates 28 g, Fiber 2 g, Total fat 1.5 g (Saturated 0 g, Monounsaturated 0 g, Polyunsaturated 1 g), Cholesterol 0 mg, Sodium 150 mg.
▲ *1 Bread*

Farfalle with Shrimp and Scallops

Fresh and satisfying, this pasta dish is quickly prepared.

    ½ cup (2½ oz/75 g) finely chopped onion
    3 cloves garlic, minced
    3 tablespoons olive oil

    ½ cup (4 fl oz/125 ml) dry white wine
    3 large tomatoes, peeled and seeded
    1 cup (8 fl oz/250 ml) tomato purée
    1 teaspoon fennel seeds
    ¼ cup (2 fl oz/60 ml) half-and-half (half milk and half cream)
    ½ lb (250 g) medium shrimp (prawns), shelled and deveined
    ½ lb (250 g) scallops
    2 tablespoons Pernod (optional)
    ¼ teaspoon salt
    freshly ground pepper to taste
    1 lb (500 g) farfalle (bow-tie pasta), cooked al dente and drained
    ¼ cup (¼ oz/7 g) fresh tarragon leaves

1. In a large skillet, sauté the onion and garlic in the olive oil until soft but not browned. Deglaze pan with the wine, and add the tomatoes, purée and fennel seeds. Simmer for 30 minutes, until slightly thickened.
2. Add the half-and-half, shrimp and scallops. Simmer for 5–7 minutes, until the seafood is firm and opaque. Finish with the Pernod and season with the salt and pepper.
3. Toss the seafood mixture with the pasta, sprinkle with the tarragon and serve immediately.

Serves 6

---

1 serving: Calories 480, Protein 26 g, Carbohydrates 69 g, Fiber 4 g, Total fat 11 g (Saturated 2 g, Monounsaturated 6 g, Polyunsaturated 1.5 g), Cholesterol 75 mg, Sodium 240 mg, Iron 30%, Vitamin A 25%, Vitamin C 60%.
▲ *2 Bread, 1 Meat*

Sautéed Salmon and Lentils with Warm Raspberry Vinaigrette

Spring is the perfect time for this heart-healthy salad. Choose your favorite tender greens, or serve the lentils inside a radicchio leaf. Both lentils and salmon are great sources of potassium, vitamin B$_6$ and other key nutrients. The salmon also provides omega-3 fatty acids and the lentils valuable fiber.

    1 cup (7 oz/220 g) green lentils, rinsed and drained
    1 carrot, diced very small
    1 turnip, diced very small
    ½ cup (2½ oz/75 g) finely minced onion
    4 tablespoons (2 fl oz/60 ml) safflower oil
    4 salmon fillets, ½ in (12 mm) thick, about ¾ lb (375 g) total
    1 shallot (white onion), very finely chopped
    6 tablespoons (3 fl oz/90 ml) raspberry vinegar
    ¼ teaspoon salt
    freshly ground pepper to taste
    2 cups (2 oz/60 g) mesclun (mix of tender greens: mâche, frisée, arugula and the like)
    4 sprigs fresh chervil

1. Preheat oven to 300°F (150°C).
2. Place the lentils with 3 cups (24 fl oz/750 ml) of water in a large saucepan, and bring to a boil. Reduce to a simmer, and add the carrot, turnip and onion. Cook for 20 minutes, until the lentils are tender but not mushy. Drain, and set aside.
3. In a large skillet, heat 2 tablespoons of the oil, and sear the salmon over high heat for 2 minutes on each side. Transfer the fillets to an ovenproof platter, cover and keep warm in the oven for 5 minutes.
4. Add the shallot to the juices in the skillet, and sauté until soft. Deglaze the pan with 4 tablespoons of the vinegar, and reduce slightly. Season with the salt and pepper. Pour the warm vinaigrette over the lentils, reserving 4 teaspoons to pour over the salmon fillets. Toss the lentils well.
5. Toss the mesclun with the remaining raspberry vinegar and remaining oil.

6. Place the mesclun on half of each plate; spoon the lentils on the other half. Arrange a salmon fillet on top of the lentils, and spoon 1 teaspoon of the remaining vinaigrette over each fillet. Garnish the salmon with the chervil, and serve at once.
Serves 4

1 serving: Calories 450, Protein 32 g, Carbohydrates 38 g, Fiber 8 g, Total fat 20 g (Saturated 2 g, Monounsaturated 3.5 g, Polyunsaturated 13 g), Cholesterol 50 mg, Sodium 240 mg, Iron 30%, Vitamin A 100%, Vitamin C 30 %.
▲ *1 Vegetable, 1 Meat*

Clockwise from top right: Swedish Rye Bread; Farfalle with Shrimp and Scallops; Sautéed Salmon and Lentils with Warm Raspberry Vinaigrette

Multigrain Currant Scones with Rose-Petal Cream

Multigrain Currant Scones with Rose-Petal Cream

This hearty scone boasts a higher-than-usual protein content due to the use of amaranth flour. Available in health food stores, amaranth is a seed high in calcium and iron. When combined with other grains, its amino acid lysine provides a complete protein. If amaranth is not available, just use all-purpose flour. Serve the scones with a bowl of fresh strawberries.

1½ cups (7½ oz/235 g) all-purpose (plain) flour
1 cup (5 oz/155 g) whole-wheat (wholemeal) flour
1 cup (3 oz/90 g) uncooked oatmeal (rolled oats)
¼ cup (1½ oz/45 g) amaranth flour
¼ cup (¾ oz/20 g) wheat or oat bran
⅓ cup (3 oz/90 g) sugar plus 1 tablespoon
1 tablespoon baking powder
1½ teaspoons baking soda (bicarbonate of soda)
1¾ cups (14 fl oz/425 ml) buttermilk or fresh milk plus
   1½ tablespoons lemon juice

2 teaspoons finely grated orange zest
1 cup (6 oz/185 g) dry currants
3 tablespoons low-fat (1-percent) milk
2 cups rose-petal cream (recipe follows)

1. Preheat an oven to 400°F (200°C). Line a baking sheet with parchment paper.
2. In a large mixing bowl, combine the all-purpose flour, whole-wheat flour, oats, amaranth flour and bran. Add ⅓ cup (3 oz/90 g) of the sugar, the baking powder and the baking soda, and mix well.
3. In a medium bowl, mix the buttermilk, orange zest and currants. Add to the dry ingredients, stirring just until moistened. Do not overmix.
4. Transfer the dough to a lightly floured work surface and roll 1 in (2.5 cm) thick. Cut into 3-in (7.5-cm) rounds with a biscuit cutter, and place the rounds on the baking sheet.
5. Brush the tops of the scones with the milk, and sprinkle with the remaining sugar. Bake for 20 minutes, until the scones are golden brown. Serve hot from the oven with the rose-petal cream.

Makes 12 scones

1 scone per serving: Calories 210, Protein 6 g, Carbohydrates 44 g, Fiber 4 g, Total fat 1.5 g (Saturated .5 g, Monounsaturated .5 g, Polyunsaturated .5 g), Cholesterol 0 mg, Sodium 200 mg.
▲ 2 Bread

ROSE-PETAL CREAM

2 cups (16 fl oz/500 ml) plain low-fat yogurt without thickeners or stabilizers, strained overnight in the refrigerator
3 tablespoons honey, or to taste
1 tablespoon rosewater
fresh rose petals

1. In a medium mixing bowl, blend together the yogurt, honey and rose water.
2. Transfer to a serving dish, and sprinkle the rose petals on top.
Makes 2 cups (16 fl oz/500 ml)

1 heaping tablespoon per serving: Calories 40, Protein 2 g, Carbohydrates 7 g, Fiber 0 g, Total fat 1.5 g (Saturated 1 g, Monounsaturated .5 g, Polyunsaturated 0 g), Cholesterol 0 mg, Sodium 25 mg.
▲ *½ Milk*

BEVERAGES / UNITED STATES

Strawberry-Rhubarb-Orange Smoothie

This refreshing fruit shake is perfect for an afternoon snack or breakfast starter and is a good source of calcium, surprisingly from the rhubarb.

2 cups (8 oz/250 g) strawberries
1 recipe rhubarb-orange compote (recipe on page 95)
2 cups (16 fl oz/500 ml) freshly squeezed orange juice
10 ice cubes

1. Combine all the ingredients in a blender, and process until smooth. Serve immediately.
Serves 6

1 glass per serving: Calories 160, Protein 2 g, Carbohydrates 40 g, Fiber 4 g, Total fat 1 g (Saturated 0 g, Monounsaturated 0 g, Polyunsaturated 0 g), Cholesterol 0 mg, Sodium 5 mg, Vitamin C 180%, Calcium 10%.
▲ *2 Fruit*

BREAKFAST / UNITED STATES

Southwestern Breakfast Strata with Roasted Tomatillo Salsa

This is a wonderful do-ahead brunch dish. Make it the night before, then bake and serve it in an attractive soufflé dish or casserole. It can also be prepared in individual dishes—just reduce the cooking time to 35–40 minutes.

1 recipe chicken sausage squares (recipe on page 164)
8 egg whites
1½ cups (12 fl oz/375 ml) low-fat (1-percent) milk
5 flour tortillas made without lard

1½ cups (12 fl oz/375 ml) roasted tomatillo salsa (recipe follows)
¼ cup (1 oz/30 g) grated white cheddar cheese (optional)

1. Lightly oil a 6-cup (48-fl oz/1.5-l) soufflé or baking dish.
2. Crumble the chicken sausage into a bowl and set aside. In a pourable container, whisk together the egg whites and milk. Set aside.
3. Place a layer of tortillas in the soufflé dish. Sprinkle with some crumbled sausage, and pour some egg mixture over the top. Repeat the layers, finishing with a tortilla. Cover with tomatillo salsa. Refrigerate overnight.
4. Preheat an oven to 350°F (180°C). Sprinkle the casserole with the cheese. Bake in a bain-marie, with hot water reaching halfway up the side of the soufflé dish, for about 1 hour until firm. Serve hot, or cool to room temperature.
Serves 8

1 serving: Calories 220, Protein 20 g, Carbohydrates 20 g, Fiber 1 g, Total fat 6 g (Saturated 1 g, Monounsaturated 1.5 g, Polyunsaturated 3 g), Cholesterol 35 mg, Sodium 210 mg.
▲ *1 Bread, 1 Meat*

ROASTED TOMATILLO SALSA

Cover and refrigerate this salsa until you are ready to serve it. Salsa is also delicious with raw vegetables or home-baked tortilla chips (see the sopa de lima *recipe on page 71).*

8–10 fresh tomatillos, husks removed
1 jalapeño chili pepper or more to taste (optional)
zest of 1 lemon
3 tablespoons lemon juice

1. Preheat an oven to 350°F (180°C).
2. Place the tomatillos on a lightly oiled baking sheet. Add the jalapeño if desired. Roast for 20–25 minutes, or until golden brown and soft.
3. In a blender or food processor, purée the tomatillos and jalapeño until smooth. Add the lemon zest and juice, and mix well.
Makes 2 cups (16 fl oz/500 ml)

¼ cup per serving: Calories 10, Protein 0 g, Carbohydrates 3 g, Fiber 1 g., Total fat 0 g (Saturated 0 g, Monounsaturated 0 g, Polyunsaturated 0 g), Cholesterol 0 mg, Sodium 0 mg.

Left to right: Strawberry-Rhubarb-Orange Smoothie, Southwestern Breakfast Strata with Roasted Tomatillo Salsa

Mole Poblano de Guajolote

TURKEY WITH CHILI SAUCE

This turkey stew with a spicy glaze is a traditional Mexican festival dish. Serve it with warm flour tortillas. Every mole recipe is different. Adjust the seasonings to your personal taste, and create your own version. If fresh mulato *or dried* poblano *chilies are not available, substitute more of the dried* ancho *chilies, but add a little fresh jalapeño (hot green) chili to liven the dish up. The mole sauce can also be served with chicken or duck.*

 **8 lb (4 kg) turkey, skin and fat removed and meat cut into
  serving pieces**
 **2 cups (16 fl oz/500 ml) chicken stock (see glossary),
  heated to boiling**
 1 carrot, peeled and cut into ½-in (12-mm) pieces
 1 onion, cut into ½-in (12-mm) pieces
 2 cloves garlic, smashed
 3 dried *poblano* (mild) chilies
 2 dried *ancho* chilies
 4 dried *mulato* chilies
 ¼ cup (1½ oz/45 g) raisins
 1-in (2.5-cm) piece of cinnamon stick
 2 whole cloves
 ¼ teaspoon whole coriander seeds
 ¼ teaspoon anise seeds
 2 tablespoons sesame seeds, toasted
 1 corn tortilla, broken into pieces
 3 ripe tomatoes, peeled
 ¼ cup (1¼ oz/35 g) *pepitas* (hulled pumpkin seeds), toasted
 1 oz (30 g) Mexican chocolate or unsweetened chocolate

1. Preheat an oven to 350°F (180°C). Place the turkey pieces in a roasting pan with the chicken stock, carrot, onion and garlic. Cover, and roast for 45 minutes, or until the turkey is tender. Remove the turkey pieces with tongs. Strain the vegetables, reserving the cooking liquid and set aside 1½ cups (12 fl oz/375 ml). Return the rest of the cooking liquid and the turkey pieces to the pan, and keep warm.

2. To make the mole, while the turkey is roasting, soak the dried chilies and raisins in warm water for at least 30 minutes. Drain. Purée the mixture in a blender with 1 cup (8 fl oz/250 ml) of the cooking liquid that was set aside. Transfer the purée to a medium saucepan, and simmer for 10 minutes.

3. In a medium skillet, combine the cinnamon stick, cloves, coriander and anise seeds. Toast over medium heat until lightly colored and fragrant. Remove to cool. Grind finely in a spice grinder along with 1 tablespoon of the sesame seeds. Place in a blender with the tomatoes, *pepitas*, tortilla, reserved cooking vegetables, and remaining ½ cup (4 fl oz/125 ml) of the cooking liquid that was set aside. Blend until smooth. Add to the chili purée. Crumble the chocolate into the mixture, and simmer for 30 minutes, stirring occasionally.

4. Place the turkey pieces on a warm serving platter. Cover with the mole, sprinkle with the remaining sesame seeds and serve at once.
 Serves 10

---

1 serving: Calories 330, Protein 45 g, Carbohydrates 12 g, Fiber 2 g, Total fat 11 g (Saturated 4 g, Monounsaturated 3 g, Polyunsaturated 3.5 g), Cholesterol 110 mg, Sodium 110 mg, Iron 25%, Vitamin C 180%.
▲ *1 Vegetable, 2 Meat*

Chicken Paprikás

Lecsó is a mixture of peppers that can be made ahead and frozen, then pulled out at the last minute to make a quick paprikás. *Serve the chicken over noodles or rice. This beautiful one-dish meal provides generous amounts of protein, many B vitamins and zinc, as well as iron, vitamin A and vitamin C.*

 2 lb (1 kg) chicken pieces, skin and fat removed
 1 recipe *lecsó* (recipe on page 132)
 1 cup (8 fl oz/250 ml) chicken stock (see glossary)
 ½ teaspoon dried marjoram
 12 oz (375 g) egg noodles
 ½ cup (4 fl oz/125 ml) plain low-fat yogurt
 1 tablespoon flour mixed with 1 tablespoon water
 paprika to taste

1. Heat the chicken pieces, *lecsó*, chicken stock and marjoram in a large stockpot. Cover, and simmer for 30–35 minutes, or until the chicken is tender.

2. Ten minutes before the chicken is done, cook the noodles. Drain them, and place on a platter. Remove the chicken and vegetables with a slotted spoon, arrange them over the noodles and keep warm.

3. Add the yogurt to the chicken cooking liquid, and heat through. Whisk in the flour, and simmer to thicken slightly, about 3 minutes. Adjust the seasoning, adding paprika, if desired. Pour the sauce over the chicken, and serve immediately.
 Serves 6

---

1 serving: Calories 465, Protein 34 g, Carbohydrates 58 g, Fiber 5 g, Total fat 11 g (Saturated 2.5 g, Monounsaturated 5 g, Polyunsaturated 2.5 g), Cholesterol 130 mg, Sodium 310 mg, Iron 35%, Vitamin A 55%, Vitamin C 340%.
▲ *2 Bread, 1 Vegetable, 1 Meat*

Top to bottom: Chicken Paprikás; Turkey with Chili Sauce, served with rice

Top to bottom: Cream of Carrot and Leek Soup, Graham Rusks,
Terra Cotta Chicken Breasts with Confetti

Graham Rusks

*Rusks, twice-baked crispy little breads, are great for picnics or midday
snacks. They keep well in an airtight container for a week or more.*

1 package (¼ oz/7 g) active dry yeast
1½ teaspoons sugar
4 tablespoons (2 fl oz/60 ml) safflower oil

¾ cup (6 fl oz/180 ml) warm low-fat (1-percent) milk
½ teaspoon salt
1½ cups (7½ oz/235 g) graham (whole-wheat/
   wholemeal) flour
1 tablespoon caraway seeds
1¾ cups (9 oz/280 g) all-purpose (plain) flour

1. Line a baking sheet with parchment.
2. In a large mixing bowl, dissolve the yeast and sugar in ¼ cup
   (2 fl oz/60 ml) of warm water (105°–115°F/41°–46°C).

3. Add the oil, milk, salt, graham flour and caraway seeds. Stir until the dough is not lumpy. Add the all-purpose flour, ½ cup (2½ oz/75 g) at a time.

4. Turn onto a lightly floured work surface, and knead until the dough is smooth and not sticky. Divide into 16 equal pieces, and form into balls. Roll between your palms to elongate slightly. Place the rolls on the baking sheet, and let rise, covered with plastic wrap, until doubled, about 45 minutes.

5. While the rolls are rising, preheat an oven to 450°F (230°C). Bake the rolls for 10 minutes, until golden brown. Remove from the oven, and cool on a rack. Reduce the oven temperature to 400°F (200°C).

6. Split each roll in half lengthwise across the middle of the height, and return the halves to the baking sheet, cut sides down. Continue to bake for 10 minutes.

7. Allow to cool, and air dry overnight.
   Makes 32 rusks

---

2 rusks per serving: Calories 130, Protein 4 g, Carbohydrates 20 g, Fiber 2 g, Total fat 4 g (Saturated .5 g, Monounsaturated .5 g, Polyunsaturated 3 g), Cholesterol 0 mg, Sodium 80 mg.
▲ *1 Bread*

POULTRY / MEXICO

Terra Cotta Chicken Breasts with Confetti

This rustic-looking chicken with a chili-orange glaze is quite simple to prepare. Serve it with tortillas and ice-cold cervezas (beers).

    2 whole chicken breasts, skinned, boned and cut in half
    2 cups (16 fl oz/500 ml) chicken stock (see glossary)
    3 tablespoons white wine
    2 dried mild red chilies, seeded
    2 shallots (white onions), minced
    3 cloves garlic, minced
    2 tablespoons vegetable oil
    ½ cup (4 fl oz/125 ml) dry white wine
    3 cups (24 fl oz/750 ml) freshly squeezed orange juice, reduced to 1 cup (8 fl oz/250 ml)
    2 tablespoons minced fresh cilantro (fresh coriander)
    salt and freshly ground pepper to taste
    1 zucchini (courgette), green part only, cut into tiny dice
    ½ cup (3 oz/90 g) sweet corn kernels
    1 red bell pepper (capsicum), seeded and cut into tiny dice

1. Preheat an oven to 350°F (180°C).

2. In a skillet, poach the chicken breasts in the chicken stock for 6–7 minutes. Remove the chicken to a baking dish, reserving the stock, and sprinkle the breasts with the 3 tablespoons of white wine. Cover and bake for 10–15 minutes as you prepare the glaze.

3. Soak the dried chilies in the reserved chicken stock for 20 minutes. Purée the chilies and stock in a blender until smooth. Set aside.

4. Sauté the shallots and garlic in the oil until soft but not browned. Add the ½ cup (4 fl oz/125 ml) dry wine, and cook, reducing to a

glaze. Add the reduced orange juice and the chili purée. Reduce again to thicken slightly. Remove from the heat. Add the cilantro, salt and pepper.

5. Coat the chicken breasts with the glaze, and sprinkle them with the zucchini, corn and red pepper, like confetti, to garnish.
   Serves 4

---

1 serving: Calories 360, Protein 30 g, Carbohydrates 30 g, Fiber 2 g, Total fat 11 g (Saturated 2 g, Monounsaturated 3 g, Polyunsaturated 5 g), Cholesterol 75 mg, Sodium 80 mg, Vitamin A 35%, Vitamin C 100%.
▲ *1 Vegetable, 1 Meat*

SOUPS / UNITED STATES

Cream of Carrot and Leek Soup

A "creamy" soup can be achieved by puréeing cooked vegetables instead of adding heavy (double) cream. The carrots make this soup very nutrient-rich, providing many times the day's requirement of vitamin A, as well as lots of fiber and B vitamins. This versatile recipe is delicious in autumn as well, made with cauliflower or butternut squash instead of carrots. Other edible flowers include specially grown, pesticide-free pansies, Johnny-jump-ups and calendulas. If you have asthma, hay fever or allergies, avoid edible flowers.

    1 tablespoon cumin seeds
    2 tablespoons safflower oil
    3 leeks, white part cut into ¼-in (6-mm) slices
    3 lb (1.5 kg) large carrots, peeled and sliced
    4 cups (32 fl oz/1 l) chicken stock (see glossary)
    ½ cup (4 fl oz/125 ml) low-fat (1-percent) milk
    ¼ teaspoon salt
    freshly ground white pepper to taste
    6 fresh nasturtium flowers

1. Toast the cumin in a hot, dry skillet, shaking constantly over medium heat for 2 minutes. Grind the seeds into a coarse powder in a spice grinder, or crush them with a rolling pin. Set aside.

2. In a medium stockpot or Dutch oven, heat the oil. Add the leeks, and cook over medium heat until soft, about 5 minutes. Add the cumin, reserving ½ teaspoon for garnish, and cook an additional 2 minutes, stirring occasionally. Add the carrots and stock. Bring to a boil, reduce to a simmer and cook, covered, until the carrots are tender, about 25 minutes.

3. Purée in a blender or food processor until smooth. Return the mixture to the pot, pour in the milk and warm over medium-low heat for about 5 minutes. Season with the salt and pepper, and pour into warm bowls. Garnish each with a sprinkle of the reserved cumin and a nasturtium flower. Serve immediately.
   Serves 8

---

1 cup per serving: Calories 150, Protein 3 g, Carbohydrates 26 g, Fiber 6 g, Total fat 5 g (Saturated 1 g, Monounsaturated 1 g, Polyunsaturated 3 g), Cholesterol 0 mg, Sodium 150 mg, Vitamin A 960%, Vitamin C 40%.
▲ *2 Vegetable*

Braid of Salmon and Sea Bass with Red Pepper and Sorrel Sauces

This simple, yet elegant, presentation of two seafood favorites uses sauces that take off from the traditional beurre blanc *(white butter sauce) often served with seafood. The butter has been cut drastically, yet the flavor is sustained by the addition of sweet pepper and tart sorrel. You may also try substituting other herbs, such as basil or cilantro, for the sorrel.*

1 lb (500 g) salmon fillet, cut lengthwise into eight ½-in-by-5-in (12-mm-by-13-cm) strips

½ lb (250 g) sea bass fillet, cut lengthwise into four ½-in-by-5-in (12-mm-by-13-cm) strips

¾ cup (6 fl oz/180 ml) dry white wine

pinch of salt

freshly ground white pepper to taste

1 shallot (white onion), minced

2 cups (16 fl oz/500 ml) vegetable stock (see glossary)

1 tablespoon fresh lemon juice

2 tablespoons unsalted butter

1 large red bell pepper (capsicum), roasted, peeled and puréed (see glossary)

1 cup (1 oz/30 g) fresh sorrel leaves

¼ teaspoon salt

1. Preheat an oven to 400°F (200°C). Lightly oil a baking sheet.
2. Make a braid with 2 strips of salmon and 1 strip of sea bass. Trim the ends evenly. Repeat to make a total of 4 braids. Place the braids on the baking sheet, and sprinkle with the wine, pinch of salt, and pepper.
3. Bake for 10 minutes, or until firm and opaque.
4. While the fish is baking, place the shallot and wine in a saucepan over medium heat, and reduce to a bubbly glaze. Add the vegetable stock, and reduce to half the volume. Whisk in the lemon juice and butter, 1 tablespoon at a time. Heat through.
5. Divide the sauce in half. Whisk the red pepper into one half of the sauce, and purée the sorrel with the other half in a blender. Season with the ¼ teaspoon salt and white pepper.
6. Nap each plate with the 2 sauces, and place a cooked braid on top.
Serves 4

1 braid with sauces per serving: Calories 300, Protein 35 g, Carbohydrates 5 g, Fiber 1 g, Total fat 14 g (Saturated 5 g, Monounsaturated 4.5 g, Polyunsaturated 3.5 g), Cholesterol 100 mg, Sodium 350 mg, Vitamin A 70%, Vitamin C 120%.
▲ *1 Meat*

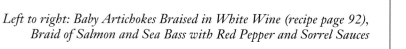

Left to right: Baby Artichokes Braised in White Wine (recipe page 92), Braid of Salmon and Sea Bass with Red Pepper and Sorrel Sauces

Top to bottom: Chicken Avgolemono, Hot and Sour Soup

Baby Artichokes Braised in White Wine

Small Mediterranean purple artichokes are beautiful for this dish, but even full-size artichokes will braise nicely if you trim and quarter them lengthwise, remove the choke and allow 20–30 minutes longer for cooking. Serve braised artichokes as a side dish or a simple first course.

8 baby artichokes
1 lemon, cut in half
3 tablespoons olive oil

1 cup (5 oz/155 g) finely chopped onion
3 cloves garlic, minced
2 carrots, peeled and diced
¾ cup (6 fl oz/180 ml) dry white wine
½ cup (4 fl oz/125 ml) vegetable stock (see glossary)
bouquet garni: 1 sprig parsley, 1 sprig thyme, 1 bay leaf
¼ teaspoon salt
freshly ground pepper to taste

1. Trim the tops of the artichokes, and remove the coarse outer leaves. Cut the bases of 4 artichokes flat so they will stand upright. Cut the remaining artichokes in half lengthwise, and remove the fine center leaves. Cut in half lengthwise again, to create quarters. Rub all the cut surfaces with the lemon.

2. In a large skillet or Dutch oven, heat the olive oil. Add the onion, garlic and carrots, and cook over medium heat until the onion is soft but not browned, about 3 minutes. Add the wine to deglaze the pan, and reduce the liquid by one-third over high heat.

3. Add the vegetable stock, and return to a boil. Reduce to a simmer; add the bouquet garni, salt, pepper and whole artichokes, standing up. Simmer, covered, for 20 minutes. Add the cut artichokes, and continue to simmer, stirring occasionally, until they are tender, 25–30 minutes more. Serve immediately, or cool to room temperature and serve, with braising liquid.

Serves 4   *Photograph pages 90–91*

---

1 serving: Calories 220, Protein 5 g, Carbohydrates 28 g, Fiber 4 g, Total fat 11 g (Saturated 1.5 g, Monounsaturated 8 g, Polyunsaturated 1 g), Cholesterol 0 mg, Sodium 280 mg, Vitamin A 210%, Vitamin C 45%.
▲ *2 Vegetable*

SOUPS / VIETNAM

Hot and Sour Soup

Pepper is the "hot" and lime is the "sour" in this soup. Increase or decrease these ingredients to get the balance to your taste.

6 medium Chinese dried shiitake mushrooms, soaked in hot water for 20 minutes
5 cups (40 fl oz/1.25 l) chicken stock (see glossary)
½ lb (250 g) shrimp (prawns), shelled and deveined (reserve shells)
2 stalks lemongrass, white bulb cut into ½-in (12-mm) lengths
1 carrot, finely julienned
4 green (spring) onions, thinly sliced
½ teaspoon grated lime zest
1 cup (3 oz/90 g) straw mushrooms, or an equal amount canned
3 tablespoons cornstarch (cornflour) dissolved in ¼ cup (2 fl oz/60 ml) cold chicken stock (see glossary)
2 tablespoons soy sauce
1 tomato, peeled, seeded and diced
1 cup (4 oz/125 g) mung bean sprouts
¼ cup (2 fl oz/60 ml) freshly squeezed lime juice
1 teaspoon freshly ground pepper
½ teaspoon sesame oil

1. Drain the shiitake mushrooms and rinse them in clear water once or twice. Remove and discard the stems. Cut the mushrooms into thin slivers, and set aside.

2. Heat the chicken stock with the reserved shrimp shells. Bring to a boil. Reduce the heat, and simmer for 10 minutes; with a slotted spoon, remove and discard the shrimp shells. Add the lemongrass, shiitake mushrooms, carrot and green onions. Simmer, covered, for 5 minutes, until the carrot is tender.

3. Add the shrimp, lime zest and straw mushrooms, and simmer 2–3 minutes, until the shrimp are pink and firm.

4. Combine the cornstarch mixture with the soy sauce, and add in a steady stream to the soup, stirring gently as it thickens slightly.

Add the tomato, mung bean sprouts, lime juice and pepper, adjusting to taste, and remove from the heat.

5. Add the sesame oil, and serve immediately.

Serves 6

---

1 cup per serving: Calories 130, Protein 11 g, Carbohydrates 17 g, Fiber 2 g, Total fat 3 g (Saturated .5 g, Monounsaturated 1 g, Polyunsaturated 1 g), Cholesterol 55 mg, Sodium 350 mg, Vitamin A. 70%, Vitamin C 20%.
▲ *1 Vegetable, ½ Meat*

POULTRY / GREECE

Chicken Avgolemono

This egg-and-lemon sauce is similar to the traditional avgolemono *soup. It is wonderful with seafood as well. Serve this dish over orzo or rice.*

3 cups (24 fl oz/750 ml) chicken stock (see glossary)
1 cup (4 oz/125 g) chopped onion
1 carrot, peeled and cut into ½-in (12-mm) pieces
1 rib celery, cut into ½-in (12-mm) pieces
4 cloves garlic, smashed
1 bay leaf
1 sprig thyme
2 lb (1 kg) chicken pieces, skin and fat removed
3 lemons
2 eggs, separated
¼ cup (½ oz/15 g) minced fresh dill
pinch of salt
freshly ground pepper to taste
1 tablespoon cornstarch, dissolved in 2 tablespoons chicken stock (optional)

1. In a large stockpot, bring the chicken stock to a boil. Add the onion, carrot, celery, garlic, bay leaf and thyme. Reduce to a simmer, and add the chicken and the juice of 1 lemon. Simmer until the chicken is tender, about 30 minutes. Remove the chicken; drain and set aside the vegetables, reserving the stock in the stockpot. Discard the bay leaf and thyme.

2. In a mixing bowl, beat the egg whites until frothy. Add the yolks and then the juice of the 2 remaining lemons, whisking constantly. Slowly add 2 cups (16 fl oz/500 ml) of the reserved stock, whisking constantly. Return the egg mixture to the stockpot, and cook until slightly thickened, stirring constantly. Do not boil. Add the dill, and season with the salt and pepper. The sauce will be thin; if a thicker sauce is desired, add the cornstarch, and cook until thickened.

3. Return the chicken and vegetables to the sauce, and warm them through. Transfer to a serving dish, and serve immediately.

Serves 4

---

1 serving: Calories 280, Protein 38 g, Carbohydrates 13 g, Fiber 2 g, Total fat 9 g (Saturated 3 g, Monounsaturated 3 g, Polyunsaturated 2 g), Cholesterol 220 mg, Sodium 250 mg, Vitamin A 110%, Vitamin C 50%.
▲ *1 Vegetable, 1 Meat*

APPETIZERS / FRANCE

Seafood Terrine with Asparagus Sauce

This elegant starter also makes a lovely light lunch, served on a bed of blanched green beans or fresh greens.

¾ lb (375 g) scallops
¾ lb (375 g) salmon fillet
¼ lb (125 g) shrimp (prawns), shelled and deveined
juice of ½ lemon
¼ cup (2 fl oz/60 ml) dry white wine
¼ cup (2 fl oz/60 ml) half-and-half (half milk and half cream)
2 eggs
¼ teaspoon cayenne pepper
½ cup (2½ oz/75 g) pimiento (canned sweet pepper), diced
3 tablespoons minced fresh tarragon
1 tablespoon minced fresh chervil
sprigs of chervil for garnish
3 cups (24 fl oz/750 ml) asparagus sauce (recipe follows)

1. Preheat an oven to 350°F (180°C). Lightly oil an 8-cup (64-fl oz/2-l) pâté or soufflé dish.
2. In a food processor, purée the scallops, salmon, shrimp, lemon juice, wine, half-and-half, eggs and cayenne until smooth, pulsing so as not to heat the mixture too much. Add the pimiento, tarragon and minced chervil, and mix well.
3. Transfer the mixture to the oiled dish. Cover the purée with a layer of lightly oiled parchment paper to keep it from drying out. Place the dish in a bain-marie, and bake for 1 hour.
4. Serve warm or cold, garnished with the chervil sprigs, and pass a bowl of asparagus sauce.

Serves 12

One 2-oz slice with ¼ cup sauce per serving: Calories 120, Protein 15 g, Carbohydrates 4 g, Fiber 0 g, Total fat 5 g (Saturated 2 g, Monounsaturated 1.5 g, Polyunsaturated 1 g), Cholesterol 85 mg, Sodium 90 mg, Vitamin C 20%.
▲ *1 Meat*

ASPARAGUS SAUCE

1 tablespoon unsalted butter
1 tablespoon flour
2 cups (16 fl oz/500 ml) chicken stock (see glossary)
1 cup (8 oz/250 g) chopped asparagus, blanched (see glossary)
2 tablespoons half-and-half (half milk and half cream)

1. Melt the butter in a saucepan. Add the flour, and cook for 2–3 minutes. Do not brown. Add the chicken stock, and cook over medium heat, whisking constantly, until thickened. Cool. Purée until smooth in a blender with the asparagus and half-and-half. Strain and serve.

Makes 3 cups (24 fl oz/750 ml)

¼ cup sauce per serving: Calories 20, Protein 1 g, Carbohydrates 2 g, Fiber 0 g, Total fat 2 g (Saturated 1 g, Monounsaturated .5 g, Polyunsaturated 0 g), Cholesterol 5 mg, Sodium 90 mg.
▲ *1 Meat*

Individual Angel Food Cakes

The ultimate no-fat, no-dietary-cholesterol dessert, individual angel food cakes are great substitutes for shortcake all year-round. Serve with rhubarb-orange compote (recipe follows) or other fruit in season.

½ cup (2 oz/60 g) cake (soft-wheat) flour
¾ cup (6 oz/185 g) superfine (castor) sugar
1 tablespoon finely grated orange zest
6 large egg whites
½ teaspoon lemon juice
½ teaspoon cream of tartar
1 teaspoon vanilla extract (essence)
1 tablespoon confectioners' (icing) sugar

1. Preheat an oven to 350°F (180°C). Set six 1-cup (8-fl oz/250-ml) ramekins on a baking sheet.

2. On a piece of parchment or waxed paper, sift together the cake flour and ¼ cup (2 oz/60 g) of the superfine sugar; sift again to aerate. Add the orange zest. Set aside.

3. Place the egg whites in a nonreactive bowl, and beat until foamy, using an electric mixer. Add the lemon juice, and sprinkle the cream of tartar over the top. Beat the eggs just to soft peaks. Add the remaining superfine sugar 2 tablespoons at a time, beating constantly, until the eggs have more than doubled in volume. Beat in the vanilla.

4. With a balloon whisk, fold the flour mixture, 2 tablespoons at a time, into the egg mixture. Do not overmix.

5. Scoop the batter into the ramekins, filling them two-thirds full. Bake 35–40 minutes, until the cakes are golden and their tops spring back when lightly touched.

6. Remove from the oven, invert on a rack and let rest for 10 minutes. Loosen the sides with a sharp knife, and remove the cakes from the ramekins to finish cooling on the rack. When they are cool, dust them with the confectioners' sugar, and serve.

Serves 6

1 cake per serving: Calories 150, Protein 4 g, Carbohydrates 34 g, Fiber 0 g, Total fat 0 g (Saturated 0 g, Monounsaturated 0 g, Polyunsaturated 0 g), Cholesterol 0 mg, Sodium 55 mg.
▲ *1 Bread*

RHUBARB-ORANGE COMPOTE

1 lb (500 g) fresh rhubarb stalks, cut into 2-in (5-cm) lengths
½ cup (4 oz/125 g) sugar
½ cup (4 fl oz/125 ml) freshly squeezed orange juice
1 teaspoon grated orange zest
2 oranges, peeled, seeded and sliced crosswise

1. Combine the rhubarb, sugar, orange juice and orange zest in a medium saucepan. Simmer for 30 minutes, until the rhubarb is tender.

2. Remove from the heat, and add the orange slices. Chill until ready to serve.

Makes about 3¼ cups (26 fl oz/810 ml)   *Photograph page 97*

½ cup per serving: Calories 110, Protein 1 g, Carbohydrates 27 g, Fiber 3 g, Total fat 0 g (Saturated 0 g, Monounsaturated 0 g, Polyunsaturated 0 g), Cholesterol 0 mg, Sodium 3 mg, Vitamin C 70%.
▲ *1 Fruit*

Les Fleurs Farcies

STUFFED ZUCCHINI FLOWERS

Squash blossoms are spring's reminder of the summer's bounty of zucchini to come. This recipe uses the outer skin of zucchini (courgettes) and Japanese eggplant (aubergine). You can freeze the centers for use later in soups or stocks.

24 baby zucchini (courgettes) with flowers attached
¼ cup (2 fl oz/60 ml) olive oil
3 shallots (white onions), finely minced
2 cloves garlic, finely minced
2 zucchini (courgettes), outer skin (⅛ in/3 mm deep) removed and skin cut into tiny dice (reserve centers for another use)
1 Japanese eggplant (aubergine), outer skin (⅛ in/3 mm deep) removed and skin cut into tiny dice (reserve center for another use)
1 red bell pepper (capsicum), cut into tiny dice
5 large leaves fresh basil, cut into very fine chiffonade
1 teaspoon fresh parsley, finely minced
salt and freshly ground pepper to taste

1. Preheat an oven to 350°F (180° C). Lightly oil a baking sheet.

2. Rinse the insides of the zucchini flowers. Trim the stem ends, and blanch the zucchini for 10 seconds in boiling salted water. Immerse them immediately in ice water to stop cooking. Drain on paper towels.

3. To prepare the ratatouille, heat the olive oil, and sauté the shallots and garlic until soft but not browned. Add the zucchini skins, eggplant skin and red pepper, and sauté lightly, about 2 minutes. Add the basil, parsley, salt and pepper.

4. Fill each flower with a spoonful of the ratatouille. Twist the flower ends slightly, and place the zucchini on the baking sheet. Season with salt and pepper.

5. Cover tightly with foil, and bake for 10 minutes, just until tender. Do not overcook.

Serves 8

3 zucchini per serving: Calories 80, Protein 1 g, Carbohydrates 3 g, Fiber 1 g, Total fat 7 g (Saturated 1 g, Monounsaturated 5 g, Polyunsaturated .5 g), Cholesterol 0 mg, Sodium 0 mg, Vitamin C 50%.
▲ *1 Vegetable*

Kasekuchen von Schwedt

CHEESECAKE WITH BRANDIED CHERRIES

Quark is a fresh cheese made in Germany and first tasted by this author in a little town called Schwedt an der Oder, in eastern Germany near the border of Poland. A combination of cottage cheese and ricotta cheese makes a reasonable substitute. This cake is a pleasure at cherry blossom time. The muesli *crust is a nice low-fat innovation.*

> 1¼ cups (7½ oz/225 g) *muesli* (recipe on page 177), finely ground in a food processor
> ½ cup (2 oz/60 g) finely grated apple
> 2 tablespoons unsalted butter or margarine, melted
> 2 cups (16 oz/500 g) *quark*, or 1 cup (8 oz/250 g) low-fat cottage cheese and 1 cup (8 oz/250 g) low-fat ricotta
> 1 cup (8 fl oz/250 ml) low-fat (1-percent) milk
> ½ cup (4 oz/125 g) sugar
> 2 eggs
> 1 teaspoon vanilla extract (essence)
> 1 tablespoon grated lemon zest
> ½ cup (2 oz/60 g) dried cherries, snipped in half

1. Preheat an oven to 350°F (180°C). Lightly oil the bottom and sides of a 9-in (23-cm) springform pan (cake tin).
2. In a medium bowl, mix together the *muesli*, apple and butter. Press into the bottom of the springform pan. Bake 13–15 minutes, until golden brown. Cool on a rack.
3. In a blender, combine the *quark*, milk, sugar, eggs and vanilla. Blend well. Stir in the lemon zest and dried cherries. Pour into the springform pan, and bake 1¼ hours, until the filling is set. Cool on a rack.
Serves 8

1 serving: Calories 240, Protein 12 g, Carbohydrates 32 g, Fiber 2 g, Total fat 8 g (Saturated 4.5 g, Monounsaturated 2.5 g, Polyunsaturated .5 g), Cholesterol 75 mg, Sodium 190 mg.
▲ *½ Bread, ½ Milk*

BRANDIED CHERRIES

These cherries can be stored in the refrigerator for a month, or you may can them for longer storage. They are delicious alone or served with kasekuchen von Schwedt *(recipe above).*

> 1 lb (500 g) fresh cherries
> 1 cup (8 oz/250 g) sugar
> ¼ cup (2 fl oz/60 ml) white wine vinegar
> 3 whole cloves
> 1 cinnamon stick
> ½ cup (4 fl oz/125 ml) brandy

1. Remove the pits and stems from the cherries. Set the fruit in a medium bowl.
2. In a medium saucepan, combine the sugar, vinegar and ¼ cup (2 fl oz/60 ml) of water; bring to a boil, stirring until the sugar

is dissolved. Add the cloves and cinnamon stick, and simmer for 5 minutes.
3. Remove from the heat, add the brandy and pour over the cherries. Cool and then refrigerate them overnight before serving.
Makes about 4 cups (32 fl oz/1 l)

½ cup per serving: Calories 170, Protein 1 g, Carbohydrates 35 g, Fiber 1 g, Total fat 0 g (Saturated 0 g, Monounsaturated 0 g, Polyunsaturated 0 g), Cholesterol 0 mg, Sodium 0 mg.
▲ *1 Fruit, 1 Fat/Sugar*

Ginger Roulade with Fresh Strawberry Sauce

This low-fat cake is filled with spring's finest. Not only are strawberries a beacon of the summer fruit to come, but they are also good for you, providing almost all of the day's requirement of vitamin C in a ⅔-cup (2¾-oz/85-g) serving.

> 6 cups (1½ lb/750 g) strawberries, thinly sliced
> 1½ cups (12 oz/375 g) sugar
> 2 teaspoons cornstarch (cornflour) dissolved in 1 tablespoon water
> 5 large eggs, separated
> ¼ teaspoon cream of tartar
> ¾ cup (2½ oz/75 g) sifted cake flour
> 2 teaspoons cinnamon
> 1 teaspoon ground ginger
> 2 tablespoons confectioners' (icing) sugar
> fresh strawberry sauce (recipe follows)
> 12 strawberries, left whole for garnish

1. Preheat an oven to 350°F (180°C). Line a 10-by-15-in (25-by-38-cm) jelly roll (Swiss roll) pan with parchment paper, leaving excess paper overlapping one edge. Lightly oil the parchment paper.
2. To make the filling, combine half of the sliced strawberries with ½ cup (4 oz/125 g) of the sugar in a medium saucepan. Cook over medium heat for 10 minutes, stirring constantly. Add the cornstarch mixture, and simmer for 5 minutes, continuing to stir, until slightly thickened. Remove to cool.
3. To make the cake, in a medium nonreactive bowl, whisk the egg whites until frothy. Add the cream of tartar, and whisk to soft peaks. Add ½ cup (4 oz/125 g) of the remaining sugar, 2 tablespoons at a time, whisking constantly, until the whites form stiff but not dry peaks.
4. In a large bowl, beat the egg yolks with the remaining ½ cup (4 oz/125 g) of sugar until light.
5. In a small bowl, sift together the flour, cinnamon and ginger.
6. Fold the flour mixture into the egg yolk mixture, taking care not to overwork the batter. Gently fold in the egg whites, and spread

Clockwise from top: Individual Angel Food Cakes with Rhubarb-Orange Compote (recipe page 95); Cheesecake with Brandied Cherries; Ginger Roulade with Fresh Strawberry Sauce

the batter evenly on the pan. Tap the pan on a counter to release air bubbles. Bake for 12 minutes, until the cake is lightly colored and firm to the touch.

7. Place a piece of parchment on a work surface, and sprinkle it with a little of the confectioners' sugar. Invert the cake straight from the oven onto this parchment. Peel off the baking parchment.

8. Spread the strawberry filling mixture to within 1 in (2.5 cm) of the edges of the cake. Top with the remaining sliced strawberries, evenly distributed. Roll the cake from the long side, as tightly as possible without cracking it. Trim the ends with a serrated knife. Place it seam side down on a serving platter, and dust with the remaining confectioners' sugar. Let it stand 1 hour before serving.

9. To serve, slice the roll crosswise, 1 in (2.5 cm) thick. Nap each plate with 2 tablespoons of strawberry sauce, place a slice of cake on the sauce and top with a fresh strawberry.

Serves 12

1 slice with 2 tablespoons strawberry sauce per serving: Calories 210, Protein 4 g, Carbohydrates 43 g, Fiber 3 g, Total fat 3 g (Saturated .5 g, Monounsaturated 1 g, Polyunsaturated .5 g), Cholesterol 90 mg, Sodium 30 mg, Vitamin C 120%.
▲ *1 Bread, 1 Fruit*

FRESH STRAWBERRY SAUCE

2 cups (8 oz/250 g) strawberries, tops removed
2 tablespoons confectioners' (icing) sugar
juice of 2 oranges

1. Place the strawberries in a blender with the confectioners' sugar and orange juice. Purée, and pass through a strainer to remove the seeds. Chill until ready to use.

Yield 2 cups (16 fl oz/500 ml)

⅓ cup per serving: Calories 20, Protein 0 g, Carbohydrates 4 g, Fiber 1 g, Total fat 0 g (Saturated 0 g, Monounsaturated 0 g, Polyunsaturated 0 g), Cholesterol 0 mg, Sodium 0 mg, Vitamin C 35%.

Summer

Fruits and vegetables abound in this, the season of salads. Dress fresh greens from the garden with a vinaigrette made with tomatoes right off the vine. Try a lemon vinaigrette with a platter of crudités, a colorful collection of raw and blanched bite-sized vegetables.

Hot soups are fine for the winter months, but summer calls for cool varieties. From Denmark comes *yoghurtsuppe*—low-fat yogurt blended with cucumber, radishes and green (spring) onions and seasoned with fresh dill, tarragon and mint. Or try cold pineapple soup, an explosion of tropical tastes and colors, including ruby red pomegranate seeds.

As the days get longer, fire up the grill to cook spicy chicken, skewered seafood and all manner of vegetables—especially sweet corn in the husk. Complement the meal with a fresh fruit sangria or a spicy fruit salsa. For breakfasts and desserts, go for the berries: cobblers, crumb cakes, crêpes and sauces.

Yoghurtsuppe

A morning walk in the garden will yield a refreshing chilled soup for lunch on a hot summer day. If you are substituting dried herbs for the fresh, use one-third the amount. Low-fat yogurt is even higher than milk in calcium, a nutrient needed by adults as well as children.

1 cucumber, seeded and cubed

10 radishes, thinly sliced

2 cups (16 fl oz/500 ml) plain low-fat yogurt

1 cup (8 fl oz/250 ml) chicken stock (see glossary)

1 green (spring) onion, minced

1 tablespoon minced fresh dill

1½ teaspoons minced fresh tarragon

½ teaspoon minced fresh mint

salt and freshly ground white pepper to taste

4 sprigs fresh dill for garnish

1. Combine all but the last ingredient. Chill well before serving. Garnish each bowl with a sprig of dill.

    Serves 4

---

1 cup per serving: Calories 90, Protein 7 g, Carbohydrates 11 g, Fiber 1 g, Total fat 2 g (Saturated 1.5 g, Monounsaturated .5 g, Polyunsaturated 0 g), Cholesterol 5 mg, Sodium 90 mg, Calcium 20%.
▲ *1 Milk*

Persian-Style Basmati Rice

Basmati rice is probably the most familiar of the aromatic long-grain rices. With origins in India, it has found its way to most parts of the world. It is quite low in the starches that make rice sticky, which is why it is often used for pilaf. It has a nutty flavor and a wonderful aroma as it cooks.

2 cups (14 oz/440 g) *basmati* rice, rinsed well and
    soaked overnight

1 cinnamon stick

3 whole cloves

2 tablespoons safflower oil

½ cup (2 oz/60 g) chopped onion

¼ cup (1 oz/30 g) pistachios, shelled and coarsely chopped

zest of 1 orange

½ cup (3 oz/90 g) dried currants or golden raisins

1 tablespoon unsalted butter, melted

1 potato, peeled and sliced lengthwise ⅛ in (3 mm) thick

1. Preheat an oven to 350°F (180°C).

2. In a medium saucepan, bring 3 cups (24 fl oz/750 ml) of water to a boil. Add the rice, cinnamon and cloves, and reduce to a simmer. Cook for 10 minutes, stirring occasionally. Drain any excess water, and set the rice aside.

3. Heat the oil in a large, heavy, ovenproof casserole or Dutch oven with a cover. Sauté the onions, pistachios and orange zest until the onions are golden brown, about 5 minutes. Remove with a slotted spoon, and stir into the rice. Add the currants to the rice, and mix.

4. Brush the sides and bottom of the casserole with the melted butter. Arrange the potato slices in the bottom, fitting tightly. Spoon in the rice, packing it tightly in the bottom and pressing it down. Using the handle of a wooden spoon, make 3 deep holes through the rice to allow steam to escape. Cover the rice with a damp, clean towel to absorb the steam, and cover the casserole tightly.

5. Bake for 50 minutes. Remove from the oven, and let the casserole stand for 10 minutes.

6. Uncover, and remove the towel. Place a large serving platter on top, and invert the casserole to serve.

    Serves 6

---

1 cup per serving: Calories 380, Protein 7 g, Carbohydrates 67 g, Fiber 2 g, Total fat 9 g (Saturated 1.5 g, Monounsaturated 2.5 g, Polyunsaturated 4 g), Cholesterol 5 mg, Sodium 5 mg, Iron 20%.
▲ *2 Bread*

Hummus

Tahini is essentially a sesame seed butter, rich in protein and calcium, but also very high in fat. In this version of hummus we use mostly chick-peas, to keep the fat content low. To reduce it even further, you can serve the hummus combined with an equal amount of plain nonfat yogurt. It's delicious as a sandwich spread, vegetable dip or, most familiarly, with falafel (recipe on page 78).

¼ lb (125 g) dried chick-peas (garbanzo beans),
    soaked overnight

2 cups (16 fl oz/500 ml) chicken stock (see glossary)

2 cloves garlic

juice of 1 lemon

1 tablespoon tahini (sesame seed paste)

⅛ teaspoon salt

2 teaspoons olive oil

½ teaspoon paprika

2 tablespoons minced fresh parsley

1. In a medium saucepan, simmer the chick-peas in the chicken stock for 2 hours, or until very tender. Drain, reserving the chicken stock. Place the chick-peas in a food processor with the garlic, lemon juice, tahini and salt. Purée until smooth. Add the reserved chicken stock, a little at a time, to achieve the consistency desired.

2. Spoon onto 4 serving plates, and make a well in each with the back of a spoon. Place ½ teaspoon of the olive oil in each well. Sprinkle the paprika and parsley on top to garnish.

    Serves 4

½ cup per serving: Calories 160, Protein 7 g, Carbohydrates 21 g, Fiber 2 g, Total fat 7 g (Saturated 1 g, Monounsaturated 3 g, Polyunsaturated 2 g), Cholesterol 0 mg, Sodium 90 mg.
▲ *½ Meat*

Clockwise from top: Persian-Style Basmati Rice, Baba Ghanouj, Hummus, Yoghurtsuppe

VEGETABLES / MIDDLE EAST

Baba Ghanouj

Roasted eggplant makes a wonderful spread for sandwiches or dip for vegetables.

2 large eggplants (aubergines)
juice of 2 lemons
2 tablespoons tahini (sesame seed paste)
2 cloves garlic, finely minced
¼ teaspoon salt
freshly ground white pepper to taste
2 tablespoons finely chopped parsley

1. Preheat an oven to 400°F (200°C). Lightly oil a baking sheet.
2. Cut the eggplants in half, and place them cut side down on the baking sheet. Roast them for 40 minutes, or until soft and shriveled. Remove to cool.
3. Scoop out the pulp, discarding the seeds, and place the pulp in a food processor with the lemon juice, tahini and garlic. Process until smooth. Season with the salt and pepper.
4. Transfer to a serving bowl, and sprinkle with the parsley.
Serves 6

½ cup per serving: Calories 70, Protein 2 g, Carbohydrates 10 g, Fiber 2 g, Total fat 3 g (Saturated .5 g, Monounsaturated 1 g, Polyunsaturated 1 g), Cholesterol 0 mg, Sodium 110 mg.
▲ *1 Vegetable*

Left to right: Coal-Roasted Corn and Grilled Vegetables with Jalapeño Oil, Mustard-and-Onion-Crusted Catfish with Corn Salsa

1 zucchini (courgette), cut into 1-in (2.5-cm) slices
1 fennel bulb, cut into 8 wedges
8 mushrooms, cleaned and stemmed
16 cloves garlic
freshly ground pepper to taste

1. Preheat a grill. Soak the ears of corn for 1 hour in water, leaving the husks on.
2. To make the prickly pear glaze, in a medium saucepan, cook the prickly pears in water until very tender, about 20 minutes. Purée in a blender, and return the purée to the saucepan. Add the sugar, vinegar and minced garlic, and cook until thickened, about 5 minutes. Pour into a serving dish and allow to cool.
3. To make the jalapeño oil, in a small saucepan, heat the olive oil. Add the jalapeño, and cook over low heat for 30 seconds. Remove from the heat to cool; stir in the cumin and cilantro, and set aside.
4. Alternate the bell pepper, onion, eggplant, zucchini, fennel, mushrooms and garlic cloves on 8 skewers. Place the ears of corn on the coals or rack of the grill, and roast them for 10 minutes, turning frequently. Brush the vegetable skewers lightly with jalapeño oil, season them with the ground pepper and grill them with the corn for another 5 minutes, turning them to grill evenly.
5. Husk the corn, cut each ear in half and brush lightly with jalapeño oil. Serve the corn and skewers immediately with the cactus glaze.
Serves 8

1 skewer per serving: Calories 240, Protein 3 g, Carbohydrates 44 g, Fiber 3 g, Total fat 7 g (Saturated 1 g, Monounsaturated 5 g, Polyunsaturated 1 g), Cholesterol 0 mg, Sodium 20 mg, Vitamin C 50%.
▲ *2 Vegetable, 1 Fat/Sugar*

VEGETABLES / UNITED STATES

Coal-Roasted Corn and Grilled Vegetables with Jalapeño Oil

Try the southwestern way with summer vegetables glazed with prickly pear sauce. In the autumn or winter, you can blanch and skewer seasonal vegetables such as brussels sprouts, carrots, potatoes, butternut squash and beets, and broil them for 4–5 minutes, turning from side to side each minute.

4 ears (cobs) of corn, husks intact and silks removed
½ cup (3½ oz/105 g) peeled and coarsely chopped prickly pears
1 cup (8 oz/250 g) sugar
¼ cup (2 fl oz/60 ml) white wine vinegar
3 cloves garlic, minced
¼ cup (2 fl oz/60 ml) olive oil
1 jalapeño chili pepper, finely minced
¼ teaspoon ground cumin
2 tablespoons finely minced fresh cilantro (fresh coriander)
1 red bell pepper (capsicum), cut into 1-in (2.5-cm) pieces
1 red (Spanish) onion, cut into 1-in (2.5-cm) pieces
1 Japanese eggplant (aubergine), cut into 1-in (2.5-cm) slices

SEAFOOD / UNITED STATES

Mustard-and-Onion-Crusted Catfish with Corn Salsa

Halibut or salmon also tastes right at home with this mustard-and-onion coating. The corn salsa can be prepared up to 6 hours ahead and refrigerated. This recipe uses a generous amount of fish. Smaller fillets will yield lower amounts of calories and nutrients.

CORN SALSA
6 ears (cobs) corn
½ cup (1½ oz/45 g) sliced green (spring) onion
1 red bell pepper (capsicum), diced
1 jalapeño chili pepper, minced
juice of 1 lime
¼ teaspoon salt
freshly ground pepper to taste
CRUSTED CATFISH
3 large red (Spanish) onions, julienned
2 tablespoons coarse-grained mustard

2 tablespoons plus 1 teaspoon olive oil
4 catfish fillets, about 6 oz (185 g) each

1. Preheat an oven to 350°F (180°C). Lightly oil a baking sheet.
2. To prepare the corn salsa, remove the corn from the cob; rinse the kernels several times to remove starches, and blanch for 30 seconds. Drain well; mix with the green onion, bell pepper and jalapeño. Add the lime juice, salt and pepper. Set aside in a serving bowl.
3. To prepare the fish, spread the red onions on the baking sheet, and bake until golden brown, about 10 minutes. Remove from the oven to cool.
4. Mix together the mustard and 1 teaspoon of the olive oil, and pat one-half of the mixture onto 1 side of the catfish fillets. Press half of the onions into the mustard coating on the fish.
5. In an ovenproof skillet, heat the 2 tablespoons of olive oil. Place the catfish fillets, coated side down, in the pan; cook over medium heat for 2 minutes. While the fillets are cooking, pat mustard and onions onto their top sides. Carefully turn the fillets, and place the skillet in the oven for 8 minutes, or until the fish are firm and opaque. Serve at once with the corn salsa.
Serves 4

---

1 fillet with ¼ salsa per serving: Calories 470, Protein 37 g, Carbohydrates 45 g, Fiber 8 g, Total fat 17 g (Saturated 3 g, Monounsaturated 9 g, Polyunsaturated 3.5 g), Cholesterol 100 mg, Sodium 380 mg, Vitamin A 25%, Vitamin C 100%.
▲ *1 Vegetable, 2 Meat*

APPETIZERS / UNITED STATES

Crudités with Lemon Vinaigrette

A colorful and seasonal display of vegetables with a tangy dipping sauce.

¼ lb (125 g) broccoli florets
¼ lb (125 g) cauliflower florets
¼ lb (125 g) asparagus, trimmed to 4-in (10-cm) lengths
3 carrots, peeled and cut into narrow 4-in (10-cm) lengths
1 small jícama (yam bean), peeled and cut into narrow 4-in (10-cm) lengths
2 cups (12 oz/375 g) cherry tomatoes
¼ lb (125 g) snow peas (mangetouts)
2 red bell peppers (capsicums), cut into narrow 4-in (10-cm) lengths
6 oz (185 g) *enoki* mushrooms
2 heads Belgian endive (witloof/chicory), leaves separated
¼ cup (2 fl oz/60 ml) fresh lemon vinaigrette dipping sauce (recipe follows)

1. To brighten the color and remove the raw taste, blanch the broccoli, cauliflower, asparagus and carrots by dropping them into boiling water for 30–60 seconds, depending on size. Plunge immediately into ice water to stop cooking. Drain well.

2. Arrange all the vegetables on a platter with a dipping bowl. Pour the dipping sauce into the bowl, and serve.
Serves 8

---

1 serving: Calories 115, Protein 4 g, Carbohydrates 21 g, Fiber 4 g, Total fat 3 g (Saturated 0 g, Monounsaturated .5 g, Polyunsaturated 2 g), Cholesterol 0 mg, Sodium 25 mg, Vitamin A 190%, Vitamin C 170%.
▲ *2 Vegetable*

FRESH LEMON VINAIGRETTE

This sauce can also be used as a salad dressing. Concentrated chicken stock reduces the amount of oil in the vinaigrette.

½ cup (4 fl oz/125 ml) chicken stock (see glossary)
¼ cup (2 fl oz/60 ml) fresh lemon juice
¼ cup (2 fl oz/60 ml) white wine vinegar
½ cup (4 fl oz/125 ml) safflower oil
2 teaspoons finely grated lemon zest
2 teaspoons fresh dill, stems removed
freshly ground white pepper to taste

1. Cook the chicken stock until it is reduced to ¼ cup (2 fl oz/60 ml). Cool.
2. In a medium mixing bowl, combine the stock, lemon juice and vinegar. While whisking, slowly drizzle in the oil. Stir in the lemon zest and dill; season with the pepper.
Makes 1¼ cups (10 fl oz/310 ml)

---

2 tablespoons per serving: Calories 80, Protein 0 g, Carbohydrates 1 g, Fiber 0 g, Total fat 9 g (Saturated 1 g, Monounsaturated 1 g, Polyunsaturated 7 g), Cholesterol 0 mg, Sodium 0 mg.
▲ *1 Fat/Sugar*

Crudités with Lemon Vinaigrette

Provençal Fresh Tomato and Basil Tarts

In Provence this pizzalike tart is likely to be prepared on a puff pastry shell. A yeast pastry crust provides an alternative lower in fat.

yeast pastry crust (recipe follows)
½ cup (4 fl oz/125 ml) fresh tomato purée
1 tablespoon dried basil
2 tablespoons olive oil
2 large fresh tomatoes, sliced ¼ in (6 mm) thick
1 teaspoon minced fresh thyme
1 teaspoon sugar
salt and freshly ground pepper to taste
4 large leaves of basil, cut into chiffonade

1. Preheat an oven to 375°F (190°C).
2. Follow the instructions 1–4 for the yeast pastry crust.
3. Prick the yeast pastry crust dough with a fork. Set aside.
4. Strain and reserve the liquid from the tomato purée. Mix together the strained purée, dried basil and olive oil. Brush the mixture evenly onto the pastry circles, extending to within ½ in (12 mm) of the edge.
5. Arrange the tomato slices on top of the tarts, sprinkle with the thyme, sugar, salt and pepper and bake for 20 minutes, basting once or twice with the reserved tomato purée liquid to prevent the tarts from drying out. The crusts should be lightly browned.
6. Remove from the oven, sprinkle with the fresh basil and serve immediately.
   Serves 8

¼ tart per serving: Calories 410, Protein 10 g, Carbohydrates 65 g, Fiber 3 g, Total fat 12 g (Saturated 2 g, Monounsaturated 4 g, Polyunsaturated 6 g), Cholesterol 30 mg, Sodium 180 mg, Iron 20%, Vitamin C 20%.
▲ 2 Bread, 1 Vegetable

YEAST PASTRY CRUST

1 package (¼ oz/7 g) active dry yeast
¼ cup (2 oz/60 g) sugar
1 cup (8 fl oz/250 ml) lukewarm low-fat (1-percent) milk (approximately 105°F/40°C)
¼ cup (2 fl oz/60 ml) safflower oil
1 egg
4½ cups (1¼ lb/625 g) unbleached all-purpose (plain) flour
½ teaspoon salt

1. In a small bowl, dissolve the yeast and sugar in the milk. Let stand 5 minutes, or until the yeast foams. Stir in the oil and egg, and set aside.
2. In a large mixing bowl, stir together the flour and salt. Add the yeast mixture, mixing to incorporate all of the flour, until the dough is no longer lumpy.
3. Turn the dough onto a lightly floured work surface, and knead until smooth and elastic, about 5 minutes. Return it to a clean, lightly oiled bowl, cover and let rise until doubled in volume, about 1½ hours.
4. Punch the dough down, cut it into 2 equal pieces and form into balls. On a floured work surface, roll each ball into a 9-in (23-cm) circle, ⅛ in (3 mm) thick. Transfer to 2 lightly oiled pie pans, and let rest 10 minutes.
5. Fill and bake according to recipe.
   Makes 2 crusts

⅛ of one crust per serving: Calories 180, Protein 5 g, Carbohydrates 31 g, Fiber 1 g, Total fat 4 g (Saturated .5 g, Monounsaturated .5 g, Polyunsaturated 2.5 g), Cholesterol 15 mg, Sodium 85 mg.
▲ 1 Bread

Jacques Pépin's Leeks with Tomato and Olive Oil

This recipe first appeared in Today's Gourmet *(KQED, Inc., 1991), the companion cookbook to Jacques Pépin's PBS television series of the same name. Fresh leeks are cooked just until tender and served lukewarm or at room temperature with a tangy tomato vinaigrette.*

4 medium-to-large leeks (about 1¼ lb/625 g), trimmed and washed
1 ripe tomato, peeled, seeded and cut into ¼-in (6-mm) pieces
3 tablespoons virgin olive oil
1 tablespoon red wine vinegar
1 tablespoon Dijon-style mustard
1 teaspoon Worcestershire (Maggi) sauce
½ teaspoon salt
¼ teaspoon freshly ground black pepper

1. In a stainless steel saucepan, bring 2 cups (16 fl oz/500 ml) of water to a boil. Add the leeks, bring back to a boil, cover and boil gently 10 minutes, or until tender.
2. Drain the leeks, reserving the stock for soup. When they are cool enough to handle, squeeze them to extract and reserve most of the remaining liquid.
3. Cut the leeks into 2-in (5-cm) pieces, and arrange the pieces in a gratin dish, mixing them to combine the white and green parts.
4. Mix together the tomato, oil, vinegar, mustard, Worcestershire sauce, salt and pepper. Spoon the mixture over the leeks. Serve lukewarm or at room temperature.
   Serves 4

1 serving: Calories 180, Protein 2 g, Carbohydrates 20 g, Fiber 2 g, Total fat 11 g (Saturated 2 g, Monounsaturated 7 g, Polyunsaturated 1 g), Cholesterol 0 mg, Sodium 440 mg, Vitamin C 40%.
▲ 1 Vegetable, 1 Fat/Sugar

Top to Bottom: Provençal Fresh Tomato and Basil Tarts, Jacques Pépin's Leeks with Tomato and Olive Oil

Top to bottom: Andalusian Gazpacho, Grilled Spicy Chicken

Grilled Spicy Chicken

The custom of enjoying tapas, *a spicy assortment of appetizers, has spread beyond the borders of Spain. Many restaurants and bars now serve typical little dishes such as marinated mushrooms, stuffed peppers and squares of thick omelettes, as well as this grilled spicy chicken. The drink of choice is chilled Manzanilla, a light dry sherry from Andalusia.*

    1 whole chicken breast, boned and skinned
    2 tablespoons fresh lime juice
    1 tablespoon olive oil
    1 tablespoon honey
    ½ teaspoon ground coriander
    ½ teaspoon hot paprika
    2 cloves garlic, finely minced
    1 red bell pepper (capsicum), cut into 1-in (2.5-cm) chunks
    1 yellow bell pepper (capsicum), cut into 1-in (2.5-cm) chunks
    ½ lb (250 g) button mushrooms
    16 artichoke hearts, marinated in olive oil
    ¼ teaspoon salt
    freshly ground pepper to taste
    ¼ cup (⅓ oz/10 g) chopped fresh cilantro
       (fresh coriander) (optional)

1. Soak 16 wooden skewers in water for 30 minutes. Cut the chicken breast crosswise into ½-in (12-mm) strips. Set aside.
2. In a shallow dish, combine the lime juice, olive oil, honey, coriander, paprika and garlic.
3. Place the chicken on the skewers, alternating with the red and yellow peppers, mushrooms and artichoke hearts; pour the sauce over the skewers, and marinate in the refrigerator overnight, or at least 1 hour.
4. Season the chicken and vegetables with the salt and pepper. Grill the skewers over medium heat (or broil them in a broiler), turning once and brushing with marinade until the chicken is browned and firm, about 2 minutes on each side.
5. Arrange the skewers on a platter, sprinkle with the cilantro if desired and serve immediately.
Serves 16

1 skewer per serving: Calories 80, Protein 9 g, Carbohydrates 8 g, Fiber 1 g, Total fat 2 g (Saturated .5 g, Monounsaturated .5 g, Polyunsaturated .5 g), Cholesterol 20 mg, Sodium 115 mg, Vitamin C 110%.
   ▲ *1 Vegetable, ½ Meat*

Andalusian Gazpacho

Gazpacho *literally means* soaked bread. *There are many versions of the ingredients for this soup, from grapes and almonds to seafood and meat stocks. Hot or cold, spicy or mild, it is delicious with toasted bread rubbed with cloves of garlic.*

    1 red bell pepper (capsicum), seeded and coarsely chopped
    1 green bell pepper (capsicum), seeded and coarsely chopped
    1 English (hothouse) cucumber, peeled and diced
    1 lb (500 g) tomatoes, peeled and coarsely chopped
    2 slices day-old bread, crust removed, soaked 5 minutes in
       water, then squeezed
    2 cloves garlic
    2 green (spring) onions, sliced
    2 tablespoons olive oil
    1 tablespoon sherry wine vinegar
    1 tablespoon fresh parsley, minced
    ½ teaspoon paprika
    ¼ teaspoon salt

1. Place half of the red pepper, green pepper and cucumber in a blender or food processor, reserving the other half for garnish. Add the remaining ingredients to the blender and process until smooth.
2. Chill at least 2 hours before serving. Ladle into chilled bowls, and garnish each with a spoonful of reserved vegetables.
Serves 6

1 cup per serving: Calories 90, Protein 2 g, Carbohydrates 11 g, Fiber 2 g, Total fat 5 g (Saturated .5 g, Monounsaturated 3.5 g, Polyunsaturated .5 g), Cholesterol 0 mg, Sodium 150 mg, Vitamin A 30%, Vitamin C 100%.
   ▲ *2 Vegetable*

Cold Pineapple Soup

Chilled soups are excellent lunch fare, but this one is especially nice for brunch as well.

    1 large ripe pineapple, peeled, cored and sliced
    1 papaya, peeled and cut into cubes
    zest of 1 lime
    juice of 2 limes

2 tablespoons tequila (optional)
4 tablespoons (2 oz/60 g) sugar
1 mango, peeled and sliced
1 star fruit (carambola) or kiwi, peeled and sliced
seeds of 1 pomegranate, about ½ cup (2½ oz/75 g)

1. In a food processor or blender, purée the pineapple and papaya, reserving ¼ cup (2 fl oz/60 ml) of each to garnish the soup. Add the lime zest, half of the lime juice, the tequila and half of the sugar, and blend until smooth. Chill for 2 hours before serving.
2. Toss the mango, carambola, reserved pineapple and reserved papaya in the remaining lime juice and sugar, and chill.
3. Just before serving, pour the fruit purée into serving glasses. Arrange the sliced fruits on top and sprinkle with the pomegranate seeds.
Serves 6

---

1 cup per serving: Calories 190, Protein 2 g, Carbohydrates 48 g, Fiber 5 g, Total fat 1 g (Saturated 0 g, Monounsaturated 0 g, Polyunsaturated .5 g), Cholesterol 0 mg, Sodium 5 mg, Vitamin A 45%, Vitamin C 120%.
▲ *2 Fruit*

BREAKFAST / MEXICO

Sweet Corn Cakes, Poached Eggs and Summer Fruit Salsa

Summer fruit salsa is simply a blend of fresh fruits and savory onion and chili flavors. The nopales *(cactus pads) are much easier to prepare than they appear. Simply scrape the eyes and stickers off with a sharp knife or potato peeler, and rinse. If your market doesn't sell* nopales, *substitute any fresh seasonal fruit or pepper—kiwi is good.*

FRUIT SALSA
    1 papaya, peeled
    ¼ lb (125 g) small *nopales*
    1 mango, peeled and diced
    ½ cup (2½ oz/75 g) peeled and diced jícama (yam bean)
    ½ cup (2 oz/60 g) diced red (Spanish) onion
    1 red bell pepper (capsicum), seeded and diced
    1 jalapeño chili pepper, seeded and minced
    1 orange, peeled and sliced into wedges
    juice of 1 orange
    salt and freshly ground pepper to taste
CORN CAKES
    1½ cups (9 oz/280 g) sweet corn kernels
    3 eggs
    3 cups (24 fl oz/750 ml) low-fat (1-percent) milk
    3 tablespoons safflower oil
    1 cup plus 2 tablespoons (5¾ oz/165 g) flour
    1 cup plus 2 tablespoons (4½ oz/140 g) *masa harina*
    1½ teaspoons baking powder
    ¼ teaspoon salt
    2 tablespoons sugar
POACHED EGGS
    1 tablespoon freshly squeezed orange juice
    6 eggs

1. To make the fruit salsa, remove the seeds from the papaya, reserving 3 tablespoons of seeds. Dice the papaya, and set aside.
2. Remove any stickers and imperfections from the *nopales*, trim the edges, rinse and dice. Steam over boiling water for 2 minutes, then refresh in ice water. Drain well.
3. In a large mixing bowl, combine the papaya and reserved papaya seeds, *nopales*, mango, jícama, onion, bell pepper, jalapeño, orange wedges and orange juice. Season with the salt and pepper. Let stand for 30 minutes.
4. To prepare the corn cakes, mix together the corn, eggs, milk and oil.
5. In a large mixing bowl, combine the flour, *masa harina*, baking powder, salt and sugar. Add the corn mixture, and stir gently until just mixed.
6. In a nonstick frying pan, drop spoonfuls as you would for pancakes, and cook about 1 minute on each side, turning once. Keep the corn cakes warm in an oven until you are ready to serve them.
7. To prepare the eggs, heat 1 in (2.5 cm) of water to boiling in a skillet. Add the orange juice, and reduce to a simmer. Break the eggs, one at a time, into a small dish, and gently slip each one into the water. Cook until the whites are firm, about 5 minutes. Remove with a slotted spoon.
8. Serve at once, placing an egg over 2 corn cakes with salsa spooned on the side.
Serves 6

---

2 corn cakes, 1 egg, ⅔ cup salsa per serving: Calories 520, Protein 21 g, Carbohydrates 72 g, Fiber 8 g, Total fat 18 g (Saturated 4 g, Monounsaturated 4.5 g, Polyunsaturated 7 g), Cholesterol 335 mg, Sodium 270 mg, Iron 25%, Calcium 30%, Vitamin A 70%, Vitamin C 70%.
▲ *2 Bread, 1 Fruit, 1 Vegetable, ½ Meat, ½ Milk*

Top to bottom: Cold Pineapple Soup; Sweet Corn Cakes, Poached Eggs and Summer Fruit Salsa

Fava Bean Saláta

Serve this as a salad, or purée it for a delicious dip with wedges of pita bread (recipe on page 78) and vegetables. It provides almost half of your daily need for fiber and lots of B vitamins.

1 lb (500 g) shelled fresh fava beans or fresh lima beans

8 cups (64 fl oz/2 l) chicken stock (see glossary)

1 cup (4 oz/125 g) chopped onion

2 cloves garlic, minced

1 carrot, peeled and diced

2 small zucchini (courgettes), cut crosswise into ½-in (12-mm) slices

½ cup (4 fl oz/125 ml) lemon juice

¼ cup (2 fl oz/60 ml) olive oil

½ teaspoon salt

freshly ground pepper to taste

¼ cup (1 oz/30 g) chopped red (Spanish) onion

½ cup (2 oz/60 g) sliced celery

1 teaspoon minced mint leaves

¼ cup (⅓ oz/10 g) minced parsley

4 cups (4 oz/120 g) purslane or arugula (rocket) or other green of choice

2 tomatoes, cut into wedges

1. Wash the fava beans, and place them in a large pot with the chicken stock, onion, garlic and carrot. (You may put the fava

Top to bottom: Souvlaki with Dill-Scented Yogurt, Fava Bean Saláta

beans in a cheesecloth (muslin) pouch so you can easily remove them later.) Simmer for 30 minutes. Add the zucchini, and cook 10 minutes, or until the beans are tender. Drain, and set aside to cool. When cool, remove the skins from the fava beans. (It is not necessary to remove the skins from lima beans.) Return the beans to the zucchini mixture.

2. In a large mixing bowl, combine the lemon juice and olive oil. Season with the salt and pepper. Add the cooled bean mixture, red onion, celery, mint and half of the parsley. Toss.

3. Mix the purslane with the bean mixture and arrange on a platter. Garnish with the remaining parsley and the tomatoes, and serve at room temperature or chilled.

Serves 8

1 cup per serving: Calories 310, Protein 17 g, Carbohydrates 43 g, Fiber 10 g, Total fat 9 g (Saturated 1.5 g, Monounsaturated 6 g, Polyunsaturated 1.5 g), Cholesterol 0 mg, Sodium 180 mg, Iron 25%, Vitamin A 60%, Vitamin C 40%.

▲ *1 Vegetable, 1 Meat*

POULTRY / GREECE

Souvlaki with Dill-Scented Yogurt

Souvlaki—skewers of marinated chicken—are the perfect summer food. Serve them with ripe sliced tomatoes and red (Spanish) onions, garden-fresh cucumbers and a bowl of radishes. Wrap these all up in pita bread (recipe on page 78) that has been warmed on the grill.

SOUVLAKI

½ cup (4 fl oz/125 ml) extra virgin olive oil

juice of 3 lemons

3 cloves garlic, minced

2 teaspoons minced fresh oregano

1 teaspoon minced fresh thyme

4 bay leaves

¼ teaspoon salt

freshly ground pepper

1½ lb (750 g) chicken breast, skinned, boned and cut into 1-in (2.5-cm) cubes

DILL-SCENTED YOGURT

½ cup (4 fl oz/125 ml) plain low-fat yogurt

1½ teaspoons fresh dill, minced

1. In a large nonreactive bowl, combine the olive oil, lemon juice, garlic, oregano, thyme, bay leaves, salt and pepper. Set aside 3 tablespoons to be used for basting, and use the rest to marinate the chicken, refrigerated, overnight.

2. To make the dill-scented yogurt, combine yogurt and dill. Refrigerate until ready to use.

3. Preheat a grill or broiler. Soak eight 6-in (15-cm) skewers in water for 20 minutes. Place the chicken pieces on the skewers and grill, basting with the marinade, until the chicken is darkened and crisp on the outside, about 6 minutes. Move the chicken 2 in (5 cm) away from the heat source and cook until done inside, about 6–8 minutes longer.

4. Brush the chicken lightly with the reserved 3 tablespoons of marinade, remove from the skewers and serve immediately with the dill-scented yogurt.

Serves 4

2 skewers plus 2 tablespoons yogurt per serving: Calories 290, Protein 41 g, Carbohydrates 3 g, Fiber 0 g, Total fat 11 g (Saturated 2 g, Monounsaturated 7 g, Polyunsaturated 1.5 g), Cholesterol 110 mg, Sodium 150 mg.
▲ *1 Meat*

GRAINS / FRANCE

Socca

CHICK-PEA–FLOUR PANCAKE

In Nice, socca, *a savory chick-pea–flour pancake, is sold in the Cours Saleya market, delivered fresh and hot from a basket on wheels pulled by a bicycle. You must be ready to purchase—the supply goes fast. The flour is available in most health food stores and is very rich in folacin, a B vitamin necessary for cell division.* Socca *makes an excellent accompaniment to* les fleurs farcies *(recipe on page 95) or a Niçoise salad (recipe on page 68).*

1⅓ cups (7 oz/220 g) chick-pea (garbanzo bean) flour
½ teaspoon salt
2 cloves garlic, very finely minced
½ teaspoon ground cumin
2 tablespoons olive oil

1. In a medium mixing bowl, whisk the chick-pea flour a little at a time into 1 cup (8 fl oz/250 ml) cold water. Whisk in the salt, garlic and cumin. Cover, and let stand for 1 hour.
2. About 10 minutes before the hour is over, preheat an oven to 450°F (230°C). Oil a 12-in (30-cm) pizza pan with 1 tablespoon of the olive oil.
3. Stir the batter, and pour into the pizza pan to a thickness of ¼ in (6 mm). Drizzle the remaining tablespoon of olive oil over the top. Bake until golden and crisp, about 20 minutes. Cut into 8 wedges and serve at once, right from the pan.

Serves 4

2 wedges per serving: Calories 220, Protein 8 g, Carbohydrates 26 g, Fiber 3 g, Total fat 9 g (Saturated 1 g, Monounsaturated 6 g, Polyunsaturated 1.5 g), Cholesterol 0 mg, Sodium 300 mg.
▲ *2 Bread*

SOUPS / FRANCE

French Market Soup

Summer is the height of tomato season, and very ripe tomatoes make the best soup. This basic tomato-basil soup gets its remarkable color from the addition of a little beet. Delicious and nutrient-rich on its own, it is also the perfect base for other market-fresh items—seafood, eggplant (aubergine), zucchini (courgettes), other herbs, and sprouted or fresh legumes, to mention a few. Increase the liquid, and you can add pasta or rice.

Left to right: French Market Soup, Chick-Pea–Flour Pancake

2 tablespoons olive oil
2 onions, chopped
2 cloves garlic, minced
3 cups (24 fl oz/750 ml) chicken stock (see glossary)
1 carrot, peeled and sliced
2 ribs celery, thinly sliced
¼ cup (4 oz/125 g) peeled and chopped beet (beetroot)
2 lb (1 kg) ripe tomatoes, peeled, cored, seeded and coarsely chopped
2 tablespoons tomato paste (purée)
salt and freshly ground pepper to taste
3 tablespoons fresh basil leaves, cut into chiffonade

1. In a stockpot, heat the olive oil. Add the onions and garlic, and cook until soft. Add the chicken stock, carrot, celery and beet, and bring to a boil. Reduce to a simmer, and cook until the vegetables are tender, about 10 minutes.
2. Add the tomatoes and tomato paste, and simmer until the soup begins to thicken, about 15 minutes. Purée in a blender until smooth. Return to the stockpot, season with the salt and pepper and heat through.
3. Pour into warmed soup bowls, sprinkle with the basil and serve.

Serves 6

1 cup per serving: Calories 120, Protein 3 g, Carbohydrates 16 g, Fiber 4 g, Total fat 6 g (Saturated 1 g, Monounsaturated 4 g, Polyunsaturated 1 g), Cholesterol 0 mg, Sodium 40 mg, Vitamin A 90%, Vitamin C 60%.
▲ *2 Vegetable*

Clockwise from left: Adzuki-Bean-and-Brown-Rice Burgers, Vegetable Cocktail, Crustless Corn-and-Jicama Quiche

Vegetable Cocktail

A juicer is the best appliance for this drink, but a food processor or blender will also do. The key flavor in the recipe is the tomatoes. They should be ripe, soft and juicy. If you have a juicer, try adding celery, beet and carrot as well.

2 lb (1 kg) ripe tomatoes

¼ cup (2 fl oz/60 ml) crushed ice

½ lb (250 g) spinach leaves, chopped

1 red bell pepper (capsicum), roasted, peeled and seeded (see glossary)

1 English (hothouse) cucumber, peeled

2 teaspoons freshly squeezed lemon juice

salt and freshly ground white pepper to taste
1 teaspoon red hot pepper (Tabasco) sauce (optional)

1. Chop the tomatoes coarsely, saving as much juice as possible; place in a blender with the crushed ice, and purée. Pass through a fine strainer to remove the seeds and pulp, pressing to extract as much juice as possible. Return the juice to the blender. Add the remaining ingredients one at a time, blending after each addition, until smooth.
2. Adjust the seasonings to taste, and chill slightly before serving.
Serves 8

---

1 glass per serving: Calories 35, Protein 2 g, Carbohydrates 8 g, Fiber 3 g, Total fat 0 g (Saturated 0 g, Monounsaturated 0 g, Polyunsaturated 0 g), Cholesterol 0 mg, Sodium 35 mg, Vitamin A 60%, Vitamin C 90%.
▲ *1 Vegetable*

GRAINS / UNITED STATES

Adzuki-Bean-and-Brown-Rice Burgers

Vegetarians love these grain burgers, which are crisp on the outside and soft on the inside. Combining beans and rice provides a complete protein.

¼ cup (2 oz/60 g) adzuki beans, soaked overnight
¼ cup (2 oz/60 g) brown rice
2 tablespoons soybean flakes
1 carrot, grated
2 cups (16 fl oz/500 ml) vegetable stock (see glossary)
1 tablespoon olive oil
½ cup (2 oz/60 g) chopped onion
2 cloves garlic, minced
¾ cup (2¼ oz/65 g) sliced mushrooms
1 egg, lightly beaten
2 tablespoons wheat germ
½ teaspoon soy sauce
freshly ground pepper to taste
½ cup (2½ oz/70 g) all-purpose (plain) flour
3 tablespoons plain low-fat yogurt
2 tablespoons Dijon mustard
6 whole-wheat burger buns
6 leaves red-leaf lettuce
2 tomatoes, sliced

1. In a medium saucepan, cook the beans, brown rice, soybean flakes and carrot in the vegetable stock for 40 minutes. Drain well.
2. Heat the olive oil, and sauté the onion and garlic until golden, about 5 minutes. Add the mushrooms, and cook until the liquid has evaporated. Add the bean mixture, and cool.
3. Place the mixture in a food processor. Pulse until just evenly chopped. Do not overprocess to a purée. Stir in the egg and wheat germ; season with the soy sauce and pepper. Fold in the flour.
4. Heat a nonstick frying pan. Form 6 patties, using one-sixth of the mixture for each, and cook over medium heat

until firm and golden brown, about 10 minutes, turning after 3 minutes on each side.
5. Mix the yogurt and mustard, and spread on the buns; add the burger patties, and serve with the lettuce and sliced tomatoes.
Serves 6

---

1 sandwich per serving: Calories 330, Protein 12 g, Carbohydrates 53 g, Fiber 4 g, Total fat 8 g (Saturated 2 g, Monounsaturated 3.5 g, Polyunsaturated 1.5 g), Cholesterol 55 mg, Sodium 510 mg, Vitamin A 80%, Vitamin C 20%.
▲ *2 Bread, 1 Vegetable, ½ Meat*

BREAKFAST / UNITED STATES

Crustless Corn-and-Jícama Quiche

Make this quiche a day ahead, and serve it heated or at room temperature for brunch. It's delicious with fresh tomato vinaigrette (recipe on page 116) or a fresh tomato salsa.

2 tablespoons olive oil
1 cup (5 oz/155 g) finely chopped onion
½ lb (250 g) mushrooms, sliced
2 large tomatoes, peeled, seeded and coarsely chopped
½ cup (3 oz/90 g) corn kernels
½ cup (2½ oz/75 g) peeled and diced jícama
3 eggs plus 2 egg whites
1½ cups (12 fl oz/375 ml) low-fat (1-percent) milk
2 teaspoons Dijon mustard
1 tablespoon minced fresh cilantro (fresh coriander)
1 teaspoon minced fresh parsley
½ teaspoon minced fresh oregano
¼ teaspoon salt
½ teaspoon paprika
¼ cup (1 oz/30 g) grated skim-milk mozzarella

1. Preheat an oven to 375°F (190°C). Lightly oil a 9-by-9-in (23-by-23-cm) baking dish.
2. In a large skillet, heat the olive oil, and sauté the onion until soft, about 5 minutes. Add the mushrooms, and cook until all liquid has evaporated. Stir in the tomatoes, corn and jícama, place in the baking dish and set aside.
3. In a medium mixing bowl, combine the eggs, egg whites, milk, mustard, cilantro, parsley, oregano, salt and paprika. Mix well. Pour over the vegetables, stirring gently to distribute evenly.
4. Sprinkle with the mozzarella, and bake for 35–40 minutes, until the top is lightly browned and a knife inserted in the center comes out clean. Cool for 10 minutes on a rack before slicing to serve.
Serves 6

---

1 serving: Calories 170, Protein 10 g, Carbohydrates 14 g, Fiber 2 g, Total fat 9 g (Saturated 2.5 g, Monounsaturated 5 g, Polyunsaturated 1 g), Cholesterol 115 mg, Sodium 260 mg, Vitamin C 30%.
▲ *1 Vegetable, ½ Milk*

Top to bottom: Summer Potato Salad, Seared Cured Salmon

Halstrad Gravlax

SEARED CURED SALMON

Chef Staffan Terje cures and then sears this fillet of salmon. Start a day ahead to cure the fish properly. The purpose of curing the salmon in salt is to draw out the moisture and firm the fish. Most of the salt and sugar used in the cure is removed. The seared gravlax *can be served simply with this spicy mustard sauce and a colorful vegetable summer salad.*

CURED SALMON
  1½ cups (12 oz/375 g) sugar
  ¾ cup (6 oz/170 g) coarse sea salt or kosher salt
  ½ cup (¾ oz/20 g) finely chopped fresh dill
  ¼ cup (¾ oz/20 g) white or black peppercorns, crushed
  ¼ cup (½ oz/15 g) juniper berries, crushed
  2 lb (1 kg) fresh salmon fillet, center cut, with skin on
MUSTARD SAUCE
  ½ cup (4 fl oz/125 ml) sweet and hot mustard
  juice of 1 lemon
  2 tablespoons chopped dill
  ⅓ cup (3 fl oz/80 ml) canola oil
  ¼ teaspoon salt
  freshly ground pepper to taste

1. To make the curing mixture, mix together the sugar, salt, finely chopped dill, peppercorns and juniper berries. Let stand for 30 minutes.

2. Remove the scales and any small bones from the salmon.
3. Cover the bottom of a nonreactive dish (large enough to hold the salmon) with one-quarter of the curing mixture. Place the salmon in the dish, skin side down, and cover with the remaining curing mixture. Cover with plastic wrap, and let stand at room temperature for 1 hour. Refrigerate for 12 hours.
4. Scrape off and discard the curing mixture. Wipe the salmon with a clean, damp cloth.
5. Remove the salmon skin, cut it into 1-in (2.5-cm) strips and set it aside. Cut the salmon straight across into 1-in (2.5-cm) slices.
6. To make the mustard sauce, whisk together the mustard, lemon juice, chopped dill and 1 tablespoon of water. Slowly add the oil, whisking constantly. Season with the salt and pepper.
7. Heat a well-seasoned cast iron or nonstick pan until very hot. Sear the slices of salmon for 30 seconds on each side. Arrange the slices on a serving platter.
8. In the same pan, cook the strips of salmon skin over medium heat until crisp. Sprinkle them over the seared salmon, and serve at once with the mustard sauce.
Serves 6

---

1 serving: Calories 390, Protein 33 g, Carbohydrates 4 g, Fiber 0 g, Total fat 26 g (Saturated 3 g, Monounsaturated 14 g, Polyunsaturated 7 g), Cholesterol 95 mg, Sodium 820 mg.
▲ *1 Meat, 1 Fat/Sugar*

Summer Potato Salad

Chef Staffan Terje recommends serving this fresh salad with seared gravlax *(preceding recipe).*

  1 lb (500 g) small new potatoes
  ½ lb (250 g) asparagus, cut into 3-in (7.5-cm) pieces and blanched (see glossary)
  2 large ripe tomatoes, peeled and cut into wedges
  1 red (Spanish) onion, halved and thinly sliced
  3 tablespoons white wine vinegar
  2 tablespoons finely chopped fresh dill
  ¼ cup (⅓ oz/10 g) finely cut chives
  ½ teaspoon sugar
  pinch of salt
  freshly ground pepper to taste
  ⅓ cup (3 fl oz/80 ml) canola oil

1. Cook the potatoes, unpeeled, until tender, about 15 minutes. Drain and cool. Cut them into ¼-in (6-mm) slices, and place in a large bowl with the asparagus, tomatoes and onion.
2. In a small bowl, whisk together the vinegar, dill, chives, sugar, salt and pepper. Add the oil slowly, whisking constantly.
3. Toss the vegetables with the dressing, and keep covered at room temperature until ready to serve.
Serves 8

¾ cup per serving: Calories 150, Protein 2 g, Carbohydrates 16 g, Fiber 2 g, Total fat 9 g (Saturated 1 g, Monounsaturated 5 g, Polyunsaturated 3 g), Cholesterol 0 mg, Sodium 25 mg, Vitamin C 25%.
▲ *1 Vegetable*

Marinated Clams and Mussels

Fresh clams and mussels are found in abundance in the Atlantic. Look for ones that are tightly shut or that close tightly when tapped. If you can't use them immediately, store them covered with a damp towel in the coldest part of your refrigerator. Use them within a day or two.

Don't be put off by the amount of coarse salt in this recipe: only a little of it is absorbed; the rest is drained off. If sodium is a concern, substitute 1 tablespoon lemon zest for the capers.

12 mussels, scrubbed with a stiff brush and debearded
12 clams, scrubbed with a stiff brush
3 tablespoons coarse salt
2 tablespoons plus ⅓ cup (3 fl oz/80 ml) olive oil
½ cup (2 oz/60 g) chopped onion
3 tablespoons chopped fresh parsley
1 teaspoon minced fresh thyme
¾ cup (6 fl oz/180 ml) red wine
1 cup (7 oz/220 g) long-grain rice, cooked according to package directions (approximately 3 cups/15 oz/ 465 g cooked)
2 tablespoons red wine vinegar
2 tablespoons capers, drained
2 tomatoes, peeled, seeded and diced
salt and freshly ground pepper to taste

1. Place the scrubbed mussels and clams in cold water, and add the coarse salt. Soak for 10 minutes; drain well.

2. In a large skillet, heat 2 tablespoons of the olive oil. Add the onion, and sauté until soft but not browned. Add 2 tablespoons of the parsley, the thyme, red wine, mussels and clams. Cover and cook over high heat, shaking the pan occasionally, until all of the mussels and clams have opened, about 5 minutes. Remove the mussels and clams, and set them aside. Add ½ cup (2½ oz/75 g) of the cooked rice to the skillet, and continue to cook until thickened, about 10–15 minutes.

3. While the rice mixture is cooking, preheat an oven to warm. Pull the meat from the mussel and clam shells, reserving the shells. Place the mussel and clam meat in a nonreactive bowl, and add the ⅓ cup (3 fl oz/80 ml) olive oil and the vinegar; let marinate for 15 minutes.

4. Add the capers, tomatoes and remaining parsley to the rice mixture, and season with the salt and pepper. Spoon some of the rice mixture into half of each shell.

5. With a slotted spoon, drain the mussels and clams, and place a mussel or clam on top of the rice in its appropriate shell. Keep them warm in the oven until ready to serve.

6. Spread the remaining rice on a serving platter, and make a small well in the center for any leftover rice filling. Arrange the mussels and clams on the rice, and serve immediately.
Serves 4

1 serving: Calories 310, Protein 10 g, Carbohydrates 44 g, Fiber 2 g, Total fat 10 g (Saturated 1.5 g, Monounsaturated 7 g, Polyunsaturated 1 g), Cholesterol 15 mg, Sodium 720 mg, Iron 40%, Vitamin C 30%.
▲ *1 Bread, 1 Meat*

Salmon-Yaki

After marinating, this fresh summer grill is ready in minutes. Serve it over short-grain rice with a simple green salad.

2 tablespoons lemon juice
¼ cup (2 fl oz/60 ml) soy sauce
¼ cup (2 fl oz/60 ml) *mirin* (sweet cooking sake)
¼ cup (2 fl oz/60 ml) sake
1 lb (500 g) salmon fillet, cut into 4 pieces
2 tablespoons minced chives
1 lemon, cut into wedges

1. In a medium bowl, combine the lemon juice, soy sauce, *mirin* and sake, and marinate the salmon in the mixture for at least 30 minutes in the refrigerator.

2. Preheat a grill or broiler.

3. Grill or broil the salmon 2 minutes on each side. Sprinkle with the chives, and serve at once, with a lemon wedge on the side.
Serves 4

1 piece per serving: Calories 200, Protein 24 g, Carbohydrates 1 g, Fiber 0 g, Total fat 10 g (Saturated 2 g, Monounsaturated 5 g, Polyunsaturated 2 g), Cholesterol 70 mg, Sodium 260 mg.
▲ *1 Meat*

Left to right: Marinated Clams and Mussels, Salmon-Yaki

Couscous

Couscous is a tiny semolina pasta. Regular (as opposed to instant) couscous is cooked for over an hour in a couscoussier, *a pot designed especially for this purpose. A deep pot with a colander set in it can be used as a steamer instead. This recipe calls for quick-cooking couscous and does not require special equipment.*

1 tablespoon olive oil
1 cup (4 oz/125 g) chopped onion
4 cloves garlic, minced
1 red bell pepper (capsicum), finely chopped
1¾ cups (14 fl oz/430 ml) chicken stock (see glossary)
1½ cups (9 oz/280 g) quick-cooking couscous
¼ teaspoon salt
freshly ground pepper to taste
½ lb (250 g) broccoli rabe (rapini)

1. In a large skillet, heat the olive oil. Add the onion, 3 cloves of the garlic and the bell pepper, and sauté until tender, about 3 minutes. Add 1½ cups (12 fl oz/375 ml) of the chicken stock, and bring to a boil. Add the couscous, cover and remove from the heat to stand for 5 minutes.

2. In a medium skillet, heat the remaining chicken stock with the remaining garlic, the salt and the pepper. Add the broccoli rabe, and simmer for 5 minutes.

3. Fluff the couscous with a fork, and place it on a serving platter. Make a long, narrow indentation in the middle. Arrange the broccoli rabe in the middle, and spoon the cooking liquid over the couscous. Serve at once.

Serves 6

1 cup per serving: Calories 230, Protein 8 g, Carbohydrates 42 g, Fiber 2 g, Total fat 3 g (Saturated .5 g, Monounsaturated 2 g, Polyunsaturated .5 g), Cholesterol 0 mg, Sodium 115 mg, Vitamin A 25%, Vitamin C 100%.
▲ *2 Bread*

Vegetable Tian with Fresh Tomato Vinaigrette

Used in Provence, a tian *is an oval or rectangular earthenware dish in which layers of vegetables and meat are gratinéed and served at room temperature or chilled. Hearty enough for a vegetarian main dish, this recipe can also be a delightful first course. Although it calls for 4 small dishes, it is just as nicely presented in a single 4-cup (32-fl oz/1-l) dish. The ingredients offer a beta-carotene bonanza, providing your whole day's requirement of vitamins A and C, and are an excellent source of iron.*

2 tablespoons olive oil
2 cups (10 oz/300 g) finely chopped onion
4 cloves garlic, finely minced
4 tomatoes, peeled, seeded and coarsely chopped
1 tablespoon minced fresh basil
2 teaspoons minced fresh parsley
1 teaspoon minced fresh thyme
1 teaspoon minced fresh mint
¼ teaspoon salt
freshly ground pepper to taste
2 potatoes, peeled, very thinly sliced and blanched 3 minutes (see glossary)
4 red bell peppers (capsicums), roasted, peeled and seeded (see glossary)
8 leaves Swiss chard (silverbeet), blanched quickly to soften, with rib removed (see glossary)
2 tablespoons grated Parmesan cheese
¼ cup (2 fl oz/60 ml) fresh tomato vinaigrette (recipe follows)

1. Preheat an oven to 375°F (190°C). Lightly oil four 1-cup (8-fl oz/250-ml) *tians* or gratin dishes.

2. In a large nonstick skillet, heat the olive oil. Sauté the onion until just golden brown, about 5 minutes. Add the garlic, and cook until soft but not browned, about 2 minutes. Add the tomatoes and cook for 2 minutes. Add the basil, parsley, thyme and mint; season with the salt and pepper. Stir to combine, and remove from the heat.

3. Cut the potato slices, red peppers and chard leaves into 3-in (7.5-cm) squares, or to fit the *tian* dishes.

4. Spoon one-third of the onion-tomato mixture into the *tian* dishes. Alternate layers of potato slices, tomato mixture, chard leaves and red peppers, finishing with a spoonful of tomato mixture. Sprinkle with the Parmesan cheese.

5. Cover with foil, and bake for 10 minutes. Remove the foil and bake until the cheese browns, about 15 minutes. Cool on a rack. Spoon 1 tablespoon of fresh tomato vinaigrette over each *tian*, and serve at room temperature or chilled.

Serves 4

1 cup with dressing per serving: Calories 240, Protein 7 g, Carbohydrates 34 g, Fiber 6 g, Total fat 11 g (Saturated 2 g, Monounsaturated 7 g, Polyunsaturated 1.5 g), Cholesterol 2 mg, Sodium 430 mg, Iron 20%, Vitamin A 110%, Vitamin C 350%.
▲ *2 Vegetable, 1 Fat/Sugar*

FRESH TOMATO VINAIGRETTE

1 tablespoon red wine vinegar
½ teaspoon coarse-grained mustard
1 shallot (white onion), minced
2 tablespoons extra virgin olive oil
1 large tomato, peeled, seeded and diced
1 tablespoon fresh basil, cut into chiffonade
salt and freshly ground pepper to taste

1. In a mixing bowl, combine the vinegar, mustard and shallot. Drizzle in the olive oil, whisking constantly. Stir in the tomato and basil; season with the salt and pepper.

Makes ¾ cup (6 fl oz/180 ml)

2 tablespoons per serving: Calories 50, Protein 0 g, Carbohydrates 2 g, Fiber 0 g, Total fat 5 g (Saturated .5 g, Monounsaturated 3.5 g, Polyunsaturated .5 g), Cholesterol 0 mg, Sodium 35 mg.
▲ *1 Fat/Sugar*

Left to right: Vegetable Tian with Fresh Tomato Vinaigrette, Couscous

Top to bottom: Marie Simmons's Oven-Roasted Vegetables with Gemelli; Skewered Seafood and Porcini Mushrooms; Italian Bread Salad

Marie Simmons's Oven-Roasted Vegetables with Gemelli

Marie Simmons, columnist and author of a number of books, including Italian Light Cooking, *suggests adapting this recipe to the seasonal availability of vegetables. For a spring version, try asparagus, carrots, zucchini (courgettes), shallots (white onions) and fresh dill. The important thing is to have 6 cups (3 lb/1.5 kg) or more of raw vegetables, since they cook down to half that amount.*

2 red bell peppers (capsicums), halved, seeded and cut into ½-in (12-mm) wedges

1 eggplant (aubergine), stemmed and cut into ½-by-2-in (12-mm-by-5-cm) strips

1 green zucchini (courgette), trimmed and cut into ½-in (12-mm) diagonal slices

1 yellow zucchini (courgette) or summer squash, trimmed, cut into ½-in (12-mm) diagonal slices

1 large red (Spanish) onion, halved lengthwise and cut into ½-in (12-mm) wedges

4 cloves garlic, halved and bruised with the side of a knife

¼ cup (2 fl oz/60 ml) extra virgin olive oil

4 Roma (plum/egg) tomatoes, quartered lengthwise

¼ teaspoon salt

freshly ground black pepper to taste

½ cup (½ oz/15 g) lightly packed torn fresh basil leaves

1 lb (500 g) *gemelli* or other short, broad pasta

2 tablespoons freshly grated *parmigiano reggiano* (Italian Parmesan cheese)

1. Preheat an oven to 425°F (220°C).
2. Place the bell peppers, eggplant, green and yellow zucchini, red onion and garlic in a large baking pan or sheet pan. Drizzle with the oil, and toss to coat. Roast the vegetables 30 minutes, stirring once or twice so they cook evenly. Add the tomatoes, and roast until the vegetables begin to char on the edges, about 30 minutes more. Remove from the oven, sprinkle with the salt and pepper and add the basil leaves.
3. Meanwhile cook the pasta in about 8 cups (64 fl oz/2 l) of boiling water until al dente (tender but firm to the bite). Ladle out and reserve about ½ cup (4 fl oz/125 ml) of the pasta cooking liquid. Quickly drain the pasta in a colander; do not rinse with water, and do not allow to stand.
4. Turn the pasta into a large, shallow bowl or deep platter. Spoon the roasted vegetables on top. Using a rubber spatula, gather all the juices and drops of oil in the roasting pan, and add to the pasta. Drizzle with half of the reserved pasta cooking liquid; toss to blend. Add the remaining liquid, if the pasta seems dry. Sprinkle with the cheese, and serve at once.

Serves 8

---

1 cup per serving: Calories 320, Protein 9 g, Carbohydrates 52 g, Fiber 4 g, Total fat 8 g (Saturated 1.5 g, Monounsaturated 5 g, Polyunsaturated 1 g), Cholesterol 0 mg, Sodium 110 mg, Vitamin A 30%, Vitamin C 80%.

▲ *1 Bread, 1 Vegetable*

SALADS / ITALY

Panzanella

ITALIAN BREAD SALAD

This salad is designed to make use of leftover bread. If you are using fresh bread, lightly toast it before cutting it into cubes. The longer this salad stands, the more dressing the bread absorbs. Serve at room temperature.

3 cups (6 oz/170 g) Italian bread, cut into ½-in (12-mm) cubes

2 ripe tomatoes, seeded and cut into ½-in (12-mm) pieces

1 cup (6 oz/185 g) yellow pear tomatoes, cut in half

1 cucumber, peeled, seeded and cut into ½-in (12-mm) chunks

½ cup (2 oz/60 g) green bell pepper (capsicum), seeded and cut into ½-in (12-mm) pieces

½ cup (2½ oz/75 g) finely chopped red (Spanish) onion

3 cloves garlic, finely minced

¼ cup (2 fl oz/60 ml) red wine vinegar

1 cup (1 oz/30 g) fresh basil leaves

¼ cup (2 fl oz/60 ml) olive oil

⅛ teaspoon salt

freshly ground pepper to taste

3 sprigs fresh basil for garnish

1. In a large mixing bowl, combine the bread cubes, red tomatoes, yellow tomatoes, cucumber, bell pepper and red onion.
2. In a blender or food processor, purée the garlic, vinegar and 1 cup (1 oz/30 g) of basil until smooth. With the machine running, slowly drizzle in the olive oil. Season with the salt and pepper.
3. Toss the dressing with the bread and vegetable mixture, garnish with the basil sprigs and serve at once.

Serves 6

¾ cup per serving: Calories 160, Protein 3 g, Carbohydrates 16 g, Fiber 2 g, Total fat 9 g (Saturated 1 g, Monounsaturated 7 g, Polyunsaturated 1 g), Cholesterol 0 mg, Sodium 150 mg, Vitamin C 50%.

▲ *1 Bread, 1 Vegetable*

SEAFOOD / ITALY

Spiedini ai Frutti di Mare Monterosso

SKEWERED SEAFOOD AND PORCINI MUSHROOMS

The Italian Riviera has a bounty of fresh seafood. Serve these glorious fruits of the sea with orzo with wild mushrooms (recipe on page 166).

12 prawns or jumbo shrimp, shelled and deveined

24 large sea scallops

6 large porcini (boletus) mushrooms, cut into quarters

¼ cup (2 fl oz/60 ml) extra virgin olive oil

juice of 1 lemon

2 teaspoons minced fresh thyme

2 cloves garlic, minced

freshly ground pepper to taste

1. Soak 12 wooden skewers in water for 30 minutes.
2. Thread each skewer with 1 prawn, 2 scallops and 2 pieces of porcini. Place in a flat, shallow dish.
3. In a small bowl, combine the olive oil, lemon juice, thyme and garlic. Mix well, and pour over the skewers. Let marinate for at least 1 hour, or overnight in the refrigerator.
4. Preheat a grill or broiler.
5. Remove the skewers from the marinade, and season them with the pepper. Grill for 4–5 minutes, turning frequently and brushing with the marinade, until the prawns are pink and the scallops are firm and opaque. Serve immediately.

Serves 6

---

2 skewers per serving: Calories 160, Protein 26 g, Carbohydrates 3 g, Fiber 0 g, Total fat 4 g (Saturated .5 g, Monounsaturated 2 g, Polyunsaturated 1 g), Cholesterol 135 mg, Sodium 210 mg.

▲ *1 Meat*

Tuscan-Style Rosemary Chicken

In Tuscany, flattened whole chickens are cooked between two pieces of terra cotta to yield a crisp outside and a moist interior. The terra cotta utensil, called a mattone, *is heated and cooks on top of the stove. Our version uses utensils available in most kitchens. The chicken skin is also removed to lower the fat content of the dish.*

1 whole 3-lb (1.5-kg) chicken
1 lemon, cut in half
¼ teaspoon salt
freshly ground pepper to taste
4 teaspoons olive oil
1 tablespoon fresh rosemary leaves

1. Cut the chicken lengthwise through the backbone, and flatten the two sides by pressing the breastbone. Remove and discard the skin from the breast, legs and thighs. Rub the meat with 1 lemon half. Season with the salt and pepper.
2. Heat a large cast-iron or nonstick skillet, and add 2 teaspoons of the olive oil. When the oil is very hot, place the flattened chicken, bone side up, in the pan. Brush the remaining oil over the top of the chicken, and sprinkle with the rosemary.
3. Place a flat plate or another skillet on top of the chicken, and weight it with a large can of food or two bricks. Cook for 35 minutes over medium heat, turning every 10 minutes.
4. Squeeze the juice of the other lemon half over the chicken, and serve immediately.
Serves 4

1 serving: Calories 270, Protein 35 g, Carbohydrates 1 g, Fiber 0 g, Total fat 14 g (Saturated 3 g, Monounsaturated 7 g, Polyunsaturated 2.5 g), Cholesterol 110 mg, Sodium 250 mg.
▲ *1 Meat*

Pomodori Ripieni

STUFFED TOMATOES

Pomodori ripieni *make an appetizing side dish to serve with grilled poultry or seafood. They are a good source of vitamins C and A.*

8 firm, ripe tomatoes
1 cup (5 oz/155 g) minced onion
1 cup (2 oz/60 g) stemmed and coarsely chopped Swiss chard (silverbeet)
½ cup (2½ oz/75 g) diced yellow bell pepper (capsicum)
3 cloves garlic, minced
3 tablespoons dry bread crumbs
3 tablespoons fresh parsley, minced
1 teaspoon fresh thyme, minced

½ teaspoon fresh marjoram, minced
¼ teaspoon salt
freshly ground pepper to taste
3 tablespoons freshly grated Parmesan cheese

1. Preheat an oven to 375°F (190°C). Lightly oil a large, shallow baking dish.
2. Cut the tomatoes in half horizontally. Loosen the pulp by slicing inside the edge with a sharp knife, taking great care not to pierce the outer flesh. Scoop the seeds and pulp into a large mixing bowl. Place the tomato halves in a baking dish.
3. Add the onion, chard, bell pepper, garlic, bread crumbs, parsley, thyme and marjoram to the reserved tomato pulp, and mix well. Season with the salt and pepper. Spoon into the tomato halves, and sprinkle the Parmesan over the tops.
4. Bake for 30 minutes, until golden brown on top. Serve at once, or cool to serve later at room temperature.
Serves 8

1 tomato (2 halves) per serving: Calories 60, Protein 3 g, Carbohydrates 11 g, Fiber 2 g, Total fat 1 g (Saturated .5 g, Monounsaturated .5 g, Polyunsaturated 0 g), Cholesterol 2 mg, Sodium 150 mg, Vitamin A 20%, Vitamin C 80%.
▲ *1 Vegetable*

Bruschette con Caponata alla Siciliana

SICILIAN TOAST WITH EGGPLANT RELISH

This chunky eggplant relish can be made ahead and served hot or cold. Salting eggplant before cooking draws out excess moisture and gives the eggplant a denser texture, so that it absorbs less oil when cooked. Most of the salt is rinsed off before cooking.

1 eggplant (aubergine), about 1 lb (500 g), peeled and cut into ½-in (12-mm) cubes
1 teaspoon salt
¼ cup (2 fl oz/60 ml) olive oil
4 ribs celery, thinly sliced
1 onion, diced
3 cloves garlic, minced
1 tablespoon capers
2 tablespoons pine nuts, toasted
2 tablespoons raisins
2 teaspoons sugar
¼ cup (2 fl oz/60 ml) red wine vinegar
1 cup (6 oz/185 g) peeled and diced ripe tomato
salt and freshly ground pepper to taste
16 slices fresh country-style bread, toasted
1 cup (1½ oz/40 g) chopped fresh basil

Clockwise from top: Tuscan-Style Rosemary Chicken; Stuffed Tomatoes, Sicilian Toast with Eggplant Relish

1. Arrange 3 layers of paper towels on a sheet pan. Spread the eggplant on top, and sprinkle it with the teaspoon of salt. Let stand for 10 minutes. Rinse, and pat dry with paper towels.

2. In a large sauté pan, heat the olive oil, and cook the celery, onion and garlic until golden, about 3–4 minutes. Add the eggplant, and cook 2–3 minutes, until soft.

3. Add the capers, pine nuts, raisins, sugar and vinegar. Cook until the vinegar evaporates, about 3 minutes.

4. Add the tomato, and heat through, about 2 minutes. Season with the salt and pepper.

5. Spoon over the toasted bread slices, and top with the basil. Serve hot or cold.

Serves 8 (2 slices each)

2 slices per serving: Calories 280, Protein 8 g, Carbohydrates 44 g, Fiber 4 g, Total fat 8 g (Saturated 1 g, Monounsaturated 6 g, Polyunsaturated 1 g), Cholesterol 0 mg, Sodium 600 mg.

▲ *2 Bread, 2 Vegetable*

Broa

WHOLE-WHEAT CORN BREAD

Serve this hearty corn bread with soups and salads.

- 1¼ cups (10 fl oz/310 ml) low-fat (2-percent) milk
- 1 package (¼ oz/7 g) active dry yeast
- 1½ teaspoons sugar
- 1 tablespoon olive oil
- ½ cup (2½ oz/75 g) stone-ground yellow cornmeal (yellow maize flour)
- ½ cup (2½ oz/75 g) whole-wheat (wholemeal) flour
- 1 teaspoon salt
- 2–2½ cups (10–12½ oz/315–390 g) all-purpose (plain) flour

1. Heat ⅔ cup (5 fl oz/160 ml) of the milk to 105°–115°F (40°–46°C). Dissolve the yeast and sugar in the milk, and let stand 5 minutes to proof. Add the oil.
2. Place the cornmeal and whole-wheat flour in a large mixing bowl. Add the yeast mixture, and stir until smooth. Let rise, covered with a towel, for 1 hour.
3. Punch down the dough. Add the remaining milk, the salt and 1 cup (4 oz/125 g) of the all-purpose flour. Stir until smooth. Turn onto a floured work surface, and continue to add all-purpose flour, ½ cup (2 oz/60 g) at a time, kneading until the dough is smooth and not sticky.
4. Form the dough into a ball. Place it in a lightly oiled bowl, cover, and let rise for 1 hour, until doubled in bulk.
5. Line a baking sheet with parchment paper, and dust it with flour. Punch down the dough, knead it a few times, form it into an oval loaf and place it on the baking sheet. With a sharp razor, slash an *X* across the top of the loaf. Cover and let rise for 1 hour, until doubled in bulk.
6. Preheat an oven to 375°F (190°C).
7. Bake for 30 minutes. Cool on a wire rack before slicing.
Makes 12 slices

1 slice per serving: Calories 130, Protein 5 g, Carbohydrates 24 g, Fiber 4 g, Total fat 2 g (Saturated .5 g, Monounsaturated 1 g, Polyunsaturated .5 g), Cholesterol 5 mg, Sodium 210 mg.
▲ *1 Bread*

Sea Scallops with Cucumber Sauce

A cool and refreshing summer salad that is low in calories and high in vitamin C.

- 2 cups (16 fl oz/500 ml) vegetable stock (see glossary)
- ¾ lb (375 g) sea scallops, muscle removed
- 2 large cucumbers and 1 medium cucumber
- 1 shallot (white onion), chopped
- 1 tablespoon freshly squeezed lemon juice
- 2 teaspoons fresh parsley, minced
- ½ teaspoon fresh mint, minced
- ⅛ teaspoon sea salt
- freshly ground white pepper to taste
- 2 cups (4 oz/125 g) frisée (tender yellow inner parts of chicory/curly endive)

1. In a medium saucepan, bring the stock to a boil. Reduce to a simmer, add the scallops and cook for 1–2 minutes, until they are firm and opaque. Remove the scallops to cool, reserving 2 tablespoons of stock for the sauce. Cut the scallops into ½-in (12-mm) slices, and chill.
2. To prepare the cucumber sauce, peel the 2 large cucumbers, reserving the peel. Halve the cucumbers lengthwise, and scrape out the seeds. Cut the flesh into 1-in (2.5-cm) pieces, and place them in a food processor or blender. Add the shallot, reserved stock, lemon juice and parsley, and purée until smooth. Stir in the mint, season with the salt and pepper, and refrigerate until ready to serve.
3. Blanch the reserved cucumber peel for 30 seconds, and refresh it immediately in iced water. Pat dry with paper towels, and cut into thin lengthwise strips for garnish. Set aside.
4. Slice the unpeeled medium cucumber ⅛ in (3 mm) thick crosswise. Arrange the frisée in the center of a serving platter, and encircle it with cucumber slices. Place the scallops in the center and some cucumber peel on top. Serve chilled, with cucumber sauce on the side.
Serves 4 *Photograph page 124*

1 serving: Calories 110, Protein 16 g, Carbohydrates 10 g, Fiber 2 g, Total fat 1 g (Saturated 0 g, Monounsaturated 0 g, Polyunsaturated .5 g), Cholesterol 30 mg, Sodium 220 mg, Vitamin C 25%.
▲ *1 Vegetable, 1 Meat*

Paella

Paella is customarily made in a paella pan, a wide, deep two-handled skillet, but any large skillet may be used. The three essential ingredients are rice, olive oil and saffron. Everything else is garnish, and these embellishments vary greatly from region to region in Spain, depending upon the seasonal and regional availability of ingredients.

- 3 tablespoons olive oil
- 3 cloves garlic, minced
- 8 fresh artichoke hearts (leaves and choke removed)
- 2 medium leeks, white part only, julienned
- 1 green bell pepper (capsicum), julienned
- 1 red bell pepper (capsicum), julienned
- 1½ cups (12 fl oz/375 ml) chicken stock (see glossary)
- ½ teaspoon saffron threads, crushed in a mortar
- ½ cup (3½ oz/110 g) Valencia or medium-grain rice
- 4 tomatoes, peeled and coarsely chopped
- ½ lb (250 g) monkfish (anglerfish), cut into 2-in (5-cm) pieces
- ½ lb (250 g) red snapper, cut into 2-in (5-cm) pieces
- ½ lb (250 g) squid, cleaned and cut into ¼-in (6-mm) slices
- 12 clams, cleaned

Top to bottom: Whole-Wheat Corn Bread, Paella

12 mussels, debearded and cleaned
8 shrimp (prawns), peeled and deveined
1½ lb (750 g) lobster, parboiled for 2 minutes and
**   split lengthwise**
1 cup (5 oz/155 g) fresh peas
¼ cup (¼ oz/8 g) fresh cilantro (fresh coriander) leaves

1. In a paella pan or large skillet, heat the olive oil. Add the garlic, artichoke hearts, leeks, green pepper and red pepper, and sauté until soft, about 3 minutes. Add the chicken stock, and bring to a boil. Reduce to a simmer, add the saffron and rice, and let simmer for 10 minutes. Add the tomatoes, monkfish, snapper and squid; cook for 5 minutes. Add the clams and mussels, and simmer for 3–5 minutes, until all shells have opened. Add the prawns, lobster and peas; cook for 2 minutes. Remove from the heat, cover and let stand for 10 minutes.

2. Garnish with the cilantro, and serve from the paella pan.
   Serves 8

---

1 serving: Calories 370, Protein 45 g, Carbohydrates 25 g, Fiber 2 g, Total fat 9 g (Saturated 1.5 g, Monounsaturated 4.5 g, Polyunsaturated 1.5 g), Cholesterol 230 mg, Sodium 160 mg, Iron 30%, Vitamin A 25%, Vitamin C 90%.

▲ *1 Vegetable, 1 Meat*

Szechwan-Style Duck Salad

The Chinese chicken salad we are most familiar with is made with roasted chicken and cucumber. In this version duck is used, and honeydew melon offers a sweet contrast to the spicy sauce. It is likely that melons originated in Asia; there is evidence of them dating from 1000 B.C. Leftover barbecued duck (or chicken) works well in this dish.

DRESSING

2 cloves garlic

1 teaspoon grated ginger

1 tablespoon chopped fresh cilantro (fresh coriander)

1 tablespoon Chinese sesame paste or tahini if sesame paste is unavailable

1 tablespoon soy sauce

2 teaspoons Chinese sesame oil

1 tablespoon dry sherry

1 teaspoon rice vinegar

2 teaspoons sugar

½ teaspoon chili paste

¼ teaspoon ground Szechwan peppercorns

Top to bottom: Sea Scallops with Cucumber Sauce (recipe page 122), Szechwan-Style Duck Salad

SALAD

3 cups (9 oz/280 g) shredded Napa cabbage

1 lb (500 g) roasted duck or chicken meat, skinned and shredded

1 cup (4 oz/125 g) mung bean sprouts, blanched for 30 seconds (see glossary)

1 honeydew melon, peeled and cut into ¼-in (6-mm) slices

½ lb (250 g) snow peas (mangetouts), strings removed, blanched for 10 seconds (see glossary)

1 carrot, peeled and coarsely grated

1. To make the dressing, in a blender or food processor, blend together the garlic, ginger, cilantro, sesame paste, soy sauce, sesame oil, sherry, vinegar, sugar, chili paste and peppercorns.

2. To assemble the salad, place the cabbage in a deep bowl. Place the duck meat in the center. Arrange the bean sprouts, melon slices, snow peas and carrot in circles around the duck.

3. Drizzle dressing over the salad and chill or serve at once.

Serves 6

1 serving: Calories 300, Protein 22 g, Carbohydrates 29 g, Fiber 4 g, Total fat 12 g (Saturated 4 g, Monounsaturated 4 g, Polyunsaturated 2.5 g), Cholesterol 65 mg, Sodium 230 mg, Vitamin A 80%, Vitamin C 140%.
▲ *1 Fruit, 1 Vegetable, 1 Meat*

Blue-Corn Fettuccine with Roasted Corn and Red Pepper Pesto

Fettuccine made with blue cornmeal and cayenne gives this dish its southwestern feeling. If you don't have time to roll out fettuccine, substitute ready-made fresh or dried pasta of your choice.

FETTUCCINE

2 cups (10 oz/315 g) unbleached all-purpose (plain) flour

1 cup (5 oz/155 g) blue cornmeal (blue maize flour)

½ teaspoon cayenne pepper

1 tablespoon safflower oil

4 eggs

PESTO

3 ears (cobs) of corn with husks

2 red bell peppers (capsicums), roasted, peeled and seeded (see glossary)

¼ cup (⅓ oz/10 g) fresh cilantro (fresh coriander) leaves

3 tablespoons pine nuts, toasted

2 tablespoons safflower oil

1 cup (4 oz/125 g) coarsely chopped onion

3 cloves garlic, minced

1½ cups (12 fl oz/375 ml) chicken stock (see glossary)

¼ teaspoon salt

freshly ground pepper to taste

1. To make the fettuccine, in a large bowl, mix together the flour, cornmeal and cayenne pepper. Make a well, and add the oil and

Blue-Corn Fettuccine with Roasted Corn and Red Pepper Pesto

eggs. With a fork, stir the flour into the eggs, working from the center of the bowl out, until all of the flour is incorporated. Turn the mixture onto a floured work surface, and knead, adding flour as needed, until the dough is smooth and no longer sticky. Place it in a plastic bag, and let it rest 15 minutes.

2. Roll the dough, one-quarter at a time, as directed under *Pastas* in the glossary. Cut into ¼-in (6-mm) strips. Spread on a floured work surface until ready to use.

3. To make the pesto, preheat a grill to medium hot. Remove the silks from the ears of corn, keeping the husks intact. Soak the ears in warm water for 15 minutes. Roast the corn over the grill, turning frequently, for 5 minutes. Remove, and cool. Cut the kernels from the cob, and set aside.

4. In a food processor, purée the red peppers. Add 3 tablespoons of the cilantro and 1 tablespoon of the pine nuts and process to a smooth paste. Set aside.

5. In a medium skillet, heat the oil, and sauté the onion and garlic until soft but not browned. Add the chicken stock, puréed pepper mixture and corn. Simmer for 5–7 minutes, until slightly thickened.

6. Cook the fettuccine in boiling water for 5 minutes, until al dente. Drain and transfer to a serving bowl. Season the sauce with the salt and pepper. Pour it over the pasta, sprinkle with the remaining pine nuts and cilantro leaves, and serve at once.

Serves 6

1 serving: Calories 440, Protein 14 g, Carbohydrates 65 g, Fiber 5 g, Total fat 15 g (Saturated 2.5 g, Monounsaturated 3.5 g, Polyunsaturated 7 g), Cholesterol 145 mg, Sodium 150 mg, Iron 25%, Vitamin A 40%, Vitamin C 90%.

▲ *2 Bread, 1 Vegetable*

Top to bottom: Mediterranean-Style Lavash Rolls, Basil-Stuffed Methow Trout on a Bed of Caramelized Onions, Millet with Papaya and Orange-Mustard Vinaigrette

Mediterranean-Style Lavash Rolls

Lavash rolls are a hearty addition to an appetizer buffet. They can also be served for a light lunch. The yogurt cheese used in this recipe is a versatile base and an excellent substitute for sour cream. Add any variety of ingredients to it to use for dips, thickening soups, and spreads.

4 rounds *lavash* (recipe on page 159)
1 eggplant (aubergine), thinly sliced
¼ teaspoon salt
¾ cup (6 fl oz/180 ml) yogurt cheese (recipe follows)

4 large tomatoes, thinly sliced
1 head green-leaf lettuce
1 English (hothouse) cucumber, thinly sliced
¼ cup (¼ oz/7 g) mint leaves, minced
salt and freshly ground pepper to taste

1. Preheat a grill or broiler.
2. Lightly moisten the *lavash*, and wrap it in a damp towel for 25 minutes.
3. Sprinkle the eggplant slices with salt. Let stand for 20 minutes. Rinse, and pat dry. Place the slices on the grill or a lightly oiled baking sheet, and grill or broil 1 minute on each side.
4. Lay the softened *lavash* on a work surface. Spread each round with

one-third of the yogurt cheese. Make a layer of tomatoes, then half of the lettuce, then the cucumber and finish with the eggplant. Top with a thin layer of the remaining yogurt cheese. Sprinkle with the mint leaves and the salt and pepper.

5. Roll the bread up like a pinwheel, as tight as possible while keeping the layers in place. Wrap the roll tightly in plastic wrap, and refrigerate for at least 1 hour.

6. Remove the roll from the plastic wrap, place it on a cutting board, cut it into 1-in (2.5-cm) slices and arrange them on a platter lined with the remaining lettuce leaves.
   Serves 8 (4 rolls cut into 6–8 slices)

3–4 slices per serving: Calories 350, Protein 7 g, Carbohydrates 36 g, Fiber 4 g, Total fat 10 g (Saturated 1.5 g, Monounsaturated 7 g, Polyunsaturated 1 g), Cholesterol 0 mg, Sodium 35 mg, Vitamin A 20%, Vitamin C 40%.
▲ *1 Bread, 1 Vegetable*

YOGURT CHEESE

1 cup (8 fl oz/250 ml) plain low-fat yogurt without gelatin or stabilizers

1. Line a colander with cheesecloth (muslin), and place it over a large bowl. Place the yogurt in the cheesecloth; refrigerate and let it drain overnight.
   Yield ¾ cup (6 fl oz/180 ml)

¾ cup per serving: Calories 140, Protein 12 g, Carbohydrates 16 g, Fiber 0 g, Total fat 4 g (Saturated 2.5 g, Monounsaturated 1 g, Polyunsaturated 0 g), Cholesterol 15 mg, Sodium 160 mg, Calcium 40%.
▲ *1 Milk*

SEAFOOD / UNITED STATES

Basil-Stuffed Methow Trout on a Bed of Caramelized Onions

In the Methow Valley of the Pacific Northwest, streams burble and chuckle with clean, clear water and sparkling rainbow trout. What could be better than a little fly-fishing and a campground grill?

4 tablespoons (2 fl oz/60 ml) olive oil
1 lb (500 g) onions, very thinly sliced
¼ cup (2 fl oz/60 ml) balsamic vinegar
¼ teaspoon salt
freshly ground pepper to taste
4 whole trout, 10–12 oz (315–375 g) each, cleaned
8 large fresh basil leaves

1. Preheat a grill. Soak hickory chips in water for 30 minutes.

2. Heat 3 tablespoons of the oil in a large skillet. Add the onions, and cook until golden brown, stirring frequently, about 20 minutes. Add the vinegar, and cook until reduced and syrupy, about 2 minutes. Season with the salt and pepper, and set aside on a serving platter.

3. Brush the trout inside and out with the remaining olive oil. Place 2 basil leaves inside each fish. Sprinkle the hickory chips on the fire, and grill the trout until browned, about 4 minutes on each side. Remove to the platter over the caramelized onions, and serve at once.
   Serves 4

---

1 trout per serving: Calories 280, Protein 22 g, Carbohydrates 11 g, Fiber 2 g, Total fat 17 g (Saturated 2.5 g, Monounsaturated 11 g, Polyunsaturated 2.5 g), Cholesterol 55 mg, Sodium 180 mg.
▲ *1 Vegetable, 1 Meat*

GRAINS / ZIMBABWE

Millet with Papaya and Orange-Mustard Vinaigrette

Millet is the grain used for couscous in most of Africa, although packaged instant couscous is usually semolina. Millet is higher in B vitamins and minerals than brown rice or wheat is. This mild-flavored and crunchy grain adds fiber as well as nutrients to a meal. Papaya is one of the most delicious and antioxidant-rich fruits, providing vitamins A, C and E in abundance.

4 green (spring) onions, minced
2 teaspoons minced ginger
1 tablespoon coarse-grained mustard
¼ cup (2 fl oz/60 ml) freshly squeezed orange juice
¼ cup (2 fl oz/60 ml) sunflower oil
⅛ teaspoon salt
freshly ground pepper to taste
1 ripe papaya, peeled
2 oranges, peeled, seeded and cut into wedges
1 green papaya, peeled, seeded and grated coarsely
1 cup (7 oz/220 g) whole or cracked millet
3 cups (24 fl oz/750 ml) chicken stock (see glossary)

1. To make the orange-mustard vinaigrette, in a medium mixing bowl, combine the green onions, ginger, mustard and orange juice. Slowly drizzle in the sunflower oil, whisking constantly. Season with the salt and pepper. Set aside.

2. Remove the seeds from the ripe papaya, reserving 2 tablespoons of them, and slice the fruit ½ in (12 mm) thick. Combine the papaya slices, orange wedges, and grated green papaya. Toss with ¼ cup (2 fl oz/60 ml) of the vinaigrette. Set aside.

3. Cook the millet in simmering chicken stock for 20 minutes, covered. Drain any excess liquid, and toss the millet with the remaining vinaigrette. Place the millet on a serving platter, spoon the papaya mixture into the center and sprinkle with the reserved papaya seeds. Serve immediately.
   Serves 8

---

1 serving: Calories 210, Protein 4 g, Carbohydrates 30 g, Fiber 5 g, Total fat 9 g (Saturated 1 g, Monounsaturated 1.5 g, Polyunsaturated 6 g), Cholesterol 0 mg, Sodium 65 mg, Vitamin A 25%, Vitamin C 100%.
▲ *1 Bread, 1 Fruit*

GRAINS / BOLIVIA

Humita

QUINOA, CORN AND POTATOES STEAMED IN CORN HUSKS

Quinoa was one of the Incan staple foods, along with corn and potatoes, and has probably been in existence for thousands of years. It has the highest protein content of any grain, and its protein provides an excellent balance of the essential amino acids. It should be thoroughly rinsed before cooking, as it has a bitter coating that acts as a natural insect repellant.

> **12 fresh or dried corn husks**
> **½ cup (3 oz/90 g) quinoa**
> **1 medium potato, peeled and cut into ¼-in (6-mm) dice**
> **1 cup (4 oz/125 g) chopped onion**
> **2 cups (12 oz/370 g) fresh corn kernels**
> **¼ cup (⅓ oz/10 g) chopped fresh cilantro (fresh coriander)**
> **½ teaspoon salt**
> **freshly ground pepper to taste**

1. Soak the corn husks in warm water for 20 minutes.
2. Rinse the quinoa thoroughly. Place it in a saucepan with 1 cup (8 fl oz/250 ml) of water, the potato, and ½ cup (2 oz/60 g) of the onion. Bring to a boil, reduce to a simmer and cook for 12–15 minutes, until all the water is absorbed and the grains are transparent. Add the corn, the remaining onion and the cilantro. Season with the salt and pepper.
3. Spoon the mixture into the corn husks, fold the husks to close

them and place them in a steamer. Steam over boiling water for 15 minutes. Serve immediately.
Serves 6

2 husks per serving: Calories 130, Protein 4 g, Carbohydrates 27 g, Fiber 4 g, Total fat 1 g (Saturated 0 g, Monounsaturated 0 g, Polyunsaturated 1 g), Cholesterol 0 mg, Sodium 220 mg.
▲ *½ Bread, 1 Vegetable*

POULTRY / JAMAICA

Jerked Chicken

The spicy marinade in this dish is well known in the Caribbean. It varies from island to island but is usually a blend of sweet spices and peppers. Adjust the seasoning to your taste.

> **½ teaspoon ground cinnamon**
> **½ teaspoon ground allspice**
> **¼ teaspoon ground ginger**
> **¼ teaspoon ground nutmeg**
> **¼ teaspoon ground cloves**
> **½ teaspoon minced jalapeño chili pepper**
> **4 green (spring) onions, roughly chopped**
> **1 tablespoon olive oil**
> **salt and freshly ground pepper to taste**
> **4 half chicken breasts, skinned**

1. In a mortar, blend together the cinnamon, allspice, ginger, nutmeg, cloves, jalapeño and green onions.

2. Add the olive oil, salt and pepper.
3. Rub the paste on the chicken breasts, cover and marinate overnight in the refrigerator.
4. Preheat a grill, and grill the chicken 10 minutes on each side.
   Serves 4

---

*½ breast per serving: Calories 180, Protein 27 g, Carbohydrates 2 g,
Fiber 1 g, Total fat 7 g (Saturated 2 g, Monounsaturated 4 g,
Polyunsaturated 1 g), Cholesterol 75 mg, Sodium 65 mg.*
▲ *1 Meat*

PASTAS / ITALY

Orecchiette alla Barese

BARI-STYLE PASTA WITH CLAMS, SPINACH AND TOMATOES

*Bari is a coastal port in the southeastern region of Apulia, an area rich
in seafood from the Adriatic. One of the most popular pastas of the
region is* orecchiette, *which gets its name from its shape, like little ears.
It is very easy to make and can also be found dried in most Italian
groceries or gourmet food stores. Clams make this recipe an excellent
source of iron and a good source of zinc and other minerals.*

1 cup (5 oz/155 g) unbleached all-purpose (plain) flour
2 cups (10 oz/315 g) whole-wheat (wholemeal) flour
3 dozen clams, scrubbed
3 tablespoons olive oil
4 cloves garlic, minced
½ cup (2 oz/60 g) chopped onion
½ lb (250 g) fresh spinach, coarsely chopped
3 ripe tomatoes, peeled, seeded and coarsely chopped
1 tablespoon minced fresh parsley
¼ teaspoon salt
freshly ground pepper to taste
3 tablespoons grated *pecorino* cheese

1. To make the *orecchiette*, mix the flours together. Make a well in
   the center, and add 1 cup (8 fl oz/250 ml) water, stirring to
   incorporate. Turn the dough onto a floured work surface and
   knead, adding flour as needed, until smooth and no longer sticky.
   Cut into 4 pieces, cover and let rest 15 minutes. Roll each piece
   into a long sausage shape, about ½ in (12 mm) thick. Cut crosswise
   into ⅛-in (3-mm) slices. Press the center of each slice firmly with
   a floured thumb so that the edges curl up to resemble an ear. Let
   the *orecchiette* dry on a floured work surface until ready to use.
2. Place the clams in a large pot with 1 in (2.5 cm) of water. Cover
   and cook over high heat for 1 minute. Remove the clams that have
   opened; cook any remaining clams a few seconds longer, until
   they open. When the clams are cool enough to handle, remove
   the meat from the shells, catching and reserving any stock in the
   shells. Rinse the clam meat well, to remove any sand, and chop
   coarsely. Set aside. Strain the cooking stock through cheesecloth
   (muslin) or a fine-mesh seive, to remove sand, and reserve.
3. In a large skillet, heat the olive oil. Sauté the garlic and onion until
   lightly golden. Add the spinach, and cook for 1 minute. Add the
   tomatoes and reserved clam stock; bring to a boil. Reduce to a

simmer, and add the *orecchiette*. Cook for 3–4 minutes, until the
pasta is al dente. Add the reserved clams, parsley, salt and pepper.
Sprinkle the *pecorino* on top, and serve immediately.
Serves 6 *Photograph page 4*

---

*1¼ cups per serving: Calories 350, Protein 17 g, Carbohydrates 52 g,
Fiber 8 g, Total fat 9 g (Saturated 2 g, Monounsaturated 5 g,
Polyunsaturated 1 g), Cholesterol 20 mg, Sodium 200 mg, Iron 60%,
Vitamin A 60%, Vitamin C 40%.*
▲ *2 Bread, 1 Vegetable, 1 Meat*

APPETIZERS / ITALY

Grilled Pizza Carciofi

*Semolina flour gives this crust a crackery texture, which holds up nicely
to grilling. Any variety of toppings may be used. Grilling the pizza
keeps the topping fresh and moist; oven baking sometimes dries it out.
If sodium is a concern, reduce the salt to 1 teaspoon.*

1 package (¼ oz/7 g) active dry yeast
2 tablespoons sugar
3½ cups (18½ oz/575 g) all-purpose (plain) flour
½ cup (2½ oz/75 g) semolina flour
1 tablespoon salt
4 tablespoons (2 fl oz/60 ml) olive oil
4 oz (125 g) part-skim mozzarella cheese, grated
2 artichoke hearts, steamed and sliced
2 Roma (plum/egg) tomatoes, sliced
1 tablespoon rosemary leaves

1. Dissolve the yeast and sugar in 1½ cups (12 fl oz/375 ml) of
   warm water (105°–115°F/40°–46°C). Let stand until foamy,
   about 5 minutes.
2. In a large mixing bowl, combine the all-purpose flour, semolina and
   salt. Make a well in the center, and add the yeast mixture and
   3 tablespoons of the olive oil. Work the liquids into the flour mixture
   until the dough is stiff. Turn it onto a lightly floured work surface,
   and knead until smooth and not sticky. Shape into a ball, place in
   a lightly oiled bowl, cover with a towel and let rise for 30 minutes.
3. Punch the dough down, and divide it into 8 balls. Let them rest,
   covered, for 45 minutes.
4. Preheat a grill, and brush the rack with olive oil.
5. Roll the balls into 6-in (15-cm) circles, and brush them lightly
   with 1 teaspoon of the remaining olive oil. Sprinkle the mozzarella onto each pizza, leaving a ½-in (12-mm) border free of
   topping. Arrange the artichoke hearts and tomato slices on top,
   and brush lightly with the remaining olive oil. Sprinkle with the
   rosemary leaves.
6. Grill over medium-high heat for 6–8 minutes, until the dough is
   firm and lightly browned and the cheese is melted, or bake at
   450°F (230°C) for 10 minutes.
   Makes eight 6-in (15-cm) pizzas *Photograph page 4*

---

*1 pizza per serving: Calories 340, Protein 11 g, Carbohydrates 55 g,
Fiber 3 g, Total fat 8 g (Saturated 2 g, Monounsaturated 4.5 g,
Polyunsaturated 1 g), Cholesterol 10 mg, Sodium 950 mg.*
▲ *1 Bread, 1 Vegetable, ½ Milk*

Clockwise from top: Cantonese Bamboo-Steamed Flounder; Barbecued Shrimp on Sugarcane with Spicy Peanut Sauce; Spicy Sour Vegetables

Barbecued Shrimp on Sugarcane with Spicy Peanut Sauce

This delightfully fresh appetizer typifies the Vietnamese love for fresh vegetables. The sugarcane imparts a subtle sweetness while providing a vehicle to barbecue the shrimp paste. If fresh sugarcane is not available, use canned sugarcane.

PEANUT SAUCE

    1 teaspoon peanut (groundnut) oil
    2 teaspoons minced garlic
    1 tablespoon minced fresh cilantro (fresh coriander)
    2 tablespoons dry-roasted peanuts (groundnuts)
    2 tablespoons soy sauce
    1 tablespoon sugar
    ¼ teaspoon chili paste, or to taste
    ¼ cup (2 fl oz/60 ml) chicken stock (see glossary)

SHRIMP

    1 lb (500 g) shrimp (prawns), shelled, deveined and patted dry
    4 cloves garlic
    2 green (spring) onions, cut into 1-in (2.5-cm) lengths
    1 tablespoon sugar
    1 tablespoon sesame oil
    1 tablespoon soy sauce
    1 egg white
    1 fresh or canned sugarcane, peeled and cut into six
       3-in (7.5-cm) pieces
    assorted fresh vegetables: bean sprouts, coarsely grated
       carrot and daikon radish, julienned cucumber, chopped
       fresh mint and fresh cilantro (fresh coriander)
    1 small head green-leaf lettuce
    12 sheets rice paper

1. To make the peanut sauce, heat the peanut oil in a small sauté pan, and cook the minced garlic until golden brown. Place in a blender, and add the minced cilantro, peanuts, soy sauce, sugar, chili paste and chicken stock. Blend until smooth. Transfer the sauce to a serving dish, and set aside.

2. In a food processor, make a paste of the shrimp, garlic cloves and

scallions. Add the sugar, sesame oil, soy sauce and egg white; pulse until well blended. Chill at least 20 minutes.

3. Split the sugarcane pieces into fourths lengthwise, and pat the chilled shrimp paste firmly around the middle two-thirds of each piece of cane. Place the pieces on a sheet pan, and chill until ready to cook.

4. Heat a grill or broiler, and brush it lightly with oil. Barbecue the shrimp-coated sugarcane pieces for about 5–7 minutes, turning to brown all sides lightly.

5. Arrange the fresh vegetables on a serving platter with the lettuce leaves and rice paper. Serve the shrimp with the vegetables, rice paper, bowls of warm water and peanut sauce. Guests dip a sheet of rice paper in the warm water until softened, then fill it with their choice of vegetables and bits of the barbecued shrimp pulled from the sugarcane.

---

2 pieces per serving: Calories 180, Protein 18 g, Carbohydrates 14 g, Fiber 1 g, Total fat 6 g (Saturated 1 g, Monounsaturated 2 g, Polyunsaturated 2 g), Cholesterol 115 mg, Sodium 550 mg, Vitamin A 35%.
▲ *1 Vegetable, 1 Meat*

VEGETABLES / INDONESIA

Sayur Asam

SPICY SOUR VEGETABLES

Tamarind is a bittersweet fruit with shelled pods that contain seeds. The pulp is sold in Asian, Indian and South American markets, slightly dried, in blocks. When using the whole pods, remove the shell and coarse strings. After soaking the pods in hot water for 30 minutes, knead the pulp away from the seeds. If tamarind is unavailable, substitute ¼ cup (2 fl oz/60 ml) lemon juice and 1 teaspoon sugar for the tamarind and hot water. Sayur asam is delectable as a complement to skewered grilled chicken, known as satay *in Indonesia, or serve it as a side dish over rice.*

¼ cup (4 oz/125 g) tamarind pulp
1 onion, coarsely chopped
2 cloves garlic, minced
4 cups (32 fl oz/1 l) chicken stock (see glossary)
1 bay leaf
1 tablespoon sugar
1 eggplant (aubergine), cut into 2-in (5-cm) cubes
¼ lb (125 g) green beans, ends trimmed and cut into 1-in (2.5-cm) pieces
¼ lb (125 g) cauliflower, cut into florets
2 cups (12 oz/375 g) fresh or frozen or drained canned baby corn
juice of 1 lime
¼ lb (125 g) mung bean sprouts
½ teaspoon Indonesian *sambal* paste or chili paste, or to taste

1. Break the tamarind pulp into small pieces, and pour ½ cup (4 fl oz/125 ml) of hot water over. Let stand 30 minutes, then mash with a wooden spoon. Strain, pressing to extract as much liquid as possible. Set the liquid aside, and discard the pulp.

2. In a food processor, purée the onion and garlic with ½ cup (4 fl oz/125 ml) of the chicken stock. Place the purée in a stockpot

with the remaining chicken stock, and bring to a boil. Add the bay leaf and sugar, and reduce to a simmer. Add the eggplant and green beans, and simmer, covered, for 10 minutes. Add the cauliflower, corn, and reserved tamarind juice. Cook 3–5 minutes longer, until the vegetables are tender but still firm.

3. Stir in the lime juice and bean sprouts. Add the *sambal* or chili paste, adjusting the spiciness to taste. Remove the bay leaf, and serve at once.
   Serves 8

---

1 cup per serving: Calories 100, Protein 3 g, Carbohydrates 21 g, Fiber 3 g, Total fat 1 g (Saturated .5 g, Monounsaturated .5 g, Polyunsaturated .5 g), Cholesterol 0 mg, Sodium 25 mg, Vitamin C 35%.
▲ *2 Vegetable*

SEAFOOD / CHINA

Cantonese Bamboo-Steamed Flounder

If you don't have a bamboo steamer, improvise, using a deep, covered stockpot and elevating the food on a rack at least ½ inch (12 mm) above the boiling water. Any fish will cook quickly and stay moist when you steam it. Allow less time for fillets, about 4-6 minutes, depending on the thickness.

2 lb (1 kg) whole flounder or sole, cleaned, with head and tail intact
¼ cup (2 fl oz/60 ml) rice wine
1 tablespoon soy sauce
2 teaspoons sesame oil
1 tablespoon minced fresh gingerroot
1 clove garlic, minced
4 large leaves Napa cabbage
1 carrot, cut lengthwise into thin shreds
1 piece of fresh gingerroot, about 2-in (5-cm), peeled and cut lengthwise into thin shreds
1 green (spring) onion, thinly sliced crosswise

1. Set up a bamboo steamer.

2. Rinse the flounder or sole well, and pat dry. Score the fish on both sides with deep diagonal slices, 1 in (2.5 cm) apart. Place the fish in a shallow dish.

3. In a small bowl, combine the rice wine, soy sauce, sesame oil, minced ginger and garlic. Pour over the fish, rubbing the sauce into the slices. Let marinate for 30 minutes.

4. Line the bottom of the steamer with the cabbage leaves. Arrange the fish on top, and sprinkle it with the carrot, shredded ginger and green onion.

5. Steam the fish for 7–8 minutes, or until cooked through. Serve at once from the bamboo steamer.
   Serves 4

---

1 serving: Calories 180, Protein 33 g, Carbohydrates 3 g, Fiber 1 g, Total fat 3 g (Saturated .5 g, Monounsaturated .5 g, Polyunsaturated 1 g), Cholesterol 80 mg, Sodium 210 mg, Vitamin A 120%, Vitamin C 20%.
▲ *1 Meat*

Lecsó

This versatile dish appears in many forms on tables in Hungary: as a sauce, an appetizer and a side dish to accompany poultry and seafood dishes. It freezes well for use later in chicken paprikás *(recipe on page 86).*

2 tablespoons olive oil
1 large onion, thinly sliced
½ lb (250 g) sweet red and green bell peppers (capsicums), seeded and sliced
½ lb (250 g) banana peppers, seeded and sliced
3 large fresh tomatoes, peeled, seeded and coarsely chopped
1 tablespoon medium-hot Hungarian paprika, or to taste
2 teaspoons sugar
½ teaspoon salt

1. Heat the olive oil in a large skillet. Add the onion, and cook to a light golden color, about 5 minutes.
2. Add the peppers and cook until soft but not browned, about 2–3 minutes.
3. Stir in the tomatoes, paprika, sugar and salt. Heat through.

Serves 4

---

1 cup per serving: Calories 160, Protein 4 g, Carbohydrates 22 g, Fiber 5 g, Total fat 8 g (Saturated 1 g, Monounsaturated 5 g, Polyunsaturated 1 g), Cholesterol 0 mg, Sodium 310 mg, Vitamin A 80%, Vitamin C 430%.

▲ *2 Vegetable*

Escabeche

Escabeche is a spicy, cold marinade originally used to preserve cooked meat. It also refers to the marinating of raw meats and seafood in citrus, often called "ceviche." Unfortunately, eating raw meat and seafood is not safe. We are returning to the practice of seasoning cooked meat with a delicious marinade. In this recipe, poached chicken is tossed with a cilantro pesto and served in a lemon half.

4 lemons, halved
2 cloves garlic
1 cup (1 oz/30 g) fresh cilantro (fresh coriander) leaves
⅓ cup (2 oz/60 g) pine nuts
3 tablespoons safflower oil
1 cup (8 fl oz/250 ml) chicken stock (see glossary)
1 whole chicken breast, skinned and boned
1 red bell pepper (capsicum), diced
1 ear (cob) of corn, kernels removed and blanched (see glossary)
¼ cup (1¼ oz/35 g) diced jícama (yam bean)
salt and freshly ground pepper to taste

1. Remove the pulp from the lemon halves; strain the pulp to reserve the juice, and then discard. Cut a small slice from the bottom of each lemon half so that it will sit level.
2. To make the cilantro pesto, with a food processor running, drop in the garlic. Add the cilantro leaves, pine nuts, the reserved lemon juice and the safflower oil. Process to a smooth paste, and set aside.
3. Bring the chicken stock to a boil. Add the chicken breast, and reduce the stock to a simmer. Cook for 20 minutes, until the chicken is tender. Remove the chicken from the stock to cool. Reserve the stock for another use.
4. Dice the cooled chicken. Add the red pepper, corn, jícama and cilantro pesto, and toss together well. Season with the salt and pepper. Chill at least 1 hour.
5. Spoon the chicken mixture into the lemon halves, and serve immediately.

Serves 8

½ filled lemon per serving: Calories 140, Protein 9 g, Carbohydrates 7 g, Fiber 1 g, Total fat 10 g (Saturated 1 g, Monounsaturated 2 g, Polyunsaturated 6 g), Cholesterol 20 mg, Sodium 20 mg, Vitamin C 60%.

▲ *1 Vegetable, ½ Meat*

Piperrada

Piperrada is a specialty of both Spanish and French Basque cuisines and is typically made by scrambling eggs with peppers and tomatoes. This variation offers poached eggs on top of a vegetable mixture. With crusty bread and a beverage, it is a complete meal.

2 tablespoons olive oil
½ cup (2 oz/60 g) coarsely chopped onion
2 red bell peppers (capsicums), seeded and cut into 1-in (2.5-cm) pieces
1 green bell pepper (capsicum), seeded and cut into 1-in (2.5-cm) pieces
1 yellow bell pepper (capsicum), seeded and cut into 1-in (2.5-cm) pieces
2 large fresh tomatoes (about 1 lb/500 g), peeled, seeded and cut into 1-in (2.5-cm) pieces
1 teaspoon finely minced fresh parsley
½ teaspoon finely minced fresh rosemary
¼ teaspoon salt
freshly ground pepper to taste
1 teaspoon sherry wine vinegar
4 eggs

1. In a large skillet, heat the olive oil and sauté the onion until soft, about 5 minutes. Stir in the red, green and yellow peppers, and cook 5 minutes. Add the tomatoes, parsley and rosemary; continue to cook for 10 minutes. Season with the salt and pepper, and place on serving dishes. Keep warm until ready to serve.
2. Heat 1 in (2.5 cm) of water to boiling in a skillet. Add the vinegar, and reduce to a simmer. Break the eggs, one at a time, into a small dish, and gently slip each one into the water. Cook until the whites are firm, about 5 minutes. Remove with a slotted spoon, and place on top of the vegetable mixture. Serve immediately.

Serves 4

---

1 serving: Calories 180, Protein 8 g, Carbohydrates 11 g, Fiber 3 g, Total fat 13 g (Saturated 2.5 g, Monounsaturated 7 g, Polyunsaturated 1.5 g), Cholesterol 220 mg, Sodium 220 mg, Vitamin A 60%, Vitamin C 250%.

▲ *1 Vegetable, ½ Meat*

Clockwise from top: Lecsó, Piperrada, Escabeche

Hong Kong Fresh Watermelon Juice

The summer heat can be draining in Hong Kong. The best shopping is done at the night market in Kowloon, where juice makers cut fruit and juice it while you wait. Nothing can quench a thirst like cold watermelon juiced on the spot.

5 lb (2.5 kg) watermelon, chilled

1. Remove the peel, and cut the melon into 2-in (5-cm) pieces. Pass them through a juicer, or remove the seeds, purée the watermelon in a blender, and strain the purée. Drink at once.
   Makes 8 glasses

1 glass per serving: Calories 90, Protein 2 g, Carbohydrates 20 g, Fiber 2 g, Total fat 1 g (Saturated .5 g, Monounsaturated 0 g, Polyunsaturated 0 g), Cholesterol 0 mg, Sodium 6 mg, Vitamin A 20%, Vitamin C 45%.
▲ *1 Fruit*

Grilled Plantains with Pigeon Peas and Rice

Pigeon peas (gungo peas) and rice are staples on most Caribbean islands. You can substitute kidney beans if the peas are not available. Plantains are delicious to eat at each stage of ripening. The riper they are, the sweeter they taste. For this recipe, pick some that are not overripe, still firm enough to hold their shape when grilled.

1 cup (5 oz/155 g) fresh pigeon peas or ¾ cup (6 oz/185 g) dried kidney beans, soaked in water overnight
2 cups (16 fl oz/500 ml) chicken stock (see glossary)
¾ cup (6 fl oz/180 ml) coconut milk (coconut water)
2 cloves garlic, minced
3 green (spring) onions, thinly sliced
1 cup (7 oz/220 g) long-grain white rice
salt and freshly ground pepper to taste
3 tablespoons olive oil
1 onion, finely chopped
5 cloves garlic, mashed
1 tablespoon grated fresh gingerroot
⅓ cup (3 fl oz/80 ml) freshly squeezed orange juice
4 large yellow-ripe plantains, peeled

1. Place the pigeon peas or the soaked, drained kidney beans in a large saucepan with the chicken stock, coconut milk and minced garlic. Bring to a boil. Reduce to a simmer, and cook for 20 minutes (45 minutes for the kidney beans).

Top to bottom: Hong Kong Fresh Watermelon Juice; Grilled Plantains with Pigeon Peas and Rice; Flying Fish with Lime, Guava and Pineapple Glaze

2. Add the green onions and rice, and cook, covered, for 20 minutes, or until all the liquid has been absorbed.
3. Season with the salt and pepper, and keep warm as you prepare the plantains.
4. Heat the olive oil in a medium nonstick sauté pan. Add the onion, and sauté until translucent.
5. In a small bowl, mix together the mashed garlic, ginger, orange juice and salt to taste. Stir into the onions, and heat through. Set aside.
6. Slice each plantain diagonally into 4 pieces. Skewer and brush with the garlic-orange oil. Grill slowly, basting and turning frequently.
7. Serve the plantains over the peas and rice.
   Serves 8

1 cup plus 2 plantain slices per serving: Calories 390, Protein 6 g, Carbohydrates 71 g, Fiber 2 g, Total fat 12 g (Saturated 6 g, Monounsaturated 4 g, Polyunsaturated 1 g), Cholesterol 0 mg, Sodium 15 mg, Vitamin A 30%, Vitamin C 70%.
▲ *1 Bread, 1 Fruit, ½ Meat*

Flying Fish with Lime, Guava and Pineapple Glaze

While flying fish conjure memories of sparkling Caribbean waters, sole or trout would also be quite tasty prepared this way. If you don't have a bamboo steamer, improvise, using a deep, covered stockpot and elevating the food on a rack at least ½ inch (12 mm) above the boiling water.

1 fresh pineapple, peeled, cored and cubed
1 ripe guava, peeled and seeded
2 cloves garlic, finely minced
1 teaspoon grated fresh gingerroot
¼ teaspoon minced jalapeño chili pepper (optional)
zest of ½ lime
juice of 3 limes
6 flying fish or sole fillets, about 2 lb (1 kg)
3 green (spring) onions, thinly sliced

1. In a blender, purée the pineapple and guava with the garlic, ginger, jalapeño, lime zest and lime juice.
2. Transfer the purée to a saucepan, and cook over medium-high heat for 10 minutes, stirring frequently. Set aside.
3. Rinse the fillets, and pat dry. Roll them up, and secure each roll with a toothpick. Place the fillets in a bamboo steamer, and steam over boiling water for 10 minutes.
4. Remove the fillets to a serving platter, spoon pineapple glaze over them and garnish with the green onions.
   Serves 6

1 glazed fillet per serving: Calories 240, Protein 30 g, Carbohydrates 27 g, Fiber 4 g, Total fat 3 g (Saturated .5 g, Monounsaturated .5 g, Polyunsaturated 1 g), Cholesterol 75 mg, Sodium 125 mg, Vitamin C 100%.
▲ *1 Fruit, 1 Meat*

Streuselkuchen

CHERRY CRUMB CAKE

Cherries are magnificent in Germany in the early summer. Other seasonal fruits—plums, apples or peaches—are delicious on this cake as well.

1 package (¼ oz/7 g) active dry yeast

½ cup (4 fl oz/125 ml) warm low-fat (1-percent) milk (105°–115°F/40°–46°C)

½ cup (4 oz/125 g) sugar

3 tablespoons safflower oil

2 eggs

3¼ cups (16½ oz/515 g) all-purpose (plain) flour

¼ teaspoon salt

Left to right: Cherry Crumb Cake, Carrot-Apple-Blueberry Cake with Blueberry Sauce (recipe page 139)

1 lb (500 g) fresh cherries, halved and pitted
3 tablespoons unsalted butter
zest of ½ lemon, finely grated
½ teaspoon cinnamon

1. In the bowl of an electric mixer, combine 3 cups (15 oz/470 g) of the flour, all but ¼ cup (2 oz/60 g) of the remaining sugar and the salt. Add the yeast mixture, and, using a dough hook, beat until smooth and elastic. Place in a lightly oiled bowl and let rise, covered, until doubled in bulk, about 1 hour.
2. Preheat an oven to 375°F (190°C). Lightly oil a 10-in (25-cm) round cake pan. Dissolve the yeast in the warm milk with ½ teaspoon of the sugar. Let stand for 5 minutes, until foamy. Add the oil and eggs.
3. Punch down the dough, and knead lightly, about 5 minutes. Let rest 10 minutes, then press into the cake pan. Cover and let rise for 30 minutes.
4. Press the cherries into the dough, cut side up.
5. Rub together the remaining sugar, remaining flour, butter, lemon zest and cinnamon, until the mixture is crumbly. Sprinkle over the cake.
6. Bake for 30 minutes, until the cake is golden. Cool 10 minutes before slicing.
   Serves 12

1 serving: Calories 240, Protein 6 g, Carbohydrates 41 g, Fiber 2 g, Total fat 8 g (Saturated 2.5 g, Monounsaturated 2 g, Polyunsaturated 3 g), Cholesterol 45 mg, Sodium 65 mg.
▲ *1 Bread, 1 Fruit*

Left to right: Sangria, Tahitian Rum Punch

Sangria

Serve this wine punch in a large glass pitcher to show off its ruby red color and array of fresh fruit. Adjust the sweetness with a little sugar if the orange juice is tart. Or make a nonalcoholic fruited iced tea by adding 4 cups (32 fl oz/1 l) of brewed tea instead of the wine.

1 bottle (750 ml) dry red wine
1⅓ cups (11 fl oz/340 ml) orange juice
1 fresh peach, halved and sliced
1 small orange, halved and sliced
½ lemon, halved and sliced
1 lime, halved and sliced
½ cup (2 oz/60 g) sliced strawberries
sparkling water to taste (optional)

1. Combine all the ingredients in a nonreactive container, and let stand at least 3 hours or as long as overnight, refrigerated.
2. Transfer to a large glass pitcher, and serve additional sparkling water on the side. Provide goblets large enough to accommodate the fruit.
   Makes 6 glasses

1 glass per serving: Calories 130, Protein 1 g, Carbohydrates 12 g, Fiber 2 g, Total fat 0 g (Saturated 0 g, Monounsaturated 0 g, Polyunsaturated 0 g), Cholesterol 0 mg, Sodium 15 mg.
▲ *1 Fruit*

Tahitian Rum Punch

It's really hot during Tahiti's summer. The best thing to do is to sit in the shade, count flying fish and sip Tahitian rum punch.

1 mango, peeled, seeded and diced
1 banana, diced
1 orange, seeded and diced
1 small papaya, about ½ lb (250 g), peeled, seeded and diced
4 cups (32 fl oz/1 l) pineapple juice
2 cups (16 fl oz/500 ml) rum
1 cup (8 fl oz/250 ml) cane sugar syrup, or 1 cup (8 oz/250 g) sugar dissolved in ½ cup (4 fl oz/125 ml) boiling water and cooled
juice of 4 limes
2 vanilla beans (pods), split lengthwise
hibiscus flowers for garnish

1. Combine all the ingredients, and refrigerate for at least 3 hours. Serve over ice.
   Serves 8

1 glass per serving: Calories 370, Protein 1 g, Carbohydrates 62 g, Fiber 2 g, Total fat 0 g (Saturated 0 g, Monounsaturated 0 g, Polyunsaturated 0 g), Cholesterol 0 mg, Sodium 55 mg, Vitamin A 30%, Vitamin C 90%.
▲ *2 Fruit, 1 Fat/Sugar*

Carrot-Apple-Blueberry Cake with Blueberry Sauce

Moist ingredients such as apple and carrot in this cake cut down the need for oil or fat. You can eliminate the blueberries when they are not available, and dust the cake with confectioners' (icing) sugar instead.

1½ cups (7½ oz/235 g) all-purpose (plain) flour
½ cup (2½ oz/75 g) whole-wheat (wholemeal) pastry flour
2 teaspoons baking powder
2 teaspoons cinnamon
1 teaspoon baking soda (bicarbonate of soda)
¼ teaspoon salt
1 cup (8 oz/250 g) sugar
½ cup (3½ oz/105 g) firmly packed brown sugar
3 eggs
½ cup (4 fl oz/125 ml) buttermilk
½ cup (4 fl oz/125 ml) vegetable oil
3 carrots, coarsely grated
2 Granny Smith or pippin apples, peeled and diced
2 cups (8 oz/250 g) blueberries
3 cups (24 fl oz/750 ml) blueberry sauce (recipe follows)

1. Preheat an oven to 350°F (180°C). Lightly oil and flour a 10-cup (2½-qt/2½-l) nonstick Bundt pan.
2. In a medium mixing bowl, combine the flours. Add the baking powder, cinnamon, baking soda and salt, and mix well.
3. In a large mixing bowl, whisk together the sugar, brown sugar and eggs. Add the buttermilk, oil, carrots and apples. Blend in the flour mixture, stirring just until mixed; do not over-work. Gently fold in the blueberries, and pour the batter into the pan.
4. Bake 1 hour, or until the cake pulls away from the sides of the pan. Cool in the pan on a rack for 15 minutes. Invert onto a serving plate, and spoon the blueberry sauce on the side.
Serves 12

1 slice with sauce per serving: Calories 370, Protein 5 g, Carbohydrates 64 g, Fiber 5 g, Total fat 11 g (Saturated 1 g, Monounsaturated 6 g, Polyunsaturated 3 g), Cholesterol 55 mg, Sodium 190 mg, Vitamin A 100%.
▲ 1 Bread, 2 Fruit

BLUEBERRY SAUCE

4 cups (16 oz/500 g) blueberries
½ cup (4 oz/125 g) sugar
¼ teaspoon cinnamon
½ cup (4 fl oz/125 ml) apple juice

1. Combine 2 cups (8 oz/250 g) of the blueberries and the sugar, cinnamon and apple juice in a medium saucepan. Bring to a boil;

Tropical Fruit Platter

reduce to a simmer, and cook for 10 minutes. Purée in a blender and strain.
2. Add the remaining blueberries.
Makes 3 cups (24 fl oz/750 ml)   *Photograph page 136*

¼ cup per serving: Calories 70, Protein 0 g, Carbohydrates 16 g, Fiber 2 g, Total fat 0 g (Saturated 0 g, Monounsaturated 0 g, Polyunsaturated 0 g), Cholesterol 0 mg, Sodium 0 mg.
▲ 1 Fruit

Tropical Fruit Platter

Some tropical fruits, such as the star apple, genip, soursop and cashew fruit, are found only near their sources because they are too delicate to transport or their season is too short. Here is an exotic and sumptuous display of tropical fruits, many of which are now readily available, as cultivation extends to other areas and transportation methods improve. Create your own combination, adding seasonal domestic fruits as well, such as strawberries, watermelons, kumquats, grapes and kiwis. Coconut contains about 2 grams of saturated fat per tablespoon, but a little coconut adds tropical flavor and texture.

1 ripe papaya, about 1 lb (500 g)
1 ripe white sapote
1 ripe mango
1 pineapple, cut into quarters lengthwise, core removed
about 10 manzano bananas (ladyfingers)
1 feijoa
4 passion fruits
¼ cup (2 fl oz/60 ml) freshly squeezed lime juice
2 tablespoons flaked coconut

1. To prepare the papaya, peel it with a paring knife, and cut it in half lengthwise. Scoop out the seeds, and cut the fruit into ½-in (12-mm) slices.
2. To prepare the white sapote, cut the fruit in half through the stem, and scoop out the pulp with a melon baller.
3. To prepare the mango, cut it in half, slicing as close as possible to the large, flat pit. Slice the flesh into cubes, cutting down to, but not through, the skin on each half. Turn inside out, so that the cubes pop out, and slice off the skin.
4. To prepare the pineapple, slice along the inside of the skin to remove the flesh in one long piece, reserving the shell. Cut into ½-in (12-mm) slices and place back in the shell.
5. To prepare the bananas, peel and use whole or cut crosswise diagonally into 1-in (2.5-cm) slices.
6. To prepare the feijoa, peel it, and cut into dice.
7. To prepare the passion fruits, cut in half, and spoon out the flesh.
8. Arrange the prepared fruit on a platter. Sprinkle with the lime juice and coconut. Serve at once or after chilling.
Serves 12

1 serving: Calories 130, Protein 2 g, Carbohydrates 32 g, Fiber 4 g, Total fat 1 g (Saturated .5 g, Monounsaturated 0 g, Polyunsaturated 0 g), Cholesterol 0 mg, Sodium 10 mg, Vitamin A 25%, Vitamin C 70%.
▲ 2 Fruit

Top to bottom: Buckwheat Crêpes Filled with Berries and Cream, Cranberry Gingerade

Buckwheat Crêpes Filled with Berries and Cream

It's up to you—cream or no cream. You'll probably find that vanilla low-fat yogurt is just as good. Top the crêpes with a little toasted muesli.

1¼ cups (10 fl oz/310 ml) low-fat (1-percent) milk
2 eggs
1 tablespoon safflower oil
½ teaspoon vanilla extract (essence)
½ cup (2½ oz/75 g) all-purpose (plain) flour
½ cup (2½ oz/75 g) buckwheat flour
2 tablespoons sugar
2 cups (8 oz/250 g) fresh strawberries, sliced
2 cups (8 oz/250 g) fresh blueberries
2 bananas, sliced
½ cup (4 fl oz/125 ml) heavy (double) cream, whipped with
    2 tablespoons confectioners' (icing) sugar, or ½ cup
    (3½ oz/105 g) low-fat vanilla yogurt
1 tablespoon confectioners' (icing) sugar
fresh strawberry sauce (recipe on page 97)
3 tablespoons *muesli* (recipe on page 177), toasted at 350°F
    (180°C) for 7–10 minutes, until golden brown

1. In a blender, combine the milk, eggs, oil and vanilla. Blend well. Add the flours and sugar, and process until smooth.
2. Heat a nonstick skillet. Ladle 3 tablespoons of batter into the pan, and tip the pan to spread the batter in a thin layer. Cook for 20–30 seconds on each side, until golden. Remove the crêpes to a sheet of parchment paper to cool. Stack the cooled crêpes between pieces of parchment until ready to use.
3. In a large mixing bowl combine the strawberries, blueberries and bananas. Fold in half of the whipped cream or yogurt.
4. Spoon a generous amount of filling in the center of each crêpe. Fold up one end and fold in the sides. With one end open, place the crêpes, folded side down, on individual serving plates. Some of the filling may tumble out the open end.
5. Dust with the confectioners' sugar, and spoon some strawberry sauce on the plate. Garnish with a spoonful of the remaining cream or yogurt. Sprinkle with the toasted *muesli*, and serve at once.
Serves 8

---

1 serving with cream: Calories 270, Protein 6 g, Carbohydrates 42 g, Fiber 5 g, Total fat 10 g (Saturated 4.5 g, Monounsaturated 2.5 g, Polyunsaturated 2 g), Cholesterol 75 mg, Sodium 45 mg, Vitamin C 100%.
▲ *1 Bread, 1 Fruit, 1 Fat/Sugar*

---

1 serving with yogurt: Calories 230, Protein 7 g, Carbohydrates 42 g, Fiber 5 g, Total fat 5 g (Saturated 1 g, Monounsaturated 1 g, Polyunsaturated 2 g), Cholesterol 55 mg, Sodium 50 mg, Vitamin C 100%.
▲ *1 Bread, 1 Fruit*

Cranberry Gingerade

The principle of an infused simple syrup is used in this drink. Make extra ginger base (sugar, water and ginger), and keep it on hand in the refrigerator for a quick refreshment.

¼ cup (2 oz/60 g) sugar
¼ cup (½ oz/15 g) minced fresh gingerroot
8 cups (64 fl oz/2 l) cranberry cocktail
1 lime, cut into 8 wedges

1. Heat the sugar and ¾ cup (6 fl oz/180 ml) of water in a medium saucepan, stirring to dissolve the sugar. Add the ginger, and simmer for 5 minutes. Remove from the heat, cover and let stand until cool.
2. Strain out the ginger, and mix the liquid with the cranberry cocktail. Chill.
3. Serve over ice in chilled glasses with a lime wedge.
Serves 8

---

1 glass per serving: Calories 180, Protein 0 g, Carbohydrates 45 g, Fiber 0 g, Total fat 0 g (Saturated 0 g, Monounsaturated 0 g, Polyunsaturated 0 g), Cholesterol 0 mg, Sodium 10 mg, Vitamin C 180%.
▲ *1 Fruit, 1 Fat/Sugar*

Pacific Northwest Fresh-Picked Berry Cobbler

Summer in the Pacific Northwest wouldn't be complete without annual berry-picking expeditions. July is probably the peak month for raspberries, blackberries, currants and blueberries, and you could even find a few last strawberries. Berries of all types are good sources of fiber.

6 cups (24 oz/750 g) fresh-picked berries (yellow or red
   raspberries, mulberries, blackberries, boysenberries, red
   currants, blueberries and/or sliced strawberries)
½ cup (4 fl oz/125 ml) freshly squeezed orange juice
½ cup (4 oz/125 g) plus 2 teaspoons sugar
1 teaspoon orange zest
1 tablespoon cornstarch (cornflour) dissolved in
   1 tablespoon water
½ cup (2½ oz/75 g) all-purpose (plain) flour
pinch of salt
½ teaspoon ground cinnamon
¾ teaspoon baking powder
3 tablespoons unsalted butter

¼ cup (2 fl oz/60 ml) low-fat (1-percent) milk
½ cup (4 fl oz/125 ml) vanilla low-fat yogurt

1. Preheat an oven to 375°F (190°C). Lightly oil a 9-in (23-cm) square baking dish.
2. Clean and pick over the berries, and place them in a large mixing bowl.
3. In a medium saucepan, heat the orange juice with ½ cup (4 oz/125 g) of the sugar and the orange zest, stirring until the sugar is dissolved. Reduce to a simmer, add the cornstarch mixture and cook for 2 minutes, until slightly thickened. Pour over the berries, and gently mix. Pour into the baking dish.
4. In a large mixing bowl, combine the flour, remaining sugar, salt, cinnamon and baking powder. Cut in the butter with a pastry knife until finely blended. Add the milk, stirring just to moisten. Drop by spoonfuls around the edges of the baking dish, leaving the berries exposed in the middle.
5. Bake 35–40 minutes, until the pastry is golden brown. Serve immediately, topped with the yogurt.
Serves 8

1 serving: Calories 190, Protein 3 g, Carbohydrates 35 g, Fiber 7 g, Total fat 5 g (Saturated 3 g, Monounsaturated 1.5 g, Polyunsaturated .5 g), Cholesterol 15 mg, Sodium 60 mg, Vitamin C 50%.
▲ *1 Bread, 1 Fruit*

Pacific Northwest Fresh-Picked Berry Cobbler

Hot Apricot Soufflé

This soufflé is destined to impress. The secret is never to reveal just how easy it is. The fruit base is thickened with cornstarch, eliminating the need for egg yolks. Dried apricots can be substituted if fresh ones are not available.

1 tablespoon unsalted butter, melted
¼ cup (3 oz/90 g) plus 2 tablespoons sugar
6 ripe apricots, pitted, peeled and coarsely chopped, or 6 oz
    (185 g) dried apricots, soaked in ½ cup (4 fl oz/125 ml) hot
    water for at least 1 hour and puréed
4½ teaspoons cornstarch (cornflour) dissolved in 1 table-
    spoon cold water
2 tablespoons apricot liqueur
1 tablespoon vanilla extract (essence)
4 egg whites
pinch of cream of tartar
2 tablespoons confectioners' (icing) sugar
confectioners' (icing) sugar for decoration

1. Preheat an oven to 375°F (190°C). Lightly butter four 1-cup (8-fl oz/250-ml) soufflé ramekins, and dust them with 2 table-spoons of the sugar.
2. In a medium saucepan, combine the remaining sugar with ¼ cup (2 fl oz/60 ml) water. Bring to a boil, stirring constantly, until the sugar has dissolved. Reduce to a simmer, add the apricots or apricot purée and simmer for 5 minutes, until the apricots are tender. Add the cornstarch, and bring to a boil, stirring until thickened, about 3 minutes. Remove from the heat, and stir in the apricot liqueur and vanilla. Let cool.
3. In a nonreactive bowl, whisk the egg whites with the cream of tartar until they form soft peaks. Add the confectioners' sugar,

Peach Clafoutis

and whisk until stiff but not dry. Gently stir one-third of the egg whites into the apricot mixture to lighten it. Then fold in the remaining egg whites.
4. Spoon the mixture into the ramekins. Using your thumb and index finger, clean the edge of each ramekin so that the filling is slightly away from the edge.
5. Place the ramekins in a bain-marie. Bake for 10 minutes, until the soufflés have risen and are lightly browned.
6. Dust with confectioners' sugar, and serve at once.
   Serves 4

1 soufflé per serving: Calories 200, Protein 4 g, Carbohydrates 35 g, Fiber 1 g, Total fat 3 g (Saturated 2 g, Monounsaturated 1 g, Polyunsaturated 0 g), Cholesterol 10 mg, Sodium 55 mg, Vitamin A 30%.
▲ *1 Fruit, 1 Fat/Sugar*

Chocolate-Orange Biscotti

Finish a hearty meal with a couple of these crisp cookies and a cup of espresso. They store well, so you can make a full batch and keep them for at least 3 weeks, wrapped airtight.

½ cup (4 oz/125 g) unsalted margarine
3 cups (1½ lb/750 g) sugar
4 egg yolks
3 tablespoons grated orange zest
¼ cup (2 fl oz/60 ml) orange juice
3 cups (15 oz/470 g) all-purpose (plain) flour
1 cup (3 oz/90 g) unsweetened cocoa powder, sifted
2 tablespoons baking powder
2 teaspoons ground cinnamon
½ cup (2½ oz/155 g) pine nuts, toasted

1. Preheat an oven to 375°F (190°C). Lightly oil and flour a 10-by-15-in (25-by-38-cm) jelly roll (Swiss roll) pan.
2. With an electric mixer, beat together the margarine and sugar until well blended. Add the egg yolks, and beat until light and fluffy. Add the orange zest and orange juice, and beat until smooth.
3. In a mixing bowl, combine the flour, cocoa, baking powder, cinnamon and pine nuts.
4. Fold the dry ingredients into the batter, stirring just to blend. Spread in the jelly roll pan and bake for 15–20 minutes, until a knife inserted in the center comes out clean.
5. Remove the pan from the oven, and reduce the temperature to 300°F (150°C). Cut the cake into 4 strips lengthwise and 12 pieces crosswise, to yield 48 pieces about 1¼ by 2½ in (3 by 6 cm). Turn each piece on its side, and bake until crisp and dry, about 30–35 minutes more. Cool on racks.
   Makes 48

1 biscotti per serving: Calories 115, Protein 2 g, Carbohydrates 20 g, Fiber 1 g, Total fat 4 g (Saturated 1 g, Monounsaturated 1.5 g, Polyunsaturated 1 g), Cholesterol 20 mg, Sodium 5 mg.
▲ *1 Bread*

Left to right: Hot Apricot Soufflé, Chocolate-Orange Biscotti

DESSERTS / FRANCE

Peach Clafoutis

From the Limousin region of France comes the classic cherry clafoutis. A cross between a pudding and a cake, it can also be made with a seasonal fruit of your choice. Here is a peach version; plums are also excellent in this.

4 large fresh peaches (about 1½ lb/750 g), peeled

½ cup (4 oz/125 g) plus 2 tablespoons sugar

2 eggs

1¼ cups (10 fl oz/310 ml) low-fat (1-percent) milk

1 teaspoon vanilla extract (essence)

1 cup (5 oz/155 g) all-purpose (plain) flour, sifted

confectioners' (icing) sugar for decoration

1. Preheat an oven to 350°F (180°C). Lightly oil a 9-in (23-cm) round cake pan.
2. Cut the peaches in half and remove the pits. Arrange the halves, cut side down, snugly in the cake pan. Sprinkle with 2 tablespoons of the sugar, and set aside.
3. In a large mixing bowl, beat ¼ cup (2 oz/60 g) of the sugar and the eggs until fluffy; add the milk and vanilla. Add the flour and beat well.
4. Pour the mixture over the peaches, and bake for 20 minutes. Sprinkle with the remaining sugar, and bake for another 15–20 minutes, until the sugar has caramelized to a golden brown.
5. Cool to lukewarm, dust with confectioners' sugar and serve.

Serves 6

1 serving: Calories 240, Protein 7 g, Carbohydrates 49 g, Fiber 2 g, Total fat 3 g (Saturated 1 g, Monounsaturated 1 g, Polyunsaturated .5 g), Cholesterol 75 mg, Sodium 50 mg.

▲ *1 Bread, 1 Fruit*

Autumn

SEASON OF MISTS AND MELLOW FRUITFULNESS,
CLOSE BOSOM-FRIEND OF THE MATURING SUN;
CONSPIRING WITH HIM HOW TO LOAD AND BLESS
WITH FRUIT THE VINES THAT ROUND THE THATCH-EAVES RUN.
— **JOHN KEATS**, *TO AUTUMN*

When the vibrant green and rainbow hues of summer change to pumpkin orange, rusty red and gold, it's time for heartier fare.

Take full advantage of the season's apple harvest. Make chicken and apple pâté with the ever-popular Golden Delicious apples. Complement baked latkes with fresh spiced apples, using Granny Smiths or pippins.

As the air takes on a chill, think soups and stews. *Pistou tomate*, a French relative of Italian pesto, is a great way to use all those end-of-season ripe tomatoes. The *pistou* is a flavorful addition to a hearty vegetable soup. From Central and South America, try *Pepián verde de pollo y choclo*, a stew of chicken and corn. The secret ingredient: *pepitas* (pumpkin seeds).

Give the traditional Thanksgiving feast a new interpretation with turkey scallops with plum, sage and leek gratin. You can prepare these turkey breast fillets on the grill. Serve them with mustard-glazed chestnuts, brussels sprouts and baby carrots.

Left to right: Catalan Fish Stew, B'Stilla

B'Stilla

In Morocco, this sweet and savory phyllo tart is cooked over glowing charcoal and eaten family-style with the fingers, a symbol of brotherhood. For entertaining, individual pouches are simple to make ahead and serve as finger food, maintaining the tradition of using no utensils. Instead of the melted butter usually brushed between the layers of phyllo, this recipe calls for safflower oil to reduce the saturated fat.

2 cups (16 fl oz/500 ml) chicken stock (see glossary)

1 lb (500 g) chicken breasts, skinned and boned

1 onion, finely chopped

½ cup (1½ oz/45 g) coarsely chopped mushrooms

2 tablespoons minced fresh parsley

pinch of saffron threads

3 eggs, lightly beaten

½ cup (2¾ oz/80 g) almonds, toasted and ground

1 tablespoon sugar

1 tablespoon plus ½ teaspoon ground cinnamon

¼ teaspoon ground ginger

¼ teaspoon ground coriander

8 oz (250 g) fresh or frozen phyllo dough

3 tablespoons safflower oil

¼ cup (1 oz/30 g) confectioners' (icing) sugar

1. Preheat an oven to 400°F (200°C). Lightly oil 2 nonstick muffin pans.

2. In a large saucepan, bring the chicken stock to a boil. Add the chicken breasts, onion, mushrooms, parsley and saffron. Reduce to a simmer, and cook until the chicken is tender, about 20 minutes. Remove the chicken to cool. Continue to simmer the stock as you whisk in the eggs (they will scramble), and cook until creamy, about 10 minutes. Drain, reserving the cooking liquid. Place the egg-and-vegetable mixture in a small bowl with ½ cup (4 fl oz/125 ml) of the cooking liquid and set aside.

3. Cut the cooled chicken into small cubes and set aside.

4. Combine the almonds, sugar, ½ teaspoon of the cinnamon, the ginger and coriander in a small bowl, and set aside.

5. Cut the phyllo dough into 6-in (15-cm) squares. Brush 1 piece lightly with the oil. Repeat with 3 more pieces, stacking them with the corners slightly off center. Place each stack of 4 in a muffin cup, pressing the bottom down carefully. Repeat for the remaining cups.

6. Fill each cup with a spoonful of the egg mixture, a layer of chicken cubes and a sprinkle of the almond mixture. Fold the phyllo corners over the top, brush with a little more oil and bake 15 minutes, until golden brown.

7. Transfer the tarts to a heated platter to serve. Mix the confectioners' sugar and the remaining cinnamon, sift the mixture over the *b'stilla* tops and serve immediately.
    Makes 24

1 b'stilla per serving: Calories 110, Protein 7 g, Carbohydrates 9 g, Fiber 1 g, Total fat 5 g (Saturated 1 g, Monounsaturated 2 g, Polyunsaturated 2 g), Cholesterol 40 mg, Sodium 65 mg.
▲ *½ Bread, ½ Meat*

SOUPS / SPAIN

Catalan Fish Stew

This Spanish stew contains a mix of the freshest fish available. You might try John Dory, hake, sole, halibut and a variety of shellfish. Fish is a great source of selenium, a trace mineral that works with vitamin E to fight cell damage and aging.

½ lb (250 g) monkfish (anglerfish), cut into 2-in
    (5-cm) pieces
1 lb (500 g) grouper, cut into 2-in (5-cm) pieces
1 small squid (about 3 oz/90 g), cleaned, cut crosswise into
    rings, or 3 oz (90 g) frozen calamari
juice of 1 lemon
3 tablespoons olive oil
1 large onion, chopped
5 cloves garlic, minced
1 potato, peeled and diced
1 carrot, peeled and diced
½ cup (4 fl oz/125 ml) dry white wine
3 cups (24 fl oz/750 ml) fish stock (see glossary)
⅛ teaspoon ground saffron
½ lb (250 g) tomatoes, peeled, seeded and coarsely chopped
3 tablespoons minced parsley
¼ teaspoon salt
freshly ground pepper to taste

1. Place the monkfish, grouper and squid in a large nonreactive bowl. Toss with the lemon juice, and set aside.
2. Heat the olive oil in a large skillet. Sauté the onion and garlic until soft but not browned. Add the potato and carrot, and cook over medium-high heat for 2 minutes.
3. Deglaze the pan with the wine, and reduce until the wine has nearly evaporated.
4. In a medium saucepan, warm the fish stock. Add the saffron, and stir to dissolve. Pour the stock into the skillet, add the tomatoes and parsley, and bring to a boil. Simmer until the vegetables are tender, 10–15 minutes.
5. Add the fish, starting with the thickest and most dense ones. Simmer for approximately 5–7 minutes, or until all the fish are firm and translucent. Season with the salt and pepper. Serve at once in a warm tureen.
    Serves 6

1 cup per serving: Calories 230, Protein 24 g, Carbohydrates 13 g, Fiber 2 g, Total fat 9 g (Saturated 1 g, Monounsaturated 5 g, Polyunsaturated 1 g), Cholesterol 70 mg, Sodium 160 mg, Vitamin A 70%, Vitamin C 35%.
▲ *1 Vegetable, 1 Meat*

SEAFOOD / YUGOSLAVIA

Snapper Baked in Ripe Tomato Sauce

Ripe, sweet tomatoes can be passed through a food mill to remove the seeds and skin for this rich yet basic sauce. As the fish bakes, the sauce keeps it moist and tender.

1 whole red snapper, filleted, or four 6-oz (185-g) snapper fillets
1 tablespoon freshly squeezed lemon juice
⅛ teaspoon salt
freshly ground pepper to taste
1 tablespoon safflower oil
¼ cup (1 oz/30 g) chopped onions
2 cloves garlic, minced
½ lb (250 g) Swiss chard (silverbeet), stemmed and chopped
⅓ cup (3 fl oz/80 ml) dry red wine
1 lb (500 g) ripe tomatoes, peeled and crushed
2 tablespoons minced fresh parsley

1. Preheat an oven to 350°F (180°C). Lightly oil a shallow baking dish. Place the fish fillets in the dish, sprinkle with the lemon juice and season with the salt and pepper.
2. In a medium skillet, heat the oil. Sauté the onions and garlic until soft. Add the chard, and cook 3 minutes over low heat. Add the wine, and cook until slightly reduced, about 5 minutes. Add the tomatoes and parsley, and mix well. Simmer for 5 minutes, then pour the mixture over the fish.
3. Bake, covered, for 30 minutes, or until the fish flakes easily.
    Serves 4

1 serving: Calories 250, Protein 37 g, Carbohydrates 9 g, Fiber 2 g, Total fat 6 g (Saturated 1 g, Monounsaturated 1 g, Polyunsaturated 3.5 g), Cholesterol 65 mg, Sodium 320 mg, Vitamin A 50%, Vitamin C 70%.
▲ *1 Vegetable, 1 Meat*

Top to bottom: Snapper Baked in Ripe Tomato Sauce, Rustic Bean Soup (recipe page 150)

Rustic Bean Soup

Grilled meats are a specialty of Serbia. Here they have been included in a hearty bean soup, a meal in itself. Grilling the meat with the bone in adds flavor; removing the skin reduces fat. This is an excellent way to use leftover barbecued chicken. Serve the soup with a salad of sliced cucumbers and the last of the ripe tomatoes. You will enjoy a bonanza of fiber, protein and essential minerals.

½ lb (250 g) dried small white beans
½ lb (250 g) dried cranberry beans or pinto (borlotto or red kidney) beans
1½ lb (750 g) chicken breasts, skinned
½ lemon
freshly ground black pepper to taste
3 tablespoons olive oil
1 onion, chopped
4 cloves garlic, minced
8 cups (64 fl oz/2 l) chicken stock (see glossary)
1 potato, peeled and diced
2 carrots, peeled and diced
2 stalks celery, sliced
¼ cup (2 fl oz/60 ml) freshly squeezed lemon juice
¼ teaspoon dried thyme
¼ teaspoon salt

1. Soak all the beans overnight. Drain. Heat a grill or broiler.
2. Rub the chicken breasts with the cut lemon. Season the chicken with the pepper, and grill over medium-hot coals or broil for 12–15 minutes, turning as needed, until the juices run clear when the meat is pierced with a knife. Remove from the heat, and let stand until cool enough to handle. Remove the meat from the bones, and cut it into chunks.
3. In a large stockpot, heat the olive oil. Add the onion and garlic, and cook until lightly browned. Add the beans and chicken stock. Bring to a boil, then simmer for 1 hour.
4. Add the potato, carrots and celery. Simmer for 20 minutes, until the carrots, potato and beans are tender. Add the reserved chicken and the lemon juice, thyme, salt and pepper to taste. Heat through, and serve in warm bowls.

Serves 12   *Photograph page 149*

---

1 cup per serving: Calories 250, Protein 19 g, Carbohydrates 31 g, Fiber 5 g, Total fat 6 g (Saturated 1 g, Monounsaturated 3.5 g, Polyunsaturated 1 g), Cholesterol 30 mg, Sodium 95 mg, Vitamin A 70%.
▲ *1 Vegetable, 1 Meat*

Callaloo

GREENS AND CONCH SOUP

Callaloo (calalú) is the name of the green leaves of the taro root plant. Not readily available outside the Caribbean, it can sometimes be found canned, but a better substitute is fresh spinach or chard. Scotch Bonnet peppers are very, very hot. Wear plastic gloves when handling them,

and adjust the amount to your taste. Both the calabaza and the greens are loaded with beta-carotene, which protects body cells from changes, thus reducing the risks of heart attack, cancer, cataracts and even aging.

3 tablespoons safflower oil
1 large onion, finely chopped
½ fresh Scotch Bonnet (hot) pepper (*habañero*), seeded and finely chopped
3 cloves garlic, finely minced
4 cups (32 fl oz/1 l) chicken stock (see glossary)
1 cup (4 oz/125 g) peeled and cubed calabaza or butternut squash (½-in/12-mm cubes)
⅓ lb (155 g) cassava (yuca) or potato, peeled and cut into ¼-in (6-mm) dice
6 oz (185 g) conch meat or shellfish of your choice, cut into ½-in (12-mm) dice
6 oz (185 g) cooked chicken, diced
½ teaspoon dried thyme
¼ cup (2 fl oz/60 ml) fresh lime juice
½ lb (250 g) fresh callaloo greens or spinach leaves, chopped
salt and freshly ground pepper to taste

1. In a large stockpot, heat the safflower oil. Add the onion, Scotch Bonnet and garlic. Sauté until soft but not browned, about 5 minutes. Add the chicken stock, and bring to a boil.
2. Reduce to a simmer, add the calabaza and cook for 15 minutes. Add the cassava, conch, chicken and thyme, and simmer for 20 minutes.
3. Stir in the lime juice and callaloo greens; heat through, about 5 minutes, and season with the salt and pepper. Serve immediately.

Serves 6

---

1 cup per serving: Calories 240, Protein 17 g, Carbohydrates 20 g, Fiber 4 g, Total fat 10 g (Saturated 1.5 g, Monounsaturated 1.5 g, Polyunsaturated 6 g), Cholesterol 70 mg, Sodium 110 mg, Iron 20%, Vitamin A 90%, Vitamin C 70%.
▲ *1 Vegetable, 1 Meat*

Kalakeitto

SALMON AND FINNISH POTATO SOUP

Scandinavians enjoy salmon in many forms. Here is a simple chowderlike soup that qualifies for the label "comfort food." Try it as a light main course. Yellow Finnish potatoes are quite buttery in flavor, reducing the need to add butter to the soup, but any potato will work well.

4 cups (32 fl oz/1 l) fish stock (see glossary)
1 lb (500 g) yellow Finnish potatoes, peeled and diced
2 tablespoons unsalted butter or margarine
1 onion, chopped
3 tablespoons flour
2 cups (16 fl oz/500 ml) low-fat (1-percent) milk
¾ lb (375 g) salmon fillet, skinned, boned and cut into ½-in (12-mm) cubes
½ cup (4 fl oz/125 ml) dry white wine

Top to bottom: Greens and Conch Soup,
Salmon and Finnish Potato Soup

5 tablespoons (½ oz/15 g) minced fresh dill
salt and freshly ground white pepper to taste

1. In a large stockpot, bring the fish stock to a boil. Add the potatoes, return to a boil and simmer for 15–20 minutes, until tender.

2. In a medium saucepan, heat the butter, and sauté the onion until soft but not browned. Add the flour, and cook over medium heat for 3–4 minutes. The mixture will be thick. Add the milk, and simmer, stirring constantly, until the mixture is thickened, about 3 minutes. Add to the potatoes and stock.

3. Add the salmon and wine, and cook until the salmon is firm and opaque, about 2 minutes. Add the dill, and season with the salt and pepper. Serve immediately.

Serves 6

1 cup per serving: Calories 270, Protein 17 g, Carbohydrates 26 g, Fiber 2 g, Total fat 10 g (Saturated 4 g, Monounsaturated 4 g, Polyunsaturated 1.5 g), Cholesterol 50 mg, Sodium 80 mg.
▲ *1 Vegetable, 1 Meat, ½ Milk*

Piroshki

In Russia and Poland, these filled pastries are served with soups or on their own as a light entrée. In small sizes, they also make a satisfying, savory appetizer. Serve them with applesauce or plain yogurt mixed with a little horseradish.

PASTRY

   1 package (¼ oz/7 g) active dry yeast
   2 teaspoons sugar
   ½ cup (4 fl oz/125 ml) low-fat (1-percent) milk, warmed to
      105°–115°F (40°–46°C)
   1¾ cups (9 oz/280 g) all-purpose (plain) flour
   1 egg
   ½ teaspoon salt
   1 tablespoon safflower oil

FILLING

   3 tablespoons safflower oil
   ½ cup (2½ oz/75 g) finely chopped onion
   1 tablespoon all-purpose (plain) flour
   ½ cup (4 fl oz/125 ml) chicken stock (see glossary)
   ¼ cup (½ oz/15 g) small cauliflower florets, blanched
      (see glossary)
   ¼ cup (½ oz/15 g) small broccoli florets, blanched
      (see glossary)
   1 small rutabaga (yellow turnip or Swede) or white turnip,
      peeled, diced and blanched for 2 minutes (see glossary)
   1 small potato, peeled, diced and blanched (see glossary)
   1 large carrot, peeled, diced and blanched (see glossary)
   1 tablespoon chopped fresh parsley
   salt and freshly ground pepper to taste

1. Preheat an oven to 400°F (200°C). Line a baking sheet with parchment paper.
2. To prepare the pastry dough, dissolve the yeast and sugar in the milk. Let stand 5 minutes, until foamy. Add 1 cup (5 oz/ 155 g) of the flour, and beat until smooth. Cover, and let stand 30 minutes.
3. Mix the egg, salt and 1 tablespoon of oil. Add to the yeast mixture. Gradually mix in the remaining flour. Transfer the dough to a lightly floured work surface, and knead until it is smooth and elastic, about 5 minutes. Place it in a lightly oiled bowl, cover and let rise until doubled in bulk, about 1 hour.
4. To prepare the filling, heat the 3 tablespoons of the oil, and sauté the onion until soft. Stir in the 1 tablespoon of flour, cooking until lightly browned, about 3 minutes. Add the chicken stock, and stir until slightly thickened.
5. Stir in the cauliflower, broccoli, rutabaga, potato and carrot. Add the parsley, and season with the salt and pepper.
6. Punch down the dough, and divide it into 12 balls. On a floured work surface, roll them out to ⅛ in (3 mm) thick.
7. Place a tablespoon of filling in the center of each pastry round. Fold the dough in half and pinch the edges to seal. Press the sealed edges flat with the tines of a fork to secure. Place the piroshki on the baking sheet, and let them rise slightly, about 20 minutes.
8. Bake for 15 minutes. Lower the oven temperature to 375°F

(190°C), and bake an additional 10 minutes, until golden brown. Serve immediately.

Serves 12

1 piroshki per serving: Calories 140, Protein 4 g, Carbohydrates 20 g, Fiber 2 g, Total fat 5 g (Saturated .5 g, Monounsaturated 1 g, Polyunsaturated 3.5 g), Cholesterol 20 mg, Sodium 125 mg, Vitamin A 50%.
▲ *1 Bread*

Kasha Timbales

ROASTED BUCKWHEAT GROATS WITH LEEKS, MUSHROOMS AND RED CABBAGE

Whole or cracked buckwheat has an assertive nutty flavor and is an interesting alternative to rice. It is a rich source of magnesium, a mineral that helps to keep blood pressure in balance. Coating the kasha with an egg white before cooking helps keep the grains separate. For a creamier dish, eliminate that step. Kasha is not the same as Kashi, a commercial combination of grains. However, Kashi does make a delicious pilaf and can be substituted in this recipe with similar cooking times.

   8 large red cabbage leaves
   1 cup (6 oz/170 g) whole kasha (roasted buckwheat groats)
   1 egg white, lightly beaten
   2 cups (16 fl oz/500 ml) boiling chicken stock (see glossary)
   1 carrot, peeled and diced
   ½ teaspoon dried thyme
   3 tablespoons safflower oil
   2 leeks, white parts only, thinly sliced
   ½ lb (250 g) mushrooms, stemmed and sliced
   ¼ teaspoon salt
   freshly ground pepper to taste
   ⅓ cup (2 oz/60 g) dried currants or golden raisins
   ¼ cup (1 oz/30 g) coarsely chopped walnuts

1. Preheat an oven to 350°F (180°C). Lightly oil 8 straight-sided, ½-cup (4-fl oz/125-ml) timbales (ramekins).
2. Blanch the cabbage leaves in boiling water until pliable and just tender, about 4 minutes. Plunge them immediately into ice water, then pat them dry on clean towels. Turn a timbale upside down on each cabbage leaf, and cut a circle to fit the inside. Place the cabbage circle inside the timbale, and press it into the bottom; it will come slightly up the sides. Set aside. Mince the cabbage trimmings, and set aside.
3. In a medium mixing bowl, mix the kasha with the egg white until all grains are well coated. Heat a large skillet, and stir the kasha over high heat until the egg dries and the grains separate. Reduce the heat to low. Add the chicken stock, carrot and thyme. Simmer, covered, until the kasha is tender and has absorbed all the liquid, about 20 minutes.
4. While the kasha is cooking, heat the oil in a large skillet; add the leeks, and cook over medium heat until golden brown, about

Top to bottom: Borscht (recipe page 155); Piroshki; Roasted Buckwheat Groats with Leeks, Mushrooms and Red Cabbage

8–10 minutes. Add the mushrooms, and cook until they are soft and all liquid has evaporated, about 10 minutes. Season with the salt and pepper. Stir in the currants and reserved minced cabbage. Add the leek-mushroom mixture to the kasha, fluffing and mixing well.

5. Spoon the kasha mixture into the timbales, packing firmly. Sprinkle the walnuts on top and press lightly. Place the timbales in a bain-marie with water halfway up their sides and bake for

20 minutes, until completely heated through. Loosen the sides with a knife, and invert onto individual serving plates.

Serves 8

1 timbale per serving: Calories 200, Protein 6 g, Carbohydrates 29 g, Fiber 2 g, Total fat 9 g (Saturated 1 g, Monounsaturated 1.5 g, Polyunsaturated 6 g), Cholesterol 0 mg, Sodium 95 mg.

▲ *1 Bread*

Clockwise from left: Black Bean Salad with Jalapeño Dressing; Southwestern Poblano Chilies Stuffed with Shrimp and Crab; Tamarind-Chili Chicken

Southwestern Poblano Chilies Stuffed with Shrimp and Crab

If fresh poblanos (mild chilies) are not available, substitute their dried version, ancho chilies. Simply soak the anchos in hot water for 15 minutes, then drain and proceed.

¼ cup (2 fl oz/60 ml) plus 3 tablespoons olive oil
2 shallots (white onions), minced
2 yellow bell peppers (capsicums), roasted, peeled, seeded and diced (see glossary)
1½ cups (12 fl oz/375 ml) chicken stock (see glossary)
8 fresh *poblano* (mild) chilies, roasted, peeled and seeded (see glossary)
1 red (Spanish) onion, minced
3 cloves garlic, minced
¼ lb (125 g) shrimp (prawns), peeled, deveined and coarsely chopped
2 tablespoons minced fresh cilantro (fresh coriander)
½ lb (250 g) crabmeat, cooked and shredded
kernels from 1 ear (cob) of corn, blanched (see glossary)
1 red bell pepper (capsicum), diced
¼ cup (1 oz/30 g) *pepitas* (hulled pumpkin seeds), roasted
salt and freshly ground pepper to taste
fresh cilantro (fresh coriander) leaves for garnish

1. In a medium saucepan, heat 3 tablespoons of the olive oil, and sauté the shallots until soft. Add the yellow pepper and 1 cup (8 fl oz/250 ml) of the chicken stock; bring to a boil, reduce to a simmer and cook for 10 minutes. Purée the mixture in a blender. Return it to the saucepan, and keep it warm until ready to serve.
2. Make an opening in the side of each *poblano* chili. Set aside.
3. Heat the remaining olive oil in a medium skillet, and sauté the red onion and garlic until soft, about 3 minutes. Deglaze the pan with the remaining chicken stock, and bring to a boil. Add the shrimp, and cook until pink, about 3 minutes. Stir in the cilantro, crabmeat, corn, red pepper and *pepitas*; heat through. Season with the salt and pepper.
4. Spoon the filling into the chilies, and arrange on serving plates. Garnish with the yellow pepper sauce and cilantro leaves. Serve immediately.

Serves 8

---

1 stuffed chili per serving: Calories 230, Protein 12 g, Carbohydrates 15 g, Fiber 2 g, Total fat 15 g (Saturated 2 g, Monounsaturated 9.5 g, Polyunsaturated 2.5 g), Cholesterol 50 mg, Sodium 110 mg, Vitamin A 20%, Vitamin C 270%.
▲ *1 Vegetable, ½ Meat, 1 Fat/Sugar*

Black Bean Salad with Jalapeño Dressing

This salad makes a trendy addition to the holiday table. If cranberries are unavailable, add some red bell pepper (capsicum) for color. In the early autumn, if corn is still in the market, add the blanched kernels of one ear (cob) of corn instead of the yellow pepper. Not only is this salad high in fiber, but it also provides an abundance of important B vitamins, iron and zinc.

1 lb (500 g) black beans, soaked overnight
2 cloves garlic, minced
½ cup (2½ oz/75 g) finely chopped onion
1 carrot, peeled and diced
1 stalk celery, sliced
6 cups (48 fl oz/1.5 l) chicken stock (see glossary)
5 tablespoons (3 fl oz/80 ml) olive oil
1 cup (4 oz/125 g) fresh cranberries, blanched (see glossary)
½ cup (2½ oz/75 g) coarsely chopped yellow bell
    pepper (capsicum)
½ cup (1½ oz/45 g) thinly sliced green (spring) onions
3 tablespoons sherry vinegar
1 teaspoon sugar
1 fresh jalapeño chili pepper, roasted, peeled and diced
    (see glossary)
⅛ teaspoon salt
freshly ground pepper to taste

1. Drain and rinse the black beans. In a large stockpot, cook the beans, garlic, onion, carrot and celery in the chicken stock for 45 minutes, until the beans are tender but not mushy. Drain, reserving the stock for another use.

2. Toss the bean mixture with 1 tablespoon of the olive oil. Add the cranberries, bell pepper and green onions. Set aside.

3. In a medium mixing bowl, whisk the vinegar and sugar together until the sugar has dissolved. Drizzle in the remaining olive oil, whisking constantly. Add the jalapeño; season with the salt and pepper.

4. Pour the dressing over the bean mixture, and stir gently. Serve at room temperature, or chill.
    Serves 8

---

1 cup per serving: Calories 310, Protein 13 g, Carbohydrates 43 g, Fiber 9 g, Total fat 10 g (Saturated 1.5 g, Monounsaturated 7 g, Polyunsaturated 1.5 g), Cholesterol 0 mg, Sodium 50 mg, Vitamin A 50%, Vitamin C 40%, Iron 20%, Zinc 15%.
▲ 1 Vegetable, 1 Meat

POULTRY / INDIA

Tamarind-Chili Chicken

Buy tamarind pulp and kari *leaves in Indian grocery stores. You may also find whole tamarind pods in Asian or Latin markets.*

1 oz (30 g) tamarind pulp
2 teaspoons sugar
3 tablespoons safflower oil
4 dried red chilies
12 *kari* leaves (curry leaves)
2 onions, finely chopped
6 serrano (hot) chilies, sliced into thin rings
6 cloves garlic, minced
1-in (2.5-cm) piece of fresh gingerroot, peeled and minced
2 large tomatoes, peeled and coarsely chopped
2 lb (1 kg) chicken breasts, skinned, boned, and cut into
    2-in (5-cm) pieces

½ teaspoon turmeric
¼ cup (¼ oz/7 g) chopped fresh cilantro
    (fresh coriander) leaves

1. In a small saucepan, heat ½ cup (4 fl oz/125 ml) of water to boiling. Add the tamarind, and mash with a fork to dissolve. Add the sugar, and let stand for 30 minutes. Strain the liquid, pressing to extract as much tamarind juice as possible. Discard the pulp, and set aside the juice.

2. Heat the vegetable oil in a large skillet. Add the dried chilies, and stir until they are dark brown, about 1 minute. Add the *kari* leaves, onions, serrano chilies, garlic and ginger, and cook until the onions are soft, about 3 minutes. Add the tomatoes, tamarind juice, chicken and turmeric, and simmer for 20 minutes.

3. Transfer to a serving dish, sprinkle with the cilantro and serve at once.
    Serves 6

---

1 serving: Calories 290, Protein 37 g, Carbohydrates 14 g, Fiber 2 g, Total fat 9 g (Saturated 1 g, Monounsaturated 1.5 g, Polyunsaturated 5.5 g), Cholesterol 90 mg, Sodium 110 mg, Vitamin A 25%, Vitamin C 100%.
▲ 1 Vegetable, 1 Meat

SOUPS / RUSSIA

Borscht

Beets may have the highest sugar content of any vegetable, yet they remain low in calories. Beet greens are also full of nutrients and flavor. Whether you eat borscht hot or chilled, the brilliant color of this soup is enough to brighten a chilly day.

6 cups (48 fl oz/1.5 l) chicken stock (see glossary)
¼ cup (2 fl oz/60 ml) tomato sauce (puréed tomatoes)
2 stalks celery, thinly sliced
2 carrots, peeled and grated
1 onion, chopped
1 potato, peeled and diced
6 beets (beetroots) approximately 2 lb (1 kg), peeled
    and julienned
1 cup (3 oz/90 g) cabbage, shredded
1 cup (1 oz/30 g) stemmed and julienned beet (beetroot) greens
3 tablespoons minced fresh dill
2 teaspoons minced fresh parsley
salt and freshly ground pepper to taste
¼ cup (2 fl oz/60 ml) plain low-fat yogurt

1. In a large stockpot, heat the chicken stock with the tomato sauce, celery, carrots, onion, potato and beets. Bring to a boil; then simmer for 20 minutes, until the vegetables are tender.

2. Add the cabbage and beet greens, and cook an additional 10 minutes.

3. Add the dill, parsley, salt and pepper. Serve hot, with a spoonful of the yogurt on top.
    Serves 12   *Photograph page 153*

---

1 cup per serving: Calories 60, Protein 2 g, Carbohydrates 12 g, Fiber 2 g, Total fat 1 g (Saturated .5 g, Monounsaturated .5 g, Polyunsaturated 0 g), Cholesterol 0 mg, Sodium 110 mg, Vitamin A 80%, Vitamin C 25%.
▲ 2 Vegetable

Chapati

Many Indian breads are deep-fried. In fact, this dough can be fried to create poori, *another Indian bread. To reduce fat, however,* chapati *is cooked on a dry griddle.*

1 (5 oz/155 g) cup whole-wheat (wholemeal) flour
½ cup (2½ oz/75 g) all-purpose (plain) flour
pinch of salt
1 tablespoon olive oil

1. Sift the bran from the whole wheat flour. (Discard the bran or save it for another use.) Add the all-purpose flour and salt, and mix well.
2. Mix the oil with ⅓ cup (3 fl oz/80 ml) warm water, and add to the flour mixture, stirring well. Turn the dough onto a lightly floured work surface, and knead until smooth, about 5 minutes.
3. Form into a ball, place in a lightly oiled bowl and let rest, covered, for 1 hour.
4. Divide the dough into 4 balls. On a floured work surface, roll each ball into a 6-in (15-cm) round.
5. Heat a heavy griddle, and cook the *chapatis* one at a time, about 2 minutes on each side. Turn the *chapati* when small bubbles begin to appear.
6. While the next *chapati* is cooking, hold the cooked *chapati* with tongs over an open flame a few seconds on each side. Wrap the finished bread in foil or a towel, and keep warm until served.
Serves 4

1 round per serving: Calories 190, Protein 6 g, Carbohydrates 34 g, Fiber 4 g, Total fat 4 g (Saturated .5 g, Monounsaturated 2.5 g, Polyunsaturated .5 g), Cholesterol 0 mg, Sodium 40 mg.
▲ *1 Bread*

Eggplant Deva

Eggplant Deva is one of the specialties of the Bombay Café in Los Angeles. Co-owners Neela Paniz and David Chaparro suggest blending your own panch puran *spice using equal amounts of rye seeds, Indian brown mustard seed,* nijella *(onion seed), cumin seed, fenugreek and fennel seed. There really is no substitute for* kari *leaves except perhaps the dried version available in Indian markets.*

6 Japanese eggplants (aubergines), sliced lengthwise into
   3 equal parts (not peeled)
3 teaspoons safflower oil
¼ teaspoon salt plus salt and pepper to taste
1½ teaspoons *panch puran* (Indian spice mixture)
¼ teaspoon fennel seeds
3 fresh *kari* leaves (curry leaves)
3 tomatoes, peeled and roughly chopped
pinch of cayenne pepper

2 tablespoons plain low-fat yogurt
¼ teaspoon minced garlic
¼ teaspoon minced fresh gingerroot
1 tablespoon fresh cilantro (fresh coriander), minced

1. Heat a grill or broiler. Brush the eggplant slices lightly with 1½ teaspoons of the oil, and season with the salt and pepper. Grill 2 minutes on each side. Cool.
2. Heat the remaining oil in a nonreactive saucepan. Add the *panch puran*, fennel seeds and *kari* leaves, and stir over medium heat until the mixture starts to splatter.
3. Add the tomatoes, cayenne and ¼ teaspoon of the salt. Simmer over low heat for 15 minutes. Set aside.
4. In a small mixing bowl, stir together the yogurt, garlic, ginger and a pinch of the salt.
5. Arrange the grilled eggplants on a serving platter. Spoon the tomato mixture evenly onto each slice. Top with a spoonful of the yogurt mixture, and garnish with the cilantro.
Serves 6

3 slices per serving: Calories 65, Protein 2 g, Carbohydrates 10 g, Fiber 2 g, Total fat 3 g (Saturated .5 g, Monounsaturated .5 g, Polyunsaturated 2 g), Cholesterol 0 mg, Sodium 135 mg, Vitamin C 20%.
▲ *1 Vegetable*

Crown of Jewels

Dal, *the Indian name for legumes, is a valuable staple in India, along with rice, spices, breads and fruit. Potatoes also play an important role. A dish that combines more than one of these precious staples is one suited for royalty. If possible, start with whole spices and grind them fresh in a spice mill or coffee grinder. Fenugreek seeds have a unique, slightly bitter flavor and can be found in Indian and Middle Eastern grocery stores. This stew is delicious as a vegetarian main course with* chapatis *(recipe above).*

½ cup (3½ oz/105 g) dried mung beans, soaked overnight
¼ cup (1¾ oz/50 g) yellow split peas
¼ cup (1¾ oz/50 g) green lentils
½ teaspoon turmeric
1 teaspoon ground coriander
½ teaspoon ground cumin
½ teaspoon cayenne
1 in (2.5 cm) cinnamon stick, ground
½ teaspoon toasted fenugreek seeds, crushed
1 potato, peeled and cut into ¼-in (6-mm) dice
3 tablespoons vegetable oil
½ cup (2 oz/60 g) chopped onion
2 serrano (hot) chilies, stemmed and split lengthwise
3 cloves garlic, minced
1 large tomato, chopped
¼ cup (¼ oz/7 g) chopped fresh cilantro (fresh coriander)
⅓ cup (3 fl oz/80 ml) plain low-fat yogurt
¼ teaspoon salt
¼ cup (2 fl oz/60 ml) freshly squeezed lemon juice

Clockwise from top left: Eggplant Deva, Chapati, Crown of Jewels

1. Place the mung beans, split peas and lentils in a medium saucepan, and cover with water. Bring to a boil, then reduce to a simmer. Add the turmeric, ground coriander, cumin, cayenne, cinnamon and fenugreek, and cook for 35–40 minutes, until the legumes are tender. Add the potato, and cook 10 minutes, until tender.

2. In a large skillet, heat the oil. Sauté the onion, chilies and garlic until soft, about 5 minutes. Stir in the legume mixture, tomato, cilantro and yogurt. Add the salt and lemon juice. Serve immediately.

Serves 6

1 serving: Calories 230, Protein 10 g, Carbohydrates 31 g, Fiber 4 g, Total fat 8 g (Saturated 1 g, Monounsaturated 1 g, Polyunsaturated 5 g), Cholesterol 0 mg, Sodium 115 mg, Vitamin C 40%.

▲ *1 Vegetable, ½ Meat*

Tabbouleh

Bulgur is a form of cracked wheat. It comes in different grades of granulation; select the finest grade for tabbouleh. This substantial salad can be served as a main course. It is traditionally eaten with the hands, using romaine lettuce leaves to scoop and wrap it up.

1 cup (6 oz/185 g) fine-grain bulgur wheat
¾ cup (6 fl oz/180 ml) freshly squeezed lemon juice

¼ cup (2 fl oz/60 ml) olive oil
¼ teaspoon salt
freshly ground pepper to taste
1 cup (1½ oz/45 g) chopped flat-leaf (Italian) parsley
2 cups (12 oz/375 g) coarsely chopped tomatoes
½ cup (1½ oz/45 g) thinly sliced green (spring) onions
4 cloves garlic, minced
¼ cup (¼ oz/7 g) mint leaves
8 leaves romaine (cos) lettuce

Top to bottom: Lavash, Tabbouleh, Stuffed Grape Leaves

1. Soak the bulgur in 2 cups (16 fl oz/500 ml) of water for 30 minutes, until the bulgur is soft and the liquid is absorbed.
2. Stir in the lemon juice and olive oil. Season with the salt and pepper. Add the parsley, tomatoes, green onions and garlic. Chill at least 2 hours, stirring occasionally.
3. Just before serving, garnish with the mint leaves. Serve with the romaine lettuce.

   Serves 4 as main course, 8 as side dish

---

1 cup per (main course) serving: Calories 290, Protein 6 g, Carbohydrates 38 g, Fiber 9 g, Total fat 14 g (Saturated 2 g, Monounsaturated 10 g, Polyunsaturated 1.5 g), Cholesterol 0 mg, Sodium 170 mg, Vitamin A 35%, Vitamin C 110%.
▲ *1 Bread, 1 Vegetable, 1 Fat/Sugar*

APPETIZERS / GREECE

Dolmas

STUFFED GRAPE LEAVES

These tasty morsels are the perfect finger food and can also be served as a first course. If fresh grape leaves are not available, substitute bottled ones.

40 tender grape leaves or a 12-oz (375-g) jar, stems removed
¼ cup (2 fl oz/60 ml) olive oil
½ cup (2½ oz/75 g) finely chopped onion
½ cup (1½ oz/45 g) finely chopped green (spring) onions
1 cup (7 oz/220 g) long-grain rice
2 cups (16 fl oz/500 ml) chicken stock (see glossary)
juice of 2 lemons
1 tablespoon finely chopped dill
¼ cup (⅓ oz/10 g) finely chopped fresh parsley
2 teaspoons finely chopped fresh mint
2 tablespoons pine nuts
¼ cup (1½ oz/45 g) dried currants
¼ teaspoon salt
freshly ground pepper to taste
1 cup (8 fl oz/250 ml) dill-scented yogurt (recipe on page 110)
1 lemon, cut into wedges

1. Blanch the fresh grape leaves in boiling water for 15 seconds, or rinse the bottled grape leaves well, and blanch for 10 seconds. Drain, and pat dry. Spread the leaves on a work surface, shiny side down.
2. In a large skillet, heat 2 tablespoons of the olive oil. Sauté the onion and green onions until soft, about 3 minutes. Add the rice, and stir to coat with oil. Add the chicken stock, and bring to a boil. Reduce to a simmer, cover and cook for 12–15 minutes, until the liquid is absorbed. Remove from the heat, and stir in half of the lemon juice plus the dill, parsley, mint, pine nuts and currants. Season with the salt and pepper.
3. Place a heaping teaspoon of rice mixture at the base of a grape leaf. Roll the leaf up from the bottom 1 turn; fold in the sides, and continue to roll toward the point of the leaf. Stuff all the leaves, and arrange them snugly in a single layer in a large nonstick skillet. Sprinkle with 1 tablespoon of the remaining olive oil and

3 tablespoons of the remaining lemon juice. Add water just to cover the dolmas. Cover the skillet with a plate, and weight it over the leaves. Simmer for 35 minutes, adding water if necessary. Remove from the heat to cool.
4. Drain the dolmas, and arrange them on a platter. Sprinkle with the remaining olive oil and lemon juice. Serve at room temperature or chilled, with the dill-scented yogurt and lemon wedges.

   Serves 10 (makes about 40)

---

4 dolmas per serving: Calories 170, Protein 4 g, Carbohydrates 22 g, Fiber 1 g, Total fat 7 g (Saturated 1 g, Monounsaturated 4.5 g, Polyunsaturated 1 g), Cholesterol 0 mg, Sodium 260 mg.
▲ *1 Bread, 1 Vegetable*

BREADS / ARMENIA

Lavash

This crisp Armenian flatbread (crackerbread) is delicious with dips or spreads such as baba ghanouj *(recipe on page 103) or* hummus *(recipe on page 102). It can also be moistened to create rolled sandwiches (recipe on page 126).*

1 teaspoon active dry yeast
1½ teaspoons sugar
¼ cup (2 fl oz/60 ml) plus 1 tablespoon olive oil
1½ teaspoons salt
2–2½ cups (10–12½ oz/315–390 g) all-purpose (plain) flour
2 teaspoons sesame seeds

1. In a large bowl, proof the yeast in the sugar and 1 cup (8 fl oz/ 250 ml) of warm water (105°–115°F/40°–46°C). Let stand until foamy, about 5 minutes.
2. Add the ¼ cup (2 fl oz/60 ml) olive oil, salt and 1 cup (5 oz/ 155 g) of the flour, and stir until smooth.
3. Continue to add the flour, ½ cup (2½ oz/75 g) at a time, until the dough is stiff and not lumpy. Turn onto a lightly floured work surface.
4. Knead the dough until it is smooth and not sticky, about 10 minutes. Place it in a large lightly oiled bowl, cover and let rise until doubled in bulk, about 1 hour.
5. Preheat an oven to 375°F (190°C). Lightly oil a sheet pan.
6. Punch down and divide the dough into 4 pieces. Knead 1 piece, and form it into a ball. Let it rest 10 minutes, then roll it out to a 12-in (30-cm) circle.
7. Transfer the circle by rolling it up on the rolling pin and then unrolling it onto the sheet pan. Brush the dough lightly with some of the remaining olive oil, and sprinkle a few sesame seeds on top. Bake until the bread is crisp, about 10–12 minutes.
8. As the first bread is baking, roll out the next ball. Repeat with the remaining dough.
9. Remove the baked bread immediately to a rack to cool.

   Serves 8

½ round per serving: Calories 200, Protein 4 g, Carbohydrates 25 g, Fiber 1 g, Total fat 9 g (Saturated 1 g, Monounsaturated 6 g, Polyunsaturated 1 g), Cholesterol 0 mg, Sodium 440 mg.
▲ *1 Bread*

Pot-au-Feu du Bretagne

BRITTANY SEAFOOD

Along the northern coast of France, the abundance of seafood fairly jumps onto your plate to be eaten. The oyster and scallop beds are rich, the sea brimming with sea urchins, periwinkles, spiny lobsters, and an assortment of fish. A traditional pot-au-feu is a meat stew in which the broth is served as a first course, followed by a platter of the meat and vegetables. Here we use seafood in all its glory.

> 2 lb (1 kg) assorted fish: monkfish (anglerfish), turbot or sole, cod, mackerel, red snapper and sea bass
> 2 lb (1 kg) assorted shellfish: scallops, oysters, lobsters, crabs, clams and mussels
> 8 cups (64 fl oz/2 l) fish stock (see glossary)
> ¼ cup (2 fl oz/60 ml) safflower oil
> 4 carrots, peeled and julienned
> 2 stalks celery, thinly sliced
> 2 turnips, peeled and julienned
> 2 onions, chopped
> 1 leek, white part only, chopped
> bouquet garni: 1 sprig parsley, 1 sprig thyme, 1 bay leaf
> ¼ teaspoon salt
> freshly ground pepper to taste
> 12 thin slices French bread, toasted and rubbed with garlic
> 2 teaspoons fresh minced parsley

1. Skin and bone the fish, and cut them into 2-in (5-cm) cubes. Set aside.
2. Remove the shellfish from their shells. Strain the liquid from inside the shells, and add it to the fish stock. Scrub a few of the scallop, clam and mussel shells with a stiff brush and set aside.

Brittany Seafood

If using a lobster or crab, cook it in boiling water for 8 minutes; split it in two, crack the claws, and remove the meat. Set aside.
3. Heat the oil in a large stockpot. Sweat the carrots, celery, turnips, onions and leek until soft, about 10 minutes. Add the fish stock and bouquet garni, and bring to a boil. Reduce to a simmer, and cook until the carrots and turnips are tender, about 10 minutes.
4. Add the seafood according to the length of time needed to cook it. Dense, thick fish will take about 8–10 minutes. Add the shellfish and cooked lobster about 4 minutes before serving.
5. Drain the seafood and vegetables, replace some of the scallops, clams and mussels in their shells and arrange them on a platter, reserving the stock. Season the stock with the salt and pepper.
6. Place a slice of French bread in the bottom of each warm soup cup. Ladle in the stock, and sprinkle with the chopped parsley. Serve with the platter of seafood and vegetables.
   Serves 12

1 serving: Calories 260, Protein 25 g, Carbohydrates 20 g, Fiber 2 g, Total fat 7 g (Saturated 1 g, Monounsaturated 1.5 g, Polyunsaturated 5.5 g), Cholesterol 50 mg, Sodium 330 mg, Vitamin A 140%, Vitamin C 20%.
▲ *1 Bread, 1 Vegetable, 1 Meat*

Chicken and Apple Pâté

This hearty pâté is delicious served with freshly sliced baguettes, Dijon mustard and cornichons. Ask the meat department to grind the chicken coarsely for you, or chop it yourself in a food processor. Butter is traditional in pâtés, but you may substitute margarine if you wish. If sodium is a concern, reduce the salt to ½ teaspoon.

> 3 tablespoons unsalted butter
> 1 lb (500 g) Golden Delicious apples, peeled and diced
> 1 large onion, diced
> 2 lb (1 kg) ground chicken
> 4 eggs
> ¾ cup (3 oz/90 g) dry bread crumbs
> ⅓ cup (2 oz/60 g) dried currants
> ⅓ cup (2 oz/60 g) dried cherries, soaked in ⅓ cup (3 fl oz/80 ml) rum
> ⅔ cup (5 fl oz/160 ml) dry Marsala
> 3 tablespoons capers
> 2 teaspoons crumbled dried thyme
> 1 tablespoon freshly squeezed lemon juice
> 2 teaspoons salt
> 1 teaspoon lemon zest
> freshly ground pepper to taste

1. Preheat an oven to 350°F (180°C). Lightly oil an 8-cup (64-fl oz/2-l) terrine.
2. In a large skillet, melt the butter, and sauté the apples and onion until golden. Cool.
3. In a large bowl, combine the apple mixture with the remaining ingredients, and mix with the dough hook of a large mixer.

Left to right: Fresh Bean Soup with Tomato Pesto,
Chicken and Apple Pâté

4. Pack the mixture into the terrine and smooth with a rubber spatula.

5. Bake 45–50 minutes, or until the pâté is brown and pulling away from the sides of the terrine. Cool on a rack. Chill or serve at room temperature.

   Serves 12

---

1 slice per serving: Calories 250, Protein 20 g, Carbohydrates 19 g, Fiber 2 g, Total fat 9 g (Saturated 3.5 g, Monounsaturated 3.5 g, Polyunsaturated 1.5 g), Cholesterol 130 mg, Sodium 680 mg.

▲ *1 Fruit, 1 Meat*

SOUPS / FRANCE

Soupe au Pistou Tomate

FRESH BEAN SOUP WITH TOMATO PESTO

Pistou is a Provençal blend of fresh basil crushed with garlic and olive oil, a close relative of Italian pesto, which has Parmesan cheese and pine nuts in it. A tomato pistou is a common variation using very ripe tomatoes.

PISTOU

    1 cup (1 oz/30 g) fresh basil leaves

    1 ripe tomato, cut in half and seeded

    4 cloves garlic

    2 tablespoons extra virgin olive oil

SOUP

    8 cups (64 fl oz/2 l) chicken stock (see glossary)

    4 oz (125 g) fresh flageolets (immature kidney beans) or 2 oz (60 g) dried, soaked overnight

    4 oz (125 g) fresh red kidney beans or 2 oz (60 g) dried, soaked overnight

    4 oz (125 g) fresh *haricots verts* or green beans, ends trimmed, cut into 1-in (2.5-cm) lengths and blanched (see glossary)

    2 leeks, thinly sliced crosswise

    ½ cup (4 oz/125 g) diced zucchini (courgettes)

    2 carrots, peeled and sliced

    1 turnip, peeled and diced

    ½ teaspoon minced fresh thyme

    1 tablespoon minced fresh parsley

    1 bay leaf

    4 oz (125 g) corkscrew pasta

    salt and freshly ground pepper to taste

1. To make the tomato *pistou*, in a food processor or mortar, blend the basil, tomato and garlic. Add the olive oil, and blend until smooth. Transfer to a serving dish, and set aside.

2. In a large stockpot, bring the chicken stock to a boil. Add the flageolets and kidney beans. If using dried beans, simmer for 30 minutes before proceeding. Add the *haricot verts*, leeks, zucchini, carrots, turnip, thyme, parsley and bay leaf. Simmer for 20 minutes, or until the vegetables are tender.

3. Add the pasta to the soup, and cook for 10 minutes. Season with the salt and pepper.

4. Serve immediately, passing the tomato *pistou* for guests to add as desired to the soup.

   Serves 12

---

1 cup per serving: Calories 130, Protein 5 g, Carbohydrates 21 g, Fiber 3 g, Total fat 4 g (Saturated .5 g, Monounsaturated 2 g, Polyunsaturated .5 g), Cholesterol 0 mg, Sodium 25 mg, Vitamin A 70%, Vitamin C 20%.

▲ *1 Vegetable, ½ Meat*

Pepián Verde de Pollo y Choclo

STEW OF CHICKEN AND CORN

Pepián is a Central and South American stew made with chili peppers and nuts or seeds. It is often served over rice.

2 cups (16 fl oz/500 ml) chicken stock (see glossary)
3 lb (1.5 kg) skinned chicken pieces
1 lb (500 g) tomatillos, husks removed
1 cup (5 oz/155 g) *pepitas* (hulled pumpkin seeds), toasted
  and finely ground
5 serrano or jalapeño chili peppers
1 onion, chopped
2 cloves garlic, minced
1 cup (½ oz/15 g) fresh cilantro (fresh coriander) leaves
kernels from 4 ears (cobs) of corn (about 3 cups/18 oz/560 g)

1. Preheat an oven to 400°F (200°C). Lightly oil a shallow baking dish.
2. Heat the chicken stock in a Dutch oven or stockpot. Add the chicken pieces, and simmer, covered, for 30 minutes, or until the chicken is tender.
3. While the chicken is cooking, roast the tomatillos in the baking dish for 10 minutes, until golden brown.
4. In a blender, purée the *pepitas*, serrano chilies, tomatillos, onion, garlic and cilantro until smooth. Place in a large saucepan, and bring to a simmer. Add 1 cup (8 fl oz/250 ml) or more of the chicken cooking liquid to thin the sauce to the consistency of cream. Add the corn kernels, and cook for 5 minutes.

Stew of Chicken and Corn

5. With a slotted spoon, arrange the chicken pieces in a serving dish, and spoon the sauce over them. Serve immediately.
Serves 8

1 serving: Calories 390, Protein 47 g, Carbohydrates 20 g, Fiber 3 g, Total fat 14 g (Saturated 3 g, Monounsaturated 4.5 g, Polyunsaturated 5 g), Cholesterol 110 mg, Sodium 110 mg, Vitamin C 45%.
▲ *1 Vegetable, 2 Meat*

Breast of Duck with Pear Sauce

Choose ripe, firm pears. Seckel pears are recommended, but Bosc, Anjou and Bartlett are also good in this sauce. A quick and easy way to remove the pear core is to scoop it out with a melon baller. Serve this dish with turmeric-colored mashed potatoes (recipe on page 189) and steamed spinach.

2 whole duck breasts, split, with skin, bones and fat removed
  (about 11 oz/330 g)
¼ teaspoon salt
freshly ground pepper to taste
2 tablespoons unsalted butter
¼ cup (2 fl oz/60 ml) sauterne or dry white wine
2 pears, peeled, cored and sliced lengthwise
1 shallot (white onion), minced
½ lb (250 g) ripe pears, peeled, cored and coarsely chopped
2 cups (16 fl oz/500 ml) chicken stock (see glossary)
2 teaspoons minced thyme
1 teaspoon cornstarch (cornflour) mixed with 1 tablespoon
  chicken stock
salt to taste
2 tablespoons coarsely chopped toasted hazelnuts

1. Preheat an oven to 375°F (190°C). Lightly oil a small baking dish.
2. Season the duck breasts with the ¼ teaspoon salt and pepper to taste. In a medium sauté pan, heat the butter to a golden brown. Sauté the duck breasts 2 minutes on each side. Transfer the duck to the baking dish, and sprinkle with 2 tablespoons of the sauterne. Cover with foil, and bake for 10 minutes. Add the sliced pears to the baking dish, cover and bake 5 minutes more.
3. In the same sauté pan, cook the shallot and chopped pears for 1 minute. Deglaze the pan with the remaining sauterne and the chicken stock. Add the thyme, and simmer for 5 minutes. Stir in the cornstarch mixture, and simmer, stirring gently, for 5 minutes, until the sauce is slightly thickened and the pears are tender. Season with salt and pepper to taste.
4. Remove the duck breasts from the oven. Fan the pear slices on serving plates. Arrange the duck breasts on top. Spoon the sauce over, and sprinkle with the hazelnuts. Serve immediately.
Serves 4

1 serving: Calories 290, Protein 16 g, Carbohydrates 24 g, Fiber 4 g, Total fat 14 g (Saturated 6 g, Monounsaturated 5 g, Polyunsaturated 1.5 g), Cholesterol 80 mg, Sodium 210 mg, Iron 20%.
▲ *1 Fruit, 1 Meat*

Breast of Duck with Pear Sauce

Chicken Sausage Squares

Many butchers will grind chicken for you. If yours will not, you can do it yourself very easily with a meat grinder or even in a food processor. Serve these squares with Himmel und Erde *(recipe follows) for a light supper or brunch entrée.*

> 1 lb (500 g) ground chicken or skinned and boned chicken breasts, fat removed
> 1 pippin or Granny Smith apple, cored and coarsely grated
> 1 teaspoon ground sage
> ½ teaspoon crumbled dried thyme
> ¼ teaspoon crumbled dried oregano
> ½ teaspoon anise seed
> 2 tablespoons safflower oil
> ¾ teaspoon freshly ground pepper

1. Preheat an oven to 350°F (180°C). Lightly oil the bottom of a 9-in (23-cm) square baking dish.
2. If you are using chicken breasts, grind them in a food processor, pulsing to chop coarsely, not purée. Place the ground chicken in a medium mixing bowl. Add the apple, sage, thyme, oregano, anise seed and oil, and mix thoroughly.
3. Pat the mixture into the baking dish, sprinkle the pepper over the top and bake for 20 minutes.
4. Cut into squares, or use a 2-in (5-cm) biscuit cutter to cut rounds, and serve at once.

Serves 4

---

1 serving: Calories 205, Protein 26 g, Carbohydrates 6 g, Fiber 1 g, Total fat 8 g (Saturated 1.5 g, Monounsaturated 1.5 g, Polyunsaturated 4.5 g), Cholesterol 70 mg, Sodium 60 mg.

▲ *1 Meat*

Marion Cunningham's Raw Apple Muffins

This dense, moist muffin recipe comes from the mother of baking, Marion Cunningham, author of The Breakfast Book *and* The Fannie Farmer Baking Book, *among other works.*

> 4 cups (1 lb/500 g) diced apple (peeled or unpeeled)
> 1 cup (8 oz/250 g) sugar
> 2 eggs, lightly beaten
> ½ cup (4 fl oz/125 ml) corn oil
> 2 teaspoons vanilla extract (essence)
> 2 cups (10 oz/315 g) all-purpose (plain) flour
> 2 teaspoons baking soda (bicarbonate of soda)
> 2 teaspoons ground cinnamon

> 1 teaspoon salt
> 1 cup (6 oz/185 g) raisins
> ⅓ cup (1½ oz/45 g) broken walnuts (in large pieces)

1. Preheat an oven to 325°F (165°C). Lightly oil muffin pans to hold 16 muffins.
2. Put 3 mixing bowls on the work surface. Mix the apples and sugar in the first bowl, and set aside. Put the eggs, oil and vanilla in the second bowl, and blend well. Put the flour, baking soda, cinnamon and salt in the third bowl, and mix with a fork until blended.
3. Stir the egg mixture into the apples and sugar, and mix thoroughly. Sprinkle the flour mixture over the apple mixture, and mix well. Sprinkle the raisins and walnuts over the batter, and mix until they are evenly distributed. Spoon the batter into the muffin tins.
4. Bake for 25 minutes, or until a cake tester inserted into the center of a muffin comes out clean. Serve warm.

Makes 16 muffins

---

1 muffin per serving: Calories 240, Protein 3 g, Carbohydrates 37 g, Fiber 2 g, Total fat 9 g (Saturated 1.5 g, Monounsaturated 2.5 g, Polyunsaturated 5 g), Cholesterol 30 mg, Sodium 320 mg.

▲ *1 Bread, 1 Fruit*

Himmel und Erde

HEAVEN AND EARTH

From the heavens comes the apple and from the earth the potato. A classic combination of sweet and savory, this purée is typically served with a grilled sausage on top. If using sausage, choose bratwurst or a reduced-fat variety. Himmel und Erde *is also an excellent accompaniment to grilled chicken or duck.*

> 1 lb (500 g) potatoes, peeled and diced
> 1 lb (500 g) turnips, peeled and diced
> 2 tablespoons vegetable oil
> 2 tablespoons unsalted butter
> 1 large onion, sliced
> 1 large sweet apple, peeled, cored and diced
> 2 cloves garlic, minced
> ½ cup (4 fl oz/125 ml) chicken stock (see glossary)
> 3 tablespoons minced parsley
> ¼ teaspoon salt
> freshly ground white pepper to taste

1. Combine the potatoes and turnips in a large saucepan with water to cover. Bring to a boil, then simmer until very tender, about 20 minutes. Drain.
2. In a skillet, heat the oil and butter. Add the onion, apple and garlic, and sauté, covered, until the apple is tender, about 15 minutes. Uncover, and cook over medium-high heat until golden brown, about 10 minutes. Add the chicken stock.
3. Place half of the onion-apple mixture and all of the potato-turnip mixture in a food processor or blender, and pulse until just slightly chunky.

Clockwise from top: Marion Cunningham's Raw Apple Muffins;
Chicken Sausage Squares; Heaven and Earth

4. Stir in the reserved onion-apple mixture. Add the parsley, and
    season with the salt and pepper. Heat through, and serve at once.
    Serves 8

1 cup per serving: Calories 150, Protein 2 g, Carbohydrates 21 g, Fiber
3 g, Total fat 7 g (Saturated 2 g, Monounsaturated 1.5 g, Polyunsatu-
rated 3 g), Cholesterol 10 mg, Sodium 115 mg, Vitamin C 35%.
▲ *2 Vegetable*

PASTAS / ITALY

Baked Orzo with Wild Mushrooms

Orzo is a rice-shaped pasta that cooks very quickly. This dish may remind you of a risotto but it doesn't require constant stirring.

1¼ cups (10 fl oz/310 ml) chicken stock (see glossary)
1 oz (30 g) dried porcini (boletus) mushrooms
4 tablespoons (2 fl oz/60 ml) olive oil
1 cup (4 oz/125 g) coarsely chopped red (Spanish) onion
3 cloves garlic, minced
½ lb (250 g) fresh porcini (boletus) or shiitake mushrooms, stemmed and julienned

2 tablespoons flour
¼ teaspoon freshly grated nutmeg
¼ teaspoon salt
freshly ground pepper to taste
12 oz (375 g) orzo, cooked al dente and drained
2 oz (60 g) Parmesan cheese, grated
fresh flat-leaf (Italian) parsley for garnish

1. Preheat an oven to 375°F (190°C). Warm ¼ cup (2 fl oz/60 ml) of the chicken stock in a small saucepan, and soak the dried porcini mushrooms in it for 20 minutes.

2. In a medium skillet, heat 2 tablespoons of the oil, and sauté the onion and garlic for 2–3 minutes. Add the fresh mushrooms, and

cook for 3 minutes. Add the remaining chicken stock, and cook until the mushrooms are soft, about 5 minutes more.

3. Remove the mushrooms and onions with a slotted spoon, and set aside. Reserve the chicken stock for the sauce.

4. Drain the dried mushrooms, reserving the soaking stock, and set aside.

5. In a medium saucepan, heat the remaining 2 tablespoons of oil, and whisk in the flour. Cook over medium heat 2–3 minutes, stirring, to cook the starch from the flour. Do not brown. Add the reserved chicken stock and strained stock from the dried mushrooms. Stir well, and continue to cook over medium heat until slightly thickened. Season with the nutmeg, salt and pepper.

6. Chop the soaked dried mushrooms, and add them to the fresh sautéed mushrooms. Add the orzo, and mix well.

7. In a medium casserole dish, spoon in a thin layer of sauce. Set aside ¼ cup (2 fl oz/60 ml) of sauce; mix the remaining sauce with the mushroom-orzo mixture, and spoon it into the casserole. Top with the reserved sauce, and sprinkle with the Parmesan cheese.

8. Bake for 30 minutes. Garnish with the parsley, and serve at once.

Serves 6

---

1 serving: Calories 260, Protein 9 g, Carbohydrates 27 g, Fiber 3 g, Total fat 12 g (Saturated 3 g, Monounsaturated 8 g, Polyunsaturated 1 g), Cholesterol 10 mg, Sodium 280 mg.
▲ *1 Bread, 1 Vegetable*

Herbed Tomato Bread

This rustic-looking bread has a rich tomato flavor and is excellent with pasta. If sodium is a concern, reduce the salt to 1 teaspoon.

  4 tablespoons (2 fl oz/60 ml) olive oil
  ¼ cup (1¼ oz/35 g) minced onion
  3 cloves garlic, minced
  ½ lb (250 g) tomatoes, peeled, seeded and puréed
  1 teaspoon minced fresh oregano
  1 tablespoon minced fresh thyme
  2 tablespoons chopped fresh basil
  1 package (¼ oz/7 g) active dry yeast
  1½ tablespoons sugar
  4 cups (1¼ lb/625 g) all-purpose (plain) flour
  ½ cup (2½ oz/75 g) semolina
  1 tablespoon salt
  16 pieces of sun-dried tomato, soaked in warm water for 15–20 minutes
  8 sprigs fresh thyme

1. Heat 3 tablespoons of the olive oil in a medium skillet. Add the onion and garlic and sauté until soft but not browned, about 2 minutes. Add the puréed tomatoes, oregano, thyme and basil, and remove from the heat. Set aside.

2. Dissolve the yeast and sugar in ½ cup (4 fl oz/125 ml) of warm water (105°–115°F/40°–46°C). Let stand 5 minutes, until foamy.

3. In a large mixing bowl, place the tomato mixture, yeast mixture, and 1 cup (8 fl oz/250 ml) of warm water. Mix well; add 1 cup (5 oz/155 g) of the flour, the semolina and the salt.

4. Continue to add the remaining flour, ½ cup (2½ oz/75 g) at a time,

until the dough is soft and smooth. Turn onto a floured work surface, and knead until elastic, 7–10 minutes.

5. Shape the dough into a ball, cover and let rest 30 minutes.

6. Preheat an oven to 450°F (230°C). Lightly oil 2 baking sheets or preheat a bread stone.

7. Punch down the dough, and divide it into 4 balls. Cover, and let rest for 45 minutes.

8. Roll the balls into 6-in (15-cm) circles. Brush with the remaining olive oil, and top with the sun-dried tomatoes and sprigs of thyme. Place on the baking sheets or bread stone.

9. Bake for 10 minutes, until the edges are golden brown. Serve immediately.

Makes 4 small loaves (16 slices)

---

1 slice per serving: Calories 180, Protein 5 g, Carbohydrates 31 g, Fiber 2 g, Total fat 4 g (Saturated .5 g, Monounsaturated 2.5 g, Polyunsaturated 5 g), Cholesterol 0 mg, Sodium 480 mg.
▲ *1 Bread, 1 Vegetable*

Roasted Sweet Pepper and Arugula Salad

This colorful salad mellows as it marinates. The onion tends to soak up the vinegar and change the balance of the dressing. Refrigerate the peppers and onion in the dressing overnight, if desired, but taste and add vinegar if necessary, tossing with the arugula and parsley.

  1 large clove garlic
  2 red bell peppers (capsicums)
  2 yellow bell peppers (capsicums)
  2 tablespoons balsamic or red wine vinegar
  3 tablespoons safflower oil
  ¼ teaspoon salt
  freshly ground pepper to taste
  ½ cup (2 oz/60 g) sliced red (Spanish) onion
  2 cups (2 oz/60 g) arugula (rocket)
  ¼ cup (¼ oz/7 g) flat-leaf (Italian) parsley leaves

1. Rub a salad bowl with the garlic. Set aside.

2. Roast all the peppers over a flame or under a broiler (griller) until the skin blackens and blisters. Immerse the peppers immediately in ice water, and peel them. Remove the stems and seeds, and cut the peppers into 1-in (2.5-cm) strips lengthwise.

3. To make the dressing, place the vinegar in a glass or stainless bowl. Slowly drizzle in the oil, whisking constantly. Season with the salt and pepper.

4. In the salad bowl, toss together the peppers, onion and dressing. Let stand until ready to serve. Toss in the arugula and parsley just before serving. Serve at room temperature.

Serves 6

---

1 serving: Calories 80, Protein 1 g, Carbohydrates 5 g, Fiber 1 g, Total fat 7 g (Saturated .5 g, Monounsaturated 1 g, Polyunsaturated 5 g), Cholesterol 0 mg, Sodium 300 mg, Vitamin A 35%, Vitamin C 160%.
▲ *1 Vegetable, 1 Fat/Sugar*

Top to bottom: Thai-Style Cabbage Salad, Matsutake and Chicken with Ponzu Dipping Sauce

Matsutake and Chicken with Ponzu Dipping Sauce

Matsutake mushrooms grow in the pine forests of Japan, Korea and the American Northwest in the late autumn and winter. They have the distinct aroma of their pine origins. If they are not available, you may substitute shiitake mushrooms.

8 large *matsutake* mushrooms
2 whole chicken breasts, skinned, boned and cut into 1-in (2.5-cm) pieces

¼ cup (2 fl oz/60 ml) sake
¼ cup (2 fl oz/60 ml) low-sodium soy sauce
¼ cup (2 fl oz/60 ml) freshly squeezed lemon juice
1 tablespoon finely chopped green (spring) onion
1 teaspoon *mirin* (sweet cooking sake)
4 oz (125 g) *harusame* (rice noodles), soaked in warm water for 5 minutes
2 oz (60 g) *enoki* mushrooms

1. Preheat a grill or broiler. Cut 4 pieces of foil 12 in (30 cm) square.
2. Trim the bases of the *matsutake* stems, and cut the caps and stems into thick slices. Combine the chicken and sliced mushrooms with the sake, and marinate for 20 minutes.
3. To make the *ponzu* sauce, combine the soy sauce, lemon juice, green onion and *mirin*. Place in 4 dipping bowls, and set aside.

4. Drain the *harusame*, and arrange on 4 serving plates.
5. Divide the mushrooms and chicken into 4 portions on the foil squares, and fold the edges together to form air-tight pouches.
6. Grill or broil the pouches for 4 minutes on each side. Remove the chicken mixture, and place it on top of the *harusame*. Garnish with the *enoki* mushrooms, and serve with the *ponzu* sauce.

Serves 4

---

1 serving: Calories 270, Protein 31 g, Carbohydrates 26 g, Fiber 1 g, Total fat 4 g (Saturated 1 g, Monounsaturated 1 g, Polyunsaturated 1 g), Cholesterol 75 mg, Sodium 550 mg.

▲ *1 Bread, 1 Meat*

SALADS / THAILAND

Thai-Style Cabbage Salad

Serrano chilies are hot. Take care when handling them: wear disposable gloves, and wash your hands before you touch your eyes. Leave the chilies in slices or mince them very finely to distribute the spiciness more. Thai green curry paste is available in most Asian grocery stores. If you can't find it, substitute an equal amount of curry powder.

2 cloves garlic, finely minced
1 serrano (hot) chili pepper, seeded and thinly sliced crosswise (optional)
3 tablespoons rice vinegar
3 tablespoons freshly squeezed lime juice
2 tablespoons sugar
1 teaspoon green curry paste or curry powder
¼ cup (2 fl oz/60 ml) vegetable oil
1 lb (500 g) Napa cabbage, cut crosswise into narrow strips
1 cucumber, peeled, seeded and diced
5 green (spring) onions, thinly sliced
¼ cup (¼ oz/7 g) minced fresh cilantro (fresh coriander)
¼ cup (¼ oz/7 g) mint leaves
¼ cup (1½ oz/45 g) coarsely chopped dry-roasted peanuts (groundnuts)

1. In a medium mixing bowl, combine the garlic, chili, rice vinegar, lime juice, sugar and curry paste. Slowly add the oil, whisking constantly.
2. Toss the dressing with the Napa cabbage, cucumber, green onions and cilantro. Divide onto 8 plates, and sprinkle each serving with mint leaves and peanuts. Serve immediately.

Serves 8

---

1 cup per serving: Calories 120, Protein 2 g, Carbohydrates 8 g, Fiber 2 g, Total fat 9 g (Saturated 1 g, Monounsaturated 2 g, Polyunsaturated 6 g), Cholesterol 0 mg, Sodium 40 mg, Vitamin A 35%, Vitamin C 50%.

▲ *2 Vegetable*

Turkey Scallops with Plum, Sage and Leek Gratin

POULTRY / BRITAIN

Turkey Scallops with Plum, Sage and Leek Gratin

In fine weather, try grilling the turkey scallops. Omit the oats, and serve the plum and leek mixture as a compote.

2 turkey breast fillets, about 6 oz (185 g) each, skinned and sliced 2 in (5 cm) thick
¼ teaspoon salt
freshly ground pepper to taste
2 tablespoons safflower oil
3 leeks, white parts only, julienned
1 cup (8 fl oz/250 ml) brown chicken stock (see glossary)
1 lb (500 g) plums, halved and pitted
1 tablespoon chopped fresh sage
¼ cup (¾ oz/20 g) uncooked oatmeal (rolled oats)

1. Preheat an oven to 375°F (190°C). Lightly oil a shallow baking dish.
2. Using a meat pounder or rolling pin, pound the turkey slices between 2 sheets of plastic wrap, to an even thickness of 1 in (2.5 cm). Season with the salt and pepper.
3. In a large sauté pan, heat the oil, and brown the turkey scallops about 2 minutes on each side. Place them in the baking dish, and set aside.
4. In the same pan, sauté the leeks for 5 minutes, until soft. Deglaze the pan with the chicken stock. Add the plums and sage, and reduce until slightly thickened, about 5 minutes.
5. Spoon the plum mixture over the turkey slices, sprinkle with the oatmeal and bake for 20 minutes.

Serves 4

---

1 serving: Calories 290, Protein 23 g, Carbohydrates 32 g, Fiber 4 g, Total fat 9 g (Saturated 1 g, Monounsaturated 1.5 g, Polyunsaturated 5.5 g), Cholesterol 55 mg, Sodium 200 mg, Vitamin C 35%.

▲ *1 Fruit, 1 Meat*

Roasted Quail with Port Sauce

Ribier and Exotic black grapes are two varieties that are delicious with quail, but experiment with your choice of available grapes. While seedless grapes taste fine, seeded varieties may have more flavor. To remove the seeds, simply slice the grapes in half and lightly scrape out the seeds with the tip of a knife.

ROASTED QUAIL
- **8 fresh quail**
- **¼ teaspoon salt**
- **⅛ teaspoon freshly ground black pepper**
- **4 shallots (white onions), minced**
- **½ cup (3 oz/90 g) seeded and coarsely chopped black grapes**
- **2 tablespoons fresh lemon juice**
- **6 tablespoons (3 fl oz/90 ml) olive oil**

PORT SAUCE
- **2 cups (12 oz/375 g) halved and seeded black grapes**
- **1 cup (8 fl oz/250 ml) plus 2 teaspoons port**
- **2 cups (16 fl oz/500 ml) chicken stock (see glossary)**
- **4 shallots (white onions), minced**
- **1 tablespoon unsalted butter, at room temperature**
- **2 teaspoons cornstarch (cornflour)**
- **salt and freshly ground pepper to taste**

1. To roast the quail, preheat an oven to 450°F (230°C).
2. Season the quail inside and out with the ¼ teaspoon salt and ⅛ teaspoon pepper.
3. Mix together the 4 shallots, coarsely chopped grapes and lemon juice, and spoon 1–2 tablespoons of the mixture inside each bird. Tuck the wing tips under the backs, and truss the quail.
4. Heat the olive oil in a large roasting pan in the oven for 5 minutes. Place the quail on their sides in the roasting pan. Roast for 15 minutes, turning to the other side every 5 minutes. Place the quail breast-up and roast another 5 minutes, or until the juices run pink when the thigh is pierced. Remove the quail to a serving dish, and let rest for 5 minutes before serving.
5. To prepare the port sauce, combine the grape halves, all but 2 teaspoons of the port, the chicken stock, and the shallots in a medium saucepan. Bring to a boil, reduce the temperature and simmer 2 minutes.
6. Remove the grapes with a slotted spoon, and set aside. Bring the sauce to a boil, and cook until reduced to about 1 cup (8 fl oz/250 ml).
7. In a small bowl, mash the butter and cornstarch to a smooth paste. Add a little at a time to the sauce, whisking constantly. Boil gently for 1 minute.
8. Add the remaining 2 teaspoons (10 ml) of port, and season with the salt and pepper.
9. Spoon the sauce over the roasted quail, and serve.

Serves 4

---

1 quail with port sauce per serving: Calories 420, Protein 29 g, Carbohydrates 22 g, Fiber 1 g, Total fat 21 g (Saturated 6 g, Monounsaturated 10 g, Polyunsaturated 3.5 g), Cholesterol 110 mg, Sodium 230 mg.

▲ *1 Meat, 1 Fruit*

Wild Mushroom Soup

Puréeing cooked mushrooms yields a rich creamy soup without the cream. For an even silkier finish, pass the purée through a fine sieve. For a country-style soup, purée half of the mushroom mixture, leaving the other half in slices. This soup is delicious with Finnish graham rusks (recipe on page 88). Mushrooms are an excellent source of potassium, a mineral necessary for muscle contraction, water balance and blood pressure control.

- **½ lb (250 g) mixed wild mushrooms (shiitake, portobello, porcini/boletus, chanterelle), stems removed**
- **1 lb (500 g) white mushrooms, stems removed**
- **juice of 1 lemon**
- **6½ cups (52 fl oz/1.75 l) chicken stock (see glossary)**
- **2 oz (60 g) dried porcini (boletus) mushrooms**
- **2 tablespoons olive oil**
- **2 large shallots (white onions), minced**
- **3 cloves garlic, minced**
- **½ cup (4 fl oz/125 ml) Madeira**
- **1 teaspoon minced fresh thyme**
- **1 tablespoon minced fresh parsley**
- **½ teaspoon salt**
- **freshly ground pepper to taste**

1. Slice the wild mushrooms and white mushrooms. Reserve 12 nice-looking slices for garnish, and toss with lemon juice. Set aside.
2. In a small saucepan, warm ½ cup (4 fl oz/125 ml) of the chicken stock. Add the dried porcini mushrooms, and soak for 20 minutes.
3. In a large stockpot, heat the olive oil. Sauté the shallots and garlic until soft. Add the sliced mushrooms, and cook over medium-high heat for 10 minutes, until the mushrooms are soft and the liquid has evaporated. Drain the dried porcini, reserving the stock. Slice the porcini, and add to the stockpot.
4. Deglaze the pot with the Madeira, and reduce until thickened. Add the remainder of the chicken stock and reserved mushroom-soaking stock, and bring to a boil.
5. Reduce to a simmer, add the thyme and parsley, and simmer for 30 minutes, until the soup has thickened slightly. Purée in a blender, return to the stockpot, season with the salt and pepper and heat through. Serve at once, garnishing each bowl with 2 reserved mushroom slices.

Serves 8

---

1 cup per serving: Calories 110, Protein 3 g, Carbohydrates 12 g, Fiber 2 g, Total fat 5 g (Saturated 1 g, Monounsaturated 3 g, Polyunsaturated .5 g), Cholesterol 0 mg, Sodium 160 mg.

▲ *1 Vegetable*

Seafood Ravioli with Citrus-Herb Sauce

For very quick fresh ravioli, this recipe uses Chinese wonton wrappers. Their light flour dough is a perfect ready-made ravioli wrapper.

Clockwise from top: Wild Mushroom Soup; Roasted Quail with Port Sauce; Seafood Ravioli with Citrus-Herb Sauce

RAVIOLI

   ¼ lb (125 g) shrimp (prawns), shelled and deveined

   ¼ lb (125 g) sea bass or other firm-fleshed white fish, skinned and boned

   1 teaspoon finely minced fresh tarragon

   1 tablespoon fresh lemon juice

   freshly ground pepper to taste

   6 oz (185 g) wonton wrappers or fresh pasta dough cut into 3-in (7.5-cm) squares

   1 egg white

CITRUS-HERB SAUCE

   1 lemon

   2 limes

   4 oranges

   2 shallots (white onions), finely minced

   2 tablespoons vegetable oil

   ½ cup (4 fl oz/125 ml) dry white wine

   ¼ cup (2 fl oz/60 ml) half-and-half (half milk and half cream)

   2 teaspoons finely minced fresh tarragon

   1 tablespoon finely minced fresh parsley

   freshly ground pepper to taste

1. To prepare the ravioli, finely chop the seafood, and mix it with the tarragon, lemon juice and pepper. Place a spoonful on a wonton square, paint the edges with the egg white and cover with a second wonton wrapper, sealing the edges well. Repeat with the remaining filling and wonton wrappers. Set aside.

2. To prepare the citrus-herb sauce, remove the zest of 1 lemon, 1 lime and 1 orange, and set aside.

3. In a medium skillet, sauté the shallots in the oil until soft but not browned. Deglaze the pan with the juices of the lemon, limes and oranges and the wine. Reduce to about ½ cup (4 fl oz/125 ml). Add the half-and-half, citrus zest, tarragon and parsley. Heat through, and season with the pepper.

4. In a large pot, cook the ravioli in boiling water for 2 minutes, and drain. Serve them warm with the sauce.

   Serves 4

---

1 serving: Calories 300, Protein 18 g, Carbohydrates 39 g, Fiber 0 g, Total fat 10 g (Saturated 2 g, Monounsaturated 1.5 g, Polyunsaturated 6 g), Cholesterol 65 mg, Sodium 320 mg, Vitamin C 100%.

   ▲ *1 Bread, 1 Fruit, 1 Meat*

Top to bottom: Shrimp and Bread Stew,
Spinach-Mushroom Polenta with Salsa Cruda

SEAFOOD / PORTUGAL

Migas de Camarones

SHRIMP AND BREAD STEW

This hearty cold-weather stew of shrimp, chili peppers and tomatoes is thickened with bread.

3 cups (24 fl oz/750 ml) chicken stock (see glossary)

1 dried *ancho* (mild) chili pepper

2 fresh *poblano* (mild) or Anaheim (mild green) chilies, roasted and seeded (see glossary)

3 tablespoons olive oil

1 onion, chopped

4 cloves garlic, minced

½ cup (4 fl oz/125 ml) dry white wine

3 tablespoons freshly squeezed lemon juice

1 lb (500 g) shrimp (prawns), unpeeled

4 large tomatoes, peeled and chopped

2 cups (4 oz/125 g) fresh bread, torn into ½-in (12-mm) pieces

3 tablespoons chopped fresh cilantro (fresh coriander)

1. Warm 1 cup (8 fl oz/250 ml) of the chicken stock, and soak the dried chili pepper in it for at least 20 minutes. When the dried chili is soft, purée it with the fresh chilies in a food processor or blender, and set aside.

2. In a large skillet, heat the olive oil. Add the onion and garlic, and sauté until light golden, about 3 minutes. Add the wine, lemon juice and remainder of the chicken stock, and bring to a boil. Add the shrimp, and cook for 2 minutes, until pink and firm. Remove the shrimp with a slotted spoon. When they are cool, shell and devein them.

3. Return the cooking liquid to a boil, and reduce to about 1 cup (8 fl oz/250 ml). Add the chilies and tomatoes, and reduce to a simmer. Add the shrimp and bread, and stir well. Sprinkle with the cilantro, and serve immediately.

Serves 4

1 serving: Calories 310, Protein 21 g, Carbohydrates 25 g, Fiber 4 g, Total fat 14 g (Saturated 2 g, Monounsaturated 8.5 g, Polyunsaturated 2 g), Cholesterol 130 mg, Sodium 230 mg, Vitamin A 35%, Vitamin C 110%.

▲ *1 Bread, 1 Vegetable, 1 Meat*

Spinach-Mushroom Polenta with Salsa Cruda

A fresh tomato sauce adds contrast to the smooth polenta. Serve this right from the baking dish, or cut rounds with a 3-in (7.5-cm) biscuit cutter. Many people associate spinach with iron and strength. Unfortunately, the iron in spinach is poorly absorbed. The strength lies in the abundance of almost all vitamins and minerals that spinach provides.

> 2 tablespoons olive oil
> 4 cloves garlic, minced
> ½ lb (250 g) mushrooms, sliced
> 1 lb (500 g) fresh spinach, finely chopped
> 2 tablespoons minced fresh parsley
> ¼ teaspoon salt
> freshly ground pepper to taste
> 4½ cups (36 fl oz/1.2 l) chicken stock (see glossary)
> 1½ cups (9 oz/280 g) polenta or yellow cornmeal
>   (yellow maize flour)
> ¼ cup (1 oz/30 g) grated Parmesan cheese
> 4 cups (32 fl oz/1 l) *salsa cruda* (recipe follows)

1. Preheat an oven to 375°F (190°C). Lightly oil a 9-by-13-in (23-by-32.5-cm) baking dish.
2. In a medium skillet, heat the olive oil, and sauté the garlic until soft but not browned. Add the mushrooms and spinach; cook until the liquid has evaporated. Add the parsley, and season with the salt and pepper. Set aside to cool.
3. To prepare the polenta, bring the chicken stock to a boil in a large saucepan. Add the polenta slowly, whisking constantly. Lower the heat to medium, and cook, stirring constantly, for about 20 minutes, or until the polenta comes away from the side of the pot easily.
4. Spread the spinach mixture in the baking dish. Pour the polenta over evenly, and smooth the top. Sprinkle with the Parmesan cheese, and bake for 15 minutes. Serve immediately, or cool to room temperature. Pass a bowl of the *salsa cruda* for guests to spoon on top.
Serves 8

1 serving: Calories 195, Protein 7 g, Carbohydrates 31 g, Fiber 5 g, Total fat 6 g (Saturated 1.5 g, Monounsaturated 3 g, Polyunsaturated 1 g), Cholesterol 2 mg, Sodium 200 mg, Vitamin A 80%, Vitamin C 65%.
▲ *1 Bread, 2 Vegetable*

SALSA CRUDA

> 4 tomatoes, peeled, seeded and diced
> 2 tomatoes, peeled and puréed
> juice of 1 lemon
> 2 shallots (white onions), minced
> ¼ cup (¼ oz/7 g) chopped fresh basil leaves
> 1 tablespoon minced fresh parsley

> pinch of salt
> freshly ground pepper to taste

1. Combine all the ingredients in a serving bowl, and mix well.
Yield 4 cups (32 fl oz/1 l)

½ cup per serving: Calories 25, Protein 1 g, Carbohydrates 6 g, Fiber 1 g, Total fat 0 g (Saturated 0 g, Monounsaturated 0 g, Polyunsaturated 0 g), Cholesterol 0 mg, Sodium 30 mg, Vitamin C 35%.
▲ *1 Vegetable*

Mustard-Glazed Chestnuts and Brussels Sprouts

It is uncertain where brussels sprouts originated, but they are eaten not only in their namesake city but also in most of northern Europe and the Americas. Chestnuts are the only nuts that are low in fat, and they contain some vitamin C. Brussels sprouts are a cruciferous vegetable, rich in vitamins A and C, which have several properties that protect against cancer.

> ½ lb (250 g) fresh or canned chestnuts
> ½ cup (4 fl oz/125 ml) chicken stock (see glossary)
> 1 lb (500 g) brussels sprouts, blanched (see glossary)
> ½ lb (250 g) baby carrots, peeled and blanched (see glossary)
> ¼ cup (2 fl oz/60 ml) freshly squeezed orange juice
> 1 tablespoon unsalted butter
> 3 tablespoons firmly packed brown sugar
> 1 tablespoon coarse-grained mustard
> 1 teaspoon grated orange zest
> salt and freshly ground pepper to taste

1. Cut an *X* in the chestnuts. Immerse them in boiling water for 5 minutes, then drain, cool and peel. Set aside.
2. In a large saucepan, heat the chicken stock to boiling. Add the brussels sprouts and carrots, and reduce to a simmer. Cook for 8–10 minutes, until the vegetables are tender. Remove them with a slotted spoon, and set them aside, reserving the stock.
3. To make the mustard glaze, in the same saucepan, heat the stock, orange juice, butter and brown sugar. Cook over medium-high heat until the volume is reduced by half. Stir in the mustard and orange zest. Season with the salt and pepper.
4. Add the chestnuts, brussels sprouts and carrots to the mustard glaze. Heat through, stirring to coat the vegetables. Serve at once.
Serves 6   *Photograph page 175*

1 cup per serving: Calories 170, Protein 4 g, Carbohydrates 33 g, Fiber 8 g, Total fat 3 g (Saturated 1.5 g, Monounsaturated 1 g, Polyunsaturated .5 g), Cholesterol 5 mg, Sodium 70 mg, Vitamin A 35%, Vitamin C 150%.
▲ *2 Vegetable*

Chinese Long Beans and Mushrooms in Black Bean Sauce

The key flavor of this dish comes from the fermented, or salted, black beans, which are available in most Asian markets. These aromatic preserved black soy beans have been cooked and then cured in a seasoned brine. They are dried and packaged in plastic bags.

1 lb (500 g) Chinese long beans or fresh green beans, ends trimmed

½ cup (4 fl oz/125 ml) chicken stock (see glossary)

1 oz (30 g) dried black Chinese mushrooms, rinsed

2 tablespoons fermented black beans

2 tablespoons dry sherry

2 cloves garlic, finely minced

1 teaspoon chopped fresh gingerroot

1 teaspoon cornstarch (cornflour) mixed with 1 tablespoon mushroom soy sauce

3 tablespoons safflower oil

½ teaspoon toasted sesame oil

½ lb (250 g) shiitake mushrooms, julienned

4 green (spring) onions, thinly sliced

1. Blanch the long beans by dropping them into boiling water for 30 seconds (allow 1 minute for green beans). Plunge them immediately in ice water to stop cooking. Drain, and set aside.

Top to bottom: Chinese Long Beans and Mushrooms in Black Bean Sauce, Sweet Corn and Crabmeat Soup

2. In a small saucepan, warm the chicken stock. Soak the dried mushrooms in the stock for at least 30 minutes. Remove and chop the mushrooms into small dice; set aside. Strain the chicken stock through a very fine-mesh sieve or cheesecloth (muslin), and reserve.

3. In a small mixing bowl, combine the fermented black beans, sherry, garlic and ginger. Add the cornstarch and soy sauce mixture. Set aside.

4. Heat the safflower oil and sesame oil in a large skillet. Sauté the shiitake mushrooms for about 2 minutes. Add the diced black mushrooms, long beans, green onions and strained stock, and cook over high heat for 10 minutes to reduce the liquid slightly.

5. Stir the black bean mixture into the skillet to thicken the sauce, and serve immediately.

Serves 6

1 serving: Calories 140, Protein 3 g, Carbohydrates 17 g, Fiber 3 g, Total fat 7 g (Saturated 1 g, Monounsaturated 1 g, Polyunsaturated 5 g), Cholesterol 0 mg, Sodium 210 mg, Vitamin C 25%.
▲ *2 Vegetable*

Sweet Corn and Crabmeat Soup

This classic Chinese soup is very quickly prepared. Crabmeat is rich in zinc, an important nutrient that maintains our sense of taste and smell and aids wound healing. Other excellent sources of zinc include oysters, beef, liver, poultry and brewer's yeast.

4 cups (32 fl oz/1 l) chicken stock (see glossary)

½ teaspoon sesame oil

½ lb (250 g) fresh crabmeat

1 cup (6 oz/185 g) fresh corn kernels

¼ cup (2 fl oz/60 ml) low-fat (1-percent) milk

salt and freshly ground white pepper to taste

1 tablespoon cornstarch (cornflour) dissolved in 2 tablespoons chicken stock

2 egg whites

2 green (spring) onions, thinly sliced

1. In a large stockpot, bring the chicken stock and sesame oil to a boil. Add the crabmeat, corn and milk, and return to a boil. Reduce to a simmer, and cook for 10 minutes. Season with the salt and pepper.

2. Whisk in the cornstarch mixture, and simmer until slightly thickened.

3. Slowly pour in the egg whites, gently stirring the soup with a fork.

4. Ladle into warm serving bowls, and sprinkle with the green onions. Serve immediately.

Serves 6

1 cup per serving: Calories 100, Protein 10 g, Carbohydrates 8 g, Fiber 1 g, Total fat 2 g (Saturated .5 g, Monounsaturated 1 g, Polyunsaturated .5 g), Cholesterol 40 mg, Sodium 140 mg, Zinc 12%.
▲ *½ Meat*

Top to bottom: Duck Legs with Prunes and Armagnac; Mustard Glazed Chestnuts and Brussels Sprouts (recipe page 173)

WINGED GAME / FRANCE

Duck Legs with Prunes and Armagnac

Many recipes call for only the duck breast. Here is a way to use another delicious part of the bird. Serve this dish with couscous or pasta.

1 cup (6 oz/185 g) pitted prunes
1 cup (8 fl oz/250 ml) Armagnac
3 tablespoons safflower oil
3 shallots (white onions), minced
4 duck leg quarters, skin and fat removed
2 cups (16 fl oz/500 ml) chicken stock (see glossary)
2 sprigs fresh thyme
1 bay leaf
freshly ground pepper to taste

1. Soak the prunes in the Armagnac for at least 30 minutes.
2. In a large saucepan, heat the safflower oil, and sauté the shallots until soft, about 2 minutes. Add the duck legs, and brown lightly on all sides. Deglaze the pan with the prunes and Armagnac.
3. Add the chicken stock, thyme and bay leaf, and simmer, covered, for 1 hour. Season with the pepper, and serve at once.
Serves 4

1 duck leg with ¼ cup prune sauce per serving: Calories 500, Protein 23 g, Carbohydrates 28 g, Fiber 3 g, Total fat 21 g (Saturated 5 g, Monounsaturated 4.5 g, Polyunsaturated 9 g), Cholesterol 130 mg, Sodium 135 mg, Iron 25%, Vitamin A 20%, Vitamin C 20%.
▲ *1 Fruit, 1 Meat*

Muesli

Muesli *is the invention of a Swiss physician, Dr. Bircher-Brenner, who sought a protein-rich breakfast food. His mixture is high in fiber and a good source of vitamins and minerals.* Muesli *differs from* granola *in that the grains are eaten uncooked. In some versions the rolled oats and wheat are soaked in water for 30 minutes, then drained and mixed with the other grains, dried fruits and nuts.* Muesli *is best eaten with fresh fruit, such as grated apples, sliced bananas or straw-berries, and yogurt or a little milk.*

1 cup (3 oz/90 g) uncooked oatmeal (rolled oats)
½ cup (1½ oz/45 g) rolled wheat (wheat flakes)
¼ cup (¾ oz/20 g) wheat bran
2 tablespoons wheat germ
2 tablespoons roasted and coarsely chopped pecans (optional)

1. In a medium mixing bowl, combine all ingredients.
   Makes 2 cups (5 oz/155 g)

⅔ cup per serving: Calories 180, Protein 8 g, Carbohydrates 35 g, Fiber 6 g, Total fat 2.5 g (Saturated .5 g, Monounsaturated .5 g, Polyunsaturated 1 g), Cholesterol 0 mg, Sodium 0 mg
▲ *1 Bread*

Oven-Baked Latkes with Spiced Apples

Latkes (potato pancakes) are usually browned in oil. To reduce fat, here is an oven-baked version that is easy to prepare, especially in large numbers.

SPICED APPLES
3 Granny Smith or pippin apples, peeled, cored and diced
½ cup (4 fl oz/125 ml) apple juice
½ teaspoon finely grated lemon zest
¼ cup (2 oz/60 g) sugar
1 teaspoon freshly ground cinnamon
½ teaspoon freshly ground nutmeg
¼ teaspoon ground ginger
BAKED LATKES
6 potatoes, peeled
2 onions, finely chopped
2 eggs
1 teaspoon safflower oil
2 tablespoons finely minced fresh parsley
½ cup (2½ oz/75 g) all-purpose (plain) flour
½ teaspoon baking soda (bicarbonate of soda)
1 tablespoon freshly squeezed lemon juice
salt and freshly ground white pepper to taste
1 cup (8 fl oz/250 ml) plain nonfat yogurt

Left to right: Oven-Baked Latkes with Spiced Apples; Muesli

1. Preheat an oven to 375°F (190°C). Lightly oil a nonstick 13-by-17-in (32-by-43-cm) sheet pan.
2. To make the spiced apples, in a medium saucepan, combine the apples, apple juice, lemon zest and sugar. Bring to a boil. Reduce to a simmer, and cook until the apples are tender, about 10 minutes. Add the cinnamon, nutmeg and ginger. Set aside in a serving bowl to cool.
3. To make the latkes, grate the potatoes, and place them in a large colander. Run cool water over, stirring gently until the starch is rinsed away and the water runs clear. This will keep the potatoes from turning brown before you cook them. Drain the potatoes well, squeezing out as much water as possible.
4. In a large mixing bowl, add the onions, eggs, oil and parsley to the potatoes. Sift together the flour and baking soda, and add to the potato mixture. Season with the lemon juice, salt and pepper.
5. Spread the potato mixture on the sheet pan. Bake for 15 minutes, or until golden brown. Cool for 5 minutes.
6. Cut into approximately 4-in (10-cm) squares, and then cut those into triangles. Serve hot with the spiced apples and yogurt.
   Serves 8

3 triangles with apples and yogurt per serving: Calories 230, Protein 6 g, Carbohydrates 47 g, Fiber 4 g, Total fat 2 g (Saturated .5 g, Monounsaturated .5 g, Polyunsaturated 1 g), Cholesterol 55 mg, Sodium 125 mg, Vitamin C 25%.
▲ *1 Fruit, 1 Vegetable*

Mulled Apple Cider

The freshest tasting cider is the least treated, that is, unfiltered and unpasteurized. It is available in health food stores and at farmers' markets. If you don't have whole cloves, allspice or cardamom, use ¼ teaspoon of each ground spice. This recipe goes very well with a crackling fire and a good book.

8 cups (64 fl oz/2 l) apple cider
4 whole cloves
1 teaspoon whole allspice
1 cardamom pod, hulled
10 cinnamon sticks
1 orange, thinly sliced
freshly grated nutmeg to taste

1. Place the apple cider in a large heavy saucepan, and bring to a boil. Reduce to a simmer.
2. Place the cloves, allspice, and cardamom seeds in a piece of cheesecloth (muslin), and add to cider. Add 2 of the cinnamon sticks, and simmer for 10 minutes.
3. Ladle the hot cider into warm mugs. Put an orange slice and 1 of the remaining cinnamon sticks in each mug. Grate the nutmeg on top, and serve immediately.
   Serves 8   *Photograph page 178*

1 cup per serving: Calories 125, Protein 0 g, Carbohydrates 31 g, Fiber 1 g, Total fat 0 g (Saturated 0 g, Monounsaturated 0 g, Polyunsaturated 0 g), Cholesterol 0 mg, Sodium 5 mg.
▲ *1 Fruit*

Top to bottom: Mulled Apple Cider (recipe page 177), Baked Lady Apples with Apple Soufflé and Cinnamon-Rum Sauce

5. Chop the mixture coarsely, and place it on the sheet pan again. Bake 10–15 minutes longer, until crisp but not too dark. Cool.

6. Stir in the dates and raisins, and store in an airtight container.
   Makes 5 cups (17½ oz/550 g)

⅔ cup per serving: Calories 180, Protein 4 g, Carbohydrates 35 g, Fiber 4 g, Total fat 4 g (Saturated .5 g, Monounsaturated 1 g, Polyunsaturated 2 g), Cholesterol 0 mg, Sodium 25 mg.
▲ *1 Bread*

BREAKFAST / UNITED STATES

Granola

Granola is a more elaborate, cooked version of muesli. Besides being a wholesome cereal, it makes a great topping for desserts. Mix it with fresh fruit and yogurt for a delightful breakfast or snack.

1½ cups (4½ oz/140 g) uncooked oatmeal (rolled oats)
½ cup (1½ oz/45 g) rolled wheat (wheat flakes)
¼ cup (¾ oz/20 g) wheat bran
2 tablespoons hulled pumpkin seeds
2 tablespoons shelled sunflower seeds
1 tablespoon sesame seeds
1 cup (8 fl oz/250 ml) apple juice
¼ cup (2 fl oz/60 ml) honey
1 teaspoon vanilla extract (essence)
1 teaspoon ground cinnamon
¼ teaspoon ground cardamom
¼ teaspoon ground ginger
¼ teaspoon ground nutmeg
¼ cup (1½ oz/45 g) chopped dates
¼ cup (1½ oz/45 g) golden raisins or currants

1. Preheat an oven to 325°F (165°C). Lightly oil a sheet pan.

2. In a large mixing bowl, combine the oatmeal, rolled wheat and wheat bran. Add the pumpkin seeds, sunflower seeds and sesame seeds, and mix well.

3. In a small saucepan, combine the apple juice and honey. Cook over medium heat, stirring until the honey is dissolved. Add the vanilla, cinnamon, cardamom, ginger and nutmeg, and remove from the heat.

4. Pour the liquid into the oatmeal mixture, and stir to distribute evenly. Spread on the sheet pan, and bake for 30–35 minutes, stirring occasionally, until browned. Cool.

DESSERTS / UNITED STATES

Baked Lady Apples with Apple Soufflé and Cinnamon-Rum Sauce

Little Lady apples are available for a brief period in September and October. Rome or Golden Delicious apples are a wonderful substitute the rest of the season; just increase the baking time by 30 minutes.

BAKED APPLES AND SOUFFLÉ
12 Lady apples or 4 Rome or Golden Delicious apples
juice of 1 lemon
½ cup (4 fl oz/125 ml) apple juice
2 Gravenstein or other cooking apples, peeled, cored and diced
6 tablespoons (3 oz/90 g) sugar
½ teaspoon freshly ground cinnamon
¼ teaspoon ground nutmeg
2 egg whites
CINNAMON-RUM SAUCE
½ cup (3½ oz/105 g) firmly packed dark brown sugar
1 cinnamon stick
¼ cup (2 fl oz/60 ml) dark rum
2 teaspoons vanilla extract (essence)

1. Preheat an oven to 375°F (190°C).

2. With a melon baller, core the Lady or Rome apples, taking care not to cut the apples in half. Brush the cut areas lightly with some of the lemon juice. Place ¼ cup (2 fl oz/60 ml) of the apple juice in a baking dish just large enough to hold the apples. Set the apples in a single layer in the dish, and cover with foil. Bake the Lady apples for 15 minutes or the Rome apples for 45 minutes.

3. Meanwhile, in a medium saucepan, place the remaining apple juice, Gravenstein apples, and 4 tablespoons (2 oz/60 g) of the sugar. Cook over medium heat for 15 minutes, until the apples are very tender. Place in a blender, and purée. Add the cinnamon and nutmeg. This should yield about 2 cups (16 fl oz/500 ml) of applesauce. Set aside.

4. In a nonreactive bowl, whisk the egg whites with 1 teaspoon of the lemon juice until soft peaks form. Add the remaining sugar, and whisk until stiff but not dry. Fold the egg whites into 1 cup (8 fl oz/250 ml) of the applesauce. Remove the apples from the oven, and spoon this applesauce mixture into their cavities. Return them to the oven, and bake 8–10 minutes longer, uncovered, at 400°F (200°C), until the soufflé has risen slightly and is a pale golden brown. Strain and reserve the apple cooking liquid for the sauce.

5. To make the cinnamon-rum sauce, in a medium saucepan, heat the brown sugar, ¼ cup (2 fl oz/60 ml) of the apple cooking liquid and the cinnamon stick, stirring until the sugar dissolves.
6. Simmer, stirring occasionally, until the sauce has thickened, about 10 minutes. Stir in the rum and vanilla; pour into a warm serving bowl.
7. To serve, spoon the remaining applesauce onto 4 serving plates. Place 3 Lady apples or 1 Rome apple on each plate. Serve the warm cinnamon-rum sauce on the side.
Serves 4

---

1 serving: Calories 330, Protein 2 g, Carbohydrates 74 g, Fiber 7 g, Total fat 1 g (Saturated 0 g, Monounsaturated 0 g, Polyunsaturated 0 g), Cholesterol 0 mg, Sodium 35 mg, Vitamin C 30%.
▲ *2 Fruit, 1 Fat/Sugar*

BREAKFAST / UNITED STATES

Whole-Grain Maple Muffins

Serve these muffins straight from the oven with ½ cup (4 fl oz/125 ml) vanilla low-fat yogurt flavored with 3 tablespoons maple syrup.

2 cups (10 oz/315 g) all-purpose (plain) flour
½ cup (2½ oz/75 g) whole-wheat (wholemeal) flour
4 tablespoons (¾ oz/20 g) wheat germ
1¼ teaspoons baking powder
1¼ teaspoons baking soda (bicarbonate of soda)
pinch of salt
½ teaspoon ground cinnamon
½ cup (3½ oz/105 g) firmly packed brown sugar
¾ cup (6 fl oz/180 ml) buttermilk
2 tablespoons safflower oil
2 eggs
¼ cup (2 fl oz/60 ml) pure maple syrup
1 ripe banana

1. Preheat an oven to 350°F (180°C). Lightly oil a 12-cup muffin pan or line it with paper muffin cups.
2. In a large mixing bowl, combine the all-purpose flour, whole-wheat flour, 3 tablespoons of the wheat germ, the baking powder, baking soda, salt, cinnamon and brown sugar. Set aside.
3. In a blender, combine the buttermilk, safflower oil, eggs, maple syrup and banana. Purée until smooth.
4. Add the liquid ingredients to the dry, stirring just to mix. Do not overmix.
5. Spoon the batter into the muffin cups, filling them two-thirds full. Sprinkle the tops with the remaining wheat germ.
6. Bake for 20 minutes, until golden brown. Serve warm.
Makes 12 muffins

---

1 muffin per serving: Calories 190, Protein 5 g, Carbohydrates 34 g, Fiber 2 g, Total fat 4 g (Saturated 1 g, Monounsaturated 1 g, Polyunsaturated 2 g), Cholesterol 35 mg, Sodium 170 mg.
▲ *1 Bread*

Top to bottom: Whole-Grain Maple Muffins, Granola

Cactus Pears and White Sapote with Tequila and Lime

Cactus Pears and White Sapote with Tequila and Lime

Although the most common cactus pears in Central and North America are the fuchsia-colored fruits of the prickly pear cactus, other varieties from the Mediterranean and Asia have cream, orange, yellow and orange-red flesh. Choose firm cactus pears that have a slight give and good color. White sapote has a sweet custardlike pulp. Select firm fruit, and let it ripen for 3 days.

4 large cactus pears
3 tablespoons sugar
2 tablespoons tequila
2 white sapotes, about ½ lb (250 g) each, peeled and seeded
juice of 1 lime
3 tablespoons sugar
½ teaspoon lime zest

1. To peel the cactus pears, hold a pear with tongs, and slice ½-in (12 mm) from each end. Place the pear on one end, and slice off a strip of skin from one end to the other, steadying the pear with the tongs. Hold the peeled section of the pear with your fingers and slip off the remaining skin.

2. To make the cactus pear–tequila sauce, cut 2 of the cactus pears into ½-in (12-mm) cubes; set aside. Purée the remaining pears in a blender with the sugar and tequila. Strain the purée through a fine-mesh sieve, pressing to yield as much juice as possible. Discard the pulp, and chill the juice until ready to serve.

3. With a melon baller, scoop out balls of the pulp of 1 of the sapotes, place them in a bowl with the cactus pear cubes and chill.

4. To make the white sapote–lime sauce, scoop out the remaining pulp of both white sapotes, and place it in a blender with the lime juice and sugar. Purée until smooth. Add the lime zest, and chill until ready to serve.

5. To serve, spoon cactus pear–tequila sauce on half of each plate and white sapote-lime sauce on the other half. Spoon the chilled fruit on top.

Serves 4

1 serving: Calories 280, Protein 3 g, Carbohydrates 67 g, Fiber 4 g, Total fat 1 g (Saturated 0 g, Monounsaturated 0 g, Polyunsaturated 0 g), Cholesterol 0 mg, Sodium 15 mg, Vitamin C 60%.
▲ *1 Fruit*

Ken Hom's Northern Chinese Steamed Pears

Desserts in China are not the major attraction as they are in other countries, but they are usually quite fresh and natural. Here is a clean, simple finish for any meal, from Chinese cooking authority Ken Hom.

3 tablespoons Chinese rock sugar or granulated sugar
4 ripe but firm pears, peeled, left whole, and cored from the bottom, leaving stems intact
2 pieces Chinese cinnamon bark or cinnamon sticks

1. Prepare a steamer or place a rack in a wok or pot. Add about 2 in (5 cm) of water, and bring to a boil as you prepare the ingredients.
2. Combine the sugar with ⅓ cup (3 fl oz/80 ml) of water in a small pot, and boil until the sugar has completely dissolved. Cool slightly.
3. Place the pears, sugar water and cinnamon in a shallow bowl and set it in the steamer. Be sure water from the steamer does not flow into the bowl. Reduce the heat to a simmer, and cover the steamer tightly with a lid. Steam the pears for 15–25 minutes, until they are tender. (The cooking time will depend on the ripeness of the pears.)
4. Drain all the cooking liquid and cinnamon into a small saucepan, and boil to reduce it to a syrup. Remove and discard the cinnamon. Pour the syrup over the pears, and serve at once.
Serves 4 *Photograph page 8*

1 pear with sauce per serving: Calories 130, Protein 1 g, Carbohydrates 34 g, Fiber 4 g, Total fat 1 g (Saturated 0 g, Monounsaturated 0 g, Polyunsaturated 0 g), Cholesterol 0 mg, Sodium 0 mg.
▲ *1 Fruit*

Caramelized Bread Pudding

Bread pudding is traditionally made to use up stale bread, but why not use something fresh and delicious? Try raisin bread or another bread of your choice instead of the chocolate-cherry-almond bread used here. This pudding also is excellent served with brandied cherries (recipe on page 96).

1 tablespoon unsalted butter
½ cup (4 oz/125 g) plus 3 tablespoons sugar
2 cups (16 fl oz/500 ml) low-fat (1-percent) milk
2 eggs
1 tablespoon vanilla extract (essence)
1 teaspoon ground cinnamon
1 loaf Courtney's chocolate-cherry-almond bread (recipe on page 213), cubed

1. Preheat an oven to 350°F (180°C).
2. In an ovenproof, straight-sided skillet or casserole, heat the butter. Add 3 tablespoons of the sugar, stirring over medium heat

until it is dissolved. Continue to cook without stirring until the sugar is golden brown. Remove from the heat, and set aside.
3. Combine the milk, remainder of the sugar and eggs in a large mixing bowl. Stir in the vanilla and cinnamon. Add the bread cubes, and stir to coat all the pieces.
4. Pour the bread mixture over the caramelized sugar in its pan, pressing the bread slightly to pack it. Bake 45 minutes, until a knife inserted in the middle comes out clean.
5. Invert onto a serving plate, and serve warm.
Serves 8 *Photograph page 8*

1 serving: Calories 350, Protein 11 g, Carbohydrates 64 g, Fiber 5 g, Total fat 7 g (Saturated 2 g, Monounsaturated 3 g, Polyunsaturated 1 g), Cholesterol 60 mg, Sodium 360 mg.
▲ *1 Bread*

Strawberry-Champagne Sorbet

Tiny champagne grapes and wee alpine strawberries garnish this simple sorbet to make an elegant dessert. The strawberries are found through September at high altitudes. If those fruits are unavailable, substitute average size strawberries cut in half and small clusters of regular grapes. Alcohol can arrest the freezing process, so you have to begin with a frozen fruit base and then add the champagne. The egg white gives the sorbet added volume.

4 cups (1 lb/500 g) ripe strawberries
½ cup (4 oz/125 g) sugar
½ cup (4 fl oz/125 ml) champagne
1 egg white
4 small bunches, about 2 cups (12 oz/375 g), of champagne (Black Corinth) grapes
1 cup (4 oz/125 g) alpine strawberries (*fraises des bois*)

1. Purée the ripe strawberries in a blender or food processor. This should yield about 2 cups (16 fl oz/500 ml) of strawberry juice.
2. In a medium saucepan, combine the sugar and ¼ cup (2 fl oz/60 ml) of water; heat until the sugar dissolves. Stir into the strawberry juice, and chill well.
3. Place the strawberry base in an ice-cream freezer, and process it until it is partially frozen. Stir in the champagne.
4. Beat the egg white until it forms stiff but not dry peaks. Fold the egg white into the strawberry base, and return it to the ice-cream freezer. Process until slightly firm again. Chill in a freezer for 1 hour before serving.
5. Serve the sorbet in a flat bowl, garnished with the champagne grapes and sprinkled with the alpine strawberries.
Serves 4 *Photograph page 8*

1 serving: Calories 210, Protein 2 g, Carbohydrates 46 g, Fiber 5 g, Total fat 1 g (Saturated 0 g, Monounsaturated 0 g, Polyunsaturated .5 g), Cholesterol 0 mg, Sodium 15 mg, Vitamin C 180%.
▲ *2 Fruit*

Winter

It's the time of year for richly seasoned foods and an abundance of winter vegetables. Try a gratin of root vegetables—potatoes, Jerusalem artichokes, celery root, turnips and carrots. Potato-leek soup and curried winter squash soup take the edge off blustery winter days. Plan next year's garden over a Florentine orange and fennel salad or warm winter salad of grilled scallops and red onions with fresh grapefruit vinaigrette. (Fresh grapefruit from the South is always a welcome visitor in the snowy North.)

When the holidays approach, it's time to start thinking about a celebration feast for family and friends. Start with *Lussekatter*, the Santa Lucia buns traditionally served in Sweden on Christmas morning. Use the same dough to make braided wreaths of bread. Fill a turkey or goose with wild rice, chestnut and apple stuffing. This mixture goes well with Cornish hens, too. Cranberry-pear chutney makes leftover turkey something special. For a holiday pudding, try a warm persimmon and cranberry gratin.

Grilled Scallop Salad with Fresh Grapefruit Vinaigrette

This warm winter salad is substantial enough to serve as a light lunch.

GRAPEFRUIT VINAIGRETTE

¼ cup (2 fl oz/60 ml) freshly squeezed grapefruit juice

2 tablespoons champagne vinegar or white wine vinegar

¼ cup (2 fl oz/60 ml) safflower oil

¼ cup (1¼ oz/35 g) finely minced red (Spanish) onion

1 teaspoon grapefruit zest

¼ teaspoon salt

freshly ground white pepper to taste

SCALLOP SALAD

¾ lb (375 g) sea scallops

½ cup (2½ oz/75 g) red (Spanish) onion, cut into 1-in (2.5-cm) chunks

2 cups (4 oz/125 g) fresh spinach, cut into chiffonade

2 grapefruits, peeled, seeded and cut into sections

1. Heat a grill or broiler. Soak 8 bamboo skewers in water for 20 minutes.
2. To prepare the grapefruit vinaigrette, combine the grapefruit juice and vinegar in a medium bowl. Slowly drizzle in the safflower oil, whisking constantly. Add the minced onion and grapefruit zest; season with the salt and pepper.
3. To prepare the scallop salad, place the scallops and red onion chunks on skewers. Brush lightly with 1 tablespoon of the grapefruit vinaigrette. Grill or broil 1 minute on each side, until firm and opaque.
4. Make a bed of the spinach on a serving platter, and arrange the skewers on top. Scatter the grapefruit sections around the skewers, and drizzle with the remaining grapefruit vinaigrette. Serve at once.

Serves 4

1 serving: Calories 260, Protein 16 g, Carbohydrates 17 g, Fiber 3 g, Total fat 15 g (Saturated 1.5 g, Monounsaturated 2 g, Polyunsaturated 11 g), Cholesterol 30 mg, Sodium 310 mg, Vitamin A 40%, Vitamin C 100%.
▲ *1 Fruit, ½ Vegetable, 1 Meat*

Grilled Scallop Salad with Fresh Grapefruit Vinaigrette

Poppy Seed Crêpes with Smoked Salmon Mousse

Poppy Seed Crêpes with Smoked Salmon Mousse

These appetizer-size crêpes are a little thicker than the average crêpe, to allow you to pick them up with your fingers. If sodium is not a problem, garnish with a little spoonful of caviar.

1 cup (8 fl oz/250 ml) low-fat (1-percent) milk

1 egg

1 tablespoon safflower oil

¾ cup (3 oz/90 g) cake (soft-wheat) flour

1 tablespoon poppy seeds

1 tablespoon minced red (Spanish) onion

1 tablespoon minced chives

1 cup (8 fl oz/250 ml) plain low-fat yogurt, drained in cheesecloth overnight

4 oz (125 g) smoked salmon, puréed

2 teaspoons fresh dill, minced

2 tablespoons freshly squeezed lemon juice

2 teaspoons golden caviar (optional)

8 sprigs dill

1. In a blender, combine the milk, egg and oil. Add the flour, and process until smooth. Stir in the poppy seeds, red onion and chives.

2. Heat a large nonstick skillet. Pour eight 2-in (5-cm) circles of batter, and cook for 45–60 seconds on each side, until golden. Remove the crêpes to parchment paper to cool.

3. Blend together the yogurt, salmon, dill and lemon juice. Place in a pastry bag with a star tip, and pipe about 1 teaspoon of the mousse on each crêpe. Top with ¼ teaspoon of caviar and a sprig of dill. Serve at once.

Serves 8

---

1 crêpe per serving: Calories 120, Protein 7 g, Carbohydrates 12 g, Fiber 0 g, Total fat 4 g (Saturated 1 g, Monounsaturated 1 g, Polyunsaturated 2 g), Cholesterol 35 mg, Sodium 160 mg.

▲ *1 Bread, ½ Milk*

Top to bottom: Curried Winter Squash Soup, Orange Roughy Poached in Red Wine, Edna's Three-Color Mashed Potatoes

Edna's Three-Color Mashed Potatoes

Careers have been made on the basis of mashed potato recipes. My mother, Edna Sheldon, taught me the fine art of making mashed potatoes at a very young age. The potato is a complex carbohydrate. It's America's comfort food. It's time to have fun with it.

6 baking potatoes, peeled and cut into quarters lengthwise
1½ cups (12 fl oz/375 ml) buttermilk, warmed
2 tablespoons olive oil
salt and pepper to taste
½ teaspoon turmeric
3 tablespoons *pepita* pesto (see glossary)
2 tablespoons tomato paste (purée)

1. Place the potatoes in a large saucepan, and cover with cold water. Bring to a boil, and cook until fork tender, about 20 minutes. Drain thoroughly. Pass through a ricer or food mill, and return to the saucepan.
2. Add the buttermilk and oil, stirring over low heat to warm. Season with the salt and pepper. Divide the potatoes among 3 warm mixing bowls. Stir the turmeric into the first, the pesto into the second and the tomato paste into the third. Transfer immediately to warm serving dishes, and serve.
   Serves 8

¾ cup per serving: Calories 180, Protein 4 g, Carbohydrates 24 g, Fiber 2 g, Total fat 8 g (Saturated 1.5 g, Monounsaturated 5 g, Polyunsaturated 1 g), Cholesterol 5 mg, Sodium 75 mg.
▲ *1 Vegetable*

Orange Roughy Poached in Red Wine

Red snapper or rockfish is also an excellent choice to poach in red wine. This cooking technique can be applied to fillets as well as whole fish; just cook about 5 minutes for each inch (2.5 cm) of thickness.

2 tablespoons olive oil
3 shallots (white onions), minced
3 cups (24 fl oz/750 ml) dry red wine
3 cups (24 fl oz/750 ml) fish stock (see glossary)
bouquet garni: 1 sprig parsley, 1 sprig thyme, 1 bay leaf
** 5 peppercorns**
1 whole orange roughy, about 3 lb (1.5 kg)
2 teaspoons fresh thyme, minced

1. Heat the oil in a fish-poaching pan or other pan large enough to hold a whole fish. Add the shallots, and sauté until soft. Deglaze the pan with the wine, and reduce to half its volume.
2. Add the fish stock and bouquet garni, and bring to a boil.

Reduce to a simmer, and add the fish. Poach, turning occasionally, for 15 minutes, or until firm.
3. Transfer to a warm platter, sprinkle with the thyme and serve immediately.
   Serves 4

1 serving: Calories 160, Protein 33 g, Carbohydrates 0 g, Fiber 0 g, Total fat 2 g (Saturated 0 g, Monounsaturated 1.5 g, Polyunsaturated 0 g), Cholesterol 45 mg, Sodium 140 mg.
▲ *1 Meat*

Curried Winter Squash Soup

Many varieties of winter squash are available: Hubbard, butternut, buttercup, banana, acorn, Table Queen, and Delicata, to name a few. Some are very sweet; some are bland. Most are rich in complex carbohydrates, and the orange ones are rich in vitamins A and C. Try an assortment of squashes in this thick, spicy soup, or use just one variety. For a smooth bisque, purée the entire soup.

1 small spaghetti squash, about 1 lb (500 g)
1 small butternut squash, about 1 lb (500 g)
1 acorn squash, about 1 lb (500 g)
3 tablespoons safflower oil
3 leeks, white part only, cut in ¼-in (6-mm) slices
3 cloves garlic, minced
2 tablespoons curry powder
6 cups (48 fl oz/1.5 l) chicken stock (see glossary)
2 tablespoons minced parsley
¼ teaspoon salt
freshly ground pepper to taste
¼ teaspoon freshly grated nutmeg

1. Cut the spaghetti squash in half lengthwise; remove the seeds and fibers. Steam over boiling water until tender, about 20 minutes. Remove to cool. When the squash is cool enough to handle, scrape out the strands (like spaghetti) with a fork. Set aside.
2. Peel and seed the butternut and acorn squashes, and cut into 1-in (2.5-cm) pieces. Set aside.
3. Heat the oil in a medium stockpot over medium heat. Add the leeks and garlic; cook until soft, about 5 minutes. Add the curry powder, and cook 2 minutes, stirring occasionally. Add the raw squash pieces and stock. Bring to a boil, reduce to a simmer and cook, covered, until the squash is tender, about 30 minutes.
4. In a blender or food processor, purée two-thirds of the mixture until smooth, leaving one-third of the squash pieces whole. Return the mixture to the pot, add the spaghetti squash, and cook over medium-low heat about 5 minutes, just to warm. Season with the parsley, salt, pepper and nutmeg. Serve immediately.
   Serves 8

1 cup per serving: Calories 160, Protein 3 g, Carbohydrates 26 g, Fiber 3 g, Total fat 7 g (Saturated 1 g, Monounsaturated 1 g, Polyunsaturated 4.5 g), Cholesterol 0 mg, Sodium 100 mg, Vitamin A 90%, Vitamin C 45%.
▲ *2 Vegetable*

Cod and Julienned Vegetables in Parchment

SEAFOOD / FRANCE

Cod and Julienned Vegetables in Parchment

Cooking fish in parchment paper produces very moist and tender results. The packet is served unopened, and the drama of cutting the paper is heightened by the aromas released. If you use foil instead, substitute ¼ cup (2 fl oz/60 ml) of fish stock (see glossary) for the lemon juice.

1 cup (5 oz/155 g) peeled and julienned carrots, blanched for
   2 minutes (see glossary)
1 cup (4 oz/125 g) julienned leeks, blanched for 1 minute
   (see glossary)
½ cup (2 1/2 oz/75 g) peeled and julienned turnips, blanched
   for 2 minutes (see glossary)
1 cup (4 oz/125 g) julienned fennel
4 cod fillets (5–6 oz/155–185 g each)
juice of 1 lemon
¼ teaspoon salt
freshly ground pepper to taste
2 teaspoons minced fresh tarragon
1 tablespoon minced fresh parsley
1 tablespoon safflower oil

1. Preheat an oven to 350°F (180°C). Cut 4 pieces of parchment
   paper 12 by 12 in (30 by 30 cm).
2. Arrange the julienned vegetables on half of each parchment paper.
   Place a cod fillet on top. Sprinkle with the lemon juice; season
   with the salt, pepper, tarragon and parsley.
3. Fold the empty half of the parchment paper over the fish and
   vegetables, and cut the edges into a half-moon shape. Crimp the

edges tightly closed. Place the packets on a baking sheet, and brush the papers lightly with the oil. Bake for 12 minutes.
4. Serve at once. To open at the table, guests cut off the top of the packet, leaving the bottom in place.
Serves 4

1 packet per serving: Calories 190, Protein 27 g, Carbohydrates 11 g, Fiber 2 g, Total fat 5 g (Saturated .5 g, Monounsaturated .5 g, Polyunsaturated 3 g), Cholesterol 60 mg, Sodium 260 mg, Vitamin A 200%, Vitamin C 35%.
▲ *1 Vegetable, 1 Meat*

VEGETABLES / VIETNAM

Zen Master's Dish

This vegetarian main dish of steamed tofu and vegetables is quick and easy to prepare. Chef Ann Tran of Tran's Restaurant in Long Beach, California, suggests substituting mild bean sauce if you prefer a savory but less spicy version. Keith Tran, her husband and partner, says that the healthful preparation of this dish makes it suitable for a Zen master. Serve with steamed rice.

12 oz (375 g) firm tofu
3 tablespoons hot bean sauce or mild bean sauce
2 tablespoons sugar
½ cup (2 oz/60 g) bean threads
¼ cup (3 oz/90 g) halved and sliced tomato
¼ cup (¾ oz/20 g) fresh or canned straw mushrooms
¼ cup (1 oz/30 g) onion, cut into ½-by-1-in
   (12-by-25-mm) pieces
¼ cup (¾ oz/20 g) green (spring) onion, cut into 1-in
   (2.5-cm) pieces
¼ cup (1 oz/30 g) rib celery, thinly sliced diagonally
¼ cup (¼ oz/7 g) Chinese celery (*rau cân*) or celery leaves
2 tablespoons fresh gingerroot, peeled and julienned
freshly ground pepper to taste
5–6 leaves fresh cilantro (fresh coriander)
1 small tomato, cut into wedges

1. Slice the tofu in half across its thickness to about 1-in (2.5-cm) thick and 2-in (5-cm) wide. Place the slices end to end lengthwise, on a serving plate. Cut each of them crosswise at ½-in (12-mm) intervals, cutting not quite all the way through to the bottom.
2. In a small bowl, combine the bean sauce and sugar. Spread 1 tablespoon of the mixture over the top of the tofu.
3. Soak the bean threads in hot water for 1 minute; drain. Combine them with the sliced tomato, straw mushrooms, onion, green onion, celery, Chinese celery and ginger in a medium mixing bowl. Add the remaining bean sauce, ¼ cup (2 fl oz/60 ml) of water and the pepper. Mix well.
4. Spread the vegetable mixture over the tofu.
5. Place a Chinese bamboo steamer in a wok or over a large stockpot. Fill the wok or pot with water almost to the bottom edge of the steamer. Bring the water to a boil, and place the plate of tofu in the steamer. Cover tightly, reduce the temperature slightly and steam for 5 minutes.

6. Remove the plate of tofu from the steamer. Garnish with the cilantro and tomato wedges and serve at once.
Serves 2

---

1 serving: Calories 380, Protein 30 g, Carbohydrates 37 g, Fiber 5 g, Total fat 15 g (Saturated 2 g, Monounsaturated 3.5 g, Polyunsaturated 9 g), Cholesterol 0 mg, Sodium 45 mg, Iron 110%, Calcium 40%, Vitamin C 35%.
▲ *1 Vegetable, 2 Meat*

PASTAS / THAILAND

Rad Na

RICE NOODLES WITH CHINESE BROCCOLI

Serve this dish with the usual Thai condiments—chili paste, dried chilies, vinegared chilies and a sprinkle of chopped peanuts (groundnuts). Any noodle is good in this savory sauce, but rice noodles, whether fresh or dried, are particularly delicate. Since the fresh noodles have been cooked in the manufacturing process, they need only be reheated.

4 tablespoons (2 fl oz/60 ml) safflower oil
1 clove garlic, minced

½ lb (250 g) rice noodles, 1 in (2.5 cm) wide
1 tablespoon soy sauce
½ lb (250 g) Chinese broccoli, or broccoli, cut into bite-size pieces
1 tablespoon Chinese bean sauce
1 tablespoon sugar
1 tablespoon *nam pla* (fish sauce)
2 cups (16 fl oz/500 ml) chicken stock (see glossary)
2 tablespoons cornstarch (cornflour), dissolved in 3 tablespoons water

1. Heat 2 tablespoons of the oil in a wok over high heat. Add the garlic, and cook quickly until golden brown. Add the noodles and soy sauce, stir-frying until the noodles are hot, 2–3 minutes. Transfer to a warm platter, and keep warm.
2. Add the remainder of the oil to the wok, and heat until very hot. Add the broccoli, and stir-fry for 30 seconds. Quickly add the bean sauce, sugar, *nam pla* and chicken stock. Add the cornstarch mixture, and stir until thickened, about 3 minutes. Serve the broccoli mixture immediately over the noodles.
Serves 4

---

1 serving: Calories 380, Protein 10 g, Carbohydrates 56 g, Fiber 2 g, Total fat 15 g (Saturated 1.5 g, Monounsaturated 2 g, Polyunsaturated 11 g), Cholesterol 0 mg, Sodium 520 mg, Vitamin C 80%.
▲ *2 Bread, 1 Vegetable*

Left to right: Zen Master's Dish, Rice Noodles with Chinese Broccoli

Left to right: Pelmeni, Georgian Stuffed Cabbage

Georgian Stuffed Cabbage

Excellent as a vegetable side dish, finger-size stuffed cabbage rolls also make a savory addition to zakuski, an assortment of Russian appetizers. Or serve them floating in chicken stock or borscht broth. Cabbage, like broccoli, kale, brussels sprouts and cauliflower, is a cruciferous vegetable, containing antioxidants that protect against several forms of cancer.

1 head green cabbage

FILLING

    ¼ cup (2 fl oz/60 ml) safflower oil
    ½ cup (2 oz/60 g) chopped onion
    2 cloves garlic, minced
    ½ cup (1 oz/30 g) broccoli florets
    ½ cup (2½ oz/75 g) grated beet
    ½ cup (2½ oz/75 g) grated rutabaga (yellow turnip/Swede)
    1½ cups (12 fl oz/375 ml) chicken stock (see glossary)
    ¾ cup (5¼ oz/160 g) rice
    ¼ cup (¼ oz/7 g) parsley, minced
    ¼ cup (1½ oz/45 g) raisins

    ¼ cup (2 fl oz/60 ml) tomato sauce (puréed tomatoes)
    2 tablespoons freshly squeezed lemon juice
    ¼ teaspoon ground ginger
    ¼ teaspoon ground coriander
    ¼ teaspoon ground cinnamon
    salt and freshly ground black pepper to taste

SAUCE

    2 cups (16 fl oz/500 ml) tomato purée
    3 tablespoons brown sugar
    3 tablespoons fresh lemon juice

1. Preheat an oven to 350°F (180°C). Lightly oil a large, shallow baking dish.
2. To prepare the cabbage, remove the tough outer leaves and cut out the core.
3. Place the cabbage in enough boiling water to cover. Cook for 2–3 minutes, or until the leaves begin to separate. Pull the leaves apart, and cook an additional 1–2 minutes, until the leaves become pliable. Drain, and immerse the leaves immediately in ice water to stop the cooking.
4. Drain the leaves, and blot them dry with paper towels. Set aside.
5. To prepare the filling, heat the oil in a large skillet, and sauté the onion and garlic until light golden. Add the broccoli, beet and

rutabaga, and sauté for 1 minute, stirring. Add the chicken stock and rice, cover and simmer for 30 minutes.

6. Add the remaining filling ingredients, and mix well.

7. To stuff the cabbage, trim the heavy rib from the base of each cabbage leaf. With a sharp knife, cut a rough rectangle approximately 3 by 5 in (7.5 by 13 cm).

8. Place 1 tablespoon of filling in the center of each rectangle. Turn up 1 narrow edge, fold in the sides, and roll into a cylinder. Secure the rolls with lightweight string or toothpicks, if necessary, and place them in the baking dish. Set aside.

9. To make the sauce, in a small saucepan, heat the tomato purée, brown sugar and lemon juice. Simmer for 10 minutes.

10. Pour the sauce over the cabbage rolls, and bake for 30 minutes.

Makes 16 small rolls

---

2 rolls per serving: Calories 220, Protein 4 g, Carbohydrates 38 g, Fiber 4 g, Total fat 8 g (Saturated 1 g, Monounsaturated 1 g, Polyunsaturated 5 g), Cholesterol 0 mg, Sodium 330 mg, Vitamin C 110%.
▲ *2 Vegetable*

PASTA / RUSSIA

Pelmeni

RUSSIAN RAVIOLI

Siberian cooks stored these pasta dumplings in the snow; your freezer will work quite well. They are traditionally cooked and served in a meat broth, although the strained borscht in this version is another delicious vehicle.

1 carrot, finely diced
1 potato, finely diced
½ cup (2½ oz/75 g) finely chopped onion
juice of 1 lemon
½ lb (250 g) fresh salmon fillet
½ teaspoon dry mustard
2 teaspoons fresh dill, chopped
salt and freshly ground white pepper to taste
½ recipe pasta dough (see glossary), rolled thin
1 egg white beaten with 1 teaspoon water
8 cups (64 fl oz/2 l) borscht (recipe on page 155), strained

1. In a large saucepan or skillet, bring 4 cups (32 fl oz/1 l) of water to a boil. Add the carrot, potato, onion and all but 1 tablespoon of the lemon juice. Reduce to a simmer, and cook for 5 minutes.

2. Add the salmon, and poach for 8–10 minutes. Drain and cool the mixture.

3. Chop the salmon into very small pieces, and combine with the vegetables.

4. Mix the dry mustard with the remaining lemon juice. Add the dill, and stir into the salmon mixture. Season with the salt and pepper. Set aside.

5. With a biscuit cutter, cut the pasta dough into 2-in (5-cm) rounds.

6. Place ½ teaspoon of the salmon mixture in the center of each pasta circle. Moisten the edge of the circle lightly with the egg white mixture, and fold in half, forming a half-moon shape. Pinch the edges tightly, taking care that none of the filling breaks the seal of the edges. Place on a lightly floured baking

sheet until ready to use. (The *pelmeni* may be covered and refrigerated or frozen at this point.)

7. Heat the borscht, and keep it warm.

8. Bring a large stockpot of water to a boil. Drop in the *pelmeni* and cook for 2 minutes. Remove with a slotted spoon, and drain in a colander.

9. Transfer the cooked *pelmeni* to the borscht broth, and serve immediately.

Serves 8

---

1 serving: Calories 250, Protein 13 g, Carbohydrates 36 g, Fiber 3 g, Total fat 6 g (Saturated 1.5 g, Monounsaturated 2.5 g, Polyunsaturated 1 g), Cholesterol 75 mg, Sodium 150 mg, Vitamin A 130%, Vitamin C 35%.
▲ *½ Bread, 2 Vegetable*

GRAINS / MIDDLE EAST

Chick-Pea, Barley and Bulgur Pilaf

Cracked wheat, also known as bulgur, is best known for its appearance in tabbouleh (recipe on page 158). It is also a good partner to other grains in warm pilaf dishes such as this one, in which hulled barley (with its fiber) and chick-peas (for protein) are used to produce a nutty-tasting side dish that is a complete protein.

½ cup (3½ oz/105 g) hulled barley
5 cups (40 fl oz/1.25 l) chicken stock (see glossary)
½ cup (3½ oz/105 g) dried chick-peas (garbanzo beans), soaked overnight
½ cup (3 oz/90 g) medium-grain bulgur
2 tablespoons olive oil
2 cloves garlic, minced
1 onion, chopped
½ cup (2 oz/60 g) sliced celery
1 teaspoon ground cumin
½ teaspoon ground coriander
3 tablespoons fresh parsley, minced
¼ teaspoon salt
freshly ground pepper to taste

1. Place the hulled barley in a large stockpot with the chicken stock, and cook over medium heat for 30 minutes, stirring occasionally. Add drained chick-peas, and cook for 45 minutes. Add the bulgur, and cook for 15 minutes. Cover, and remove from the heat until ready to use.

2. Heat the oil in a large sauté pan. Add the garlic and onion, and cook over medium heat until light golden, about 5 minutes. Add the celery, and cook 2 minutes. Add the grain mixture and toss well.

3. Season with the cumin, coriander, parsley, salt and pepper. Serve at once.

Serves 6   *Photograph page 195*

---

1 cup per serving: Calories 190, Protein 5 g, Carbohydrates 30 g, Fiber 6 g, Total fat 6 g (Saturated 1 g, Monounsaturated 4 g, Polyunsaturated 1 g), Cholesterol 0 mg, Sodium 120 mg.
▲ *2 Bread*

Baked Halibut Steak Stuffed with Roasted Garlic and Sun-Dried Tomatoes

Any firm steaklike fish is suitable for stuffing. Try grilling the stuffed steaks for a hearty summer dish; just be careful not to overstuff them, and tie them with a little kitchen string.

6 heads roasted garlic (see glossary)

10 sun-dried tomatoes, soaked in warm water and julienned

1 shallot (white onion), finely minced

1 teaspoon fresh thyme, finely minced

½ cup (1 oz/60 g) fresh bread crumbs, finely ground

1 teaspoon freshly squeezed lemon juice

salt and freshly ground pepper to taste

2 lemons, sliced ⅛ in (3 mm) thick

4 fresh boned halibut steaks, 1 in (2.5 cm) thick (about 6 oz/185 g each)

salt and pepper to taste

1. Preheat an oven to 400°F (200°C).
2. To prepare the stuffing, remove the cloves from 2 of the heads of roasted garlic. Combine in a medium bowl with 8 of the sun-dried tomatoes, the shallot and the thyme. Stir in the bread crumbs, sprinkle with the lemon juice and season with the salt and pepper.
3. Lightly oil a shallow baking dish (use some of the oil from roasting the garlic), and line it with the lemon slices.
4. Cut a horizontal slash in the side of each halibut steak, slicing it almost in half. It should look like a book when the top flap is lifted open. Spread a spoonful of stuffing in the middle of the slice, and close the flap.
5. Place the stuffed steaks on top of the lemon slices in the baking dish. Brush the steaks lightly with oil from the roasted garlic, and season lightly with salt and pepper.
6. Bake, uncovered, for 15–18 minutes, until the fish is opaque.
7. Garnish each serving with a remaining head of roasted garlic, and sprinkle the remaining sun-dried tomatoes over the steaks. Serve immediately.

Serves 4

1 steak with 1 head garlic per serving: Calories 410, Protein 43 g, Carbohydrates 33 g, Fiber 2 g, Total fat 13 g (Saturated 2 g, Monounsaturated 7 g, Polyunsaturated 2.5 g), Cholesterol 80 mg, Sodium 240 mg, Calcium 25%, Vitamin C 55%.

▲ *1 Vegetable, 2 Meat*

Baked Halibut Steak Stuffed with Roasted Garlic and Sun-Dried Tomatoes

Left to right: Squabs in Seville Orange Sauce; Chick-Pea, Barley and Bulgur Pilaf (recipe page 193)

POULTRY / SPAIN

Squabs in Seville Orange Sauce

Seville oranges are bitter oranges, and they give this sauce a distinctive tartness. If Seville oranges are unavailable, use one sweet orange and one lemon instead. Serve the squabs over rice or couscous.

4 squabs

3 tablespoons olive oil

4 cloves garlic, sliced

4 Seville oranges or 1 sweet orange and 1 lemon, peeled and
   sliced crosswise

1 cup (8 fl oz/250 ml) dry white wine

2 cups (16 fl oz/500 ml) chicken stock (see glossary)

2 tablespoons flour mixed with 3 tablespoons chicken stock

1 tablespoon chopped fresh mint

¼ teaspoon salt

freshly ground pepper to taste

1. Rinse the squabs and pat them dry. Heat the olive oil in a Dutch oven or large casserole, and sauté the squabs over medium-high heat until brown on all sides, about 8–10 minutes. Reduce the heat to medium, add the garlic and oranges and cook for 1 minute. Deglaze the pan with the wine, and reduce over medium-high heat for 5 minutes; then add the chicken stock.

2. Simmer, covered, for 30 minutes, turning the squabs occasionally. Remove the squabs and orange slices to a warm serving platter, and keep warm.

3. Whisk the flour mixture into the cooking liquid; simmer for 5 minutes, whisking constantly, until slightly thickened. Add the mint, and season with the salt and pepper. Pour over the squabs, and serve at once.

Serves 4

---

1 serving: Calories 380, Protein 20 g, Carbohydrates 11 g, Fiber 2 g, Total fat 25 g (Saturated 7 g, Monounsaturated 14 g, Polyunsaturated 3 g), Cholesterol 100 mg, Sodium 230 mg, Vitamin C 45%.
▲ *1 Fruit, 1 Meat*

Risotto alla Piemontese

The addition of wine to risotto is not unusual, but generally white wine is used. Here red wine gives the risotto a rich color and unequaled flavor. The wine of choice in the northwestern region of Piedmont is Barolo, *although a Chianti or other full-bodied red wine is just as good. If you serve this risotto as a main dish, increase the portion size.*

3 tablespoons olive oil
1 cup (4 oz/125 g) chopped onion
1 cup (5 oz/155 g) cardoon, trimmed and cut into ½-in (12-mm) slices
2 cups (14 oz/440 g) Arborio rice

Top to bottom: Risotto alla Piemontese, Shrimp and Fennel Salad, Lynne Rossetto Kasper's Braised Garlic with Linguine

1 cup (8 fl oz/250 ml) dry red wine
5–6 cups (40–48 fl oz/1.25–1.5 l) simmering chicken stock
  (see glossary)
¼ teaspoon salt
freshly ground pepper to taste
¼ cup (1 oz/30 g) freshly grated Parmesan cheese
1 small white truffle (optional)

1. Heat the olive oil in a large saucepan. Add the onion and cardoon, and cook over low heat until soft and translucent but not browned, about 8 minutes. Add the Arborio rice, and sauté until opaque, about 2 minutes.
2. Add the wine, and simmer until it is absorbed. Begin adding the chicken stock 1 cup (8 fl oz/250 ml) at a time, stirring constantly and simmering until the stock is almost completely absorbed before adding more. Continue until the risotto is tender, but firm. Season with the salt and pepper.
3. Sprinkle with the Parmesan cheese and serve immediately. If the white truffle is available, shave a razor-thin bit on top of each serving.
Serves 6

---

1 cup per serving: Calories 340, Protein 7 g, Carbohydrates 57 g, Fiber 1 g, Total fat 9 g (Saturated 2 g, Monounsaturated 6 g, Polyunsaturated 1 g), Cholesterol 3 mg, Sodium 190 mg.
▲ *2 Bread, 1 Vegetable*

PASTAS / ITALY

Lynne Rossetto Kasper's Braised Garlic with Linguine

Lynne Rossetto Kasper's book The Splendid Table: Recipes from Emilia-Romagna, the Heartland of Northern Italian Food *provides an in-depth look at the food and historical influence of this part of Italy. Two regional specialties are included in this recipe:* parmigiano reggiano *cheese and balsamic vinegar. Use a high-quality commercial balsamic vinegar here or, better yet, an artisan-made balsamic. This dish uses a lot of oil, although it is oil of the most heart-healthy type. Balance the day with low-fat foods or serve smaller portions of this delicious pasta as a side dish.*

6 tablespoons (3 fl oz/90 ml) extra virgin olive oil
8 large cloves garlic, cut into ¼-in (6-mm) dice
1 lb (500 g) imported dried linguine
salt and freshly ground black pepper to taste
4 oz (125 g) freshly grated *parmigiano reggiano* (Italian
  Parmesan) cheese
8–10 teaspoons high-quality balsamic vinegar

1. To braise the garlic, in a large, heavy skillet, heat 3 tablespoons of the oil over medium-low heat. Add the garlic, and cook, covered, over the lowest possible heat for 5 minutes. Uncover, and continue cooking over low heat, stirring frequently with a wooden spatula, for about 8 minutes, or until the garlic is barely colored to pale blond and is very tender. Do not let the garlic turn medium-to-dark brown, as it will be bitter.
2. While the garlic braises, bring 6 qt (6 l) of salted water to a fierce boil, and drop in the linguine. Cook, stirring occasionally, until the pasta is al dente (tender, but still firm to the bite), up to 10 minutes. Spoon about 3 tablespoons of the cooking water into the braised garlic. Drain the pasta in a colander.
3. Remove the garlic from the heat and add the pasta. Add the remaining oil, and toss with 2 wooden spatulas. Season with the salt and pepper. Toss with all of the cheese, and turn into a warm serving bowl. As you serve the pasta, sprinkle each plateful with a teaspoon or so of the vinegar.
Serves 6 as main course, 10 as side dish

---

1 serving (main course): Calories 490, Protein 18 g, Carbohydrates 59 g, Fiber 2 g, Total fat 20 g (Saturated 6 g, Monounsaturated 12 g, Polyunsaturated 2 g), Cholesterol 15 mg, Sodium 360 mg, Calcium 30%.
▲ *2 Bread, 1 Fat/Sugar*

SALADS / ITALY

Insalata di Gamberi e Finocchio

SHRIMP AND FENNEL SALAD

This refreshing salad can be served as a starter or light lunch. Prepare it a day ahead, and refrigerate it to allow the flavors to blend further.

1 lb (500 g) shrimp (prawns), peeled and deveined
2 fennel bulbs, very thinly sliced crosswise
1 small red (Spanish) onion, sliced crosswise into rings
2 tablespoons red wine vinegar
3 tablespoons extra virgin olive oil
¼ teaspoon salt
freshly ground pepper to taste
1 teaspoon fresh thyme, minced
2 tablespoons flat-leaf (Italian) parsley
1 head radicchio, separated into leaves

1. Cook the shrimp in boiling water until firm and pink, about 2 minutes. Remove to cool.
2. Place the fennel in a large salad bowl with the shrimp and onion; set aside.
3. In a small bowl, mix together the vinegar and olive oil. Season with the salt and pepper. Add the thyme and parsley, and toss with the fennel and shrimp. Chill at least 1 hour before serving.
4. Spoon the salad into the radicchio leaves to serve.
Serves 6

---

1 serving: Calories 180, Protein 17 g, Carbohydrates 10 g, Fiber 1 g, Total fat 8 g (Saturated 1 g, Monounsaturated 5 g, Polyunsaturated 1 g), Cholesterol 115 mg, Sodium 260 mg, Vitamin C 25%.
▲ *1 Vegetable, 1 Meat*

Steamed Buns with Chicken and Vegetables

Bao, *Chinese steamed buns, are an essential element of* dim sum *and are also sold with a variety of fillings as "street food" in China. These are great do-ahead appetizers, steamed just before serving or steamed a day ahead and reheated. They are delicious with sweet green onion dipping sauce (recipe on page 72).*

> 1 package (¼ oz/7 g) active dry yeast
> 2 teaspoons sugar
> 1 tablespoon plus 2 teaspoons Chinese sesame oil
> 3½–4 cups (17½–20 oz/545–625 g) all-purpose (plain) flour
> 3 dried Chinese black mushrooms or dried shiitake mushrooms
> 1 tablespoon dried tree ear mushrooms
> 2 teaspoons soy sauce
> 2 teaspoons dry sherry
> 2 tablespoons peanut (groundnut) oil
> ½ lb (250 g) chicken breast, skinned, boned and chopped fine
> 3 green (spring) onions, minced
> 2 cloves garlic, minced
> 1 carrot, coarsely grated
> 2 teaspoons minced fresh gingerroot
> 1 tablespoon cornstarch (cornflour) dissolved in ¼ cup
>   (2 fl oz/60 ml) chicken stock (see glossary)
> 1 teaspoon baking powder
> ½ cup (1½ oz/45 g) green (spring) onions, finely sliced

1. Dissolve the yeast and sugar in ¼ cup (2 fl oz/ 60 ml) of warm water (105°–115°F/40°–46°C). Let stand until foamy, about 5 minutes. Add 1 tablespoon of the sesame oil.

2. Place 3 cups (15 oz/470 g) of the flour in large a mixing bowl, and add the yeast mixture slowly, beating until stiff. Turn the dough onto a lightly floured work surface, adding the remaining ½–1 cup (2½–5 oz/75–155 g) of flour as needed. Knead until smooth and elastic, not sticky, about 5–10 minutes. Place the dough in a bowl lightly coated with sesame oil, and let it rise, covered, until doubled in bulk, about 1 hour.

3. To prepare the filling, soak the black mushrooms and tree ear mushrooms in hot water for at least 20 minutes. Remove and discard the stems; rinse and mince the caps. Set aside.

4. Mix together the remaining sesame oil, the soy sauce and the sherry, and set aside.

5. Heat a wok, then add the peanut oil. When the oil is very hot, add the chicken breast and stir-fry until white, about 1 minute. Add the 3 minced green onions and the garlic, carrot and ginger, and stir-fry 1 minute. Add the mushrooms, and stir-fry 1 minute. Stir in the sesame-soy mixture, coating all ingredients. Add the cornstarch mixture, and stir until thickened, about 1 minute. Remove from the heat, and cool.

6. Punch down the dough and turn it onto a lightly floured work surface. Sprinkle the baking powder and ½ cup (1½ oz/45 g) sliced green onions over the dough, and work them in by kneading for 5 minutes.

7. Place a Chinese bamboo steamer in a wok or over a large stockpot. Fill the wok or pot with water almost to the bottom edge of the steamer. Remove the steamer, and set aside.

8. Cut out twelve 3-in (7.5-cm) squares of waxed paper or oiled parchment paper.

9. Cut the dough in half, and roll each half into a 12-in (30-cm) cylindrical rope. Cut each rope into 6 pieces. Pat each piece flat on a lightly floured work surface. With a rolling pin, roll each piece to approximately 4 in (10 cm).

10. Place 2 tablespoons of filling in the center of each round. Gather up and pleat the edges to close, giving a final small twist to the top to seal. Place the buns seam side down on the paper squares.

11. Arrange the buns on their papers 1½ in (4 cm) apart in the steamer tiers. Cover with a towel, and let rise 30 minutes.

12. Place the steamer tiers over boiling water in the wok or pot. Reduce the heat slightly. Steam for 15 minutes, covered tightly. Halfway through the cooking time, switch the positions of the tiers. Let stand, covered tightly, for 5 minutes, until the steam has dissipated, before serving.

Makes 12 buns

---

1 bun per serving: Calories 200, Protein 7 g, Carbohydrates 32 g, Fiber 2 g, Total fat 5 g (Saturated 1 g, Monounsaturated 2 g, Polyunsaturated 2 g), Cholesterol 5 mg, Sodium 55 mg, Vitamin A 35%.
▲ *1 Bread, ½ Vegetable*

Kung Pao Chicken

This old favorite is spicy and full of flavor. It's also quick and easy to prepare. Serve it with steamed rice for a fast after-work meal or light lunch.

> 2 tablespoons dry sherry
> 1 tablespoon cornstarch (cornflour)
> 1 teaspoon sesame oil
> freshly ground white pepper to taste
> 1½ lb (750 g) skinned and boned chicken breasts, cut into
>   bite-size pieces
> 1 tablespoon soy sauce
> 1 tablespoon rice wine vinegar
> ¼ cup (2 fl oz/60 ml) chicken stock (see glossary)
> 3 tablespoons peanut (groundnut) oil
> 5 small, whole dried red chilies
> ¼ cup (1½ oz/45 g) dry-roasted peanuts (groundnuts)
> 1 teaspoon minced garlic
> 1 teaspoon grated fresh gingerroot
> 4 green (spring) onions, cut into 1-in (2.5-cm) lengths
> 1 cup (5 oz/155 g) snow peas (mangetouts), ends trimmed

1. In a large bowl, combine 1 tablespoon of the sherry with the cornstarch, sesame oil and pepper. Add the chicken pieces, and toss well to coat. Let stand for 20 minutes.

2. In a small bowl, combine the soy sauce, vinegar, remaining sherry and chicken stock. Set aside.

3. Heat a wok or large skillet over medium-high heat. When it is

very hot, add the peanut oil, chilies and peanuts. Stir quickly, and cook until the chilies darken but before they turn black. Remove the peanuts and chilies with a slotted spoon, and drain on paper towels.

4. Add the garlic and ginger to the chili-flavored oil in the wok. Stir quickly; then add the chicken mixture. Stir-fry until the chicken is opaque, about 3 minutes. Add the green onions and snow peas, and stir-fry for 1 minute. Stir in the soy sauce mixture, and cook

until slightly thickened, about 2 minutes. Add the peanuts and chilies, and serve at once.

Serves 6

1 serving: Calories 250, Protein 29 g, Carbohydrates 6 g, Fiber 2 g, Total fat 12 g (Saturated 2 g, Monounsaturated 5 g, Polyunsaturated 4 g), Cholesterol 65 mg, Sodium 220 mg, Vitamin C 45%.

▲ *1 Meat*

Faisan Normand

NORMANDY-STYLE ROAST PHEASANT

Travel through picture-perfect Normandy in the fall, and you will see roadside stands selling apples and cider. This is one of my favorite dishes for holiday entertaining; the apple-flavored sauce is delicious with chicken or duck breasts as well.

2 pheasants, 3 lb (1.5 kg) each
¼ teaspoon salt
freshly ground pepper to taste
4 shallots (white onions), sliced
2 sprigs fresh thyme
4 cloves garlic, crushed
1 tablespoon unsalted butter
1 tablespoon olive oil
1 lb (500 g) tart, firm apples (such as pippin or Granny Smith), peeled, cored and diced
1 lb (500 g) celery root, peeled and cut into matchsticks
2 tablespoons Calvados or brandy
¼ cup (2 fl oz/60 ml) apple cider or unsweetened apple juice
2 cups (16 fl oz/500 ml) brown chicken stock (see glossary)
2 teaspoons fresh thyme, minced

1. Heat an oven to 350°F (180°C).
2. Rinse the pheasants, pat them dry and season them with the salt and pepper. Place half of the shallots with the thyme sprigs and garlic inside each pheasant.
3. In a large skillet, heat the butter and olive oil. Brown the pheasants on each side over high heat, and place them on their sides in a roasting pan. Set aside.
4. In the same skillet, sauté the apples and celery root for 2 minutes. Deglaze the pan with the Calvados. Add the cider, chicken stock and minced thyme, and simmer for 10 minutes. Drain the apples and celery root, and set aside; pour the cooking liquid over the pheasants in the roasting pan.
5. Roast the pheasants, covered, for 30 minutes, turning them from side to side every 10 minutes.
6. Add the reserved apples and celery root to the pan, stirring to coat them with the cooking juices. Turn the pheasants breast-up, and roast them, uncovered, 5–7 minutes more, until they are browned.
7. Transfer the pheasants to a warm serving platter. With a slotted spoon, arrange the apples and celery root around them. Spoon some of the juices over, and serve immediately.

Serves 8

Left to right: Potato-Leek Soup (recipe page 202); Normandy-Style Roast Pheasant; Gratin of Root Vegetables

¼ bird with sauce per serving: Calories 410, Protein 49 g, Carbohydrates 18 g, Fiber 3 g, Total fat 16 g (Saturated 5 g, Monounsaturated 8 g, Polyunsaturated 2 g), Cholesterol 100 mg, Sodium 230 mg, Iron 20%, Vitamin C 35%.

▲ 1 Fruit, ½ Vegetable, 1½ Meat

BREADS / BRAZIL

Sweet Potato Biscuits

Looking for a delicious new way to use leftover sweet potatoes? The potatoes give these biscuits a light, moist texture. Yams also work well and impart a pleasant, interesting color. Roast the pepitas on a dry baking sheet in a 300°F (150°C) oven for 10 minutes. Serve with your favorite fruit preserves.

1 cup (6½ oz/200 g) cooked sweet potatoes
4 teaspoons safflower oil
1 tablespoon sugar
1 cup (5 oz/155 g) all-purpose (plain) flour
1 tablespoon baking powder
¼ teaspoon salt
¼ cup roasted *pepitas* (hulled pumpkin seeds)

1. Preheat an oven to 375°F (190°C). Line a baking sheet with parchment paper.
2. In a large mixing bowl, mash the sweet potatoes with the vegetable oil and sugar.
3. In a medium bowl, mix the flour, baking powder, salt and *pepitas*.
4. Fold the dry ingredients into the potato mixture, stirring just until combined. Do not overmix.
5. Turn the dough onto a lightly floured work surface, and roll out until ½ in (12 mm) thick. Cut into rounds with a 2-in (5-cm) cutter, and place the rounds on the baking sheet.
6. Bake 15 minutes, until golden brown. Serve immediately.
   Makes 12 biscuits

1 biscuit per serving: Calories 90, Protein 2 g, Carbohydrates 14 g, Fiber 1 g, Total fat 3 g (Saturated .5 g, Monounsaturated .5 g, Polyunsaturated 2 g), Cholesterol 0 mg, Sodium 50 mg, Vitamin A 70%.

▲ 1 Bread

VEGETABLES / FRANCE

Gratin of Root Vegetables

Those who live on farms often store root vegetables in the ground and dig them up as needed. This simple storage principle can be applied at home without the earth: keeping the roots in a cool, dry and dark place helps them last longer. Try using other seasonal roots in this gratin, such as parsley roots, parsnips, rutabagas (yellow turnips/Swedes), and sweet potatoes.

1 potato, peeled and sliced ⅛ in (3 mm) thick
2 medium Jerusalem artichokes

Top to bottom: Sweet Potato Biscuits with fruit preserves, Black Bean Soup (recipe page 206)

1 tablespoon freshly squeezed lemon juice
1 celery root, peeled and sliced ⅛ in (3 mm) thick
1 turnip, peeled and sliced
1 carrot, peeled and diced
2 cups (16 fl oz/500 ml) low-fat (1-percent) milk
¼ teaspoon salt
freshly ground pepper to taste
freshly grated nutmeg to taste
3 tablespoons Parmesan cheese

1. Preheat an oven to 375°F (190°C). Lightly oil an 8-cup (64-fl oz/ 2-l) baking dish.
2. Rinse the potatoes until the water runs clear. Drain, and set aside.
3. Peel the Jerusalem artichokes and slice ⅛ in (3 mm) thick. Place in water to cover mixed with the lemon juice until ready to use. Then rinse until the water runs clear. Drain and set aside.
4. Arrange the potato, Jerusalem artichoke, celery root and turnip slices in the baking dish in alternating layers, sprinkling a few carrot dice on each layer.
5. Combine the milk, salt, pepper and nutmeg. Pour over the vegetables. Cover, and bake for 45 minutes, until the vegetables are tender. Remove the cover, sprinkle on the cheese and bake for 10 minutes to brown.
   Serves 6

¾ cup per serving: Calories 100, Protein 5 g, Carbohydrates 17 g, Fiber 2 g, Total fat 2 g (Saturated 1.5 g, Monounsaturated 0 g, Polyunsaturated 0 g), Cholesterol 5 mg, Sodium 230 mg, Vitamin A 70%, Vitamin C 20%.

▲ 1 Vegetable, ½ Milk

Potato-Leek Soup

Hearty winter vegetables are combined here to provide hearty winter fare. Make a double batch of this soup, and freeze half for later use.

4 tablespoons (2 fl oz/60 ml) safflower oil
4 leeks, julienned
4 cloves garlic, finely minced
3 potatoes, peeled and diced
3 cups (24 fl oz/750 ml) chicken stock (see glossary)
3 cups (24 fl oz/750 ml) low-fat (1-percent) milk
½ cup (3 oz/90 g) frozen petite corn
¼ teaspoon salt
freshly ground pepper to taste

1. Heat the oil in a large stockpot, and sauté the leeks and garlic until soft but not browned.
2. Add the potatoes and chicken stock, and bring to a boil. Reduce to a simmer, and cook 15–20 minutes, or until the potatoes are tender.
3. Purée approximately half of the mixture in a blender. Return it to the pot, and stir in the milk and corn. Heat through, and season with the salt and pepper.

Serves 8   *Photograph page 200*

1 cup per serving: Calories 200, Protein 5 g, Carbohydrates 27 g, Fiber 2 g, Total fat 9 g (Saturated 1.5 g, Monounsaturated 1.5 g, Polyunsaturated 5 g), Cholesterol 5 mg, Sodium 135 mg, Vitamin C 20%.
▲ *1 Vegetable, ½ Milk*

Insalata di Arànce

GIULIANO BUGIALLI'S ORANGE SALAD

Author and cooking instructor Giuliano Bugialli sends this recipe from his school in Florence. The vibrant color of the oranges and the refreshing taste of the fennel make this an excellent starter or a beautiful addition to a buffet.

4 large, juicy oranges
4 celery hearts
1 large fennel bulb, thinly sliced
3 tablespoons olive oil
1 teaspoon red wine vinegar
freshly ground black pepper to taste
4 walnuts, shelled and coarsely chopped (about 4 tablespoons/1 oz/30 g)

1. Peel the oranges, and carefully remove the white skin around the outside of the flesh. Cut the oranges crosswise into slices less than ½ in (12 mm) thick, and arrange them on a large serving platter.

2. Clean the celery hearts very well, removing all the strings, and cut them into ⅜-in (1-cm) squares. Arrange the celery and fennel over the oranges.
3. Mix the oil and vinegar, and drizzle the mixture over the oranges, celery and fennel; then season with a little pepper. Place a few walnut pieces on top.

Serves 8

1 serving: Calories 130, Protein 2 g, Carbohydrates 16 g, Fiber 5 g, Total fat 7 g (Saturated 1 g, Monounsaturated 4.5 g, Polyunsaturated 2 g), Cholesterol 0 mg, Sodium 55 mg, Vitamin C 100%.
▲ *1 Fruit, 1 Vegetable*

Roasted Monkfish with Rosemary Potatoes

This quick one-dish meal can be prepared with your choice of seafood.

1½ lb (750 g) red potatoes, cut into 2-in (5-cm) pieces
1 onion, sliced
2 tablespoons rosemary leaves, minced
3 tablespoons olive oil
1¾ lb (875 g) monkfish (anglerfish) fillet
¼ teaspoon salt
freshly ground pepper to taste
sprigs of rosemary for garnish

1. Preheat an oven to 400°F (200°C). Brush a large roasting pan lightly with olive oil.
2. Place the potatoes, onion, minced rosemary and 2 tablespoons of the olive oil in the roasting pan, and toss well. Bake until light golden brown and fork tender, about 25 minutes. Stir the potato mixture once during baking.
3. Brush the monkfish with the remaining oil, season it with the salt and pepper. Stir the potato mixture again, and place the fish on top. Bake for 10 minutes, or until the fish is opaque. Let the fish rest for 3–4 minutes; then place it on a cutting board.
4. Transfer the potato mixture to a serving platter. Slice the fish diagonally, and arrange the slices on top of the potatoes. Garnish with the sprigs of rosemary, and serve at once.

Serves 4

1 serving: Calories 340, Protein 29 g, Carbohydrates 37 g, Fiber 4 g, Total fat 8 g (Saturated 1 g, Monounsaturated 4.5 g, Polyunsaturated 1.5 g), Cholesterol 60 mg, Sodium 220 mg, Vitamin C 20 %.
▲ *1 Vegetable, 1 Meat*

Top to bottom: Roasted Monkfish with Rosemary Potatoes, Giuliano Bugialli's Orange Salad

Wild Rice, Chestnut and Apple Stuffing

Fill any poultry from Cornish game hens to a goose with this flavorful stuffing, or serve it as a side dish with grilled meats. Add 1 cup (4 oz/ 125 g) of cranberries with the apples for a colorful holiday version.

1 cup (6 oz/185 g) wild rice

salt to taste

4 leeks, white parts only, chopped

2 tablespoons safflower oil

½ lb (250 g) fresh chestnuts, roasted, peeled and sliced

1 cup (8 fl oz/250 ml) chicken stock (see glossary) reduced to ¼ cup (2 fl oz/60 ml)

½ cup (4 fl oz/125 ml) Calvados or dry Madeira

2 large Granny Smith or pippin apples, diced

1 tablespoon fresh sage, minced

2 tablespoons fresh thyme, minced

¼ cup (¼ oz/7 g) fresh parsley, minced

freshly ground pepper to taste

1. Stir the wild rice and salt into 4 cups (32 fl oz/1 l) boiling water. Simmer uncovered until the water is absorbed and the rice pops open, 40–45 minutes.
2. Sauté the leeks in the oil over moderate heat until soft but not browned. Add the chestnuts and chicken stock, and cook until the liquid evaporates, about 5 minutes. Raise the heat, deglaze the pan with the Calvados or Madeira and reduce again until syrupy.
3. Add the remaining ingredients, and toss with the wild rice.

Serves 8

¾ cup per serving: Calories 230, Protein 5 g, Carbohydrates 45 g, Fiber 7 g, Total fat 5 g (Saturated .5 g, Monounsaturated 1 g, Polyunsaturated 3 g), Cholesterol 0 mg, Sodium 15 mg, Vitamin C 40%.
▲ *1 Bread, ½ Fruit, ½ Vegetable*

Maple-Glazed Goose with Cranberry-Pear Chutney

Whether you roast a goose or a turkey, allow about 20 minutes per pound (500 g) for the total roasting time. Serve maple-glazed goose with cranberry-pear chutney (recipe follows) and sweet onion confit (recipe follows) and Himmel und Erde (recipe on page 164). Using turkey in this recipe reduces the fat by almost half.

STUFFED GOOSE

1 goose or turkey, about 10 lb (5 kg)

1 lemon, halved

freshly ground pepper to taste

2 teaspoons fresh rosemary, minced

wild rice, chestnut and apple stuffing (preceding recipe)

MAPLE GLAZE

3 tablespoons unsalted margarine

3 tablespoons minced fresh gingerroot

½ cup (4 fl oz/125 ml) pure maple syrup

½ cup (4 fl oz/125 ml) chicken stock (see glossary)

1. Preheat an oven to 425°F (220°C).
2. Rub the cavity of the goose or turkey with the lemon and then with the pepper and rosemary. Repeat for the outside of the bird.
3. Fill the poultry loosely with the stuffing, and tie the legs together.
4. To make the glaze, melt the margarine in a small saucepan. Add the ginger, and simmer 5 minutes. Add the maple syrup and chicken stock, and simmer 10 minutes.
5. Place the bird breast-up on a rack in a roasting pan, and brush it with the glaze. Cover, and roast for 15 minutes, then reduce the heat to 350°F (180°C), and bake for 3 hours, basting frequently, until a leg moves easily or a meat thermometer inserted in the thigh registers 180°F (82°C). Fifteen minutes before the bird is done, remove the cover. If the breast browns before the last 15 minutes, cover it with foil. To test for doneness, pierce the thigh: the juices should run clear, not pink.
6. Remove the stuffing from the cavity immediately, and transfer to a warm serving dish. Discard the fatty drippings.
7. Allow the bird to rest on a platter for 15 minutes before carving. Serve with the chutney.

Serves 8

4 oz maple-glazed goose with ¾ cup stuffing per serving: Calories 610, Protein 33 g, Carbohydrates 50 g, Fiber 7 g, Total fat 31 g (Saturated 9 g, Monounsaturated 13 g, Polyunsaturated 7 g), Cholesterol 100 mg, Sodium 100 mg, Iron 30%, Vitamin C 40%.
▲ *2 Bread, 1 Meat, 1 Fat/Sugar*

4 oz maple-glazed turkey with ¾ cup stuffing per serving: Calories 500, Protein 37 g, Carbohydrates 50 g, Fiber 7 g, Total fat 17 g (Saturated 4 g, Monounsaturated 5 g, Polyunsaturated 6 g), Cholesterol 95 mg, Sodium 95 mg, Iron 25%, Vitamin C 40%.
▲ *2 Bread, 1 Meat*

CRANBERRY-PEAR CHUTNEY

This is best if made 1–2 days ahead. It will keep 2 weeks in the refrigerator. Enjoy it as a condiment for any roasted meat.

1½ cups (12 fl oz/375 ml) white wine vinegar

1 cup (8 oz/250 g) sugar

½ cup (3½ oz/105 g) firmly packed light brown sugar

1 jalapeño chili pepper, seeded and chopped

1 lb (500 g) pears, peeled, cored and diced

1 lb (500 g) cranberries

1 onion, finely chopped

2 cloves garlic, minced

½ cup (3 oz/90 g) raisins

1 yellow bell pepper (capsicum), seeded and chopped

1 tablespoon grated fresh gingerroot

2 tablespoons lime juice

1 tablespoon lime zest

½ teaspoon mustard seed

½ teaspoon celery seed

Left to right: Wild Rice, Chestnut and Apple Stuffing; Maple-Glazed Goose and Cranberry-Pear Chutney; Sweet Onion Confit

1. In a large, heavy pot, combine the vinegar, sugars and jalapeño. Bring to a boil, stirring often, then add the remaining ingredients, mixing thoroughly. Return to a boil, reduce to a simmer and cook for 5 minutes. Do not overcook the fruit. Remove from the heat, and refrigerate.

Makes 8 cups (64 fl oz/2 l)

¼ cup per serving: Calories 60, Protein 0 g, Carbohydrates 15 g, Fiber 1 g, Total fat 0 g (Saturated 0 g, Monounsaturated 0 g, Polyunsaturated 0 g), Cholesterol 0 mg, Sodium 0 mg.

▲ *1 Fruit*

VEGETABLES / UNITED STATES

Sweet Onion Confit

Onions have a relatively high sugar content, and cooking enhances their sweetness. Especially sweet are the California Red, Maui, Vidalia and Walla Walla varieties. Typically, a confit *is a meat slowly cooked in its own fat. Sweet onion* confit *uses the principle of slow cooking to bring out natural sugars. To reduce tears, chill the onions, and then hold them under water while peeling them.*

3 tablespoons safflower oil
2 sweet onions, cut into 1-in (2.5-cm) pieces
1 leek, white part only, cut into 1-in (2.5-cm) pieces
1 shallot (white onion), minced
½ cup (4 fl oz/125 ml) Madeira
1 cup (8 fl oz/250 ml) chicken stock (see glossary)

1. In a large sauté pan, heat the oil. Add the onions and leek, and cook over medium-high heat until the onions turn golden brown, about 10 minutes. Add the shallot, reduce heat to low and cook another 10 minutes.
2. Deglaze the pan with the Madeira, and reduce the liquid until syrupy. Add the chicken stock, and continue to cook over medium-high heat until the liquid has reduced and the mixture is quite thick, about 15 minutes. Keep warm until ready to serve.

Makes 3 cups (24 fl oz/750 ml)

½ cup per serving: Calories 100, Protein 1 g, Carbohydrates 8 g, Fiber 1 g, Total fat 7 g (Saturated .5 g, Monounsaturated 1 g, Polyunsaturated 5 g), Cholesterol 0 mg, Sodium 10 mg.

▲ *1 Vegetable*

Pepper-Crusted Tuna Steaks

Any firm-fleshed fish can be substituted if tuna is unavailable. Try halibut, red snapper, sea bass or salmon.

1 teaspoon safflower oil
4 tablespoons (2 fl oz/60 ml) freshly squeezed lemon juice
1 lb (500 g) tuna steaks
1 teaspoon green peppercorns, crushed
1 teaspoon pink peppercorns, crushed
1 teaspoon black peppercorns, crushed
1 teaspoon white peppercorns, crushed
2 tablespoons unsalted butter
2 shallots (white onions), minced
1 lb (500 g) spinach, blanched for 5 seconds and drained
   (see glossary)
¼ teaspoon salt
1 lemon, cut into wedges

1. Preheat an oven to 400°F (200°C). Lightly oil a baking sheet.
2. In a small bowl, stir together the oil and 1 tablespoon of the lemon juice. Brush the tuna with the mixture.
3. In a small flat dish, combine the peppercorns. Dip both sides of the tuna into the peppercorn mixture, pressing lightly, and place the steaks on the baking sheet. Bake for 10 minutes, or until the fish is firm and opaque.
4. While the fish is cooking, melt the butter in a medium sauté pan. Add the shallots, and cook until soft; add the spinach, and sauté quickly, just to heat through. Season with the salt and remaining lemon juice.
5. Place the spinach mixture on a serving plate, and arrange the tuna steaks on top. Serve immediately with the lemon wedges.
   Serves 4

1 serving: Calories 260, Protein 30 g, Carbohydrates 8 g, Fiber 3 g, Total fat 13 g (Saturated 5 g, Monounsaturated 3.5 g, Polyunsaturated 3 g), Cholesterol 60 mg, Sodium 270 mg, Iron 30%, Vitamin A 240%, Vitamin C 30%.
▲ *1 Vegetable, 1 Meat*

Black Bean Soup

Traditionally, black bean soup is simmered with a ham bone, but smoked chicken or turkey also gives it an earthy depth. It is equally good vegetarian style. Beans join some cereals and unpeeled pears as the very best sources of fiber. Dried beans also provide valuable minerals, such as iron, potassium, phosphorus and chromium, to protect our health.

2 tablespoons olive oil
6 cloves garlic, minced
1 large onion, chopped
3 stalks celery, thinly sliced
2 carrots, peeled and thinly sliced
1 jalapeño chili pepper, minced
8 large tomatoes, peeled and puréed
½ lb (250 g) black beans, rinsed and soaked overnight
½ lb (250 g) smoked chicken or turkey, cubed
1½ teaspoons orange zest
8 cups (64 fl oz/2 l) chicken stock (see glossary)
1 tablespoon ground cumin
1 teaspoon ground coriander
salt and freshly ground black pepper to taste
¼ cup (2 fl oz/60 ml) dark rum
1 red bell pepper (capsicum), diced
1 cup (6 oz/185 g) cooked corn
¼ cup (2 fl oz/60 ml) plain low-fat yogurt or sour cream
¼ cup (1/4 oz/7 g) fresh cilantro (fresh coriander), minced

1. In a large stockpot, heat the olive oil. Add the garlic and onion, and sauté until soft but not browned.
2. Add the celery, carrots, jalapeño pepper, tomatoes, black beans, chicken, orange zest and chicken stock. Bring to a boil. Reduce to a simmer, and cook for 2 hours, uncovered, stirring occasionally.
3. In a dry skillet, combine the cumin and coriander and toast over medium heat for 1–2 minutes. Do not brown. Add to the cooked soup, and season with the salt and pepper. Stir in the rum, bell pepper and corn. Heat through.
4. Pour into warm bowls, garnish each serving with a tablespoon of the yogurt and top with the cilantro.
   Serves 12 *Photograph page 201*

1 cup per serving: Calories 190, Protein 11 g, Carbohydrates 27 g, Fiber 6 g, Total fat 5 g (Saturated 1 g, Monounsaturated 2.5 g, Polyunsaturated 1 g), Cholesterol 10 mg, Sodium 220 mg, Vitamin A 90%, Vitamin C 70%.
▲ *1 Vegetable, 1 Meat*

Deborah Madison's Orange Salad with Pickled Onions

Deborah Madison, author of Greens *and* The Savory Way, *offers this winter salad with pickled onions, watercress and olives. It provides almost half of your daily fiber requirement and lots of vitamins. Try a few drops of balsamic vinegar with the oranges if you like more tartness. If sodium is a concern, omit the olives.*

PICKLED ONIONS
1 small round red (Spanish) onion, peeled and thinly sliced
   into rings
1 teaspoon sugar
¼ teaspoon salt
10 peppercorns, slightly crushed
½ cup (4 fl oz/125 ml) white wine vinegar or
   champagne vinegar

Top to bottom: Deborah Madison's Orange Salad with Pickled Onions; Pepper-Crusted Tuna Steaks

ORANGE SALAD

    6 navel oranges
    1 lime
    1 teaspoon orange-flower water
    1 tablespoon extra-virgin olive oil (optional)
    1 bunch dark green watercress (about 5 oz/155 g)
    12 Moroccan or Niçoise olives

1. To make the pickled onions, separate the onion rings, and place them in a colander. Blanch them by pouring 4 cups (32 fl oz/1 l) of boiling water slowly over them; shake them dry.

2. In a stainless steel or glass bowl, mix the remaining ingredients with ½ cup (4 fl oz/125 ml) of cold water, stirring to dissolve the sugar. Add the blanched onions to the bowl and push them down to submerge them. If you need more liquid, add water and vinegar in equal amounts. Refrigerate for at least 20 minutes.

3. To make the orange salad, peel the oranges and lime by slicing off the tops and bottoms then sliding your knife down the sides, cutting just under the white pith. Slice the oranges crosswise into rounds about ⅓ in (1 cm) thick and the lime as thinly as possible. Arrange them on a platter or individual plates in an overlapping fashion, interspersing the lime slices among the oranges. Drizzle with the orange-flower water and olive oil.

4. Trim the large stems from the watercress to make fairly small sprigs, 2–3 in (5–7.5 cm) long at the most. Arrange them loosely around the edge of the plate. Remove the onions from their marinade, and add them and the olives to the oranges.

Serves 4

1 serving: Calories 140, Protein 3 g, Carbohydrates 32 g, Fiber 11 g, Total fat 2 g (Saturated .5 g, Monounsaturated 1.5 g, Polyunsaturated 0 g), Cholesterol 0 mg, Sodium 335 mg, Vitamin A 45%, Vitamin C 210%.

▲ *1 Fruit*

Barley, Oat and Cracked Wheat Porridge

While pearl barley tastes very nutty and flavorful and takes less time to cook than hulled barley (about 1 hour), it has had all of the bran removed. Hulled barley is fiber-rich and worth the extra cooking time. A good quick version of this porridge can be made with barley flakes, cooked as you would cook oatmeal, for only about 30 minutes.

½ cup (3½ oz/105 g) hulled barley
½ cup (1½ oz/45 g) steel-cut oats
½ cup (3 oz/90 g) cracked wheat
½ teaspoon grated orange zest
¼ cup (1 oz/30 g) granola (recipe on page 178)
1 cup (8 fl oz/250 ml) low-fat (1-percent) milk, warmed

1. Bring 5 cups (40 fl oz/1.25 l) of water to a boil. Add the barley, and reduce to a simmer. Cook, covered, for 1 hour, stirring occasionally. Remove the lid, and add the oats, cracked wheat and orange zest. Cook for 15 minutes, until the grains are tender.
2. Spoon into warm bowls, sprinkle with the granola and serve with the warm milk.
Serves 4

---

1 serving: Calories 230, Protein 9 g, Carbohydrates 46 g, Fiber 10 g, Total fat 2 g (Saturated .5 g, Monounsaturated .5 g, Polyunsaturated .5 g), Cholesterol 0 mg, Sodium 40 mg.
▲ *2 Bread*

Smoked Chicken Hash with Scalloped Potatoes

Here's a great morning-after use for leftover meat. Smoked chicken gives this hash a traditional flavor, but smoked turkey or cooked chicken is equally good. Use cooked chicken if you are limiting sodium in your diet.

1 lb (500 g) new red potatoes, unpeeled, sliced ¼ in (6 mm) thick
¾ cup (6 fl oz/180 ml) low-fat (1-percent) milk
1 tablespoon margarine, cut into small pieces
1 large baking potato, peeled and diced
1 cup (8 fl oz/250 ml) chicken stock (see glossary)
2 tablespoons olive oil
1 cup (5 oz/155 g) minced onion

2 cloves garlic
2 cups (12 oz/375 g) diced smoked chicken
½ teaspoon fresh thyme, minced
1 tablespoon fresh parsley, minced
½ teaspoon salt
freshly ground pepper to taste

1. Preheat an oven to 375°F (190°C). Lightly oil a large shallow baking dish.
2. Arrange the red potato slices in the baking dish.
3. Heat the milk to scalding, and pour it over the potatoes. Dot with the margarine, and bake for 25–30 minutes, or until the potatoes are fork tender.
4. Meanwhile, place the diced baking potato and chicken stock in a medium saucepan, and bring to a boil. Reduce to a simmer, and cook for 15 minutes, until the potato dice are tender. Drain.
5. In a large skillet, heat the olive oil, and sauté the onion and garlic until soft but not browned. Add the chicken and diced potato, and cook 5–7 minutes, until lightly browned. Add the thyme and parsley. Season with the salt and pepper.
6. Spoon the chicken hash over the scalloped potatoes, and serve at once.
Serves 6

---

1 serving: Calories 280, Protein 13 g, Carbohydrates 37 g, Fiber 3 g, Total fat 9 g (Saturated 2 g, Monounsaturated 5 g, Polyunsaturated 1.5 g), Cholesterol 25 mg, Sodium 830 mg, Vitamin C 30%.
▲ *1 Vegetable, 1 Meat*

Irish Brown Soda Bread

Many variations of soda bread are made in Ireland, and there are just as many techniques for making it. This whole-grain version is excellent for breakfast or afternoon tea. Serve it warm with blackberry jam and some good Irish breakfast tea.

2 cups (10 oz/315 g) whole-wheat (wholemeal) flour
1 cup (5 oz/155 g) all-purpose (plain) flour
2 tablespoons sugar
1 tablespoon baking powder
½ teaspoon baking soda (bicarbonate of soda)
½ teaspoon salt
1¾ cup (13 fl oz/410 ml) buttermilk, or fresh milk mixed with 1½ tablespoons lemon juice, at room temperature

1. Preheat an oven to 350°F (180°C). Lightly oil a 9-in (23-cm) round cake pan.
2. Combine the dry ingredients in a large mixing bowl, and mix thoroughly.
3. Add the buttermilk gradually, stirring to form a stiff but not dry dough.
4. Turn the dough onto a floured work surface, and knead it lightly until smooth, about 3 minutes. Do not overwork.

Top to bottom: Barley, Oat and Cracked Wheat Porridge; Smoked Chicken Hash with Scalloped Potatoes; Irish Brown Soda Bread

5. Form a round loaf, and place it in the cake pan.
6. Bake 35 minutes, or until a tester inserted in the center comes out clean.

   Makes 1 loaf (8 slices)

1 slice per serving: Calories 190, Protein 7 g, Carbohydrates 40 g, Fiber 4 g, Total fat 1 g (Saturated .5 g, Monounsaturated 0 g, Polyunsaturated .5 g), Cholesterol 0 mg, Sodium 280 mg.

▲ *2 Bread*

Clockwise from top: Sourdough French Toast with Poached Pear Sauce;
Butternut Squash Blintzes; German Apple Pancake

German Apple Pancake

Serve this piping hot first thing in the morning with maple syrup or for
brunch with cinnamon-rum sauce (recipe on page 178).

- **1 tablespoon unsalted butter**
- **2 Golden Delicious or Granny Smith apples, peeled, cored and sliced ½ in (12 mm) thick**
- **1 tablespoon sugar**
- **½ teaspoon cinnamon**

- **1 cup (5 oz/155 g) all-purpose (plain) flour**
- **1 cup (8 fl oz/250 ml) low-fat (1-percent) milk**
- **2 eggs**
- **1 tablespoon safflower oil**
- **1 teaspoon vanilla extract (essence)**
- **¼ teaspoon freshly grated nutmeg**
- **1 teaspoon freshly squeezed lemon juice**
- **½ teaspoon lemon zest**
- **2 tablespoons confectioners' (icing) sugar**

1. Preheat an oven to 450°F (230°C).
2. Melt the butter in a 10-in (25-cm) ovenproof skillet. Add the apples, and sauté until soft. Sprinkle with the sugar and cinnamon. Place in the oven to keep warm while you mix the batter.

3. In a blender, combine the flour, milk, eggs, oil, vanilla and nutmeg. Add the lemon juice and lemon zest. Remove the skillet from the oven, and pour the batter over the apple mixture. Return to the oven, and bake for 15 minutes. Reduce the heat to 375°F (190°C), and bake 10 minutes longer.

4. Remove from the oven. Dust with the confectioners' sugar, cut into wedges and serve at once.

Serves 6

---

1 serving: Calories 200, Protein 6 g, Carbohydrates 30 g, Fiber 2 g, Total fat 7 g (Saturated 2.5 g, Monounsaturated 1.5 g, Polyunsaturated 2 g), Cholesterol 80 mg, Sodium 45 mg.

▲ *1 Bread, 1 Fruit*

BREAKFAST / UNITED STATES

Sourdough French Toast with Poached Pear Sauce

Poached pears and French toast were made for each other. Try the pear sauce with desserts as well.

POACHED PEAR SAUCE
   1⅓ cups (11 oz/345 g) sugar
   1 teaspoon lemon zest
   6 ripe, firm pears, peeled, halved and cored
   2 teaspoons vanilla extract (essence)

FRENCH TOAST
   1 lb (500 g) sourdough French bread
   8 egg whites
   4 eggs
   1 tablespoon vanilla extract (essence)
   2 tablespoons sugar
   1 tablespoon safflower oil
   ¼ cup (1½ oz/45 g) dried cherries
   ¼ cup (1½ oz/45 g) dried blueberries

1. To make the sauce, in a large saucepan, combine 4 cups (32 fl oz/ 1 l) of water with the sugar and lemon zest. Bring to a boil, stirring until the sugar has dissolved. Reduce to a simmer, and add the pears. Simmer until the fruit is tender, about 20 minutes. With a slotted spoon, remove the pears to cool. Return the cooking liquid to a boil, and reduce it by half.

2. When the pears are cool, set aside 6 halves. Purée the remaining pears in a blender. Add the vanilla and about half of the cooking liquid to thin the purée to sauce consistency. Set aside.

3. To make the French toast, cut the bread into 12 slices, and set aside.

4. Whisk the egg whites until frothy. Add the whole eggs, vanilla and sugar.

5. Heat a nonstick griddle, and brush it with the oil.

6. Dip the bread into the egg mixture, and cook on the griddle until golden brown, about 2 minutes on each side.

7. To serve, spoon poached pear sauce onto each plate. Slice the

reserved pear halves. Arrange 2 pieces of French toast and slices of half a pear on each plate. Sprinkle with the dried cherries and dried blueberries, and serve immediately.

Serves 6

---

2 slices with sauce per serving: Calories 520, Protein 17 g, Carbohydrates 99 g, Fiber 6 g, Total fat 8 g (Saturated 2 g, Monounsaturated 2.5 g, Polyunsaturated 3 g), Cholesterol 150 mg, Sodium 530 mg.

▲ *2 Bread, 1 Fruit, ½ Meat, 1 Fat/Sugar*

BREAKFAST / UNITED STATES

Butternut Squash Blintzes

This sweet and savory brunch dish is delightful served with kumquats, figs and dried apricots in honeyed rosewater (recipe on page 216) and a little plain yogurt.

   1 large butternut squash, about 3 lb (1.5 kg)
   ¼ teaspoon salt
   freshly grated nutmeg to taste
   3 eggs
   1¼ cups (10 fl oz/310 ml) low-fat (1-percent) milk or water
   2 tablespoons safflower oil
   1 cup (5 oz/155 g) all-purpose (plain) flour
   1 tablespoon unsalted butter, melted

1. Preheat an oven to 400°F (200°C). Lightly oil a large shallow baking dish.

2. To make the filling, cut the squash in half lengthwise. Scoop out and discard the seeds. Place the squash, cut side down, on a baking sheet, and bake for 35–45 minutes, until very soft. Cool.

3. Peel the squash, and purée it in a blender. Season with the salt and nutmeg, and set aside.

4. To make the blintz crêpes, in a blender, combine the eggs, milk and oil. Blend well. Add the flour, and process until smooth.

5. Heat a 6-in (15-cm) nonstick crêpe pan or skillet over medium-high heat. Ladle 2 tablespoons of batter into the pan, and tip the pan to spread the batter over the whole bottom. Return to the heat, and cook until golden brown on 1 side, about 2 minutes. Turn the crêpe onto a plate, and repeat to make the rest of the crêpes. Stack the crêpes with parchment paper in between until ready to use.

6. Place each crêpe on a work surface, cooked side down. Spoon 3 tablespoons of filling near one edge of the crêpe, fold in the sides and roll up.

7. Place the blintzes in a single layer in the baking dish. Brush them with the melted butter, and bake for 15 minutes, until lightly browned.

Serves 12 (makes 24 blintzes)

---

2 blintzes per serving: Calories 140, Protein 5 g, Carbohydrates 20 g, Fiber 2 g, Total fat 5 g (Saturated 1.5 g, Monounsaturated 1 g, Polyunsaturated 2 g), Cholesterol 60 mg, Sodium 80 mg, Vitamin A 150%, Vitamin C 35%.

▲ *1 Vegetable, ½ Bread*

Arànce Caramelizzate di Malgieri

NICK MALGIERI'S POACHED ORANGES

Nick Malgieri, pastry chef and author of Great Italian Desserts, *brings us this typically Italian dessert of whole poached oranges. The slightly cooked oranges coupled with their zest and some orange liqueur create an intense orange flavor, making a satisfying, though very light, dessert.*

8 seedless oranges
1½ cups (12 oz/375 g) sugar
¼ cup (2 fl oz/60 ml) orange liqueur (Cointreau or Grand Marnier)

1. Strip the zest from the oranges with a vegetable peeler, making sure not to peel away any of the white pith. Cut the zest into ⅛-in (3-mm) shreds. Place them in a small saucepan, and cover with water. Bring to a boil over low heat. Drain the zest, place it in a bowl, cover it with cold water and set it aside.
2. Combine the sugar with ¾ cup (6 fl oz/180 ml) of water in a medium saucepan, bring to a boil and cook the syrup until it thickens slightly, about 3 minutes.
3. While the syrup is cooking, peel the oranges to expose the flesh. Submerge the oranges in the syrup, 1 or 2 at a time; lower the heat, and cook for 3–4 minutes.
4. Remove the oranges from the syrup with a slotted spoon, and place them in a serving bowl.

Top to bottom: Nick Malgieri's Poached Oranges, Courtney's Chocolate-Cherry-Almond Bread

5. Drain the shredded zest, and add it to the syrup. Cook for 2 minutes, or until the zest is translucent. Remove the zest from the syrup, and scatter it over the oranges.
6. Chill the oranges. Just before serving, sprinkle them with the orange liqueur.
Serves 8

1 orange with sauce per serving: Calories 140, Protein 1 g, Carbohydrates 31 g, Fiber 5 g, Total fat 0 g (Saturated 0 g, Monounsaturated 0 g, Polyunsaturated 0 g), Cholesterol 0 mg, Sodium 0 mg, Vitamin C 120%.
▲ *1 Fruit*

Mocha Java Sorbet

This refreshing ice is good any time of year.

6 tablespoons (3 oz/90 g) finely ground espresso beans
½ cup (4 oz/125 g) sugar
1 tablespoon Dutch-process cocoa powder
1 teaspoon vanilla extract (essence)
1 egg white

1. Place the ground espresso in the paper filter of a drip coffee maker. Pour 2½ cups (20 fl oz/625 ml) boiling water over, and let drip. Mix the hot coffee with the sugar and cocoa, stirring until the sugar has dissolved. Cool completely.
2. Pour the coffee mixture in an ice-cream freezer, and process until partially frozen. Stir in the vanilla.
3. Beat the egg white until it forms stiff but not dry peaks. Fold it into the coffee mixture, and return it to the ice-cream freezer. Process until it is slightly firm again. Freeze in a freezer for 1 hour before serving.
Makes 2½ cups (20 fl oz/625 ml)

½ cup per serving: Calories 90, Protein 1 g, Carbohydrates 21 g, Fiber .5 g, Total fat 0 g (Saturated 0 g, Monounsaturated 0 g, Polyunsaturated 0 g), Cholesterol 0 mg, Sodium 10 mg.
▲ *1 Fat/Sugar*

Chocolate Air Kisses

These light and airy cookies will satisfy your need for chocolate without the saturated fat. Make a batch to keep in an airtight container, ready to serve when you want them.

3 tablespoons Dutch-process cocoa powder
½ cup (2 oz/60 g) confectioners' (icing) sugar
4 egg whites
½ teaspoon lemon juice
½ cup (4 oz/125 g) granulated sugar

1. Preheat an oven to 225°F (110°C). Line a baking sheet with parchment paper.
2. In a medium bowl, sift together the cocoa and confectioners' sugar. Set aside.

Left to right: Chocolate Air Kisses, Mocha Java Sorbet

3. Using an electric mixer, beat the egg whites with the lemon juice until soft peaks form. Add 3 tablespoons of the granulated sugar. Beat until stiff, and then add the remaining granulated sugar.

4. Gently fold in the cocoa mixture. Place the batter in a pastry bag with a plain tip. Pipe "kisses" 1 in (2.5 cm) in diameter onto the baking sheet.

5. Bake for 2 hours or until the meringues are dry and crisp. Turn off the heat and let the cookies dry in the oven for 2 hours, or overnight if desired. Keep in an airtight container until ready to serve.
Makes 48

---

4 cookies per serving: Calories 60, Protein 1 g, Carbohydrates 14 g, Fiber .5 g, Total fat 0 g (Saturated 0 g, Monounsaturated 0 g, Polyunsaturated 0 g), Cholesterol 0 mg, Sodium 20 mg.
▲ *1 Fat/Sugar*

BREADS / UNITED STATES

Courtney's Chocolate-Cherry-Almond Bread

This bread is a favorite for breakfast in the author's house.

1½ cups (12 fl oz/375 ml) low-fat (1-percent) milk
¼ cup (2 fl oz/60 ml) molasses
2 teaspoons salt
1 package (¼ oz/7 g) active dry yeast
1 cup (2½ oz/80 g) wheat bran
1 cup (5 oz/155 g) whole-wheat (wholemeal) flour

2 tablespoons unsweetened cocoa powder
about 4 cups (1¼ lb/625 g) all-purpose (plain) flour
¾ cup (4½ oz/140 g) dried cherries
½ cup (2¼ oz/65 g) toasted slivered (flaked) almonds

1. Preheat an oven to 375°F (190°C). Lightly oil two 9-in (23-cm) loaf pans and a large mixing bowl.

2. In a small saucepan, scald the milk; remove from the heat, and stir in the molasses and salt. Let cool to lukewarm.

3. In a glass measuring cup, measure ½ cup (4 fl oz/125 ml) warm water (105°–115°F/40°–46°C), and stir in the yeast. Let it proof for 5 minutes, or until foamy.

4. In a large mixer with a dough hook, place the bran, whole-wheat flour, cocoa and 1 cup of the all-purpose flour. Add the lukewarm milk mixture and dissolved yeast. Beat well. Add the cherries and almonds.

5. Continue to beat, adding most of the remaining flour until the dough is well mixed. Turn onto a lightly floured work surface.

6. Knead the dough until it is smooth and elastic, adding more flour only if necessary. Place the dough in the oiled bowl, cover with plastic wrap and let rise in a warm place for approximately 2 hours, until doubled in size.

7. Punch the dough down, and form it into 2 loaves. Place them in the loaf pans, cover and let rise until almost doubled, about 1½ hours.

8. Bake for 40 minutes. Cool on racks.
Makes 2 loaves (36 slices)

---

1 slice per serving: Calories 100, Protein 3 g, Carbohydrates 20 g, Fiber 2 g, Total fat 1 g (Saturated 0 g, Monounsaturated .5 g, Polyunsaturated .5 g), Cholesterol 0 mg, Sodium 140 mg.
▲ *1 Bread*

*Clockwise from top left: Cloudberry Preserves (recipe page 216),
Santa Lucia Buns, Orange-Lingonberry Soufflé
Omelet with Grand Marnier Sauce*

Orange-Lingonberry Soufflé Omelet with Grand Marnier Sauce

Although France is usually associated with omelets, dessert omelets are not uncommon in Sweden. In fact, you can find omelets at almost every course of the Swedish meal. Have all the ingredients ready, whisking the eggs at the last minute. This recipe makes one large omelet to serve four.

2 oranges, peeled

½ cup (4 oz/125 g) plus 2 tablespoons sugar

1 tablespoon unsalted butter

¼ cup (1 oz/30 g) lingonberries or lingonberry preserves

1 teaspoon orange zest

4 eggs, separated

¼ teaspoon lemon juice

¼ cup (2 fl oz/60 ml) freshly squeezed orange juice

2 tablespoons Grand Marnier

2 tablespoons confectioners' (icing) sugar for garnish

1 cup (8 fl oz/250 ml) Grand Marnier sauce (recipe follows)

1. Preheat an oven to 400°F (200°C).
2. Slice the oranges between their membranes to remove just the flesh of the orange segments. Toss the segments with the 2 tablespoons of sugar.
3. Heat the butter in a 14-in (35-cm) ovenproof skillet. Brush some of the butter up the sides of the pan, so the omelet will not stick. Add the oranges, lingonberries and orange zest; cook until the sugar caramelizes to a golden color, about 10 minutes. Set aside.
4. In a nonreactive bowl, whisk the egg whites and lemon juice to soft peaks. Add ¼ cup (2 oz/60 g) of the remaining sugar, and continue to beat until stiff, but not dry.
5. In another bowl, beat the remaining ¼ cup (2 oz/60 g) of sugar with the egg yolks until light and fluffy. Add the orange juice and Grand Marnier, and mix well.
6. Gently fold the egg whites into the yolk mixture.
7. Spoon the mixture into the skillet over the orange-lingonberry mixture. Bake for 10 minutes, or until golden brown.
8. Dust with the confectioners' sugar, and serve with the Grand Marnier sauce.
   Serves 4

¼ soufflé omelet per serving: Calories 290, Protein 7 g, Carbohydrates 48 g, Fiber 3 g, Total fat 8 g (Saturated 3.5 g, Monounsaturated 3 g, Polyunsaturated 1 g), Cholesterol 230 mg, Sodium 70 mg, Vitamin C 90%.
▲ *1 Fruit, ½ Meat*

GRAND MARNIER SAUCE

1 cup (8 fl oz/250 ml) freshly squeezed orange juice

¼ cup (2 oz/60 g) sugar

2 tablespoons orange marmalade

1 tablespoon cornstarch (cornflour), blended with 1 table-spoon orange juice

3 tablespoons Grand Marnier

1. Heat the orange juice and sugar in a small saucepan, stirring until the sugar has dissolved. Add the marmalade, and stir until melted.
2. Stir in the cornstarch mixture, and simmer, stirring, until slightly thickened. Add the Grand Marnier, and serve warm.
   Makes 1 cup (8 fl oz/250 ml)

¼ cup per serving: Calories 130, Protein 0 g, Carbohydrates 34 g, Fiber 0 g, Total fat 0 g (Saturated 0 g, Monounsaturated 0 g, Polyunsaturated 0 g), Cholesterol 0 mg, Sodium 10 mg, Vitamin C 60%.
▲ *1 Fruit, 1 Fat/Sugar*

Lussekatter

SANTA LUCIA BUNS

This recipe was contributed by Gerd Jordano of Santa Barbara, California, who remembers the tradition of serving these buns to her parents on December 13, St. Lucia's Day. The dough can also be braided and formed into a festive wreath studded with raisins. Delicious with cloudberry preserves (recipe on page 216).

1 package (¼ oz/7 g) active dry yeast

⅓ cup (3 fl oz/80 ml) low-fat (1-percent) milk, scalded and cooled

5 tablespoons (2½ oz/75 g) sugar

¼ cup (2 oz/60 g) margarine, softened

2 eggs

½ teaspoon ground cardamom

½ teaspoon salt

¼ teaspoon saffron, ground

2½–2¾ cups (12½–14 oz/390–440 g) all-purpose (plain) flour

¼ cup (1½ oz/45 g) raisins

1. Preheat an oven to 350°F (180°C).
2. Dissolve the yeast in ¼ cup (2 fl oz/60 ml) warm water (105°–115°F/40°–46°C). Stir in the milk, 4 tablespoons of the sugar, 2 table-spoons of the margarine, 1 of the eggs, the cardamom, the salt and the saffron.
3. Add 1½ cups (7½ oz/235 g) of the flour, and beat until well mixed. Continue to stir in the remaining flour until the dough is too stiff to stir.
4. Turn the dough onto a floured work surface, and knead until it is smooth, about 5 minutes.
5. Place the dough in a lightly oiled bowl, cover and let rise until doubled, about 1 hour.
6. Punch down the dough, and divide into 12 equal parts. Roll each piece into an S-shaped rope; curve both ends into a coil. Place a raisin in the center of each coil.
7. Place rolls on a lightly oiled baking sheet. Melt the remaining margarine and brush the tops of the rolls.
8. Let rise until doubled, about 30 minutes. Brush buns with egg-water mixture and sprinkle with the sugar.
9. Bake for 15–20 minutes, until light golden brown.
   Makes 12 buns

1 bun per serving: Calories 180, Protein 4 g, Carbohydrates 28 g, Fiber 1 g, Total fat 5 g, (Saturated 1 g, Monounsaturated 2 g, Polyunsaturated 1.5 g), Cholesterol 35 mg, Sodium 160 mg.
▲ *1 Bread*

Kumquats, Figs and Dried Apricots in Honeyed Rosewater

Combine the season's fresh kumquats with preserved fruits for a heavenly compote. Serve it chilled in goblets or as a breakfast condiment with waffles or pancakes. Drying fruit concentrates the sugar, fiber, vitamins and minerals. While all dried fruits are rich in fiber, figs and prunes are the highest. Apricots provide extra vitamin A and iron.

    3 tablespoons honey
    2 tablespoons rosewater
    1 teaspoon lemon juice
    ½ lb (250 g) dried figs
    ¼ lb (125 g) dried apricots
    ½ cup (3 oz/90 g) golden raisins
    1 cinnamon stick
    2 star anise
    2 tablespoons pine nuts
    ¼ lb (125 g) kumquats, cut in half lengthwise and seeded

1. In a large saucepan, heat 2 cups (16 fl oz/500 ml) of water with the honey, rosewater and lemon juice. Add the figs, apricots, raisins, cinnamon stick, star anise and pine nuts, and simmer for 30 minutes.
2. Add the kumquats and simmer for 15 minutes. Remove from the heat to cool. Chill at least 3 hours or overnight

Serves 8

⅔ cup per serving: Calories 180, Protein 2 g, Carbohydrates 44 g, Fiber 7 g, Total fat 2 g (Saturated .5 g, Monounsaturated .5 g, Polyunsaturated .5 g), Cholesterol 0 mg, Sodium 5 mg, Vitamin A 20%.
▲ *2 Fruit*

Warm Persimmon and Cranberry Gratin

A creamy persimmon and cranberry pudding hides under a gratin of sliced persimmons. Hachiya and Fuyu persimmons are the most commonly available varieties. Hachiyas are bitter until they are ripe and very sweet and soft when they do ripen. Fuyus do not have that bitterness and are firmer, even when ripe. Persimmons are a good source of vitamin A in its best form, beta-carotene.

    3 large, ripe persimmons
    2 eggs
    1 cup (7 oz/220 g) firmly packed brown sugar
    ½ cup (4 fl oz/125 ml) half-and-half (half milk and half cream)
    ¾ cup (4 oz/125 g) all-purpose (plain) flour

    ½ teaspoon baking powder
    ½ teaspoon baking soda (bicarbonate of soda)
    2 teaspoons ground cinnamon
    ½ teaspoon freshly ground nutmeg
    1 cup (4 oz/125 g) fresh cranberries
    1 tablespoon unsalted butter, melted
    1 tablespoon sugar

1. Preheat an oven to 350°F (180°C). Lightly oil 8 small gratin dishes.
2. Slice 2 of the persimmons into ¼-in (6-mm) slices. Set aside.
3. Cut the remaining persimmon in half, and scoop out the pulp, removing any seeds; purée the pulp in a food processor or blender. Place the purée in a mixing bowl with the eggs and brown sugar. Mix well. Add the half-and-half, and set aside.
4. In a medium bowl, combine the flour, baking powder, baking soda, cinnamon and nutmeg. Stir into the persimmon mixture until just blended. Stir in the cranberries. Do not overmix.
5. Pour into the gratin dishes. Arrange the persimmon slices on top, brush with the melted butter and sprinkle with the sugar. Bake for 30 minutes, until a knife inserted in the center comes out clean and the sugar has browned. Serve warm.

Serves 8

1 serving: Calories 230, Protein 4 g, Carbohydrates 45 g, Fiber 1 g, Total fat 5 g (Saturated 2.5 g, Monounsaturated 1.5 g, Polyunsaturated .5 g), Cholesterol 65 mg, Sodium 125 mg.
▲ *½ Bread, 1 Fruit*

Cloudberry Preserves

Although summer is the season for these pale yellow, Arctic-grown raspberries, the preserves can be enjoyed all winter. Red raspberries are a delicious substitute.

    2 cups (16 oz/500 g) sugar
    1 lb (500 g) fresh cloudberries or red raspberries
    1 teaspoon freshly squeezed lemon juice

1. Sterilize three 8-fl oz (250-ml) jars.
2. In a large heavy saucepan, dissolve the sugar in 1 cup (8 fl oz/250 ml) of water; bring to a boil.
3. Add the cloudberries and lemon juice, and bring back to a boil. Reduce to a simmer, and cook gently for 5 minutes. Remove from the heat.
4. Ladle the cloudberries and liquid into the sterilized jars. Cover and seal, or freeze after cooling.

Makes 2½ cups (20 fl oz/625 ml)   *Photograph page 214*

2 tablespoons per serving: Calories 90, Protein 0 g, Carbohydrates 23 g, Fiber 2 g, Total fat 0 g (Saturated 0 g, Monounsaturated 0 g, Polyunsaturated 0 g), Cholesterol 0 mg, Sodium 0 mg.
▲ *1 Fat/Sugar*

Top to bottom: Kumquats, Figs and Dried Apricots in Honeyed Rosewater; Warm Persimmon and Cranberry Gratin

Glossary

AL DENTE: An Italian expression, literally "to the tooth," indicating food that has been cooked but still has firmness and bite. It is used most often in reference to pasta and to vegetables that are cooked but still crisp.

AMINO ACID: An organic acid that forms the basic structure of protein. There are 22 amino acids in various arrangements; 13 of these, called **nonessential amino acids,** can be manufactured in the body; the remaining 9, called **essential amino acids,** must be provided by dietary protein. *See also* Protein.

ANISE: An aromatic plant with seeds used in baking, confectionery and distilled liquors such as pastis and anisette. The leaves look similar to dill leaves, but taste very different; they may be used in salads and cooked dishes.

ANTIOXIDANTS: Substances that scientists have found play a significant role in disease prevention by protecting the body from "free radicals," or destructive chemicals that cause cell injury through oxidation. (You can easily see the results of oxidation in everyday life: rusting metal, rancid oil and crumbling rubber are examples.) Oxidation and the resulting changes within human cells lead to disease and can affect the aging process as well.

Antioxidants may also stop the oxidation of cholesterol, thus delaying or perhaps preventing the buildup of fatty deposits in arteries, which leads to heart attacks and strokes. Research also suggests that antioxidants may help prevent cataracts—clouding of the eye's lens due, at least in part, to oxidation of lens proteins.

Vitamins E and C are antioxidants. The provitamin (precursor) beta-carotene, one of the substances that gives yellow and orange fruits and vegetables their color, is also an antioxidant. The body changes beta-carotene into vitamin A.

Antioxidant research is ongoing. Scientists are in the process of studying selenium, zinc and other substances to determine their antioxidant properties. They are not yet sure of the optimum "dose," the best combination or the long-term side effects of huge doses of antioxidants. For now, experts recommend following the Food Guide Pyramid eating plan, especially eating 5–9 servings of vegetables and fruits each day, including at least 1 citrus fruit and 1 deep orange fruit or vegetable or dark green, leafy vegetable for vitamin C and beta-carotene. Broccoli, asparagus, avocado, peaches, mustard greens, turnip greens and kale are sources of vitamin E; it also occurs in wheat germ (in whole-wheat products), in corn, sunflower and soybean oils and in mayonnaise. Individuals who smoke have increased needs for antioxidants, particularly vitamin C.

ARUGULA (rocket): A peppery Mediterranean green used in salad. Rinse arugula very well and dry it before using. It can be briefly sautéed or stir-fried. Arugula is high in vitamins A and C and iron.

BAIN-MARIE: A French culinary term for the method of baking items in a hot water bath, that is, placing the dish containing the food to be cooked in a larger vessel containing hot water, which is placed in an oven; also the hot-water-bath vessel. This method helps to cook food evenly and to retain moisture.

BALSAMIC VINEGAR: An aromatic vinegar produced in the Emilia-Romagna region of Italy by boiling down and caramelizing the grape must and fermenting in a series of wood barrels in light and airy attics. *Artisan-quality balsamic* has been aged at least 12 years and is used by the drop as a condiment. The good-quality commercial-grade balsamic needed for recipes in this book is a blend of cooked down grape must, wine vinegar and possibly some caramel.

BEAN SAUCE: A canned product of ground soybeans available in Asian markets.

BETA-CAROTENE: One of a group of carotenoids associated with vitamin A in the body. Beta-carotene is found in dark green, leafy vegetables and in deep orange and yellow fruits and vegetables. Beta-carotene is an antioxidant thought to play a role in cancer prevention. *See also* Antioxidants, Carotene, Provitamins, Vitamins. **Beta-carotene-rich fruits and vegetables:** apricots, asparagus, broccoli, cantaloupes, carrots, green (spring) onions, greens (all varieties), lettuces, mangos, oriental cabbages, papayas, parsley, spinach, squashes (orange, winter varieties), sweet potatoes.

BLANCHING: Briefly cooking raw ingredients in boiling water, then immediately refreshing them in ice water and draining them well. The ice water stops the cooking and helps hold the color of vegetables. Blanching is also used to make it easy to peel soft-skinned fruits and vegetables such as peaches and tomatoes. Blanching time varies depending on the density of the ingredient. **Blanching times:** asparagus: 2 minutes; broccoli florets: 1 minute, brussels sprouts: 2 minutes; carrots, baby: 2–3 minutes; carrots, sliced: 1 minute; cauliflower florets: 1 minute; corn kernels: 30 seconds; cranberries: 2 minutes; green beans: 1 minute; mung bean sprouts: 30 seconds; potato, sliced or diced: 2 minutes; snow peas (mangetouts): 15 seconds; spinach: 15 seconds; Swiss chard (silverbeet): 15 seconds; tomatoes, to peel: 10 seconds; turnips or rutabagas, sliced or diced: 2 minutes; zucchini (courgettes), sliced or diced: 1 minute; zucchini (courgettes) flowers: 10 seconds.

BOUQUET GARNI: A bundle of aromatic herbs used to flavor stocks and broths. Use 2–3 sprigs of parsley, 1 bay leaf, 1 sprig of thyme and 3–4 whole black peppercorns. The ratio of herbs and spices can be varied depending on the

recipe. If the bouquet garni is to be removed from the dish before serving, wrap it in a small cheesecloth pouch.

BRAISING: Slow cooking in a covered utensil with a small amount of liquid. This method is especially good for tough ingredients such as lean meats and dense vegetables.

BULGUR: The whole grain of wheat, including the germ, that has been commercially cooked, dried and cracked into coarse, medium or fine grains.

CALORIE: The unit of energy in carbohydrate, fat and protein. A kilocalorie (kcal) is the amount of heat necessary to raise the temperature of a kilogram (kg) of water 1°C.

One gram of carbohydrate or protein provides 4 calories. One gram of fat provides 9 calories. One gram of alcohol provides 7 calories. Energy from food is needed to carry on the activities of every cell in the body. When we eat the number of calories we need, we maintain our weight. Eating too many calories promotes weight gain; eating too few results in weight loss. Diets providing less than 1200 daily calories may not provide all of the nutrients needed for good health.

Sometimes people want to know about the **percentage of calories from fat** in a particular food. Because each gram of fat provides 9 calories, a serving of food with 2 grams of fat and 50 calories has 18 calories from fat—or 36 percent. This percentage is often misused and misunderstood, however. Foods low in calories with only a little fat seem high in fat when considered from the percentage point of view. In fact, in the example above, 2 grams of fat is only about 3 percent of a typical person's fat allowance for a day.

Health experts advise that we eat no more than 30 percent of total calories over a several-day period from fat. A chart on page 18 converts various calorie levels to recommended grams of fat. Remember, 30 percent is a combined total, not an amount for a single food. In a typical day, you should balance individual foods with over 30 percent of calories from fat with ones that have little or no fat. In general, foods at the top of the Food Pyramid (fats, meats, dairy products) have 30 percent or more calories from fat, while foods from the bottom half of the Pyramid (breads, grains, fruits, vegetables) have less. Eating two foods from the bottom of the Pyramid for each food from the top is an easy way to bring your total calories from fat to 30 percent or less.

CARBOHYDRATES: Sugars, starches and most types of fiber. **Simple carbohydrates** are sugars—including glucose, fructose from fruit and vegetables, lactose from milk, and sucrose from cane or beet sugar. **Complex carbohydrates** consist primarily of starches and fiber.

Except for dietary fiber, carbohydrates are broken down by the body into glucose, which is burned for energy. Complex carbohydrates are recommended over simple sugars (especially refined sugar) because they usually contain other valuable nutrients. In addition, glucose is released into the bloodstream more slowly from starches than from sugars, thus affecting insulin production and use. This factor is especially important for diabetics.

A well-balanced diet includes 50–60 percent of calories from carbohydrates, with no more than 15 percent of total calories coming from refined sugar.

CAROTENE: A vitamin A precursor and orange pigment found in plants. *See also* Beta-carotene.

CHICKEN STOCK: The essence of chicken and vegetables, used as a flavoring base in soups, stews and sauces.

To make **chicken stock,** in a nonaluminum stockpot, place the bones of a 3-lb (1.5-kg) chicken; 1 peeled carrot, 1 stalk of celery, 1 onion (all cut into ½-in/12-mm pieces); and a bouquet garni (sprig of parsley, bay leaf, sprig of thyme and 4–5 peppercorns). Cover with 8 qt (8 l) water and bring to a boil. Reduce the temperature to a simmer, and skim impurities from the top. Simmer, uncovered, for 2 hours, skimming occasionally. Strain and chill the stock until the fat solidifies and can be removed.

Stock freezes very well. Try freezing it in 2- or 4-cup (16- or 32-fl oz/500-ml or 1-l) portions, to be used later in soups or sauces.

For **brown chicken stock,** first roast the chicken bones in a 400°F (200°C) oven for 20 minutes, or until quite browned. Then follow the recipe above.

For **rich chicken stock,** follow the recipe for chicken stock above, but simmer for 1 hour longer.

CHICK-PEAS (garbanzo beans): A legume popular in Middle Eastern cuisine. Chick-pea flour is known as *gram flour.*

CHIFFONADE: A French culinary term for thin cuts with a very sharp knife to yield narrow shredded strips, from ⅛ in (3 mm) to ½ in (12 mm) wide. Spinach, lettuces and leafy herbs may be cut into chiffonade.

CHILIES: Hot peppers commonly used in Central American, South American and Asian cuisine. To roast and peel chilies, *see* Roasting.

CHOLESTEROL: A waxy, fatlike substance manufactured in the liver and found in animal products. Although cholesterol is essential to life, it is not an essential nutrient. The body manufactures the cholesterol it needs from fat, protein and carbohydrates—at the rate of about 1000 mg a day. The cholesterol coming from food is known as **dietary cholesterol.**

The liver also manufactures **lipoproteins.** One of their functions is to transport cholesterol around the body. **Low-density lipoproteins** (LDLs) circulate cholesterol throughout the system, where it is needed for cellular functions and the production of hormones. In excess, LDLs contribute to the formation of deposits on artery walls that can lead to heart attacks and strokes. **High-density lipoproteins** (HDLs) return excess cholesterol to the liver, where it is reprocessed or excreted.

A diet rich in saturated fat can increase **blood cholesterol** (the proportion of cholesterol in the blood) to dangerous levels—as can foods rich in dietary cholesterol, although to a lesser degree. Health experts advise keeping total blood cholesterol below 200 mg per dl. Blood cholesterol is a sum of both "bad" (LDL) and "good" (HDL) cholesterol. Type of cholesterol as well as total cholesterol should be monitored as part of regular physical exams.

CLOUDBERRIES: Small, highly prized, golden wild berries that resemble small raspberries. They are found in the Scandinavian Arctic.

CONFIT: Meat preserved by being cooked slowly in its own fat.

CRUCIFEROUS VEGETABLES: A group of vegetables, named for their cross-shaped blossoms. They contain compounds that seem to activate enzymes that destroy carcinogens. The group consists of: broccoli, brussels sprouts, cabbage (all varieties), cauliflower, greens (collard, mustard, turnip), kale, kohlrabi, rutabagas (yellow turnips/Swedes), turnips.

CRUDITÉS: An assortment of raw and blanched vegetables arranged decoratively and served as an hors d'oeuvre. Crudités may include carrots, celery, broccoli and cauliflower florets, mushrooms, radishes, bell peppers (capsicums), cucumbers, tomatoes and baby vegetables.

CURRY: A blend of Indian spices that may include cloves, cumin seed, mustard seed, ginger, fenugreek, cardamom, turmeric, nutmeg, tamarind, coriander, cinnamon and dried chilies.

DAILY VALUES: The amounts of essential nutrients the government currently recommends should be provided by a 2000-calorie diet in a day. Daily Values are listed on food labels, and you can compare the percentages of Daily Value different food products provide of each nutrient. In general, the goal is for the total of all foods eaten in a day to provide 100 percent of all Daily Values. *See also* Reference diet.

DAL: An Indian word for dried split peas, lentils and beans.

DASHI: A fish and seaweed stock that is an essential ingredient in most Japanese recipes. It is available in an instant form in Asian stores. You can make it yourself by heating 4 cups (32 fl oz/1 l) of water with 1 oz (30 g) *konbu* (dried kelp). Just before the liquid boils, remove the *konbu* and add 1 oz (30 g) bonito flakes. Bring the mixture to a boil, and immediately remove from the heat. Strain before using.

DEGLAZE: To add wine, stock or citrus juice to a cooking pan after roasting or sautéing and stir to loosen the cooked-on particles, returning them to the sauce.

DEVEIN: To remove the "vein" from the back of shrimp (prawns). Remove the shell and slice along the back, just breaking the skin. Then lift out the dark vein, and rinse the shrimp.

DIM SUM: An assortment of small dishes, from noodles to dumplings, served with tea as the mid-morning or afternoon offering in Chinese teahouses.

EMULSION: A mixture of two liquids that do not blend well, such as oil and vinegar. Add the oil very slowly, drop by drop or in a thin stream, to the vinegar while whisking constantly.

ENRICHED: Having certain nutrients, which were lost when a food such as grain was processed, replaced by further processing. For example, wheat processed into white flour loses significant amounts of about 20 vitamins and minerals as well as fiber. Enrichment replaces 4 of the lost nutrients—thiamine, riboflavin, niacin and iron.

EXCHANGES: Portion sizes in a system originally developed by The American Dietetic Association and the American Diabetes Association, for use by people with diabetes or in weight-loss programs.

Unfortunately, the exchange system (which preceded other standard portions) differs somewhat from both Food Guide Pyramid serving sizes and nutrition label serving sizes. *See also* Serving.

FAT: A compound of carbon, hydrogen and oxygen atoms that provides energy to the body. Most fats found in food are **triglycerides**—three fatty acids and a glycerol molecule.

Fatty acids vary in degree of saturation according to the number of double bonds in their chemical structure. **Saturated fatty acids** have no double bonds in their carbon chain and are found primarily in animal products. Saturated fats are usually solid at room temperature. **Unsaturated fatty acids** have one (**monounsaturated**) or more (**polyunsaturated**) double bonds. Unsaturated fats come from plants and fish and are liquid at room temperature. **Monounsaturated fatty acids,** such as those in olive oil and canola oil, may help reduce blood cholesterol levels by reducing low-density lipoproteins (LDLs). Fish oil contains a polyunsaturated fatty acid called **omega-3,** which is thought to help reduce risk for heart attack and stroke. Hydrogenation of polyunsaturated oils can produce **trans fatty acids,** which have some of the properties of saturated fats.

Health experts recommend that only 30 percent of daily calories come from fat, with only 10 percent from saturated fat. *See also* Cholesterol, Hydrogenation.

TYPES OF FAT IN OILS, BUTTER AND OTHER FATS

Types of Oil, etc	Saturated Fat	Polyunsaturated Fat	Monounsaturated Fat	Cholesterol *(mg/tablespoon)*
Canola oil	6%	36%	58%	0
Safflower oil	9%	78%	13%	0
Sunflower oil	11%	69%	20%	0
Corn oil	13%	62%	25%	0
Olive oil	14%	9%	77%	0
Sesame oil	14%	42%	4%	0
Soybean oil	15%	61%	24%	0
Margarine, stick*	17%	32%	49%	0
Peanut oil	18%	34%	48%	0
Cottonseed oil	27%	54%	19%	0
Chicken fat	31%	21%	47%	11
Lard*	41%	12%	47%	12
Palm oil	51%	10%	39%	0
Beef fat	52%	4%	44%	14
Butterfat	66%	4%	30%	33
Coconut oil	92%	2%	6%	0

* The monounsaturated percentage includes some trans fatty acids. *See* Hydrogenation.

FIBER: The indigestible part of plants. Fiber falls into two categories—insoluble and soluble. **Insoluble fiber** can absorb significant amounts of water and assists in elimination. It may help prevent colon cancer. Sources of insoluble fiber are whole grains, vegetables, fruit peels, legumes, seeds and nuts.

Soluble fiber prevents the body from absorbing certain substances. It is thought to lower blood cholesterol levels and to help regulate blood sugar. Sources of soluble fiber are fruits, vegetables, seeds, brown rice, oats and oat bran.

FISH STOCK: The essence of fish and vegetables, used as a flavoring base for soups, stews and sauces.

To make **fish stock**, heat 3 tablespoons vegetable oil in a nonaluminum stockpot. Add 1 small onion, 1 carrot, 1 stalk of celery (all cut into ¼-in/6-mm pieces), and sauté for about 5 minutes, until soft. Add ½ cup (1½ oz/45 g) sliced mushrooms and 4 lb (2 kg) of nonoily fish (white fish) bones. Cook over low heat until the bones begin to fall apart, about 20 minutes. Add 2 cups (16 fl oz/500 ml) of dry white wine, and deglaze the pan. Add 8 cups (64 fl oz/2 l) of drinking water, and bring to a boil. Reduce to a simmer, add a bouquet garni (sprig of parsley, bay leaf, sprig of thyme, 4–5 peppercorns) and skim impurities from the top. Simmer uncovered for 30 minutes, skimming occasionally. Strain the stock through cheesecloth, and chill it until the fat solidifies and can be removed.

Stock freezes very well. Try freezing it in 2- or 4-cup (16- or 32-fl oz/500-ml or 1-l) portions, to be used later in soups or sauces.

FOOD GUIDE PYRAMID: A graphic representation developed by the United States Department of Agriculture (USDA) to illustrate the optimal proportion of major food groups in a diet that promotes health (see page 25).

FORTIFIED: Containing added vitamins and minerals that were not originally present (or were present in smaller amounts) in a food. Breakfast cereals are often fortified. Milk is fortified with vitamins A and D. Some fruit juices are fortified with vitamin C or calcium.

FREE RADICALS: Highly reactive atoms or molecules that have unpaired electrons that seek out other molecules with unpaired electrons. Free radicals occur naturally at the cellular level but are also caused by environmental factors such as smoking and radiation. In excess, they destroy genetic material within cells and the damage can lead to disease.

FRUCTOSE: A simple carbohydrate and the form of sugar found in most fruits and some vegetables. *See also* Carbohydrates, Sugar.

GLUCOSE: A sugar that is the primary fuel for cells, muscles and the brain. The body processes all carbohydrates—simple and complex—into glucose.

GRAM (g): A metric unit of weight; 28.35 g equals 1 oz. Many nutrients in food, such as carbohydrates, protein and fat, are measured in grams on food labels and in the nutrient analyses of recipes.

HEALTH CLAIMS: Food labels may include specific health claims if they meet criteria set by the government. At present health claims are allowed in only 7 areas:
- Foods that are low in fat, saturated fat and cholesterol may reduce risk of heart disease.
- Fruits, vegetables and grains with certain types of fiber may reduce risk of heart disease.
- Foods low in sodium may reduce risk of hypertension.
- Foods high in calcium may reduce risk of osteoporosis.
- Fruits and vegetables that are good sources of vitamin C, vitamin A or fiber may reduce the risk of some cancers.
- Grain products, fruits or vegetables that are good sources of fiber and low in fat may reduce the risk of some cancers.
- Foods low in fat may reduce the risk of some cancers.

HERBS: Leaves, flowers and other parts of certain plants used as flavoring agents in cooking. Fresh herbs have a completely different flavor than their dried versions. When possible use fresh ones. Remove the stems, as most are bitter (an exception is parsley, which has flavorful stems). Mince herbs with a very sharp knife so as not to bruise the leaves. When substituting dried herbs in a recipe, use ⅓ the fresh measurement called for. Herbs are easy to grow, and many can be preserved by freezing.

HYDROGENATION: The manufacturing process that adds hydrogen atoms to unsaturated fat, making it more solid. **Trans fatty acids** can result when polyunsaturated oils are hydrogenated or partially hydrogenated. These fatty acids are altered, reversing part of their chemical structure. Recent research indicates that trans fatty acids tend to raise blood cholesterol levels the way saturated fats do even though they are monounsaturated in structure. *See also* Fat.

JULIENNED: A French culinary term for ingredients thinly cut into sticks about ¼ in (6 mm) thick and 1 in (2.5 cm) or so in length. Vegetables may be julienned.

KASHA: Roasted buckwheat groats. Buckwheat is not related to wheat and contains very little gluten. Whole or cracked buckwheat has an assertive nutty flavor and is an interesting alternative to rice. Coating the kasha with an egg white before cooking helps keep the grains separate. For a creamier dish, eliminate that step. Kasha is not to be confused with Kashi, a commercial product that consists of a combination of grains. Kashi does make a delicious pilaf as well, however, with similar cooking times, and can be substituted for kasha.

LEAN, EXTRA LEAN (as in meat): As defined by the United States Department of Agriculture, lean meat and poultry products contain less than 10 g of fat, 4 g of saturated fat and 95 mg of cholesterol per 3½ oz serving. Extra lean foods have less than 5 g of fat, 2 g of saturated fat and 95 mg of cholesterol per 3½ oz serving.

LEGUMES: The family of vegetables that includes lentils, split peas and various dried beans, as well as peanuts (groundnuts), string beans, green peas, soybeans and alfalfa. Of the 14,000 species of legumes, only 20 or so are used as food. Legumes are high in complex carbohydrates and a number of vitamins and minerals. They are rich in soluble fiber and are very good sources of protein. Almost everyone's diet can be improved by the addition of legumes. Primitive cultures often relied on legumes and grains as food staples. Combined, they offer a protein source equal to meat, and most legumes have no fat.

In terms of food groups, string beans and green peas are treated as vegetables; the pod as well as the bean of string beans and snow peas or sugar snap peas (mangetouts) are eaten. Other legumes are in the dry beans and nuts food group with meat, poultry, fish and eggs. Soybeans are a major source of vegetable oil; soy protein is used in meat substitutes and in some infant formulas. Soy sauce, tofu and miso are also soybean products, with the fat removed. The major use of peanuts worldwide is for oil, but more than half of the peanuts grown in the United States are processed into peanut butter. Peanuts are high-fat members of the legume family.

Lentils and split peas have been around since 9000 B.C. They were among the first plants to be domesticated. Both lentils and split peas are low in fat and good protein sources. Lentils make a great substitute for all or part of the meat in chili.

Kidney beans have been cultivated in Mexico for more than 7000 years and are common in that country's cuisine as well as in Cajun and Caribbean foods. Black beans are a Cuban staple. Great northern or navy beans are the most widely used dried beans in the United States.

Chick-peas (garbanzo beans), which are higher in fat than most of their legume relatives, are popular in Indian and Middle Eastern cuisine. Humus is made primarily of chick-peas. Iron-rich lima beans are also legumes and once were a staple of the American Indian diet.

LINGONBERRY: A small, red wild berry found in the Scandinavian Arctic.

MATTONE: A terra cotta utensil used for cooking chicken as it is done in Tuscany, where flattened whole chickens are weighted and cooked between 2 pieces of terra cotta to yield a crispy outside and a moist interior. The *mattone* is heated and cooks on top of the stove.

MEAT SUBSTITUTES: Textured vegetable proteins, often made from soybeans, that can substitute for ground beef in recipes. Some meat substitutes are sold in patties or links.

MESCLUN: A combination of baby and bitter greens and mild herbs. It may contain escarole (curly endive/chicory), mâche (corn salad), dandelion leaves, arugula, chervil and/or oak-leaf lettuce.

MICROGRAM (mcg): A metric unit of weight; 1 mcg equals 1/1000 mg. This very tiny unit is used to measure some vitamins and minerals (such as biotin and manganese). *See also* Milligram.

MILLIGRAM (mg): A metric unit of weight; 1 mg equals 1/1000 g. Milligrams are the units used to measure most vitamins and minerals in food. *See also* Gram.

MINERALS: Inorganic substances that are the basic constituents of the earth's crust. They are absorbed from the earth by plants and subsequently consumed by animals, including humans. Among the 60 minerals found in the human body, 22 are considered essential to human nutrition. The 16 most important minerals, with their functions and food sources, are listed in the chart following the index.

MUSHROOMS: Domesticated and wild fungi used in cooking. Mild-flavored mushrooms, such as button, *enoki* and *cremini*, are found in most markets. Many wild mushrooms have been domesticated for cultivation. In recipes calling for wild mushrooms, purchase from a reputable picker or market. Foraging requires experience in identifying very subtle differences between edible and poisonous mushrooms. Readily available wild mushrooms include cèpe, porcini (boletus), Portobello, oyster, shiitake, morel, tree ear and chanterelle. Many of these also are sold in dried form, which packs a lot of flavor. Soak dried mushrooms for at least 20 minutes in warm chicken stock or water; strain and use the soaking liquid in the recipe, or reserve it for a future soup or sauce.

NONREACTIVE UTENSILS: Utensils made of materials, specifically stainless steel and glass, that do not have a reaction to acidic ingredients. Avoid aluminum, as it reacts with wine, citrus and other acidic ingredients to discolor the food and affect the taste.

NUTRIENT CONTENT CLAIMS: Claims about the levels of nutrients in a food. Only certain words or phrases can be used on food packages to describe the levels of nutrients. Use of these descriptions is strictly regulated by the government. See the definitions in the chart below.

NUTRIENT CONTENT CLAIM DEFINITIONS

Claim	Amount or Standard
FAT FREE	0.5 g fat or less per standard serving.
SATURATED FAT FREE	0.5 g saturated fat or less per standard serving.
CHOLESTEROL FREE	Less than 2 mg cholesterol and 2 g or less saturated fat per standard serving.
SODIUM FREE	Less than 5 mg sodium per standard serving.
CALORIES FREE	Less than 5 calories per standard serving.
SUGAR FREE	Less than 0.5 g sugar per standard serving.
LOW FAT	3 g fat or less per standard serving.
LOW SATURATED FAT	1 g saturated fat or less per standard serving.
LOW CHOLESTEROL	20 mg or less cholesterol and 2 g or less saturated fat per standard serving.
LOW SODIUM	140 mg sodium or less per standard serving.
LOW CALORIES	40 calories or less per standard serving.
HIGH FIBER	5 grams fiber or more per standard serving.
GOOD FIBER	2.5–4.9 g fiber per standard serving.
REDUCED	25% lower in the nutrient than the comparable regular (reference) food.
GOOD SOURCE	Contains 10–19% of the Daily Value per serving of the specified nutrient (i.e. good source of calcium).
HIGH, RICH IN, EXCELLENT SOURCE OF	Contains 20% or more of the Daily Value per serving of the specified nutrient (i.e. excellent source of calcium).
MORE, FORTIFIED, ADDED, ENRICHED	Contains at least 10% more of the Daily Value for protein, vitamins, minerals or fiber per serving compared with the regular (reference) food.
LIGHT, LITE	50% less fat than the regular (reference) food, or 50% less sodium than the reference food and food also is low calorie and low fat, or ⅓ fewer calories than the reference food, if the reference food contains less than 50% calories from fat. Also "Light in color," "Light in texture" if "light" is used to describe a food characteristic.

NUTRIENTS: Substances obtained from food and used in the body to promote growth, maintenance and repair. Nutrients include proteins, carbohydrates, fats, vitamins, minerals and water.

NUTRITION LABEL: A standard statement concerning nutritional content that is mandated to appear on most processed foods by mid-1994. In 1990, the United States Congress passed the Nutrition Labeling and Education Act. The Food and Drug Administration (FDA), which oversees all packaged foods, and the United States Department of Agriculture (USDA), which is responsible for labeling meat and poultry, cooperated in drafting the label.

Almost all packaged foods of nutritional significance now bear a nutrition label. Plain coffee, tea and most spices, however, are not labeled, nor are restaurant, vending, deli and bakery foods. Processed meat and poultry foods must be labeled; for raw meat and poultry, labeling is optional. Supermarkets are encouraged to offer nutrition information on raw fruits, vegetables and seafood. Foods previously exempt from listing ingredients—staples such as peanut butter, ice cream and canned fruit cocktail—now must provide a full ingredient listing and a nutrition label. *See also* Nutrient content claims.

ORGANICALLY GROWN: In reference to crops, grown without the use of pesticides or chemicals. The term *organic*, used to describe other food, has no legal meaning. The United States Department of Agriculture does not permit its use to describe meat and poultry.

OXIDATION: The combination of oxygen with another element, resulting in formation of a new substance. Rust is the result of oxidation of iron; rancidity is the result of oxidation of fat or oil. In the human body, oxidation within cells is a necessary chemical reaction. Antioxidants protect cells from damage by excessive oxidized particles called free radicals. *See also* Antioxidants, Free radicals.

PASTA: A flour-and-liquid dough rolled flat, cut into a variety of shapes and sizes and cooked in boiling water or another liquid. An excellent source of complex carbohydrates, pastas are known in many versions internationally. With the variety of flours and shapes, dried and fresh, with or without eggs, pasta is one of the world's most popular dishes.

To make **pasta dough,** place 3 cups (15 oz/470 g) all-purpose (plain) flour in a food processor fitted with a steel knife blade. In a small container with a pour spout, whisk 4 eggs with 1 tablespoon olive oil. With the food processor running, slowly add the egg mixture until the dough starts to clean the sides of the bowl (the amount of egg mixture added will depend on the humidity and the moisture content of the flour). Process for 30 seconds, and check the consistency. The dough should be moist enough to pinch together, but not sticky. Remove the dough from the processor and knead it by hand to form a ball; then place it in a plastic bag to rest.

To roll out pasta, use ¼ of the dough at a time, keeping the remaining dough in the plastic bag to avoid drying it out. Using a hand-crank pasta maker (Atlas, Marconi), start on widest setting. Put the dough through the machine 8–10 times, folding the pasta in half each time, until the dough is smooth. If it tears, it may be too wet; dust it with flour, and brush off excess. Narrow the machine setting one notch, and pass the dough through *without folding*. Follow this procedure twice at each setting; continue until the dough is the desired thickness. Allow the dough to dry out—about as long as it takes to roll out another piece— and then cut it into the desired pasta shape.

To make **spinach pasta,** clean, steam and squeeze as much water as possible from 12 oz (375 g) of fresh spinach. Process the spinach with the flour in a food processor before adding the egg mixture. Follow the recipe above, but use only 3 eggs.

To make **carrot or beet pasta,** peel and steam or cook ½ lb (250 g) of carrots or beets until tender. Proceed as for spinach pasta. To cook pasta, remember that fresh pasta takes only 1–2 minutes to cook in boiling water. Test to see if it is done to your preference. Don't overcook it.

PASTRY CRUST: A flaky shell made of flour, shortening and water. Most pastry crust recipes use a lot of butter or shortening. For an alternative, *see* Yeast pastry crust.

PERNOD: An anise-seed-flavored liqueur.

PESTO: A flavoring ingredient, usually made with Parmesan cheese, pine nuts, fresh basil, and olive oil. *Pepitas*, or hulled pumpkin seeds, which are up to 25 percent lower in total fat than pine nuts, can be substituted. Since this mixture is used in small amounts, however, the richness of the cheese and nuts is well distributed and not excessive in a portion. Try substituting fresh cilantro (fresh coriander) or sun-dried tomatoes for the basil or using safflower or a lighter vegetable oil instead of the olive oil. A lower-fat version, pesto without the cheese is also delicious.

To make ¼ cup (2 fl oz/60 ml) **pepita pesto,** in a food processor or blender place 1 clove garlic, 1 cup (1 oz/30 g) fresh basil leaves, 2 tablespoons Parmesan cheese, 1 tablespoon toasted *pepitas* and 2 tablespoons olive oil; blend until smooth. The pesto can be stored in the refrigerator, covered by a thin layer of oil floating on top. Remove the oil before using the pesto.

PHYLLO: A paper-thin dough used for strudels and wrapped foods.

POACHING: Cooking food in simmering liquid (often stock). The liquid should be hot before you introduce the meat, seafood or vegetables, so as to seal in the flavor. The flavor of the meat is lost to the broth if both are heated together (that is why chicken stock is so flavorful and the meat used to make it has no flavor). Add a drop or two of vinegar to the poaching water when poaching eggs.

PROTEIN: The structural component of muscles, bones, cartilage, skin and organs. It is formed from 22 amino acids, combining in various arrangements. The human body can manufacture only 13 amino acids, called **nonessential** because they do not have to be provided by the diet. The other 9 amino acids are **essential** because they must be supplied by food.

When a food has sufficient amounts of all 9 essential amino acids, it is called a **complete protein.** Most foods from animal sources are complete proteins. **Incomplete proteins** are typically plant foods and lack 1 or 2 essential amino acids. Two or more plant foods can be eaten together, however, to obtain all essential amino acids. Such combinations—for example, certain vegetables with certain grains—are called **complementary proteins.** Because amino acids circulate in the bloodstream for a while before forming new body protein, the complementary foods need not be eaten at the same meal.

The body needs a fresh supply of protein every day. Most Americans eat more than enough protein. Strict vegetarians, however, must be careful to eat enough vegetable and grain sources of protein to meet their need for essential amino acids.

PROVITAMINS (precursors): Compounds that can be converted in the human body into active vitamins. Beta-carotene, for example, is converted by the body into vitamin A.

QUINOA: A tiny grain that has the highest protein content among grains and contains a complete protein, with a balance of the essential amino acids. It should be thoroughly rinsed before using, as it has a bitter natural coating, saponin, that acts as an insect repellant.

RAU CÂN: A vegetable known as Chinese parsley that tastes like bitter celery leaves. Celery leaves can be substituted for it.

RECOMMENDED DIETARY ALLOWANCE (RDA): The recommended daily consumption levels of energy (calories) and selected nutrients for maintenance of health. RDAs are developed by the Food and Nutrition Board of the National Academy of Sciences/National Research Council and updated about every 5 years. RDAs are now set for energy, protein, 13 vitamins and 15 minerals. Separate recommendations are made for different sets of people and age groups—e.g., children 1–3, males 25–50, females 19–24, lactating women in first 6 months of lactation.

REDUCE: To concentrate and/or thicken a liquid by boiling. Water is evaporated, reducing the volume and intensifying the flavor.

REFERENCE DIET: A 2000-calorie diet used as the basis for nutrition labeling and Daily Values. It is a general standard for the "average" American's nutrient needs. *See also* Daily Values, Nutrition label.

REFERENCE FOOD: The standard food in a category or an average of the 3 most popular brands. This term was developed for labeling comparisons. It is the regular food that is compared to a "reduced" or "light" food. For example, a "reduced fat" blue cheese salad dressing must have at least 25 percent less fat than the regular (or reference) blue cheese dressing.

REGISTERED DIETITIAN (RD): A nutrition specialist who has completed a rigorous undergraduate program, an internship or supervised work experience, and the national registration exam administered by the Commission on Dietetic Registration. More than half of registered dietitians also have a postgraduate degree. Continuing education is required to keep the RD credential. Registered dietitians practice clinical and community dietetics, manage health care systems, work in education and research, work in the food industry and counsel individuals and groups about food and nutrition issues.

ROASTING: Cooking by exposing a food to direct heat, in an oven, for example. Meats should be seared in a pan before roasting, to seal in the flavor. Lengthy roasting may require basting to keep the food from drying out.

To roast garlic: Preheat an oven to 300°F (150°C). Score the skins of 8 heads of garlic around the middle; do not cut into the cloves. Remove the top half of the papery skins, exposing the cloves. Place the garlic heads in a small roasting pan, and pour ½ cup (4 fl oz/125 ml) olive oil over the garlic. Season with salt and freshly ground pepper to taste, add 1 teaspoon each of finely minced fresh rosemary and thyme and bake, covered, for 1 hour. Remove the cover, and bake 10–15 minutes longer, basting frequently, until the heads are very tender. Allow the garlic to cool before serving. (Serves 4–6 as an appetizer or main dish accompaniment). Reserve the oil from the pan.

Roasting also refers to the process used in peeling chilies and other peppers. **To roast peppers**, place them over a direct flame (on a gas burner, on a grill or under a broiler) and blacken the outer skin, turning the peppers to cook them evenly. Remove them from the flame, place them in a paper bag and close the bag to cool and steam the peppers. When they have cooled, peel away the blackened skin. The result is a softened, sweetened flesh that is delicious in salads, in sauces and as a garnish.

ROUX: A classic French technique for thickening liquids. Cook equal amounts of butter and flour, stirring for at least 5 minutes to eliminate the starchy flavor. Then stir in the liquid to be thickened, and cook over low heat until the mixture is the desired consistency. The longer the flour mixture cooks, the darker in color the resulting sauce will be.

SAFFRON: The dried stigmas of the crocus flower, used as an herb to lend a distinctive yellow color to food. Turmeric, or Indian saffron, can be substituted for it.

SALMONELLA: A common bacterium that is responsible for about half of all incidents of food poisoning. It is generally found in raw animal foods such as meat, eggs and chicken.

SEMOLINA: A flour made from coarsely ground hard durum wheat.

SEROTONIN: A brain chemical manufactured by the body from the amino acid tryptophan. It can affect mood.

SERVING: The amount of a food that an individual is presumed to eat at a sitting. Nutrition label serving sizes are not necessarily the same as servings recommended in the Food Guide Pyramid or in the exchange system. Some basic differences among the 3 sets of serving definitions are shown in the chart on page 24.

SEVICHE: A dish of Central and South America based on raw seafood marinated in citrus juices and mixed with chilies, onion, cilantro (coriander/ Chinese parsley) and fresh tomatoes. The citrus marinade "cooks" the raw fish; it is not further subjected to heat.

SMOKING: Exposing food to smoke in a closed container. Originally a means of preserving meats and fish, this technique is also used to infuse ingredients with an aromatic, smoky flavor. Aromatic woods, herbs and spices, such as juniper, mesquite, hickory, rosemary, pine needles, fennel, cinnamon and orange peel, are examples of materials burned for smoking.

STEARIC ACID: A saturated fatty acid found in meat and chocolate. Some research indicates that it does not raise blood cholesterol levels as other saturated fatty acids do.

SUCROSE: A combination of fructose and glucose. White table sugar, corn syrup and brown sugar contain sucrose. It also occurs naturally in some vegetables and fruits.

SUGAR: A simple carbohydrate. Essentially, all sugars are nutritionally equal, although some forms—fructose, for example—are sweeter than others. **Glucose,** the primary blood sugar, is the basic body fuel. The body converts complex carbohydrates (starches) and most fructose (fruit sugar) into glucose. *See also* Carbohydrates, Fructose, Glucose, Sucrose.

The following sugars can be found on food ingredient lists: barley malt, honey, brown sugar, invert sugar, cane sugar, lactose, corn sweetener, maltose, corn syrup, mannitol, dextrose, maple syrup, fructose, sorbitol, glucose, sorghum, grape sugar, sucrose, grape sweetener, sugar, high-fructose corn syrup.

SUPPLEMENTS: Vitamins and minerals in pill, powder or liquid form. Supplements contain nutrients, but they are not food. People suffering from vitamin/mineral deficiency may need to take supplements. In addition, pregnant and lactating women are typically advised to take a supplement. Researchers are exploring whether various nutrients in supplement form can protect against disease but do not yet know which supplements or how much is safe and effective. Currently, most experts recommend food as the preferred source of vitamins and minerals.

TAGEEN: A deep earthenware dish with a conical lid used in northern Africa for slow-cooked dishes. *Tageen* also refers to the preparation method.

TAMARIND: The podded fruit of an evergreen tree grown in tropical climates. The bittersweet pulp is separated from the seeds and dried or liquefied.

THICKENING AGENTS: Starches added to thicken sauces, purées and soups. Cornstarch, arrowroot, tapioca and potato or wheat flour are most commonly used. Combine these powdery starches with an equal amount of water or stock before adding them to the liquid to be thickened. This helps eliminate lumping.

TOASTING: A means of browning ingredients. **To toast nuts,** place them on a dry sheet pan in a 350°F (180°C) oven for 10–15 minutes, stirring once or twice, until golden brown.

TOFU: Coagulated soy milk, high in protein, that absorbs the surrounding flavors when marinated or cooked.

TRACE MINERALS: Essential mineral nutrients found in the human body in amounts less than 5 grams which is less than 1 teaspoonful in your entire body. These microminerals include chromium, fluoride, manganese, selenium and zinc.

TRYPTOPHAN: An amino acid found in protein that stimulates production of the mood-altering brain chemical serotonin.

VEGETABLE STOCK: The essence of vegetables, used as a flavoring base in soups, stews and sauces.

To make about 4 cups (32 fl oz/1 l) of **vegetable stock,** in a large, nonaluminum stockpot, heat 3 tablespoons vegetable oil. Add 8 celery stalks, 3 leeks, 2 peeled carrots, and 1 onion (all cut into 1-in/2.5-cm pieces). Cook until soft but not browned. Add 1 cup (8 fl oz/250 ml) dry white wine, and reduce to half the volume. Add 6 cups (48 fl oz/1.5 l) water, bring to a boil and skim impurities from the top. Reduce to a simmer, and add a bouquet garni (3 sprigs of parsley, 1 bay leaf, 2 sprigs of thyme, and 4 black peppercorns). Simmer, uncovered, for 1 hour, skimming occasionally. Strain through a fine strainer, pressing the vegetables to extract as much liquid as possible. Chill the stock until the fat solidifies and can be removed. For **rich vegetable stock,** follow the recipe for vegetable stock above, but simmer for 1 hour longer.

VEGETARIAN: A person who eats only or primarily plant foods. Strict vegetarians, called **vegans,** eat no foods of animal origin. **Lactovegetarians** include dairy products in their diet but no meats. **Lacto-ovovegetarians** eat eggs as well as dairy foods and plant foods. **Semivegetarians** generally eat small amounts of fish or chicken but no red meat. If their diet is planned carefully, vegetarians are at no greater risk for nutrient deficiencies than are meat eaters. Vegans must be careful to design their diets to consume sufficient proteins, vitamin B$_{12}$, calcium, iron and zinc.

VITAMINS: Organic substances necessary for many basic body functions. Vitamins must be provided by foods (or supplements); the body does not manufacture them. Their functions and sources are listed in the chart following the index.

WHOLE GRAIN: A grain that includes the germ, endosperm, bran and husk. The refining process removes the nutrient-rich germ and the fiber-rich bran and husk from grains. High in complex carbohydrates and rich in protein and fiber, whole grains include: amaranth, barley, buckwheat, millet, oats, quinoa, brown rice, white rice, rye, triticale and whole wheat.

YEAST PASTRY CRUST: A low-fat alternative for pastry. To make two 9-in (23-cm) single-crust pie shells, dissolve 1 package (¼ oz/7 g) active dry yeast and ¼ cup (2 oz/60 g) sugar in 1 cup (8 fl oz/250 ml) lukewarm milk (approximately 85°F/30°C). Let stand 5 minutes, or until the yeast foams. Add 4 tablespoons (2 fl oz/60 ml) safflower oil and 1 egg. Mix well, and set aside. In a large mixing bowl, stir together 4½ cups (22½ oz/700 g) unbleached all-purpose (plain) flour and ½ teaspoon salt. Add the yeast mixture, stirring until all the flour is incorporated and the dough is not lumpy. Turn the dough onto a lightly floured work surface, and knead until it is smooth and elastic. Return it to a clean, lightly oiled bowl, cover and let rise until double in volume, about 1½ hours. Punch the dough down, cut it into 2 equal pieces and form each into a ball. Roll each ball on a floured work surface and then transfer it to a lightly oiled pie pan. Let the crusts rest 10 minutes before you fill and bake them at 375°F (190°C) for 45–50 minutes, or according to the filling recipe.

YOGURT CHEESE: Yogurt thickened to a firmer consistency by draining moisture from it. To make it, line a colander with cheesecloth and place it over a large bowl. Place 1 cup (8 fl oz/250 ml) plain yogurt in the cheesecloth; refrigerate, and let drain overnight. The yogurt will reach the consistency of soft cheese and can be spread on crackers or sandwiches or substituted for cream cheese in some recipes. For the best results, use yogurt to which no stabilizers have been added.

ZEST: The brightly colored, thin outer skin of citrus fruits, which is full of flavorful oils.

Acknowledgments

Pamela Sheldon Johns would like to thank her husband and best friend, Courtney. Thanks to her friends and co-workers at Jordano's, including Peter; and love to Janice, Keri, Robin, Laurence, Kristin, Adrienne and Kelley for their special support. She also acknowledges invaluable support from all of the recipe testers. Without all of you, we'd still be standing over the stove.

Mary Abbott Hess is grateful for the support of Jane Grant Tougas, Sharon Gourley, the American Institute of Wine & Food, and the staffs of Computrition, Inc., the National Center for Nutrition and Dietetics, and Weldon Owen Inc. Their contributions are evident on every page.

The photographer and stylists would like to thank the following (from San Francisco unless specified): The Attic; Meredith Bowman; Bethanie Brandon Design; Gail Cohen, Berkeley; Cookin; Cyclamen Studios, Julie Sanders Designer, Berkeley; Ward Finer; Bea and Marty Glenn; Nancy Glenn; Rosie Glenn-Finer; Judy Goldsmith and Bernie Carrasco, J. Goldsmith Antiques; Stephanie Greenleigh; Sandra Griswold; Missy Hamilton; Glenda Jordan, Berkeley; Sue Fisher King; Mimi Koch; Luna Garcia, Venice; L'Osteria del forno, Susan Borgatti; Merna Oeberst; Paul Bauer, Inc.; Susan Pascal; Bob Pool, Berkeley; Dan Schuster; Smith and Hawken, Ltd., Berkeley; Tesoro, Los Angeles; Virginia Breier Gallery; WilkesHome at Wilkes Bashford; Machek Wlodarchek; The Cannery Wine Cellars.

The publishers would like to thank the following people and organizations for their assistance in the preparation of this book: Sigrid Chase, Richard VanOosterhout, Miriam Coupe, Jim Obata, Dawn Low, Janique Poncelet, Tori Ritchie, Fee-ling Tan, Jonette Banzon, Patty Hill, Angela Williams, Laurie Wertz, Wendely Harvey, Bruce Bailey, Kim Green, Tarji Mickelson, Barabara Pool Fenzl.

Photography Credits

Index

MINERALS

Calcium: Helps build and maintain strong bones and teeth; important for normal nerve and muscle functions and blood clotting; prevents osteoporosis. Food Sources: Milk, cheese, yogurt, other dairy products, tofu, sardines and canned salmon if eaten with bones, green leafy vegetables, chick-peas, other legumes, shellfish.

Chloride: Maintains normal fluid shifts; helps acid-base balance in body; forms hydrochloric acid to aid digestion. Food Sources: Table salt, soy sauce, processed foods, fish, shellfish, meat, milk, eggs.

Chromium: Important for glucose metabolism; may be necessary for insulin activity. Food Sources: Organ meats, other meats, cheese, whole grains, dried peas and beans, peanuts, corn oil, poultry, green leafy vegetables.

Copper: Aids formation of red blood cells; helps get iron into blood cells; helps produce enzymes and connective tissue. Food Sources: Shellfish, nuts, liver and other organ meats, cocoa powder, chocolate, raisins, corn oil margarine, leafy green vegetables, whole grains, legumes, seeds, nuts, poultry.

Fluorine (fluoride): Contributes to strong bones and teeth; may help prevent osteoporosis. Food Sources: Fluoridated water and foods grown or cooked in it, fish, tea.

Iodine: Necessary for forming thyroid hormone that helps regulate growth; necessary for normal cell function; prevents goiter; promotes health of skin, nails and hair. Food Sources: Primarily iodized salt, but also seafood, seaweed food products, vegetables grown in iodine-rich areas, vegetable oil, processed foods.

Iron: Essential for proper red blood cell function, oxygen transport and cellular activity. Food Sources: Red meats, liver and other organ meats, dark meat of poultry, shellfish, fish, enriched grains, fortified cereals, raisins, other dried fruits, prune juice, leafy green vegetables, legumes, nuts, molasses, egg yolks; meat forms are absorbed best.

Magnesium: Aids in bone growth; aids function of nerves and muscle, including regulation of normal heart rhythm; needed for energy metabolism and cell division. Food Sources: Nuts, legumes, seeds, spinach, oysters, wheat bran, whole grains, raw leafy green vegetables, apricots, seeds, meats, cocoa, chocolate.

Manganese: Required for bone growth and development, energy metabolism, cell function and normal reproduction. Food Sources: Nuts, whole grains, vegetables, fruits, instant coffee, tea, cocoa powder, beet greens, egg yolks, blueberries.

Molybdenum: Important for normal cell function. Food Sources: Peas, beans, cereal grains, organ meats, some dark green vegetables.

Phosphorus: Aids in bone growth and strengthening of teeth; important in energy metabolism. Food Sources: Milk, cheese, yogurt, meat, poultry, fish, egg yolks, dried peas and beans, soft drinks, nuts, whole grains; present in almost all foods.

Potassium: Promotes regular heartbeat; necessary for nerve and muscle contraction; regulates transfer of nutrients to cells; controls water balance in body tissues and cells; helps regulate blood pressure. Food Sources: Oranges, orange juice, bananas, dried fruits, tomato juice, peanut butter, spinach, winter squash, legumes, potatoes, coffee, tea, cocoa, yogurt, molasses, whole grains, meat, poultry, fish.

Selenium: Antioxidant; works with vitamin E to fight cell damage. Food Sources: Fish, shellfish, organ meats, red meat, egg yolks, chicken, garlic, tuna, tomatoes, onions.

Sodium: Helps regulate water balance in body; plays role in maintaining blood pressure; aids nerve impulses and muscle contraction. Food Sources: Table salt, salt added to processed and prepared foods, baking soda, dairy products, seasonings, soy sauce, meat, fish, pickles.

Sulfur: Present in all cells; part of many proteins; component of some vitamins and insulin; necessary for energy metabolism. Food Sources: All protein foods (meat, fish, poultry, milk, yogurt, cheese, legumes, etc.). Sulfur is part of the structure of some amino acids found in proteins.

Zinc: Promotes ability to taste and smell; aids normal growth and sexual development; important for fetal growth and wound healing; component of enzymes and insulin. Food Sources: Oysters, crabmeat, beef, liver, eggs, poultry, brewer's yeast, whole-wheat bread, legumes, wheat bran.

VITAMINS

Vitamin A (precursors include provitamin A carotenoids): Important in development of healthy eyes, skin, hair, teeth and gums; increases resistance to infection; necessary for vision; aids hormone synthesis; in carotene form, acts as antioxidant to prevent cell damage. Food Sources: Dark green leafy vegetables (spinach, greens, kale, brussels sprouts) asparagus, yellow-orange vegetables and fruits (carrots, sweet potatoes, winter squash, pumpkin, cantaloupe, apricots), liver, fortified milk, fish, fortified margarine.

Vitamin B_1 (thiamine): Necessary for healthy brain, nerve cells and functioning of heart; aids metabolism of carbohydrates, fats and proteins; supports normal appetite. Food Sources: Pork, whole grains, egg yolks, lean meats, organ meats, poultry, fish, legumes, enriched bread, nuts.

Vitamin B_2 (riboflavin): Aids in release of energy from foods; interacts with other B vitamins; supports vision and skin health. Food Sources: Milk and other dairy products, lean meats, green leafy vegetables, eggs, nuts, enriched breads and cereals.

Vitamin B_3 (niacin, nicotinic acid): Works with other B vitamins to release energy from foods. Food Sources: Meats, poultry, fish, milk and other dairy products, legumes, nuts.

Vitamin B_5 (pantothenic acid): Aids in release of energy from food and in formation of hormones and nerve regulators. Food Sources: Organ meats, whole-grain cereals, legumes, yogurt.

Vitamin B_6 (pyridoxine, pyridoxal, pyridoxamine): Helps metabolize proteins and fatty acids; aids function of nervous system and formation of red blood cells; helps convert amino acid tryptophan to niacin. Food Sources: Chicken, organ meats, pork, green leafy vegetables, whole-grain cereals and breads, bananas, potatoes, lima beans and other legumes, nuts, avocados, cabbage, cauliflower, eggs, whole grains, shellfish.

Folic acid (folacin, folate, pteroylglutamic acid): Aids in formation of genetic materials for cell nuclei, important for cell replacement; works with vitamin B_{12} to produce red blood cells. Food Sources: Broccoli, asparagus, spinach and other green leafy vegetables, liver and other organ meats, oranges, wheat bran, legumes, seeds.

Vitamin B_{12} (cyanocobalamin): Aids synthesis of DNA in developing cells, formation of red blood cells, nervous system functioning; used in treatment of pernicious anemia. Food Sources: Mainly animal products (liver and organ meats, seafood, egg yolks, aged cheeses, milk), nuts, legumes.

Biotin: Necessary to form fatty acids, metabolize protein and carbohydrate. Food Sources: Yeast, eggs, liver, milk.

Vitamin C (ascorbic acid): Helps maintain healthy bones, connective tissue, gums, capillaries and teeth; increases absorption of iron and folic acid; aids wound healing and hormone synthesis; as antioxidant prevents cell damage. Food Sources: Citrus fruits (oranges, grapefruits, tangerines, lemons, limes), berries, green leafy vegetables (broccoli, spinach, collard greens), green and red bell peppers (capsicums), tomatoes, potatoes, asparagus, papayas, mangos.

Vitamin D (calciferol and other forms): Necessary for strong teeth and bones and calcium absorption. Food Sources: Fortified milk, fatty fish (sardines), liver, egg yolks, fortified margarine; also produced by body in response to sunlight. Synthesis provides more than food.

Vitamin E (tocopherol): Helps form blood cells, muscles and healthy lung tissue; helps body use vitamin K; as antioxidant prevents cell damage. Food Sources: Wheat germ; corn, soybean, sunflower and other vegetable oils; nuts, seeds, olives, asparagus, green leafy vegetables, blueberries, peaches, corn bread.

Vitamin K (phylloquinone, menadione, menaquinone): Aids in clotting of blood and regulation of blood calcium. Food Sources: Broccoli, cauliflower, cabbage, spinach, cereal, soybeans, liver, milk; body produces about half of daily needs.

q
641.   Johns, Pamela Sheldon
5637   Healthy gourmet cookbook
JOH

45.00   4/3/95

LONGWOOD PUBLIC LIBRARY
Middle Country Road
Middle Island, NY 11953

(516) 924-6400

LIBRARY HOURS

Monday-Friday   9:30 a.m. - 9:00 p.m.
Saturday   9:30 a.m. - 5:00 p.m.
Sunday (Sept-May) 1:00 p.m. - 5:00 p.m.